D0576303

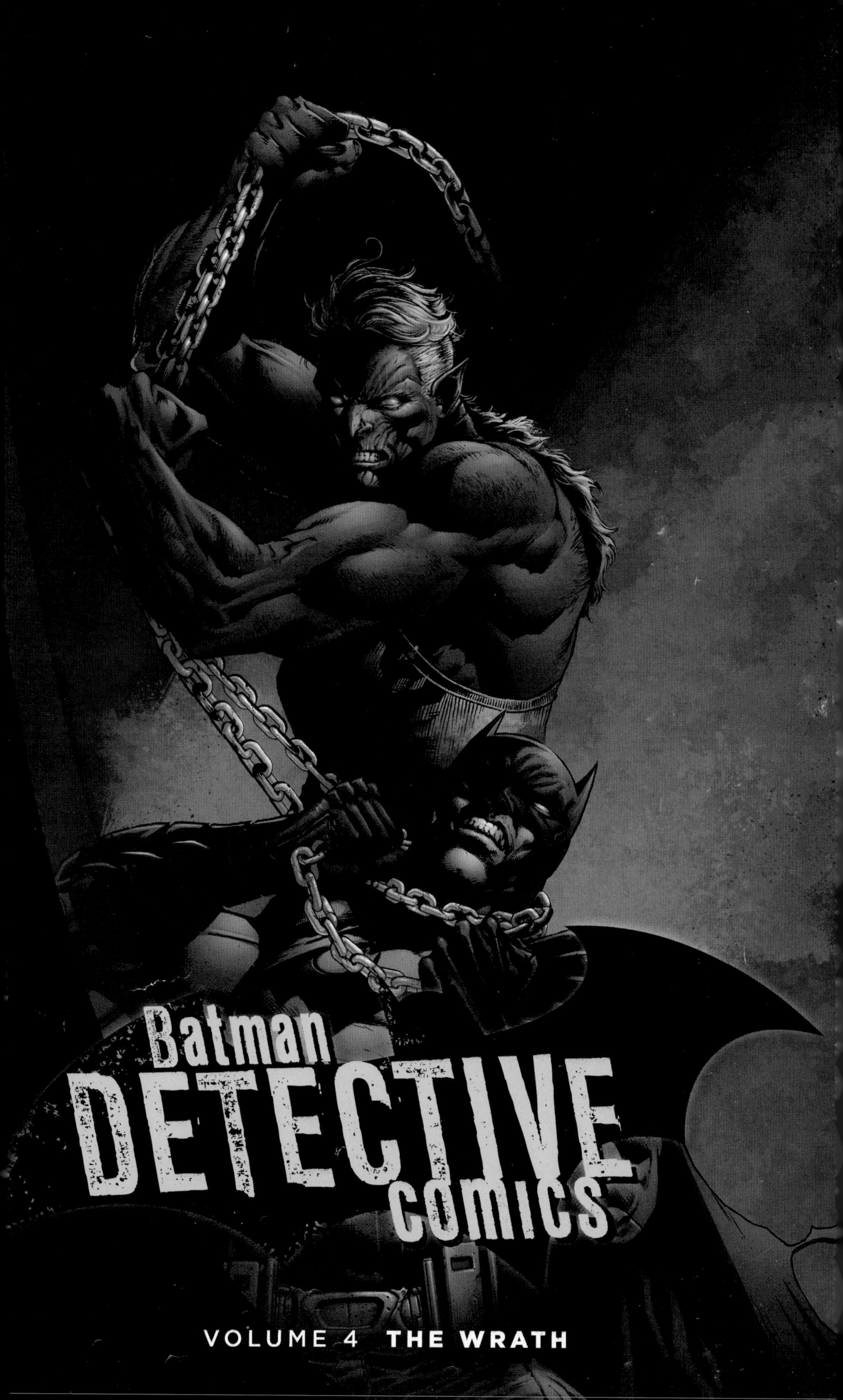
Batman
DETECTIVE
comics
VOLUME 4 THE WRATH

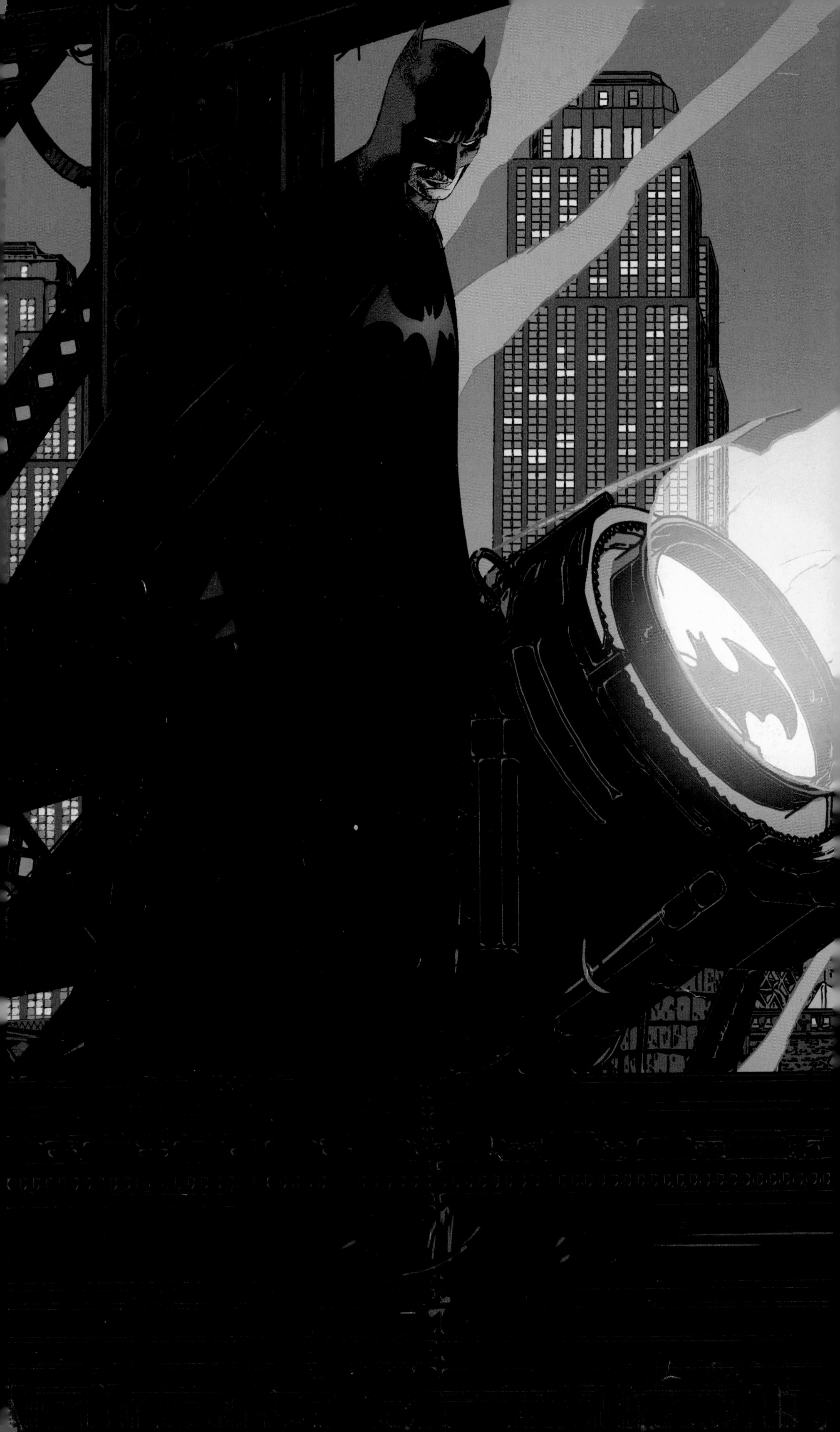

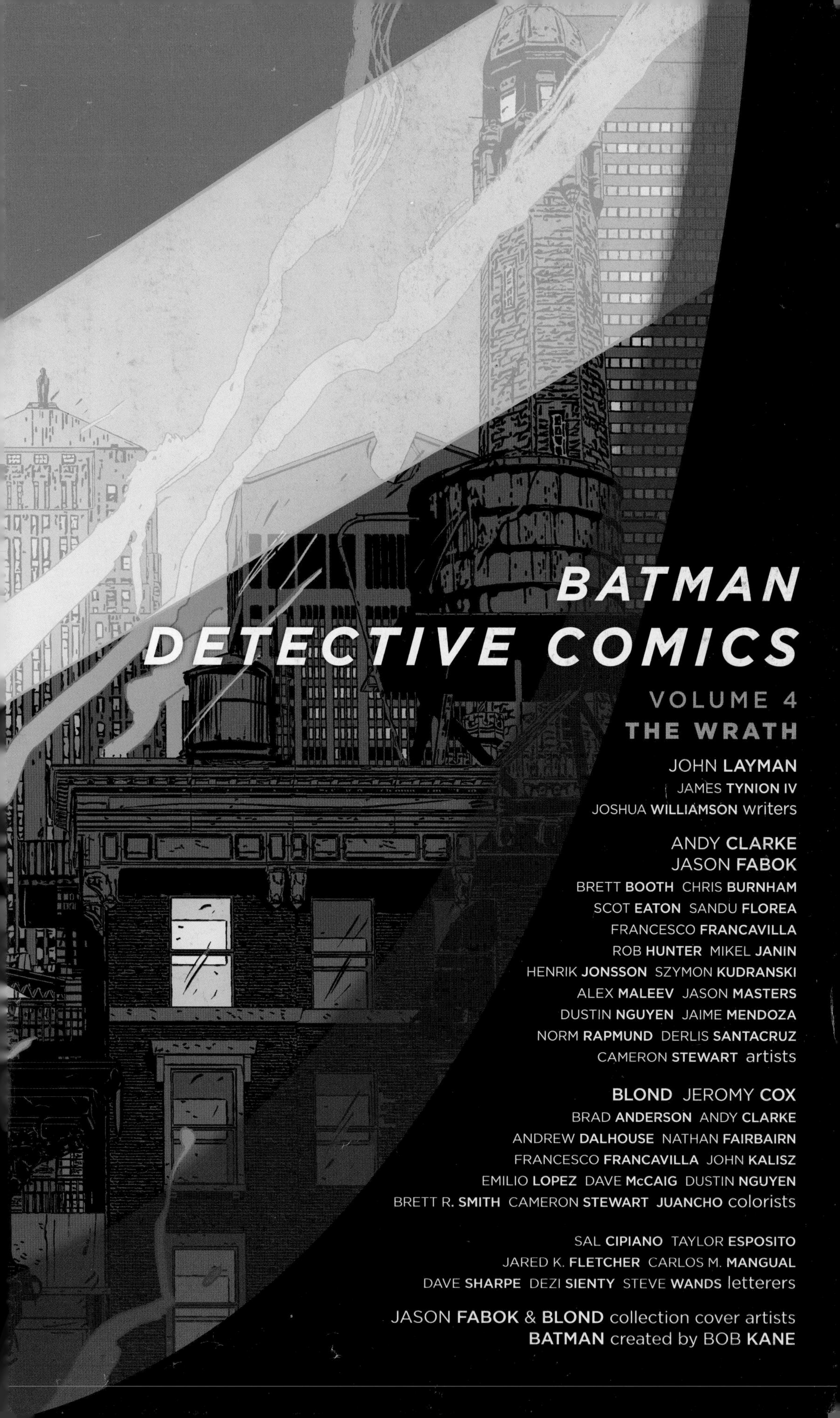

BATMAN DETECTIVE COMICS

VOLUME 4
THE WRATH

JOHN **LAYMAN**
JAMES **TYNION IV**
JOSHUA **WILLIAMSON** writers

ANDY **CLARKE**
JASON **FABOK**
BRETT **BOOTH** CHRIS **BURNHAM**
SCOT **EATON** SANDU **FLOREA**
FRANCESCO **FRANCAVILLA**
ROB **HUNTER** MIKEL **JANIN**
HENRIK **JONSSON** SZYMON **KUDRANSKI**
ALEX **MALEEV** JASON **MASTERS**
DUSTIN **NGUYEN** JAIME **MENDOZA**
NORM **RAPMUND** DERLIS **SANTACRUZ**
CAMERON **STEWART** artists

BLOND JEROMY **COX**
BRAD **ANDERSON** ANDY **CLARKE**
ANDREW **DALHOUSE** NATHAN **FAIRBAIRN**
FRANCESCO **FRANCAVILLA** JOHN **KALISZ**
EMILIO **LOPEZ** DAVE **McCAIG** DUSTIN **NGUYEN**
BRETT R. **SMITH** CAMERON **STEWART** **JUANCHO** colorists

SAL **CIPIANO** TAYLOR **ESPOSITO**
JARED K. **FLETCHER** CARLOS M. **MANGUAL**
DAVE **SHARPE** DEZI **SIENTY** STEVE **WANDS** letterers

JASON **FABOK** & **BLOND** collection cover artists
BATMAN created by BOB **KANE**

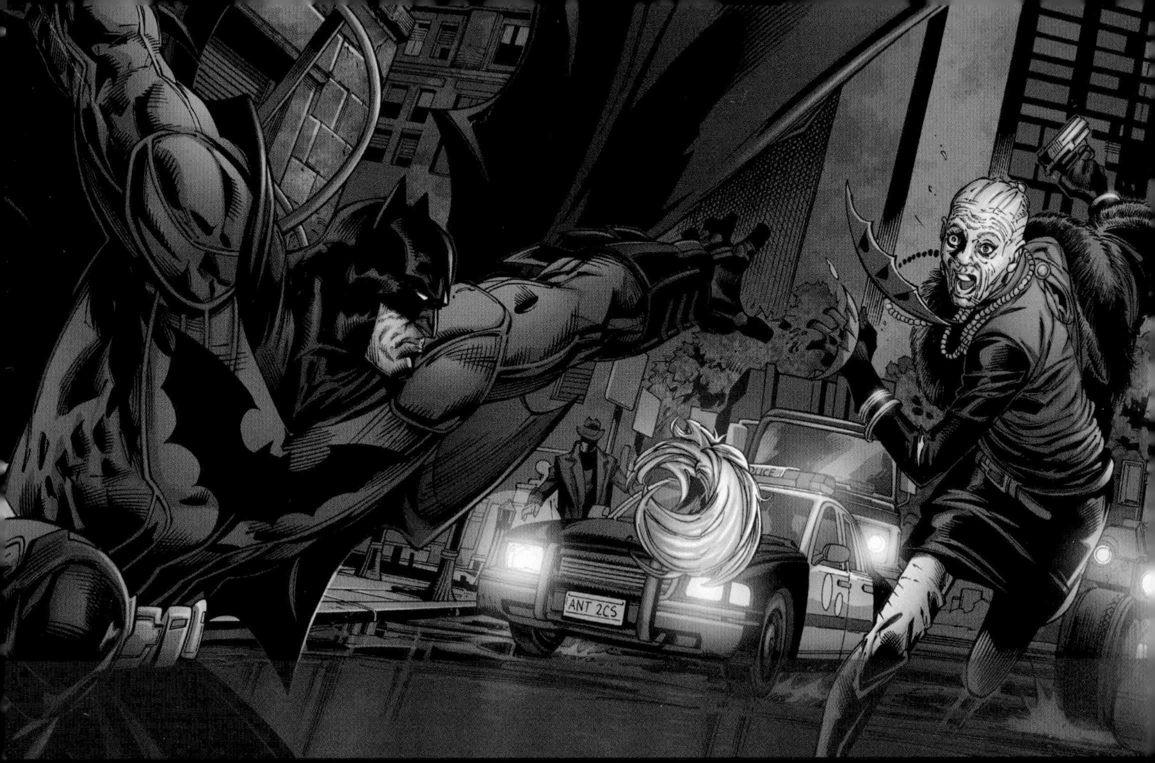
ANT 2CS

MIKE MARTS Editor - Original Series KATIE KUBERT HARVEY RICHARDS Associate Editors - Original Series
RACHEL PINNELAS Editor ROBBIN BROSTERMAN Design Director - Books
ROBBIE BIEDERMAN Publication Design

BOB HARRAS Senior VP - Editor-in-Chief, DC Comics

DIANE NELSON President DAN DIDIO and JIM LEE Co-Publishers
GEOFF JOHNS Chief Creative Officer
JOHN ROOD Executive VP - Sales, Marketing and Business Development
AMY GENKINS Senior VP - Business and Legal Affairs NAIRI GARDINER Senior VP - Finance
JEFF BOISON VP - Publishing Planning MARK CHIARELLO VP - Art Direction and Design
JOHN CUNNINGHAM VP - Marketing TERRI CUNNINGHAM VP - Editorial Administration
ALISON GILL Senior VP - Manufacturing and Operations HANK KANALZ Senior VP - Vertigo and Integrated Publishing
JAY KOGAN VP - Business and Legal Affairs, Publishing JACK MAHAN VP - Business Affairs, Talent
NICK NAPOLITANO VP - Manufacturing Administration SUE POHJA VP - Book Sales
COURTNEY SIMMONS Senior VP - Publicity BOB WAYNE Senior VP - Sales

BATMAN - DETECTIVE COMICS VOLUME 4: THE WRATH

DC Comics, 1700 Broadway, New York, NY 10019
A Warner Bros. Entertainment Company.
Printed by RR Donnelley, Salem, VA, USA. 5/23/14. First Printing.

ISBN: 978-1-4012-4633-4

SUSTAINABLE FORESTRY INITIATIVE
Certified Chain of Custody
20% Certified Forest Content,
80% Certified Sourcing
www.sfiprogram.org
SFI-01042
APPLIES TO TEXT STOCK ONLY

Library of Congress Cataloging-in-Publication Data

Layman, John, 1967-
Batman/Detective Comics. Volume 4, Wrath / John Layman ; illustrated by Jason Fabok.
pages cm. — (The New 52!)
ISBN 978-1-4012-4633-4 (hardback)
1. Graphic novels. I. Fabok, Jay. II. Title. III. Title: Wrath.
PN6728.B36L393 2014
741.5'973—dc23
2014010795

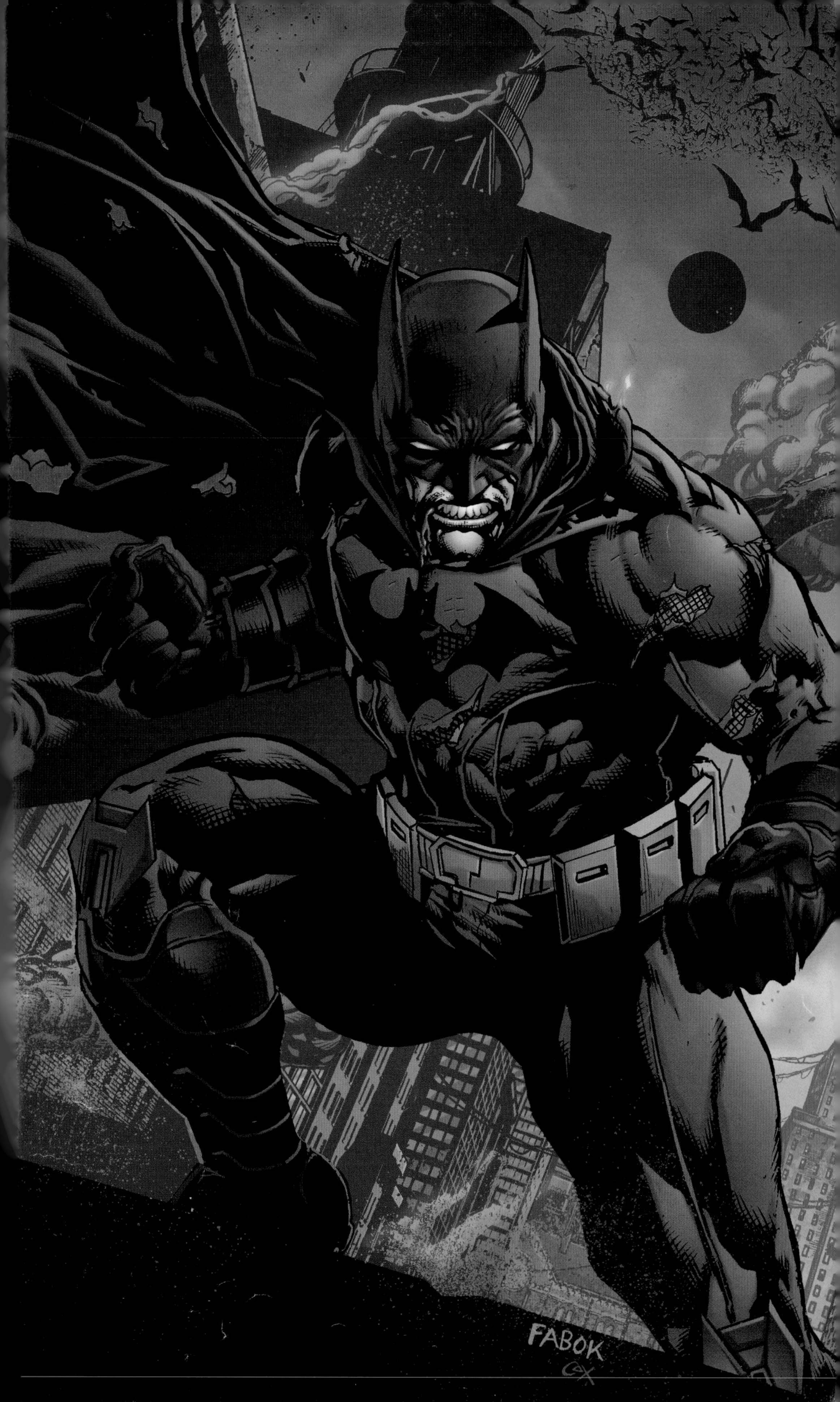
FABOK

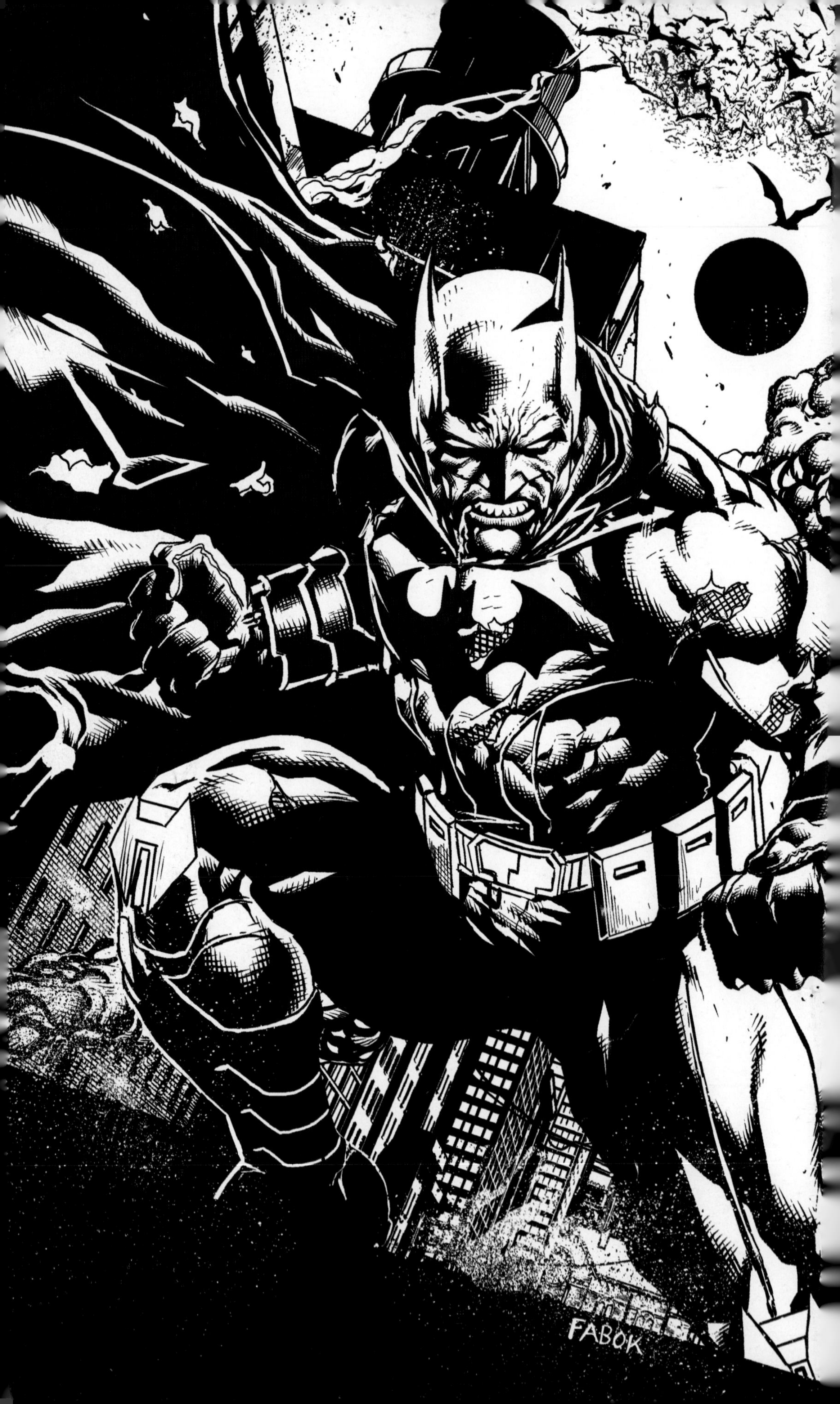
FABOK

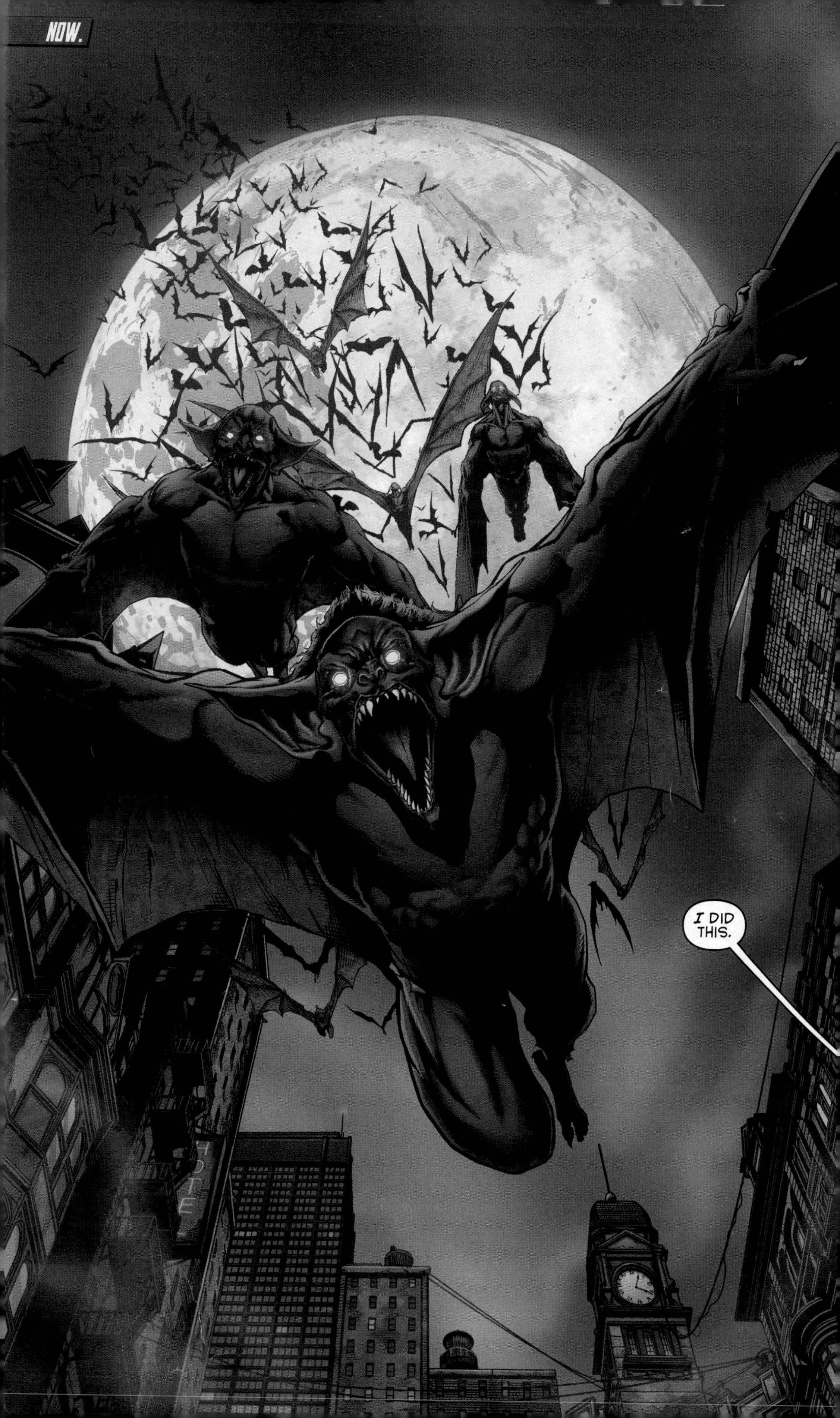
NOW.
I DID THIS.
HOTE

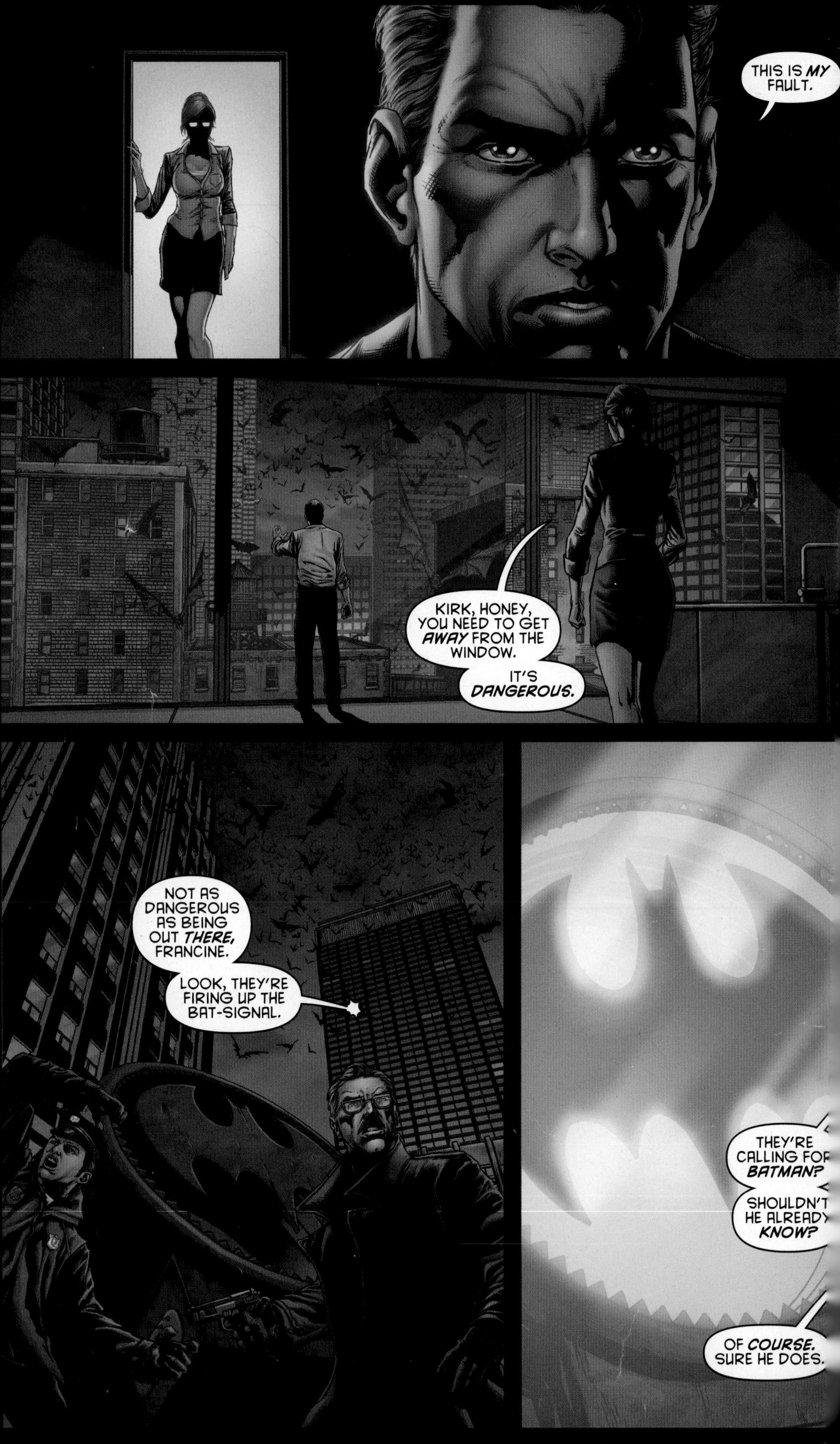
THIS IS *MY* FAULT.
KIRK, HONEY, YOU NEED TO GET *AWAY* FROM THE WINDOW.
IT'S *DANGEROUS.*
NOT AS DANGEROUS AS BEING OUT *THERE,* FRANCINE.
LOOK, THEY'RE FIRING UP THE BAT-SIGNAL.
THEY'RE CALLING FOR *BATMAN?*
SHOULDN'T HE ALREADY *KNOW?*
OF *COURSE.* SURE HE DOES.

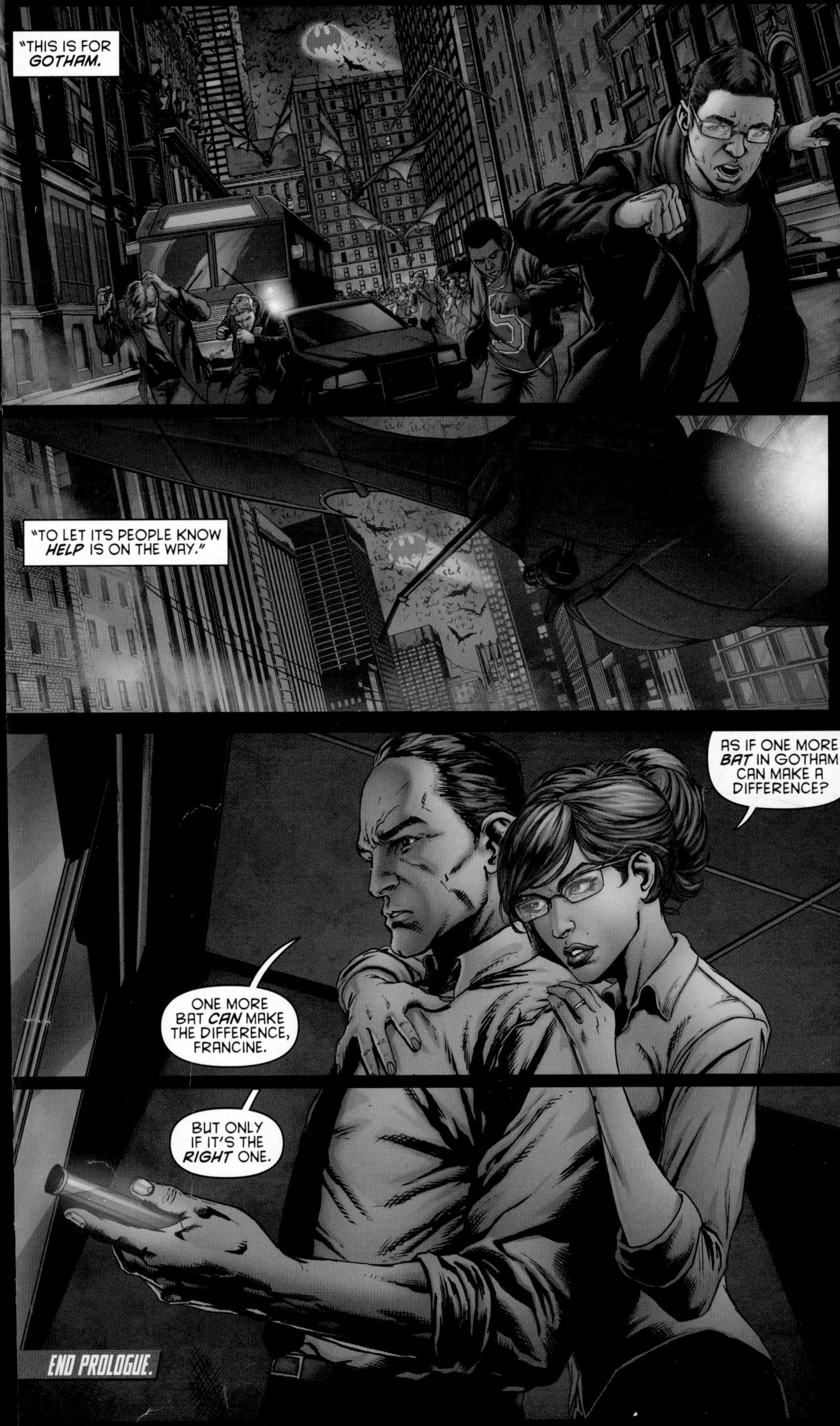
"THIS IS FOR GOTHAM.
"TO LET ITS PEOPLE KNOW HELP IS ON THE WAY."
AS IF ONE MORE BAT IN GOTHAM CAN MAKE A DIFFERENCE?
ONE MORE BAT CAN MAKE THE DIFFERENCE, FRANCINE.
BUT ONLY IF IT'S THE RIGHT ONE.
END PROLOGUE.

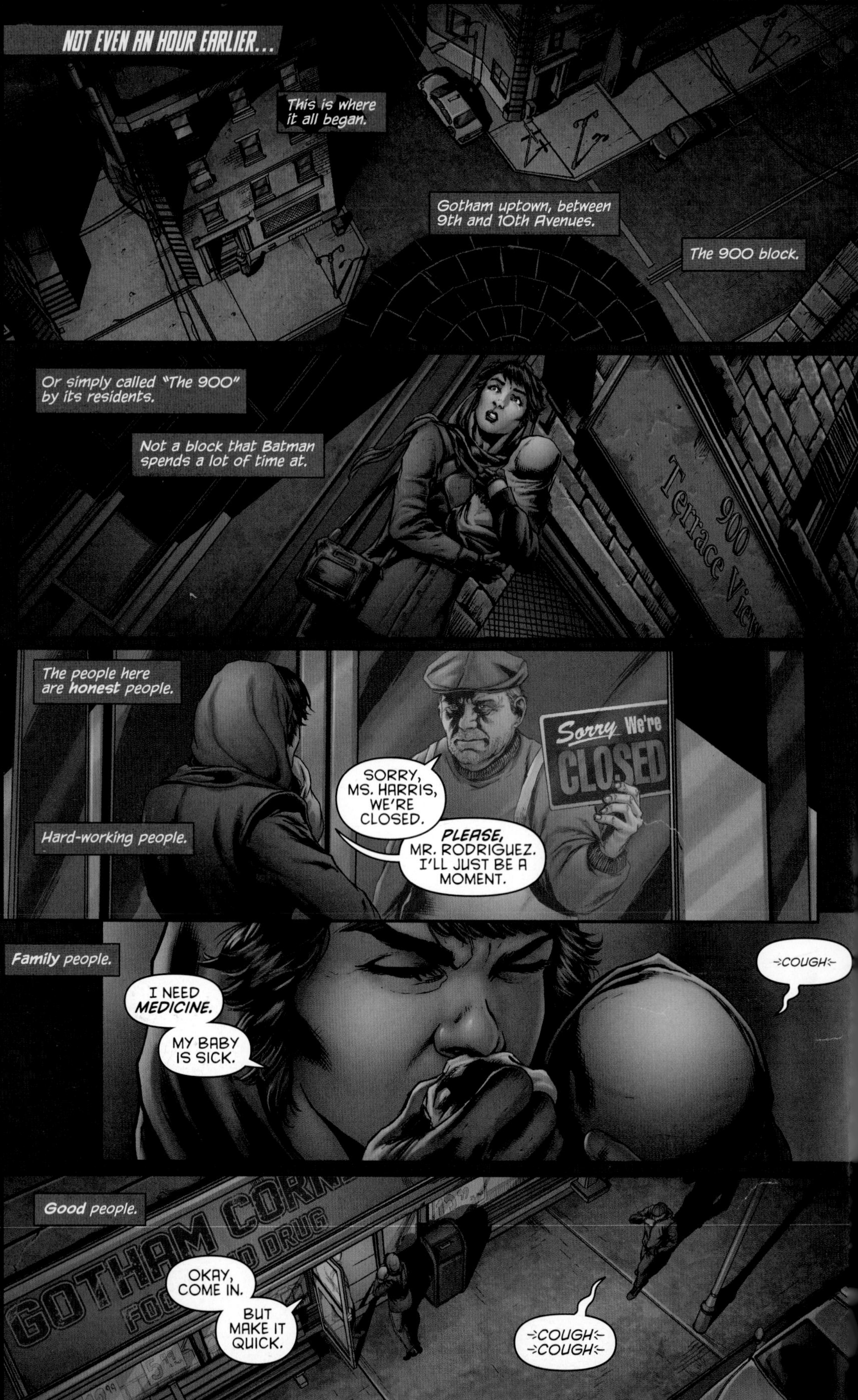
NOT EVEN AN HOUR EARLIER...
This is where it all began.
Gotham uptown, between 9th and 10th Avenues.
The 900 block.
Or simply called "The 900" by its residents.
Not a block that Batman spends a lot of time at.
900 Terrace View
The people here are **honest** people.
Hard-working people.
Sorry We're CLOSED
SORRY, MS. HARRIS, WE'RE CLOSED.
PLEASE, MR. RODRIGUEZ. I'LL JUST BE A MOMENT.
Family people.
I NEED *MEDICINE.*
MY BABY IS SICK.
COUGH
Good people.
GOTHAM CORN
FOOD AND DRUG
OKAY, COME IN.
BUT MAKE IT QUICK.
COUGH COUGH

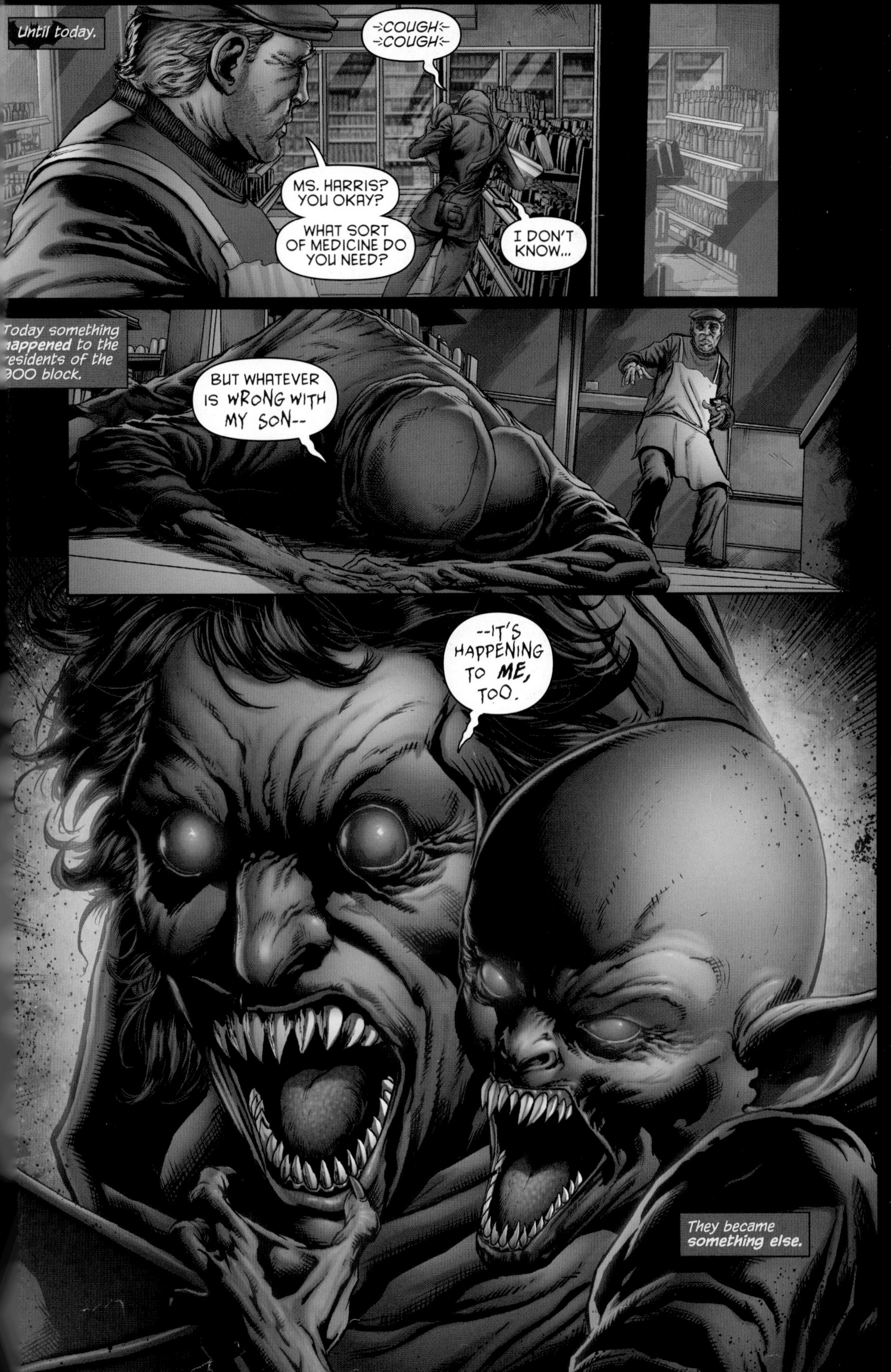
Until today.
-COUGH-
-COUGH-
MS. HARRIS? YOU OKAY?
WHAT SORT OF MEDICINE DO YOU NEED?
I DON'T KNOW...
Today something happened to the residents of the 900 block.
BUT WHATEVER IS WRONG WITH MY SON--
--IT'S HAPPENING TO ME, TOO.
They became something else.

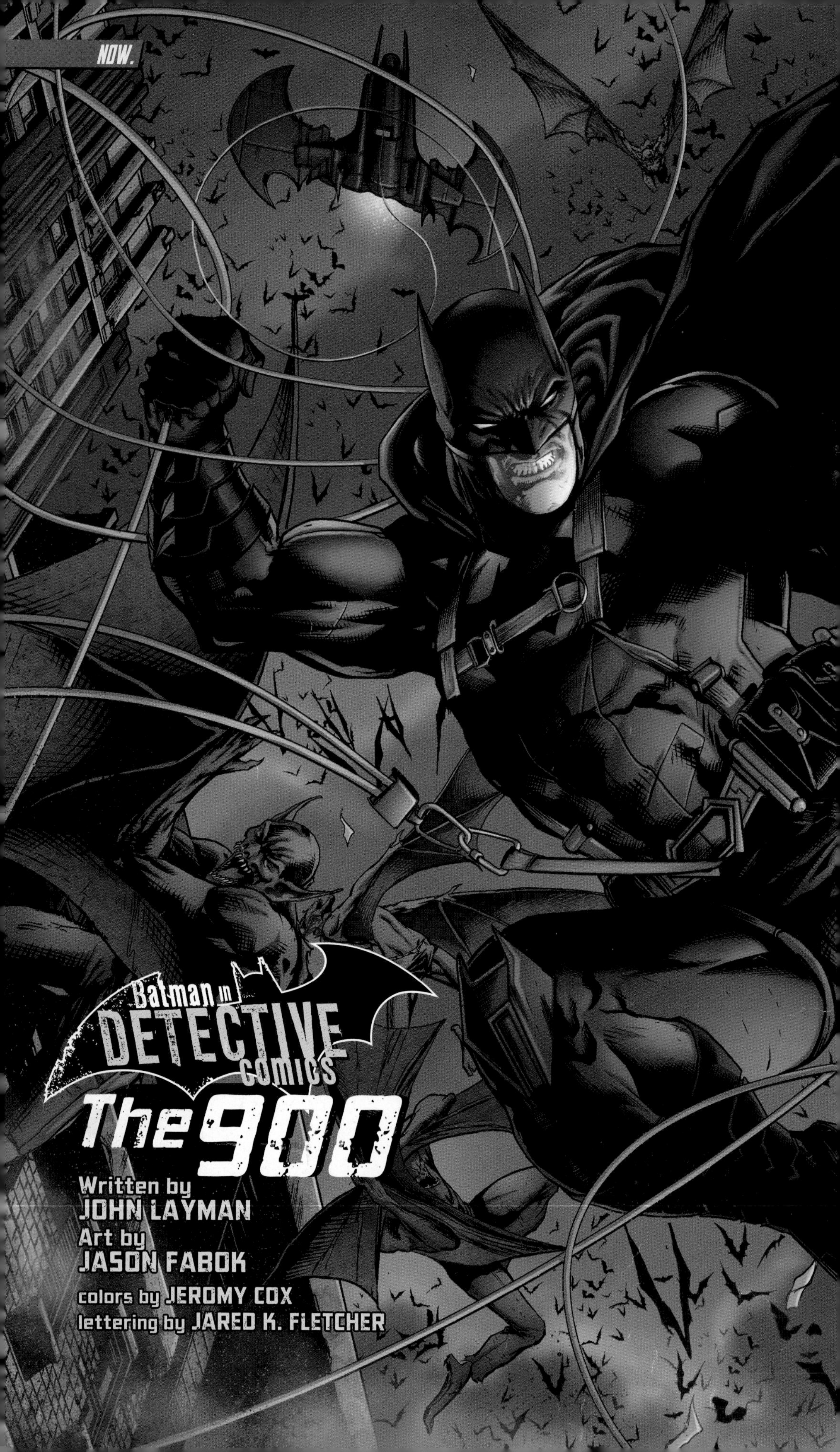
NOW.
Batman in DETECTIVE COMICS
The 900
Written by JOHN LAYMAN
Art by JASON FABOK
colors by JEROMY COX
lettering by JARED K. FLETCHER

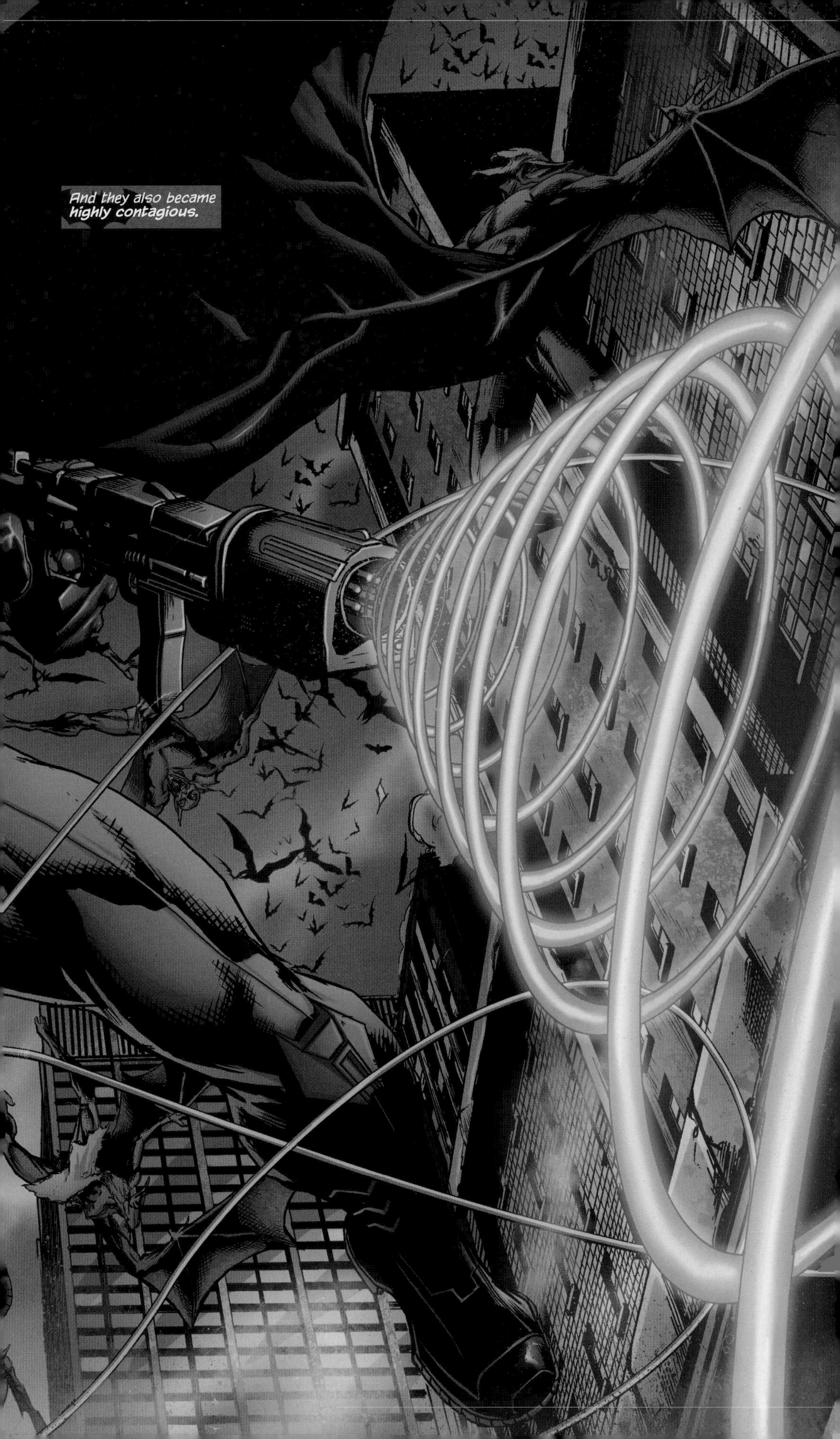
And they also became
highly contagious.

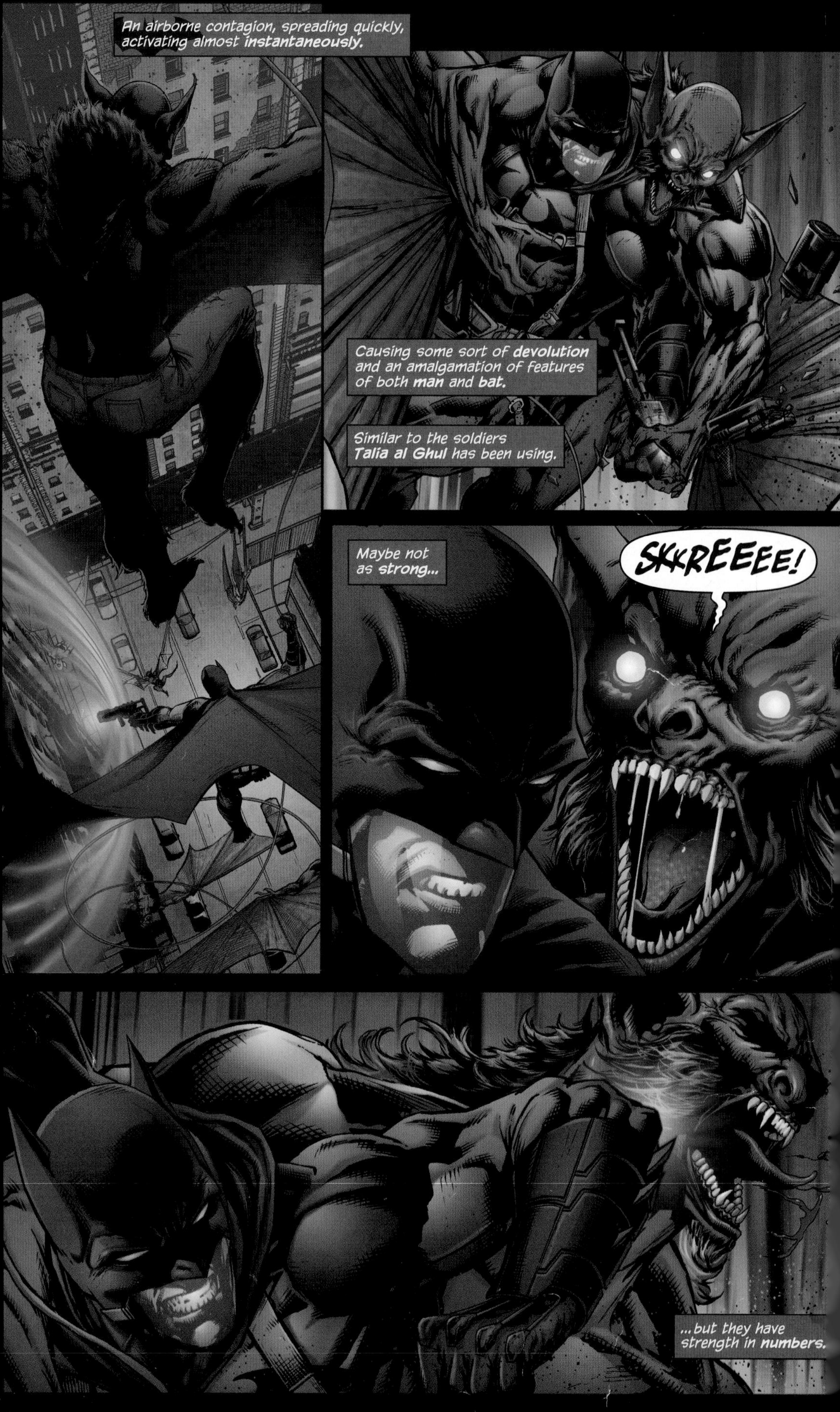
An airborne contagion, spreading quickly, activating almost **instantaneously.**
Causing some sort of **devolution** and an amalgamation of features of both **man** and **bat.**
Similar to the soldiers **Talia al Ghul** has been using.
Maybe not as **strong**...
SKKREEEE!
...but they have strength in **numbers.**

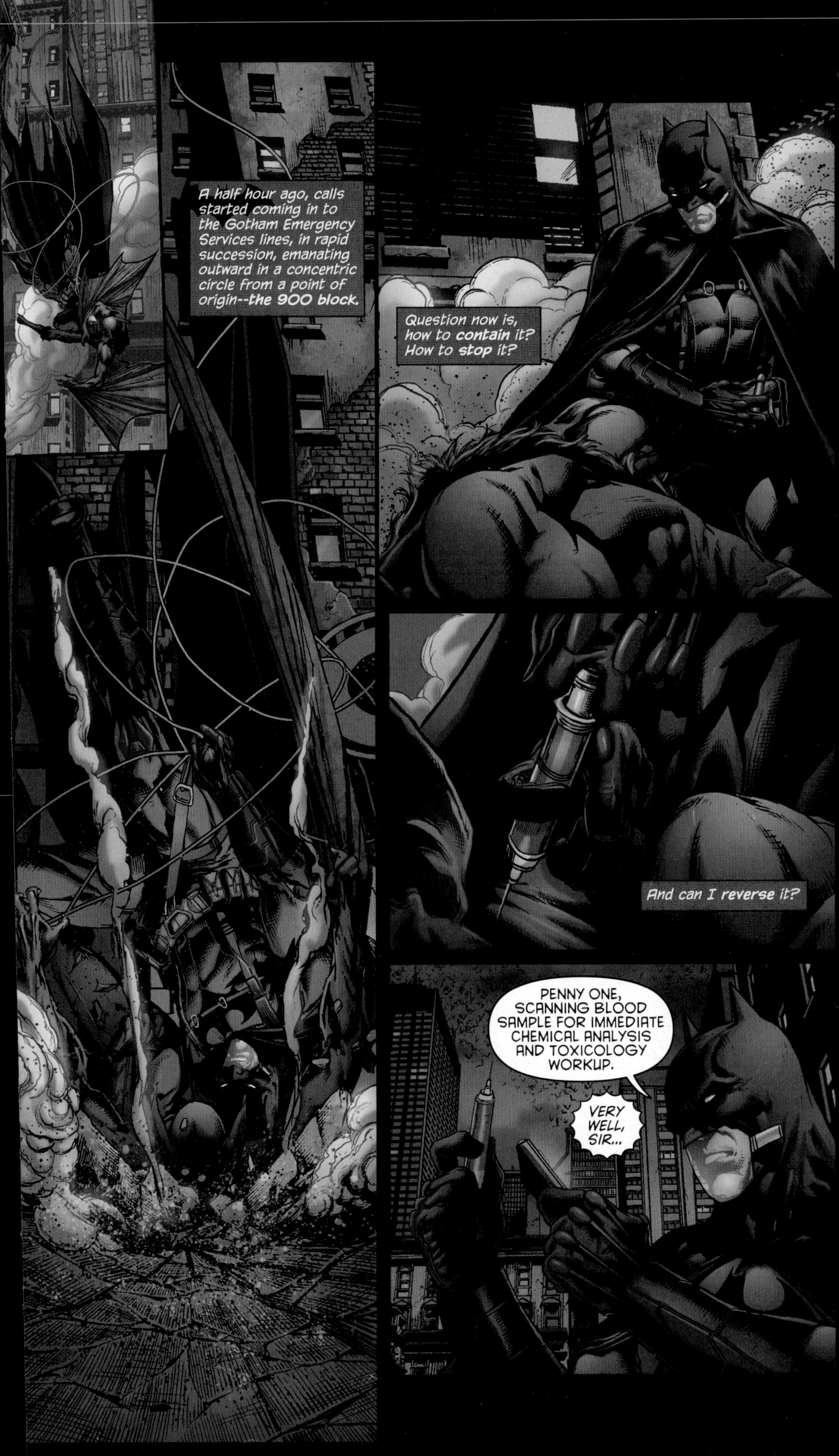
A half hour ago, calls started coming in to the Gotham Emergency Services lines, in rapid succession, emanating outward in a concentric circle from a point of origin--the 900 block.
Question now is, how to contain it? How to stop it?
And can I reverse it?
PENNY ONE, SCANNING BLOOD SAMPLE FOR IMMEDIATE CHEMICAL ANALYSIS AND TOXICOLOGY WORKUP.
VERY WELL, SIR...

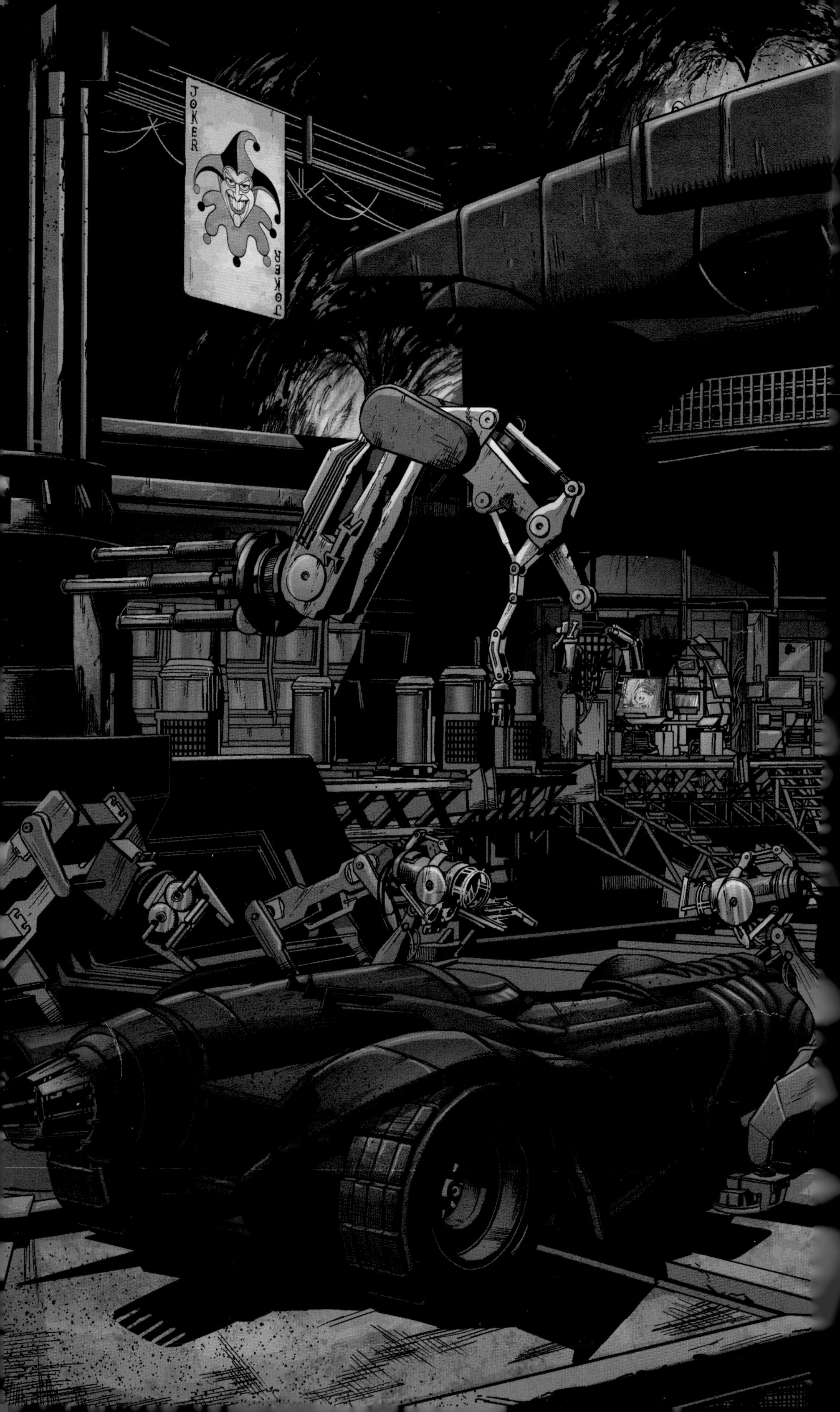
JOKER
JOKER

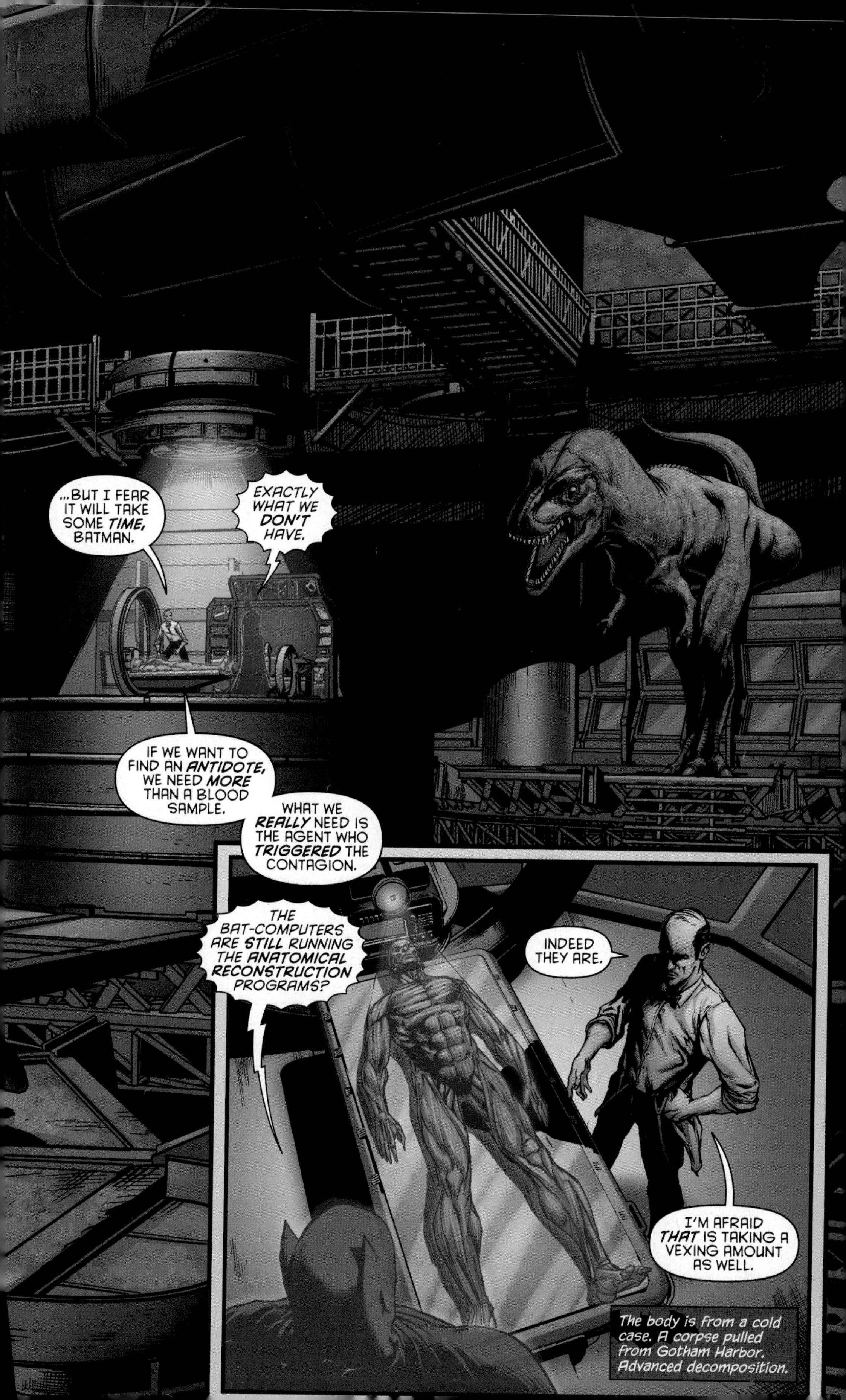
...BUT I FEAR IT WILL TAKE SOME TIME, BATMAN.
EXACTLY WHAT WE DON'T HAVE.
IF WE WANT TO FIND AN ANTIDOTE, WE NEED MORE THAN A BLOOD SAMPLE.
WHAT WE REALLY NEED IS THE AGENT WHO TRIGGERED THE CONTAGION.
THE BAT-COMPUTERS ARE STILL RUNNING THE ANATOMICAL RECONSTRUCTION PROGRAMS?
INDEED THEY ARE.
I'M AFRAID THAT IS TAKING A VEXING AMOUNT AS WELL.
The body is from a cold case. A corpse pulled from Gotham Harbor. Advanced decomposition.

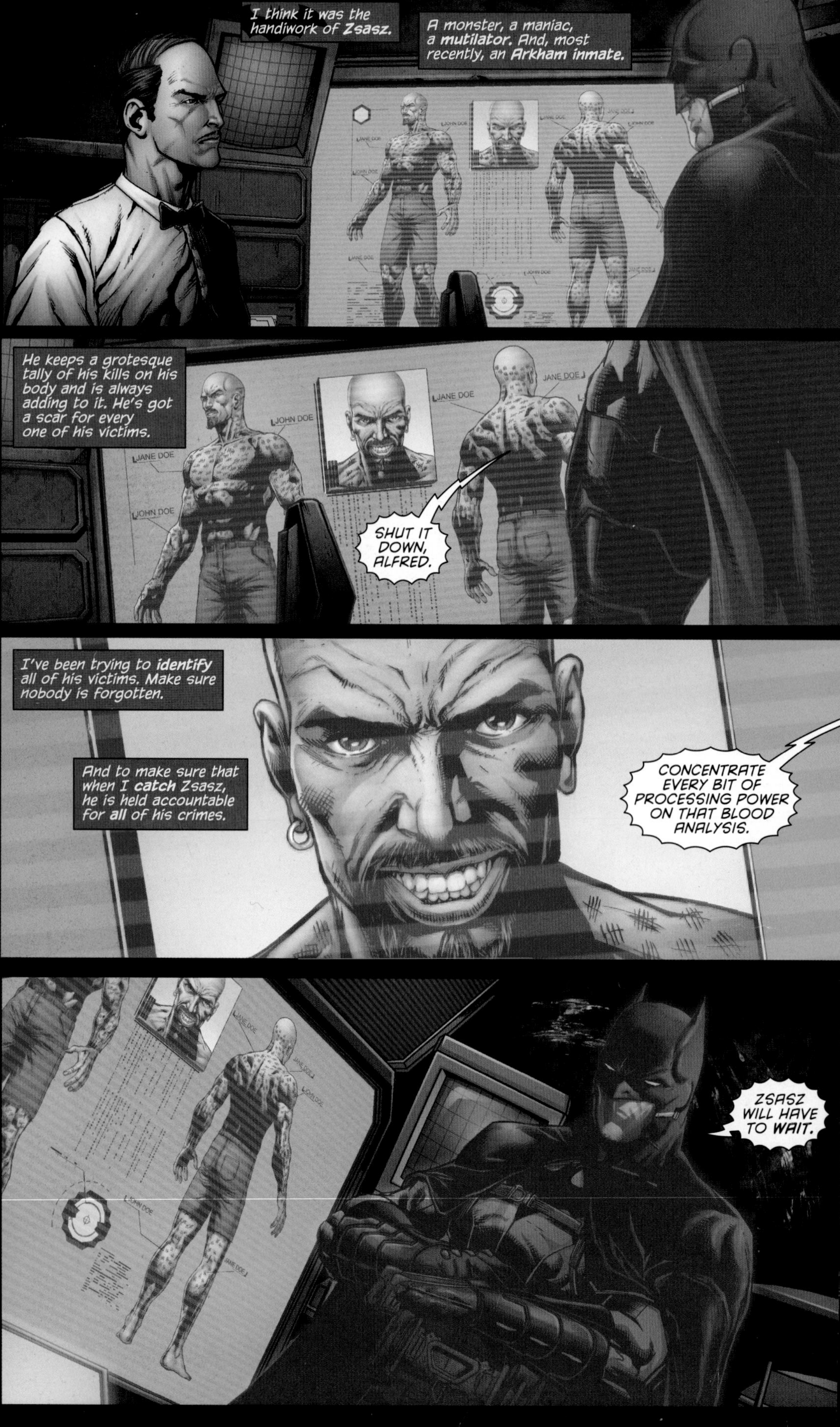
I think it was the handiwork of Zsasz.
A monster, a maniac, a mutilator. And, most recently, an Arkham inmate.
JOHN DOE
JANE DOE
He keeps a grotesque tally of his kills on his body and is always adding to it. He's got a scar for every one of his victims.
SHUT IT DOWN, ALFRED.
I've been trying to identify all of his victims. Make sure nobody is forgotten.
And to make sure that when I catch Zsasz, he is held accountable for all of his crimes.
CONCENTRATE EVERY BIT OF PROCESSING POWER ON THAT BLOOD ANALYSIS.
ZSASZ WILL HAVE TO WAIT.

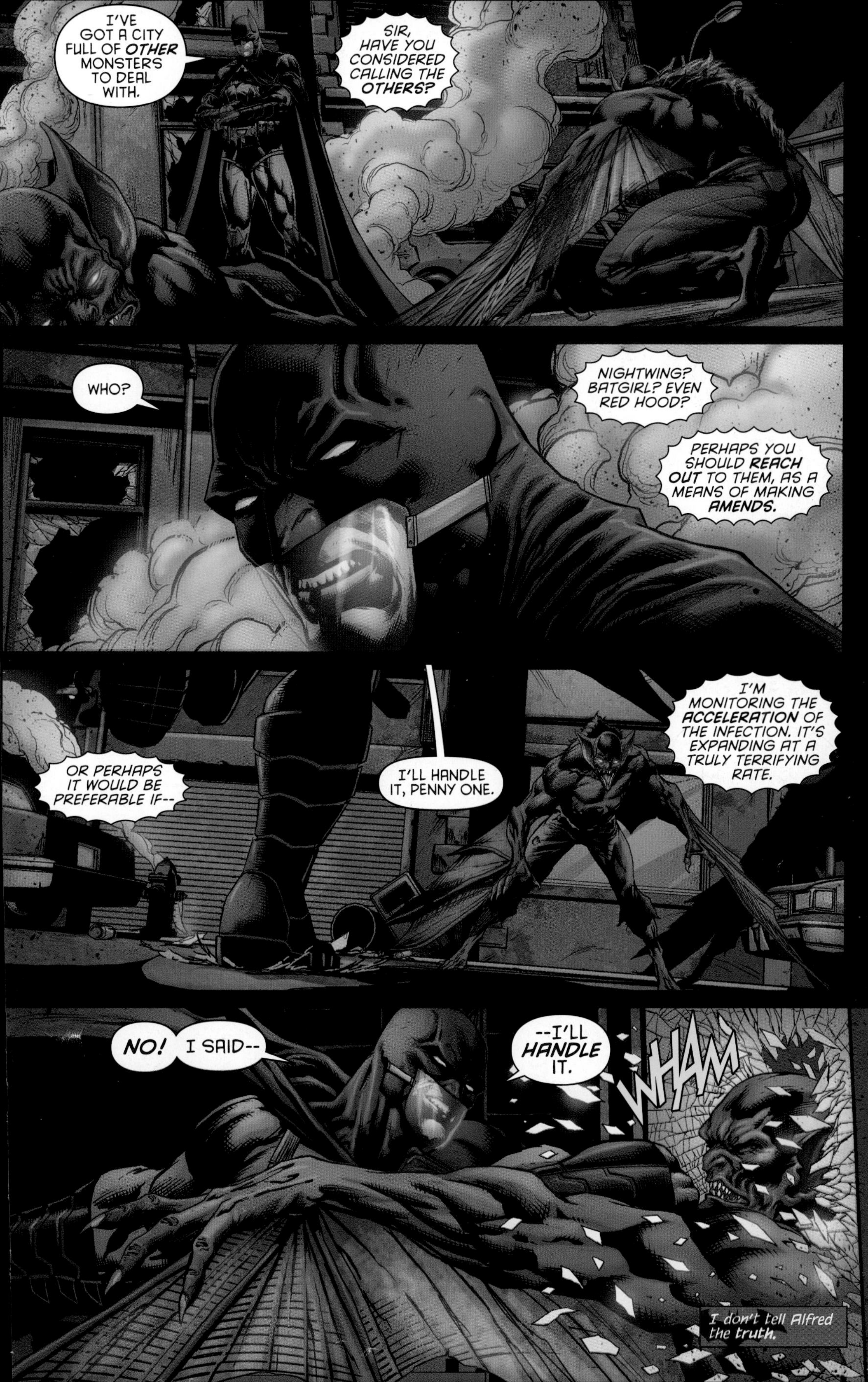
I'VE GOT A CITY FULL OF OTHER MONSTERS TO DEAL WITH.
SIR, HAVE YOU CONSIDERED CALLING THE OTHERS?
WHO?
NIGHTWING? BATGIRL? EVEN RED HOOD?
PERHAPS YOU SHOULD REACH OUT TO THEM, AS A MEANS OF MAKING AMENDS.
OR PERHAPS IT WOULD BE PREFERABLE IF--
I'LL HANDLE IT, PENNY ONE.
I'M MONITORING THE ACCELERATION OF THE INFECTION. IT'S EXPANDING AT A TRULY TERRIFYING RATE.
NO! I SAID--
--I'LL HANDLE IT.
WHAM
I don't tell Alfred the truth.

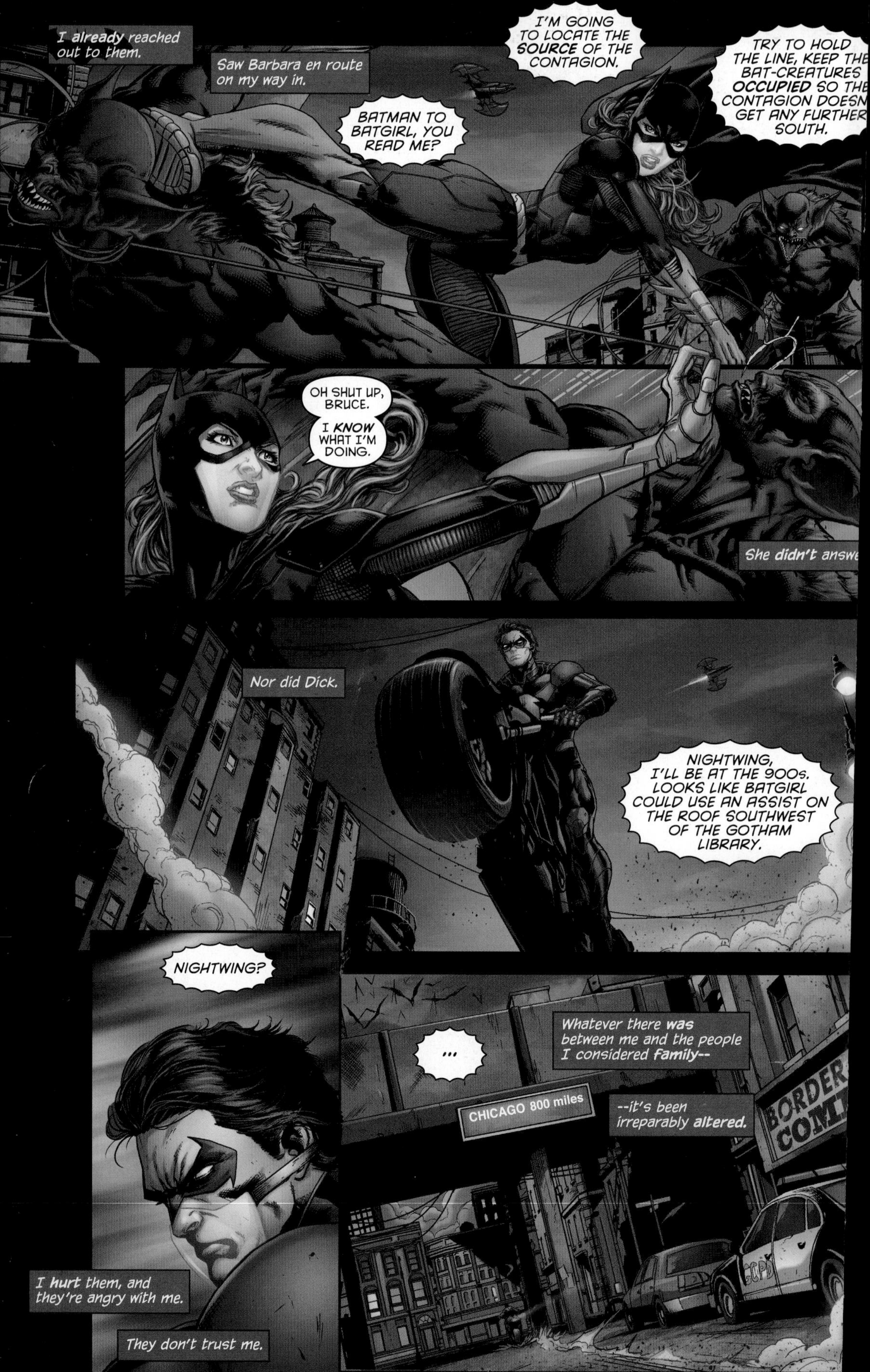

I already reached out to them.
Saw Barbara en route on my way in.
BATMAN TO BATGIRL, YOU READ ME?
I'M GOING TO LOCATE THE SOURCE OF THE CONTAGION.
TRY TO HOLD THE LINE, KEEP THE BAT-CREATURES OCCUPIED SO THE CONTAGION DOESN GET ANY FURTHER SOUTH.
OH SHUT UP, BRUCE.
I KNOW WHAT I'M DOING.
She didn't answe
Nor did Dick.
NIGHTWING, I'LL BE AT THE 900s. LOOKS LIKE BATGIRL COULD USE AN ASSIST ON THE ROOF SOUTHWEST OF THE GOTHAM LIBRARY.
NIGHTWING?
...
Whatever there was between me and the people I considered family--
CHICAGO 800 miles
--it's been irreparably altered.
BORDER COMI
GCPD
I hurt them, and they're angry with me.
They don't trust me.

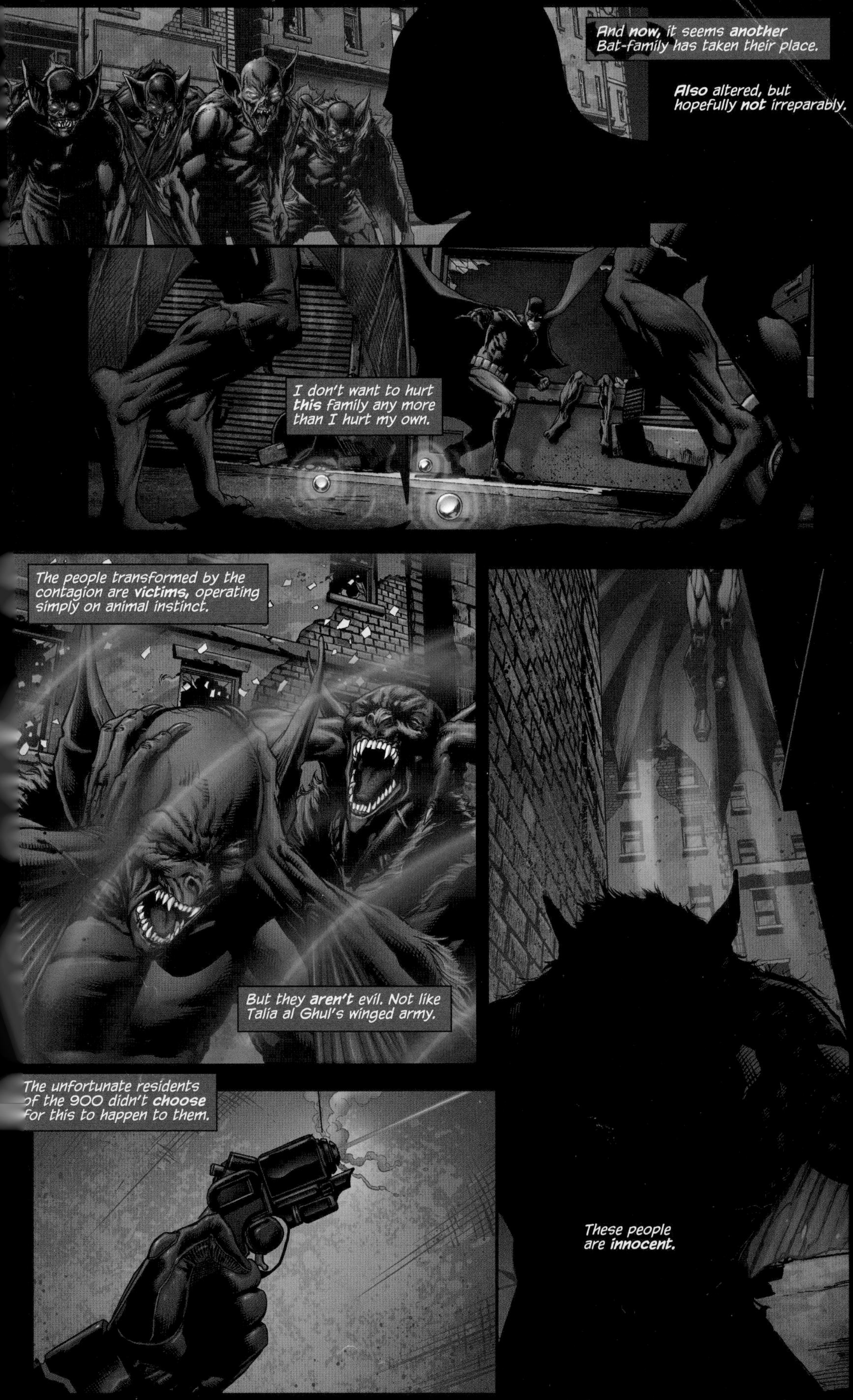

And now, it seems another Bat-family has taken their place.
Also altered, but hopefully not irreparably.
I don't want to hurt this family any more than I hurt my own.
The people transformed by the contagion are victims, operating simply on animal instinct.
But they aren't evil. Not like Talia al Ghul's winged army.
The unfortunate residents of the 900 didn't choose for this to happen to them.
These people are innocent.

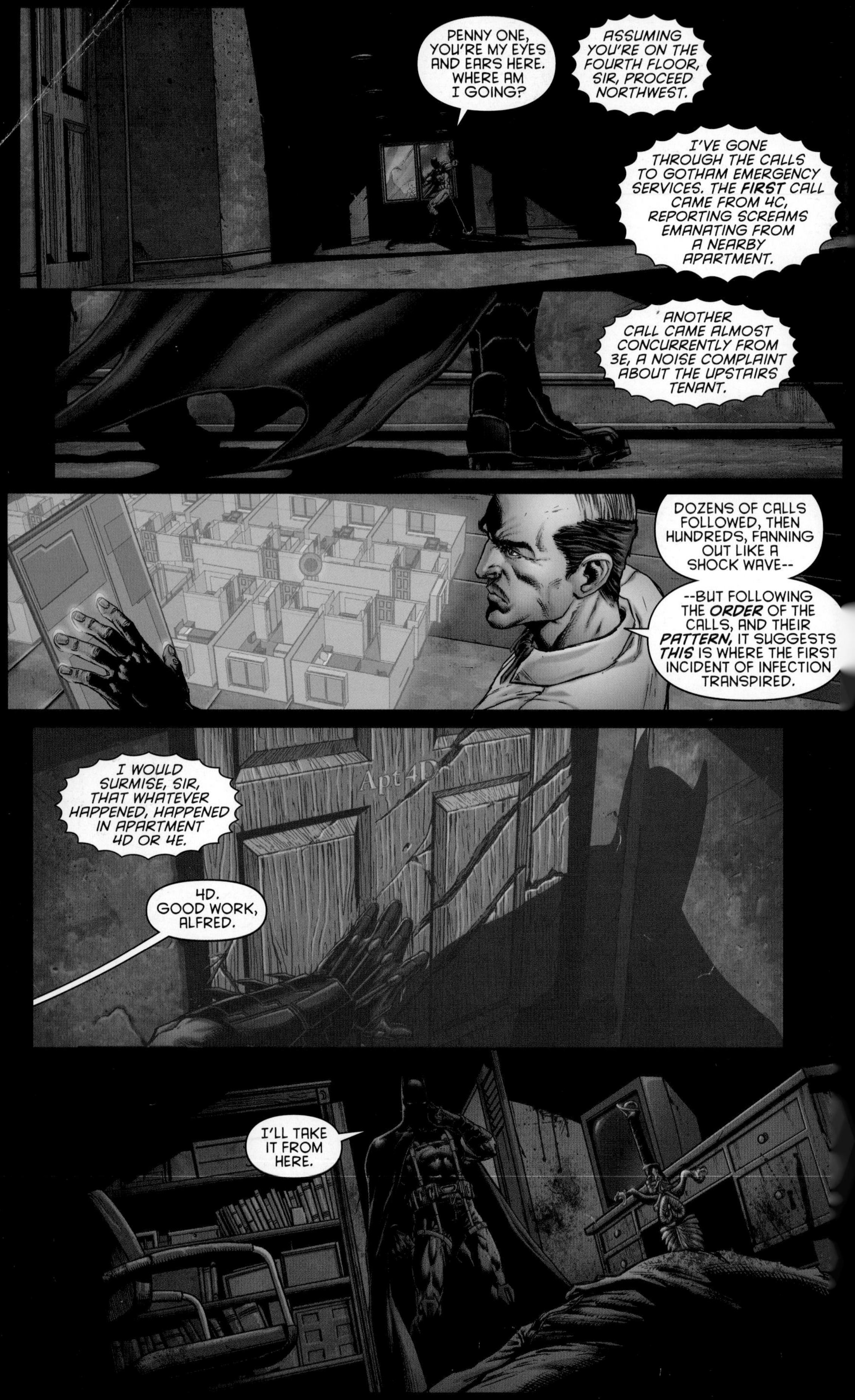

PENNY ONE, YOU'RE MY EYES AND EARS HERE. WHERE AM I GOING?
ASSUMING YOU'RE ON THE FOURTH FLOOR, SIR, PROCEED NORTHWEST.
I'VE GONE THROUGH THE CALLS TO GOTHAM EMERGENCY SERVICES. THE FIRST CALL CAME FROM 4C, REPORTING SCREAMS EMANATING FROM A NEARBY APARTMENT.
ANOTHER CALL CAME ALMOST CONCURRENTLY FROM 3E, A NOISE COMPLAINT ABOUT THE UPSTAIRS TENANT.
DOZENS OF CALLS FOLLOWED, THEN HUNDREDS, FANNING OUT LIKE A SHOCK WAVE--
--BUT FOLLOWING THE ORDER OF THE CALLS, AND THEIR PATTERN, IT SUGGESTS THIS IS WHERE THE FIRST INCIDENT OF INFECTION TRANSPIRED.
I WOULD SURMISE, SIR, THAT WHATEVER HAPPENED, HAPPENED IN APARTMENT 4D OR 4E.
Apt 4D
4D. GOOD WORK, ALFRED.
I'LL TAKE IT FROM HERE.

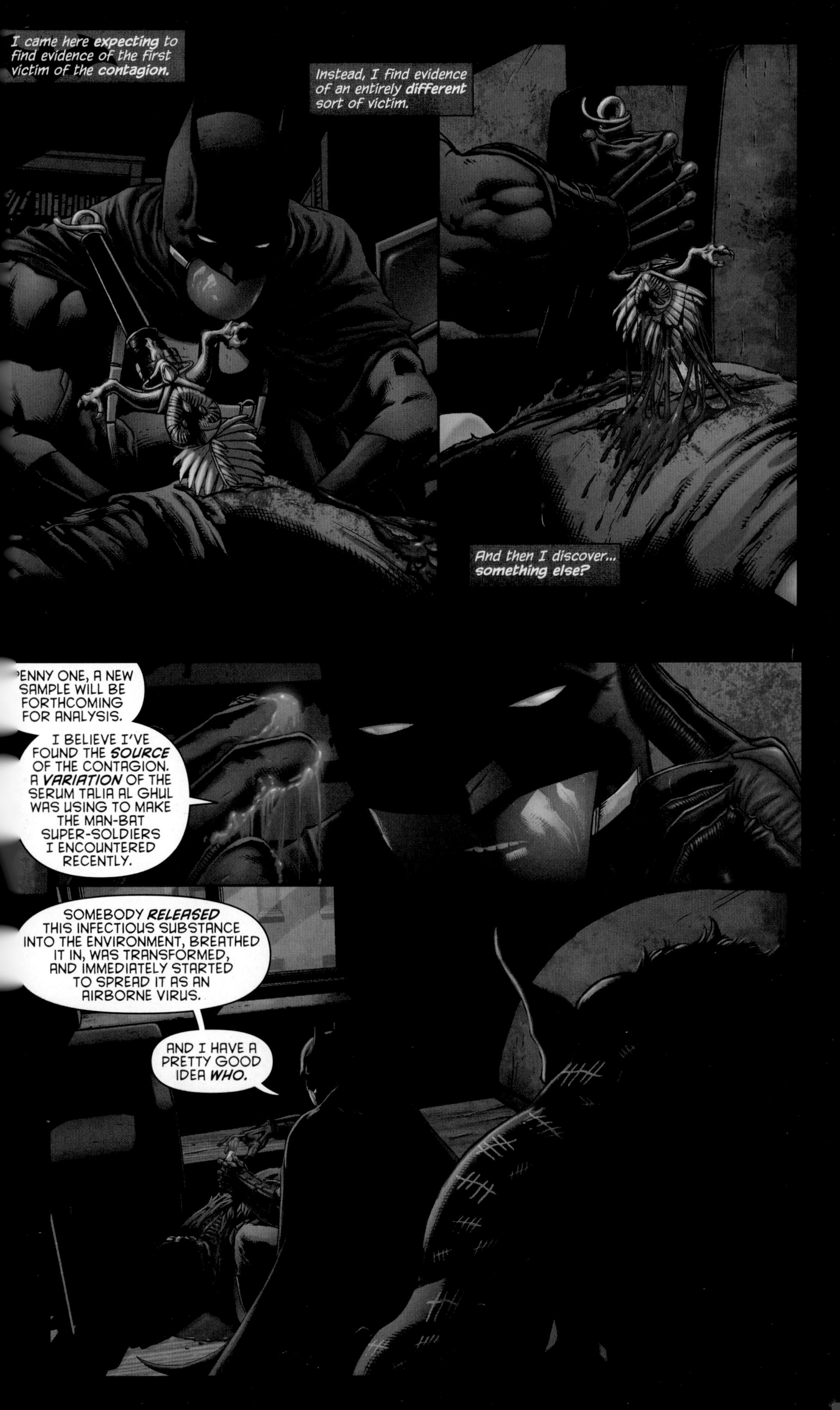

I came here expecting to find evidence of the first victim of the contagion.
Instead, I find evidence of an entirely different sort of victim.
And then I discover... something else?
PENNY ONE, A NEW SAMPLE WILL BE FORTHCOMING FOR ANALYSIS.
I BELIEVE I'VE FOUND THE SOURCE OF THE CONTAGION. A VARIATION OF THE SERUM TALIA AL GHUL WAS USING TO MAKE THE MAN-BAT SUPER-SOLDIERS I ENCOUNTERED RECENTLY.
SOMEBODY RELEASED THIS INFECTIOUS SUBSTANCE INTO THE ENVIRONMENT, BREATHED IT IN, WAS TRANSFORMED, AND IMMEDIATELY STARTED TO SPREAD IT AS AN AIRBORNE VIRUS.
AND I HAVE A PRETTY GOOD IDEA WHO.

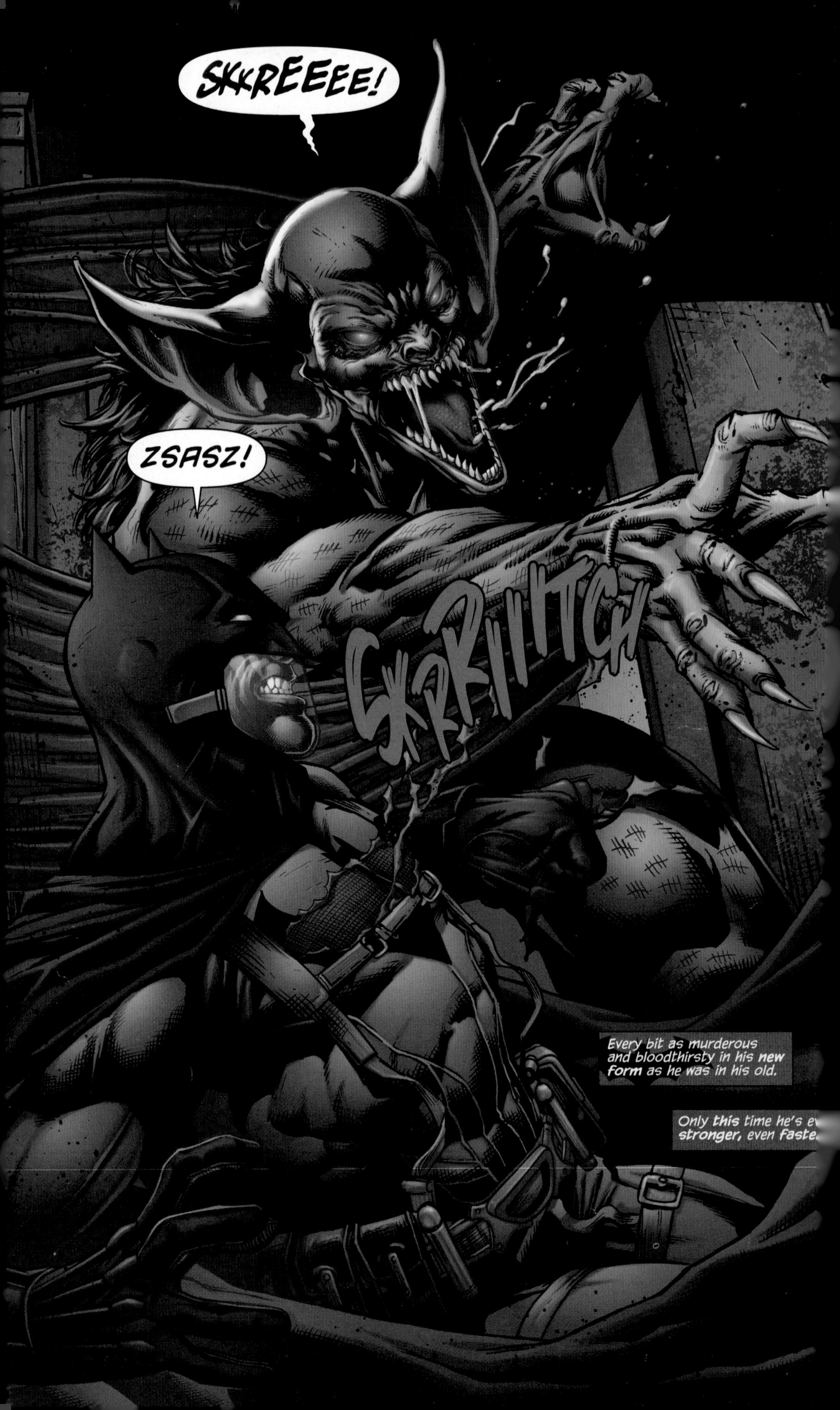
SKKREEEEE!
ZSASZ!
SKRIIITCH
Every bit as murderous and bloodthirsty in his new form as he was in his old.
Only this time he's ev stronger, even faste

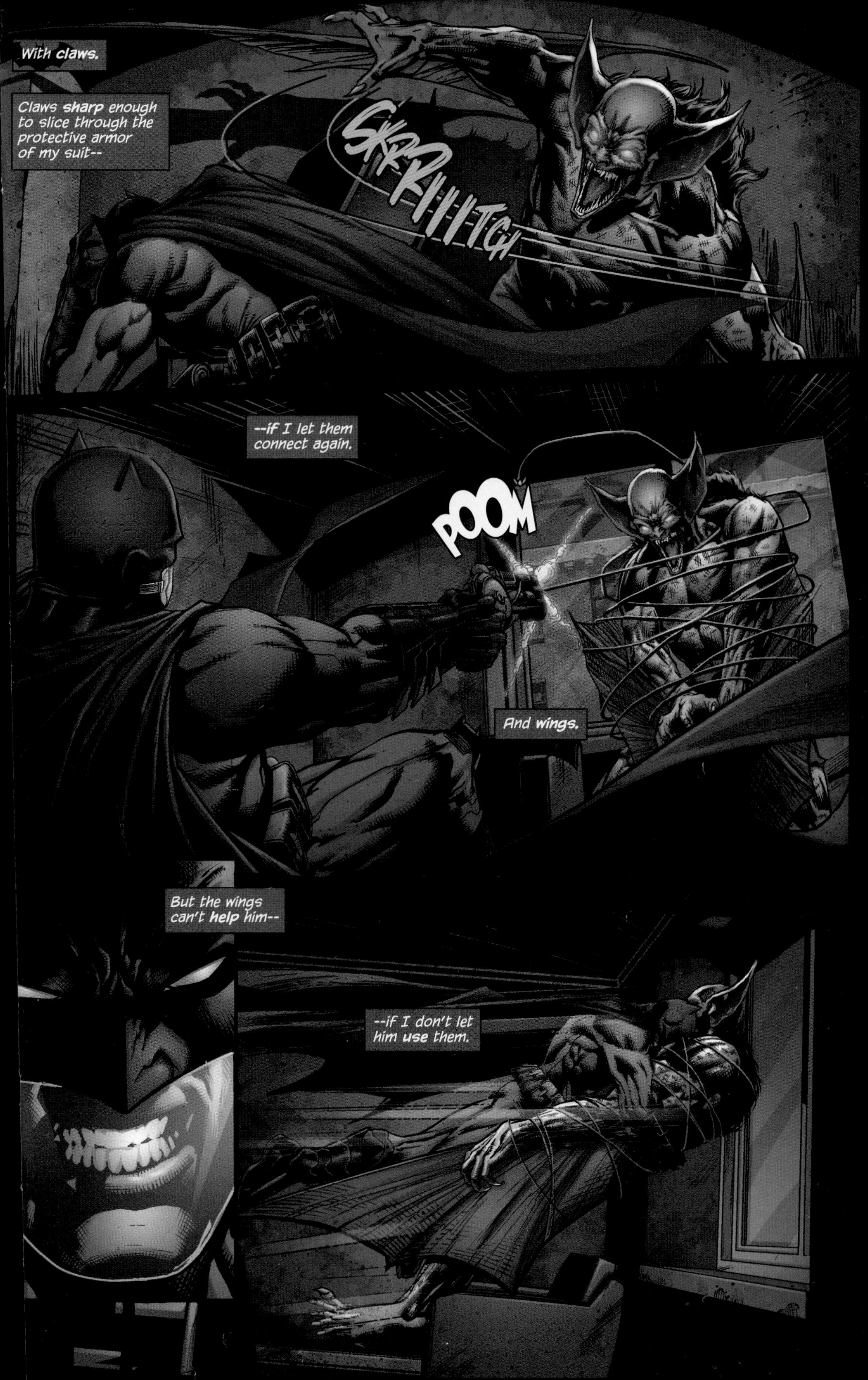

With claws.
Claws sharp enough to slice through the protective armor of my suit--
SKRRIIIITCH
--if I let them connect again.
POOM
And wings.
But the wings can't help him--
--if I don't let him use them.

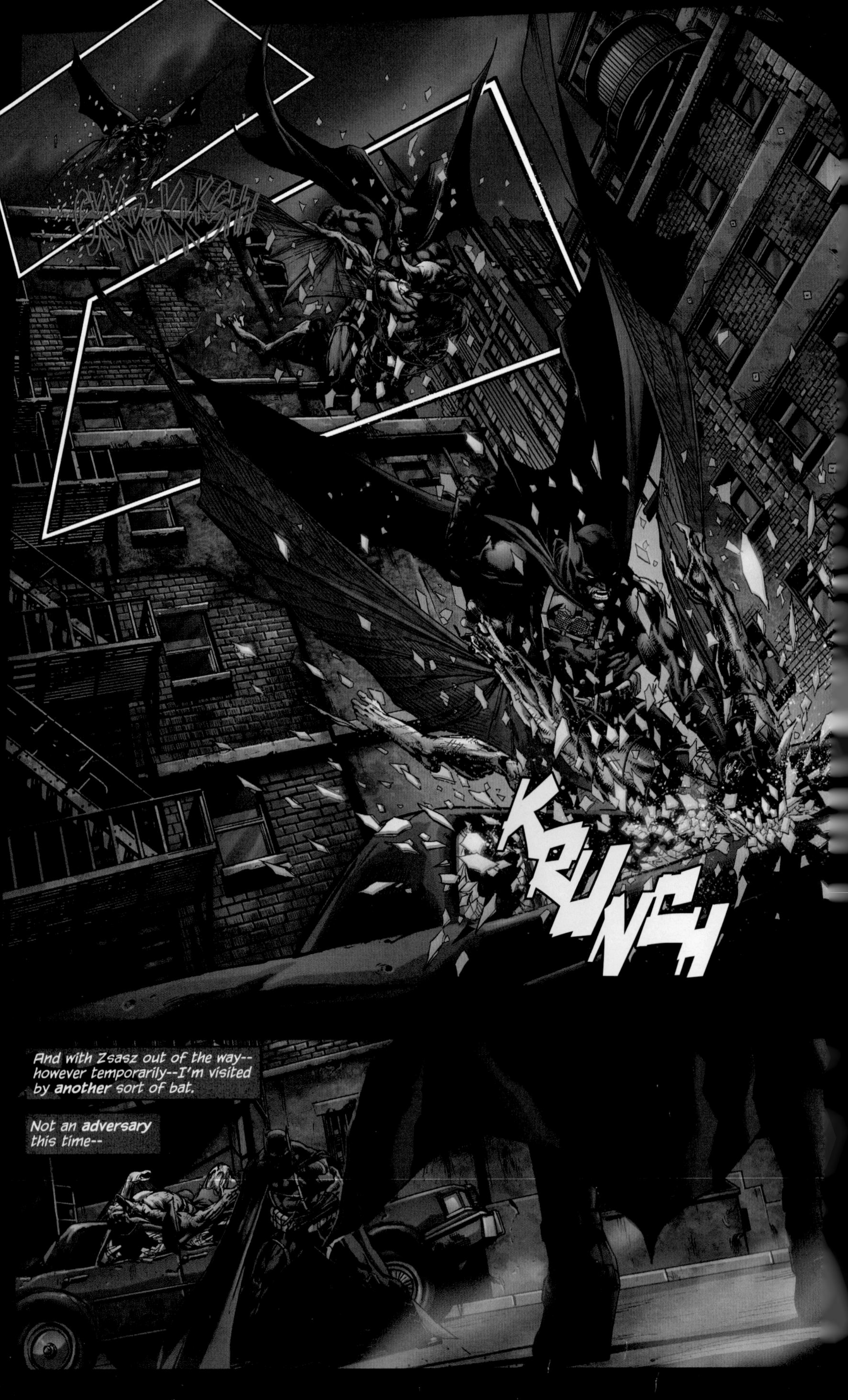
KRUNCH
And with Zsasz out of the way--however temporarily--I'm visited by another sort of bat.
Not an adversary this time--

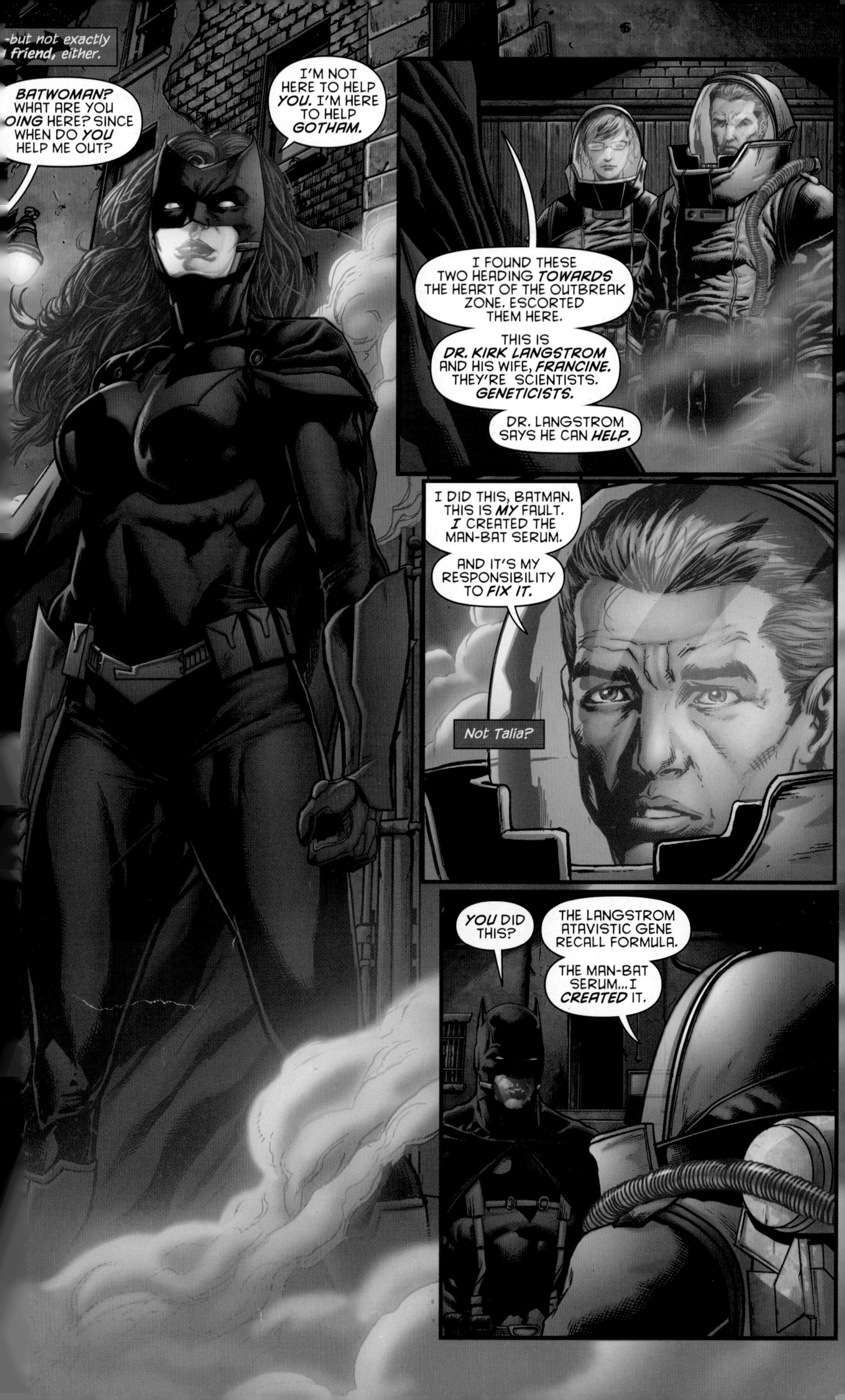

-but not exactly friend, either.
BATWOMAN? WHAT ARE YOU OING HERE? SINCE WHEN DO YOU HELP ME OUT?
I'M NOT HERE TO HELP YOU. I'M HERE TO HELP GOTHAM.
I FOUND THESE TWO HEADING TOWARDS THE HEART OF THE OUTBREAK ZONE. ESCORTED THEM HERE.
THIS IS DR. KIRK LANGSTROM AND HIS WIFE, FRANCINE. THEY'RE SCIENTISTS. GENETICISTS.
DR. LANGSTROM SAYS HE CAN HELP.
I DID THIS, BATMAN. THIS IS MY FAULT. I CREATED THE MAN-BAT SERUM.
AND IT'S MY RESPONSIBILITY TO FIX IT.
Not Talia?
YOU DID THIS?
THE LANGSTROM ATAVISTIC GENE RECALL FORMULA.
THE MAN-BAT SERUM...I CREATED IT.

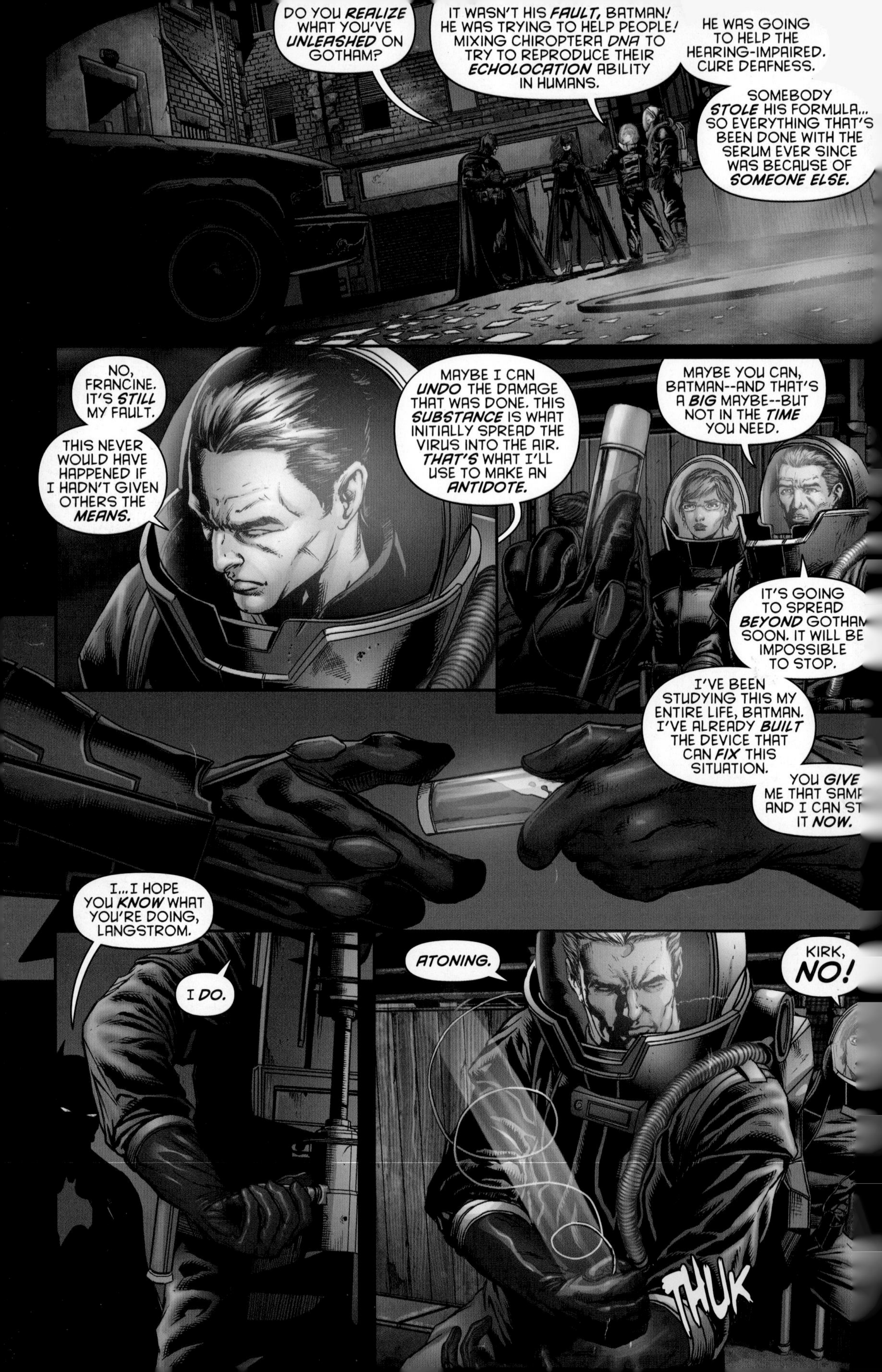

DO YOU REALIZE WHAT YOU'VE UNLEASHED ON GOTHAM?
IT WASN'T HIS FAULT, BATMAN! HE WAS TRYING TO HELP PEOPLE! MIXING CHIROPTERA DNA TO TRY TO REPRODUCE THEIR ECHOLOCATION ABILITY IN HUMANS.
HE WAS GOING TO HELP THE HEARING-IMPAIRED. CURE DEAFNESS.
SOMEBODY STOLE HIS FORMULA... SO EVERYTHING THAT'S BEEN DONE WITH THE SERUM EVER SINCE WAS BECAUSE OF SOMEONE ELSE.
NO, FRANCINE. IT'S STILL MY FAULT.
THIS NEVER WOULD HAVE HAPPENED IF I HADN'T GIVEN OTHERS THE MEANS.
MAYBE I CAN UNDO THE DAMAGE THAT WAS DONE. THIS SUBSTANCE IS WHAT INITIALLY SPREAD THE VIRUS INTO THE AIR. THAT'S WHAT I'LL USE TO MAKE AN ANTIDOTE.
MAYBE YOU CAN, BATMAN--AND THAT'S A BIG MAYBE--BUT NOT IN THE TIME YOU NEED.
IT'S GOING TO SPREAD BEYOND GOTHAM SOON. IT WILL BE IMPOSSIBLE TO STOP.
I'VE BEEN STUDYING THIS MY ENTIRE LIFE, BATMAN. I'VE ALREADY BUILT THE DEVICE THAT CAN FIX THIS SITUATION.
YOU GIVE ME THAT SAMP AND I CAN ST IT NOW.
I...I HOPE YOU KNOW WHAT YOU'RE DOING, LANGSTROM.
I DO.
ATONING.
KIRK, NO!
THUK

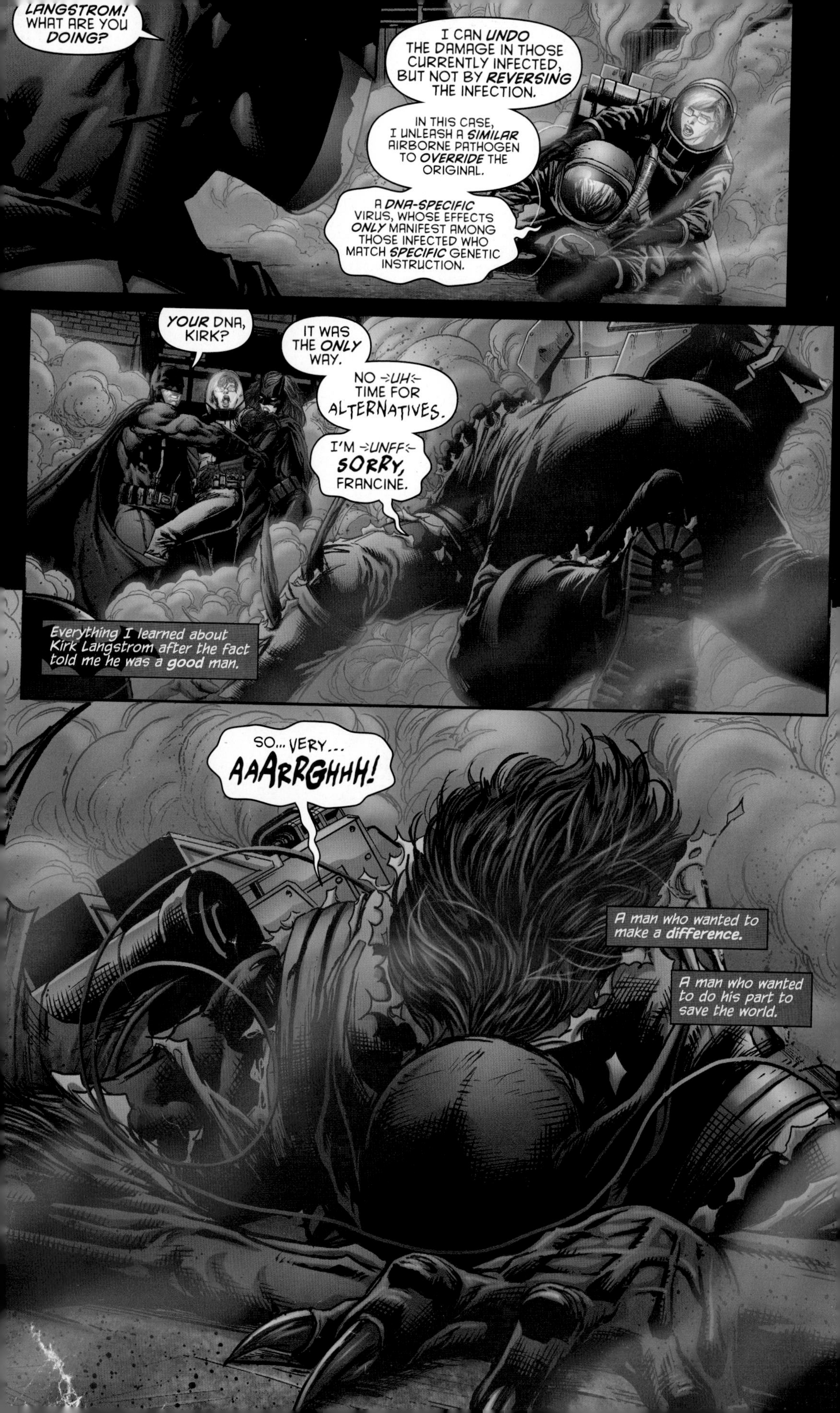
LANGSTROM! WHAT ARE YOU DOING?
I CAN UNDO THE DAMAGE IN THOSE CURRENTLY INFECTED, BUT NOT BY REVERSING THE INFECTION.
IN THIS CASE, I UNLEASH A SIMILAR AIRBORNE PATHOGEN TO OVERRIDE THE ORIGINAL.
A DNA-SPECIFIC VIRUS, WHOSE EFFECTS ONLY MANIFEST AMONG THOSE INFECTED WHO MATCH SPECIFIC GENETIC INSTRUCTION.
YOUR DNA, KIRK?
IT WAS THE ONLY WAY.
NO -UH- TIME FOR ALTERNATIVES.
I'M -UNFF- SORRY, FRANCINE.
Everything I learned about Kirk Langstrom after the fact told me he was a good man.
SO... VERY... AAARRGHHH!
A man who wanted to make a difference.
A man who wanted to do his part to save the world.

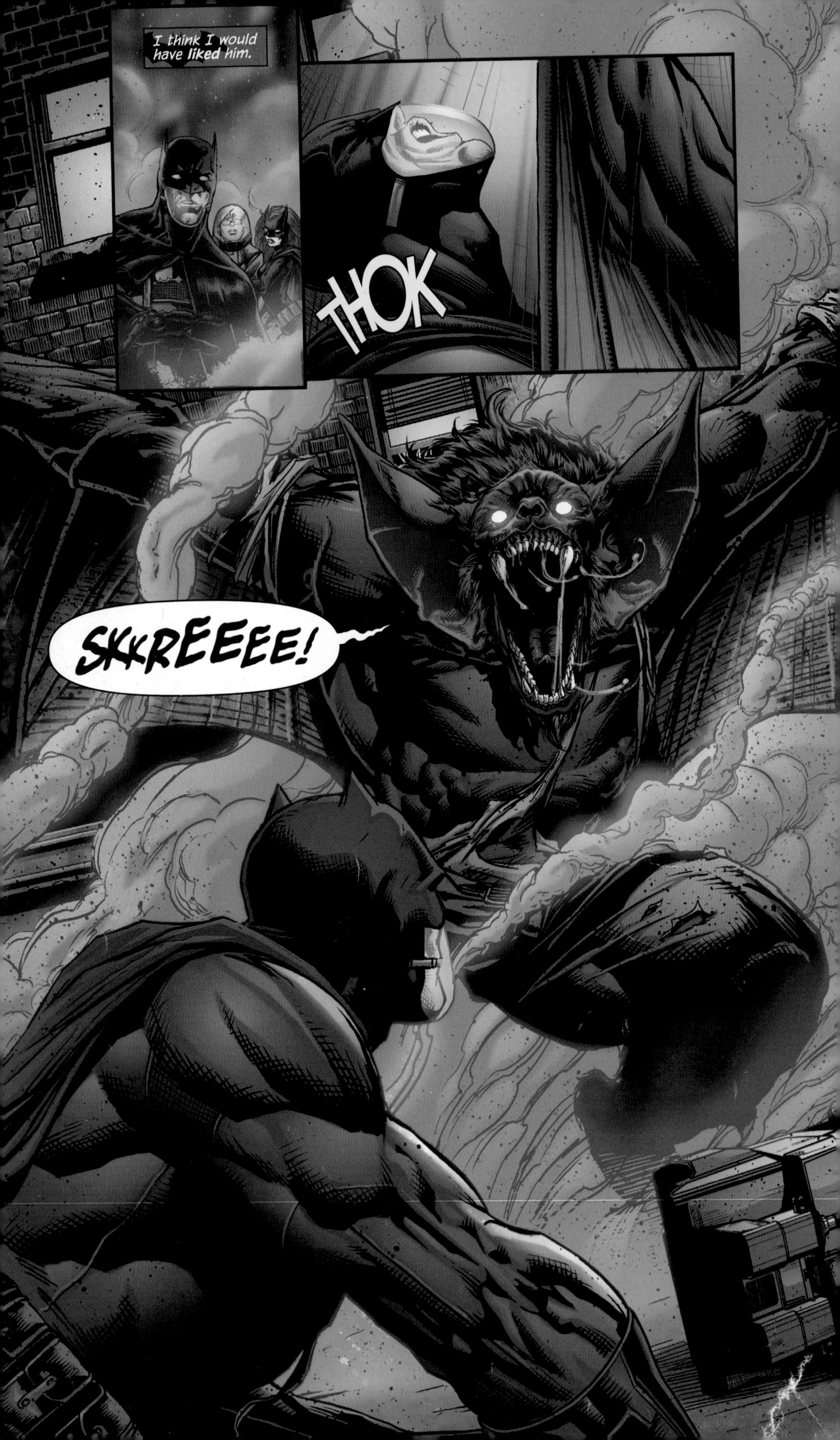
I think I would have liked him.
THOK
SKKREEEE!

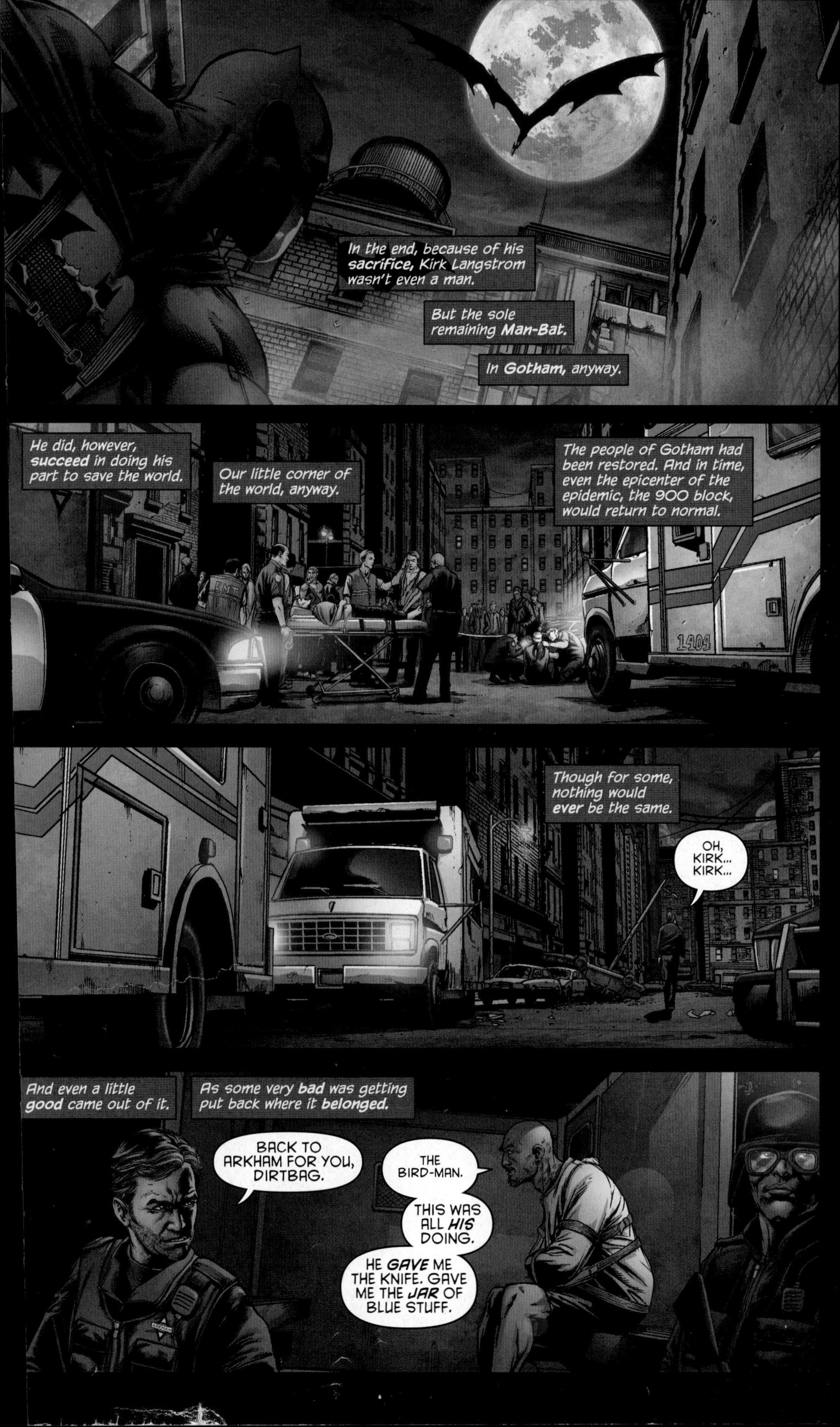

In the end, because of his sacrifice, Kirk Langstrom wasn't even a man.
But the sole remaining Man-Bat.
In Gotham, anyway.
He did, however, succeed in doing his part to save the world.
Our little corner of the world, anyway.
The people of Gotham had been restored. And in time, even the epicenter of the epidemic, the 900 block, would return to normal.
EMT
1404
Though for some, nothing would ever be the same.
OH, KIRK... KIRK...
And even a little good came out of it.
As some very bad was getting put back where it belonged.
BACK TO ARKHAM FOR YOU, DIRTBAG.
THE BIRD-MAN.
THIS WAS ALL HIS DOING.
HE GAVE ME THE KNIFE. GAVE ME THE JAR OF BLUE STUFF.

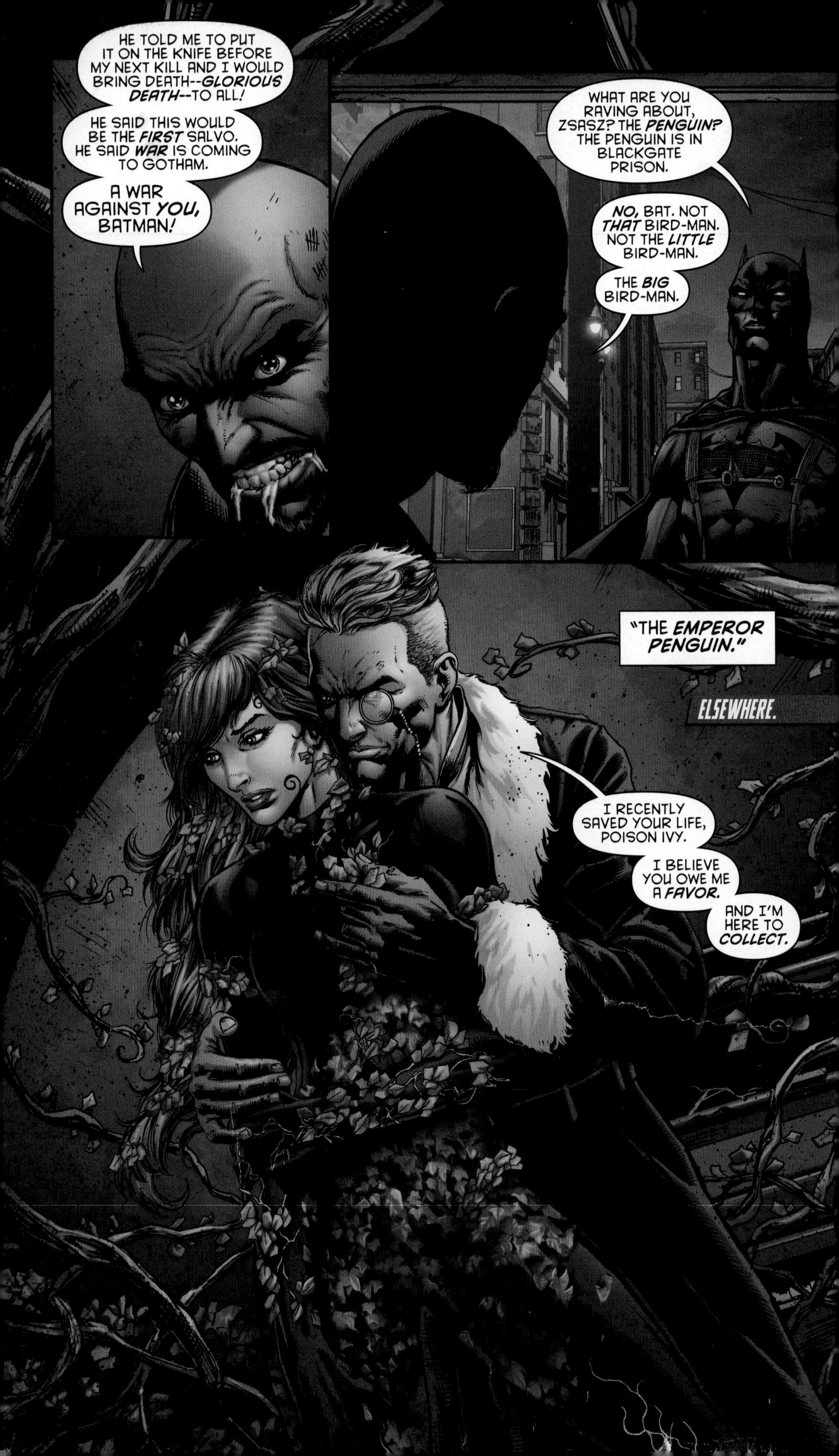
HE TOLD ME TO PUT IT ON THE KNIFE BEFORE MY NEXT KILL AND I WOULD BRING DEATH--GLORIOUS DEATH--TO ALL!
HE SAID THIS WOULD BE THE FIRST SALVO. HE SAID WAR IS COMING TO GOTHAM.
A WAR AGAINST YOU, BATMAN!
WHAT ARE YOU RAVING ABOUT, ZSASZ? THE PENGUIN? THE PENGUIN IS IN BLACKGATE PRISON.
NO, BAT. NOT THAT BIRD-MAN. NOT THE LITTLE BIRD-MAN.
THE BIG BIRD-MAN.
"THE EMPEROR PENGUIN."
ELSEWHERE.
I RECENTLY SAVED YOUR LIFE, POISON IVY.
I BELIEVE YOU OWE ME A FAVOR.
AND I'M HERE TO COLLECT.

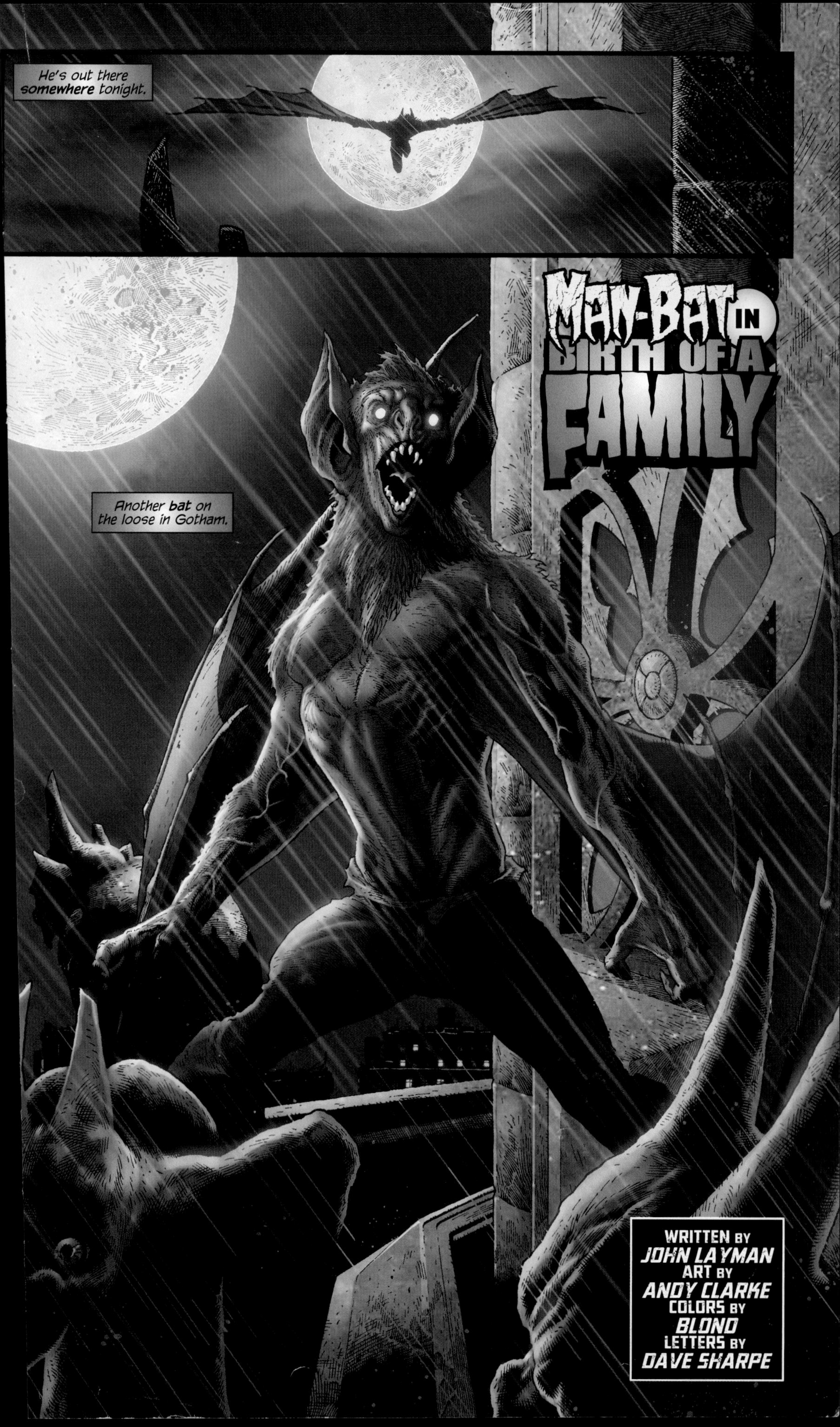

He's out there somewhere tonight.

Another **bat** on the loose in Gotham.

MAN-BAT IN BIRTH OF A FAMILY

WRITTEN BY
JOHN LAYMAN
ART BY
ANDY CLARKE
COLORS BY
BLOND
LETTERS BY
DAVE SHARPE

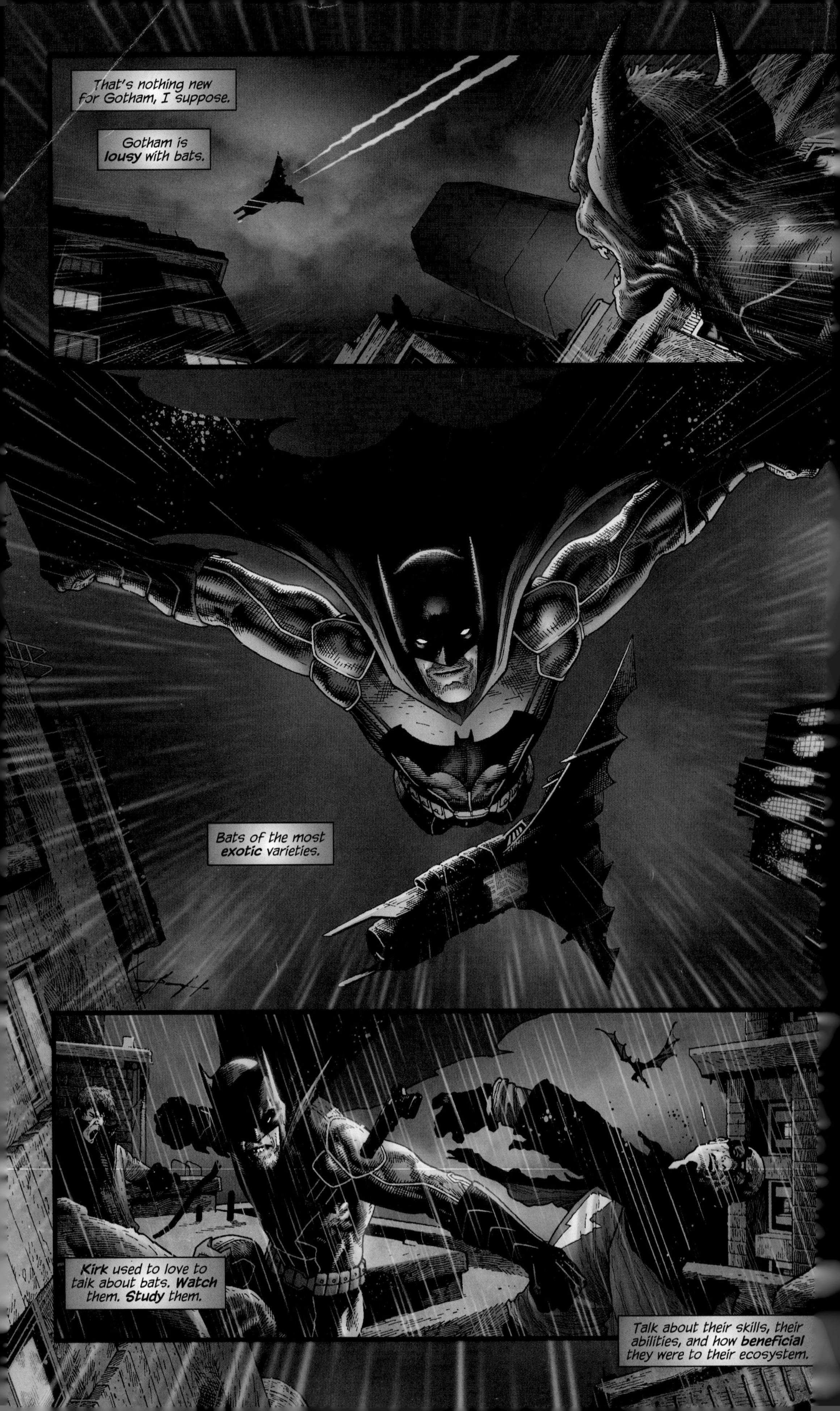
That's nothing new for Gotham, I suppose.
Gotham is **lousy** with bats.
Bats of the most **exotic** varieties.
Kirk used to love to talk about bats. **Watch** them. **Study** them.
Talk about their skills, their abilities, and how **beneficial** they were to their ecosystem.

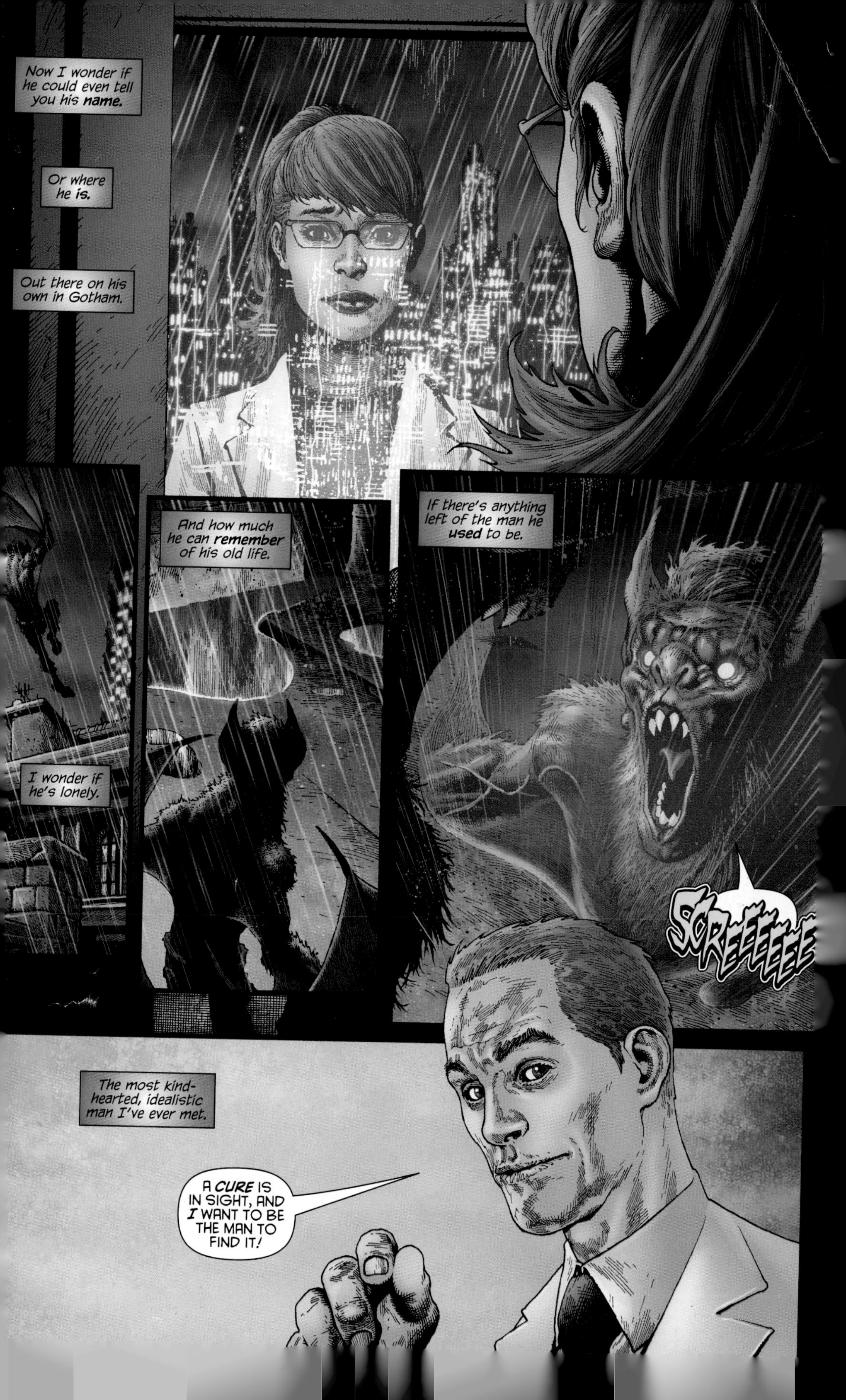

Now I wonder if he could even tell you his name.
Or where he is.
Out there on his own in Gotham.
I wonder if he's lonely.
And how much he can remember of his old life.
If there's anything left of the man he used to be.
SCREEEEEE
The most kind-hearted, idealistic man I've ever met.
A CURE IS IN SIGHT, AND I WANT TO BE THE MAN TO FIND IT!

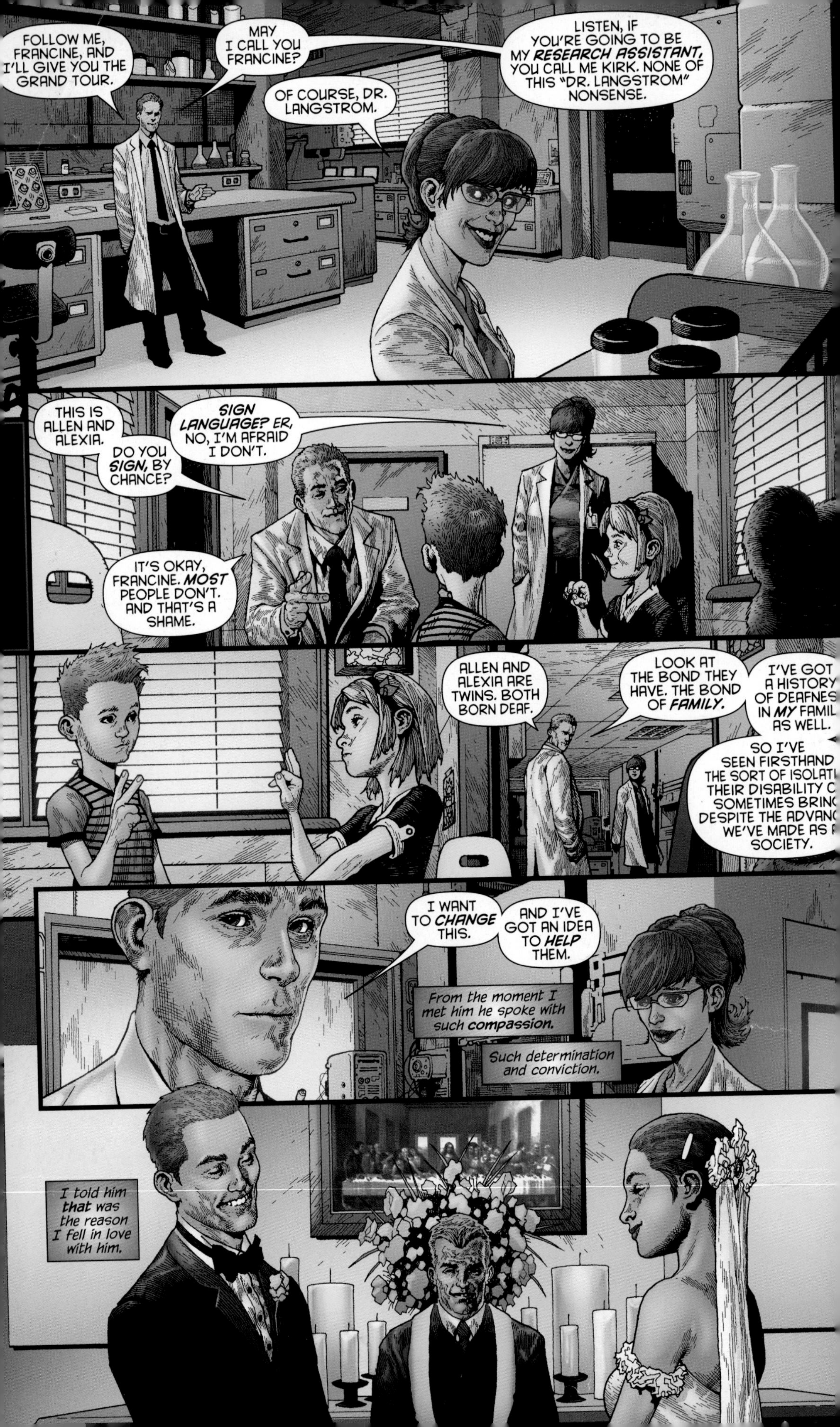
FOLLOW ME, FRANCINE, AND I'LL GIVE YOU THE GRAND TOUR.
MAY I CALL YOU FRANCINE?
OF COURSE, DR. LANGSTROM.
LISTEN, IF YOU'RE GOING TO BE MY RESEARCH ASSISTANT, YOU CALL ME KIRK. NONE OF THIS "DR. LANGSTROM" NONSENSE.
THIS IS ALLEN AND ALEXIA.
DO YOU SIGN, BY CHANCE?
SIGN LANGUAGE? ER, NO, I'M AFRAID I DON'T.
IT'S OKAY, FRANCINE. MOST PEOPLE DON'T. AND THAT'S A SHAME.
ALLEN AND ALEXIA ARE TWINS. BOTH BORN DEAF.
LOOK AT THE BOND THEY HAVE. THE BOND OF FAMILY.
I'VE GOT A HISTORY OF DEAFNES IN MY FAMIL AS WELL.
SO I'VE SEEN FIRSTHAND THE SORT OF ISOLATI THEIR DISABILITY C SOMETIMES BRINC DESPITE THE ADVANC WE'VE MADE AS SOCIETY.
I WANT TO CHANGE THIS.
AND I'VE GOT AN IDEA TO HELP THEM.
From the moment I met him he spoke with such compassion.
Such determination and conviction.
I told him that was the reason I fell in love with him.

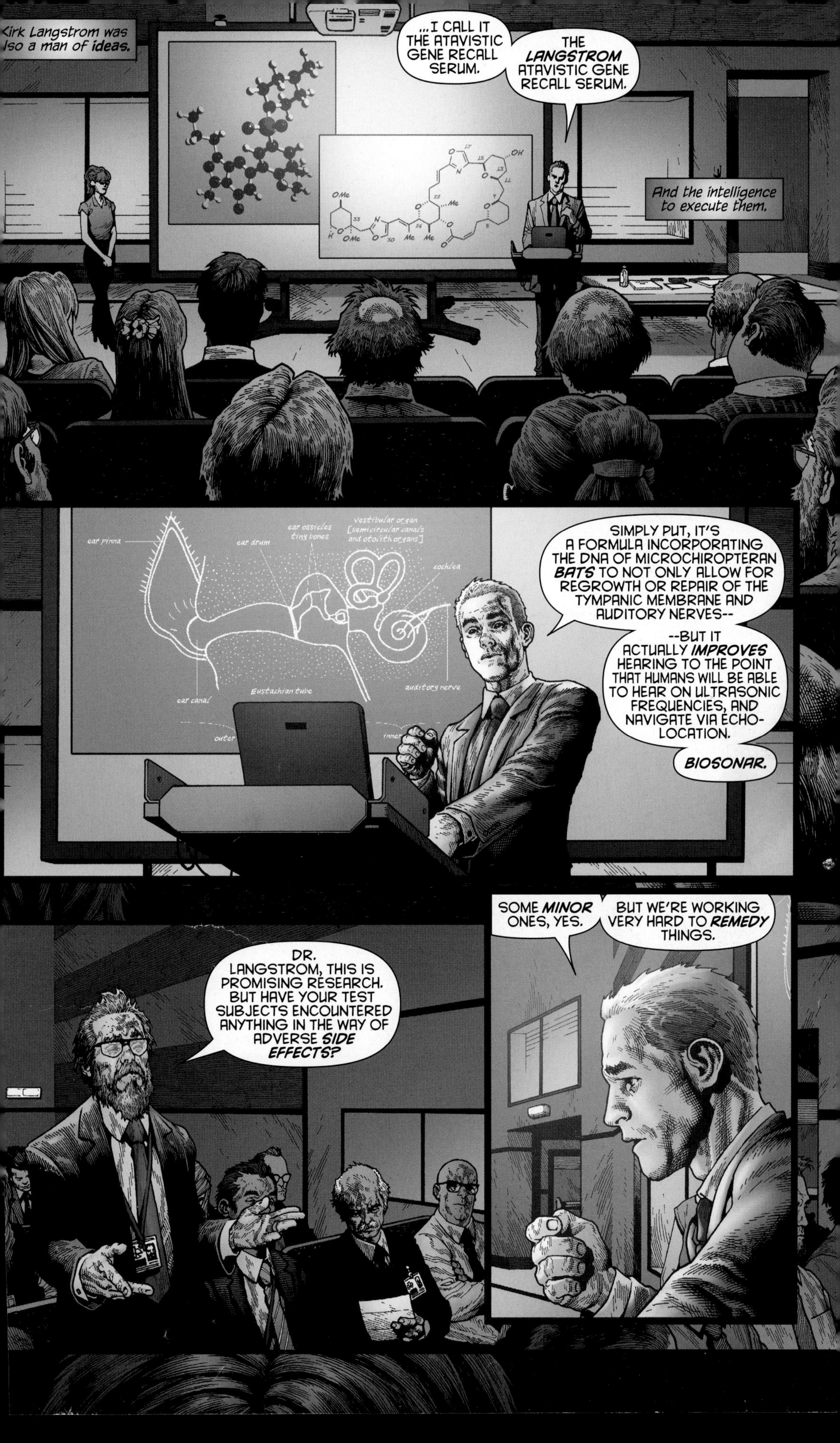

Kirk Langstrom was also a man of ideas.
...I CALL IT THE ATAVISTIC GENE RECALL SERUM.
THE LANGSTROM ATAVISTIC GENE RECALL SERUM.
And the intelligence to execute them.
ear pinna
ear drum
ear ossicles tiny bones
vestibular organ [semicircular canals and otolith organs]
cochlea
auditory nerve
Eustachian tube
ear canal
outer
inner
SIMPLY PUT, IT'S A FORMULA INCORPORATING THE DNA OF MICROCHIROPTERAN BATS TO NOT ONLY ALLOW FOR REGROWTH OR REPAIR OF THE TYMPANIC MEMBRANE AND AUDITORY NERVES--
--BUT IT ACTUALLY IMPROVES HEARING TO THE POINT THAT HUMANS WILL BE ABLE TO HEAR ON ULTRASONIC FREQUENCIES, AND NAVIGATE VIA ECHO-LOCATION.
BIOSONAR.
DR. LANGSTROM, THIS IS PROMISING RESEARCH. BUT HAVE YOUR TEST SUBJECTS ENCOUNTERED ANYTHING IN THE WAY OF ADVERSE SIDE EFFECTS?
SOME MINOR ONES, YES.
BUT WE'RE WORKING VERY HARD TO REMEDY THINGS.

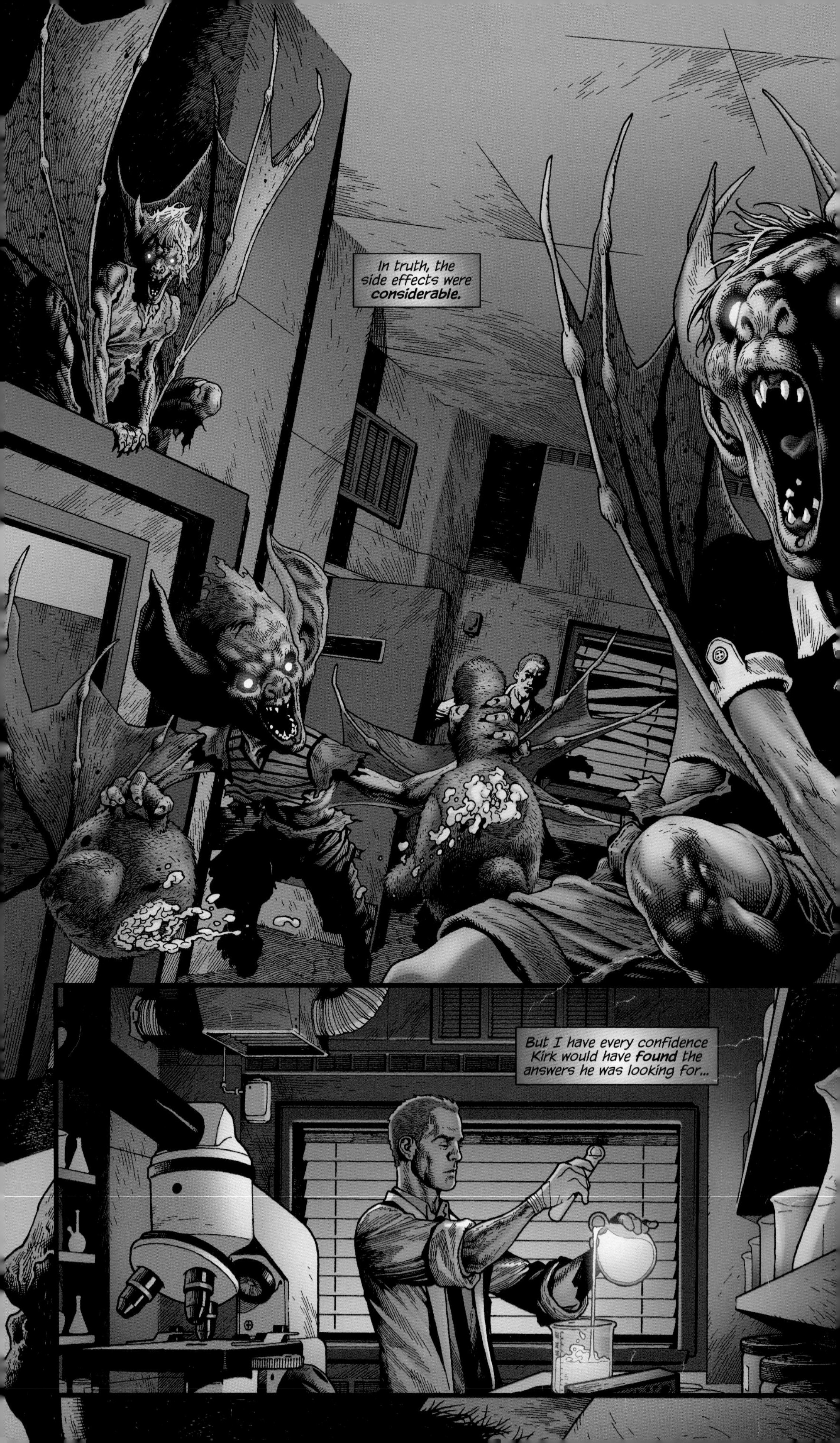
In truth, the side effects were **considerable.**
But I have every confidence Kirk would have **found** the answers he was looking for...

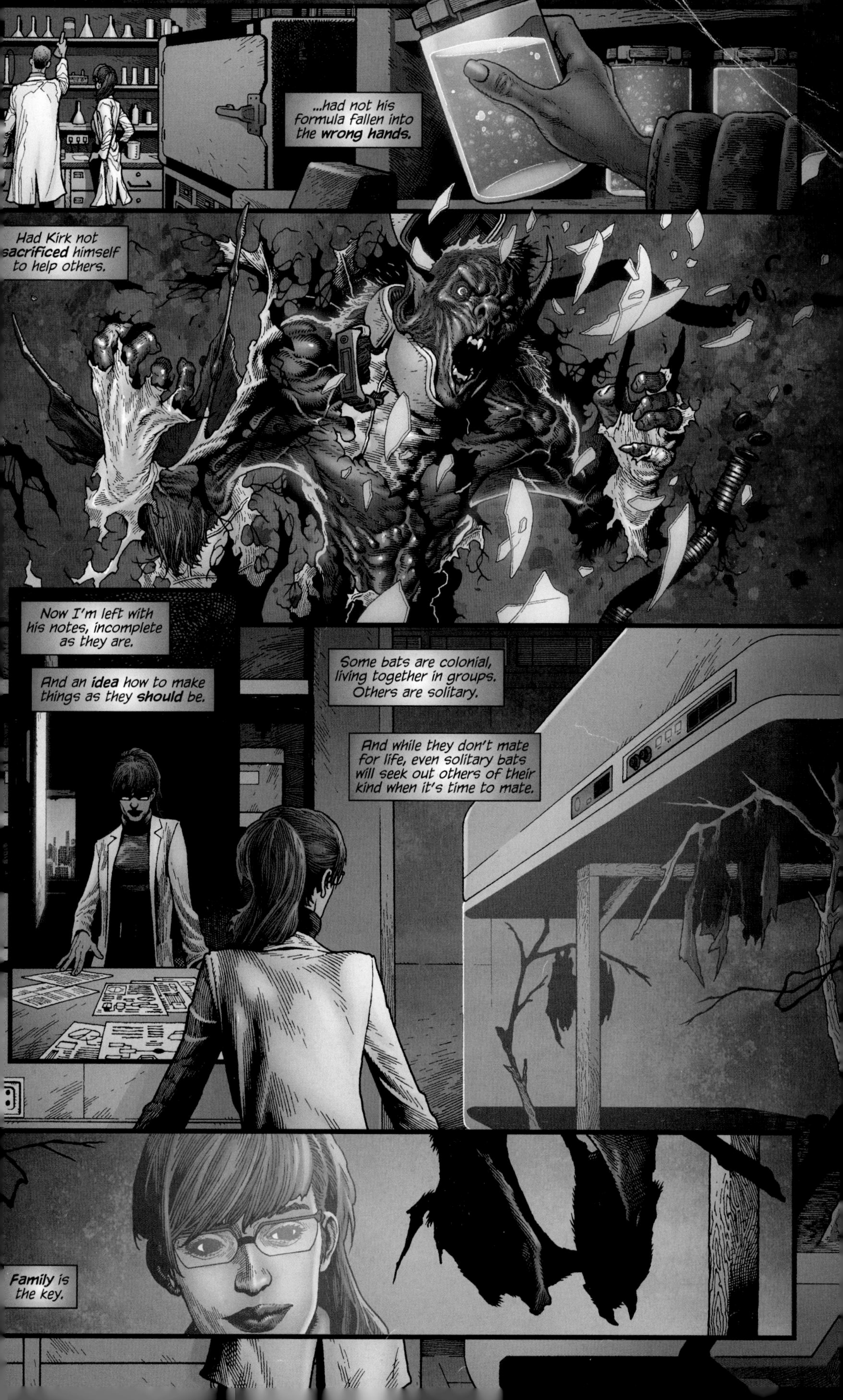

...had not his formula fallen into the **wrong hands.**
Had Kirk not **sacrificed** himself to help others.
Now I'm left with his notes, incomplete as they are.
And an **idea** how to make things as they **should** be.
Some bats are colonial, living together in groups. Others are solitary.
And while they don't mate for life, even solitary bats will seek out others of their kind when it's time to mate.
Family is the key.

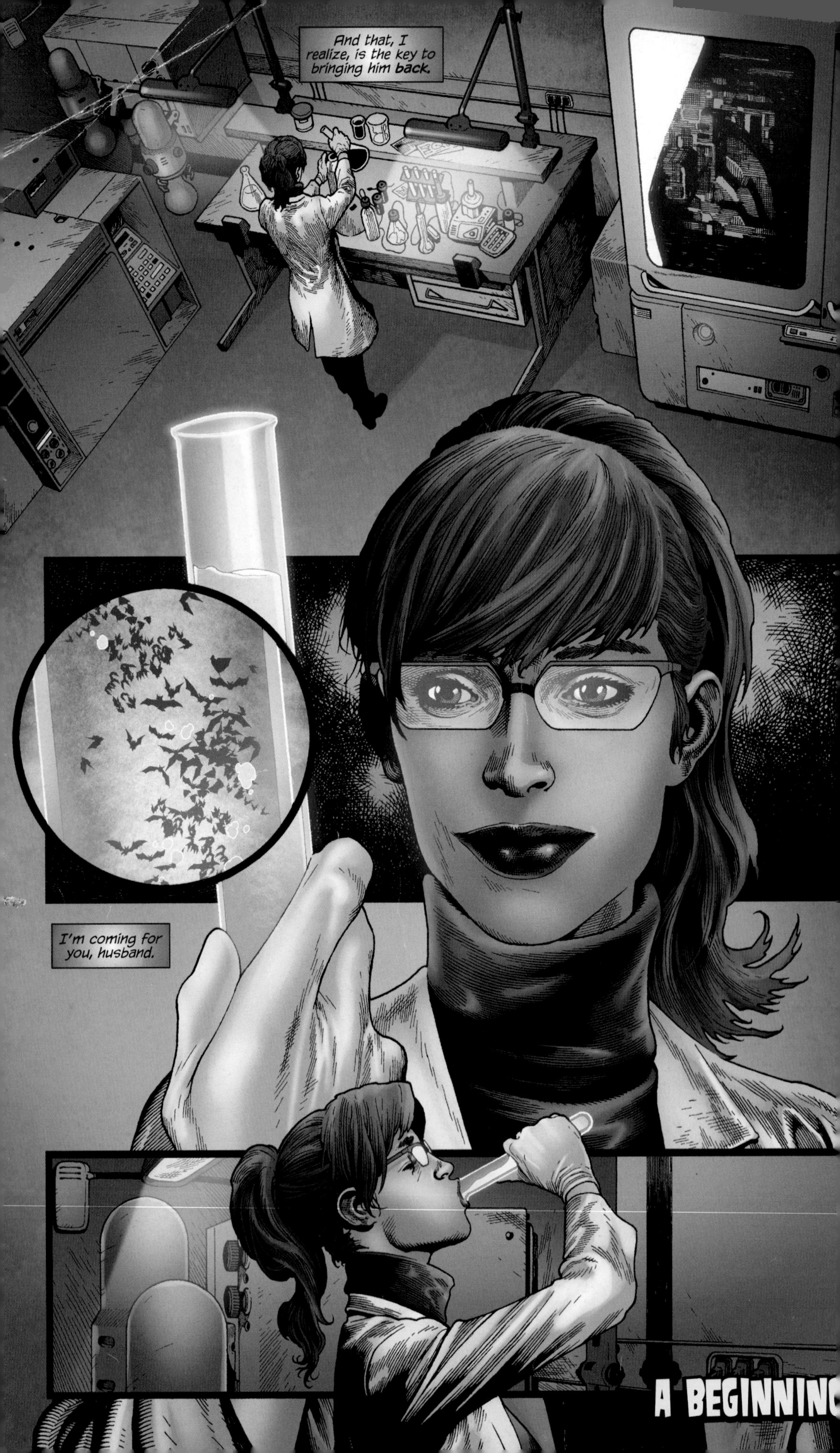
And that, I realize, is the key to bringing him back.
I'm coming for you, husband.
A BEGINNING

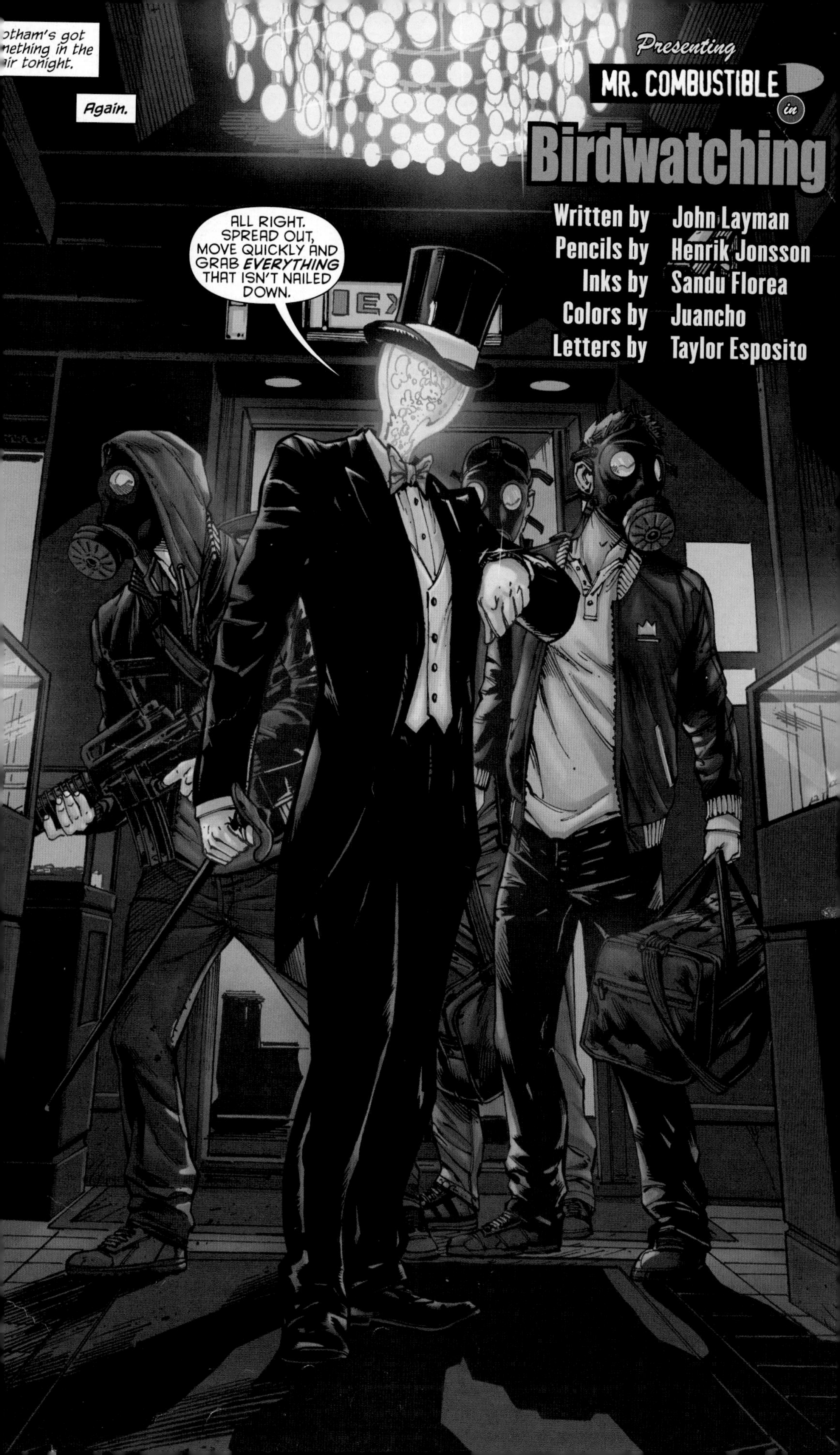

otham's got
nething in the
air tonight.
Again.
Presenting
MR. COMBUSTIBLE
in
Birdwatching
Written by John Layman
Pencils by Henrik Jonsson
Inks by Sandu Florea
Colors by Juancho
Letters by Taylor Esposito
ALL RIGHT. SPREAD OUT, MOVE QUICKLY AND GRAB *EVERYTHING* THAT ISN'T NAILED DOWN.

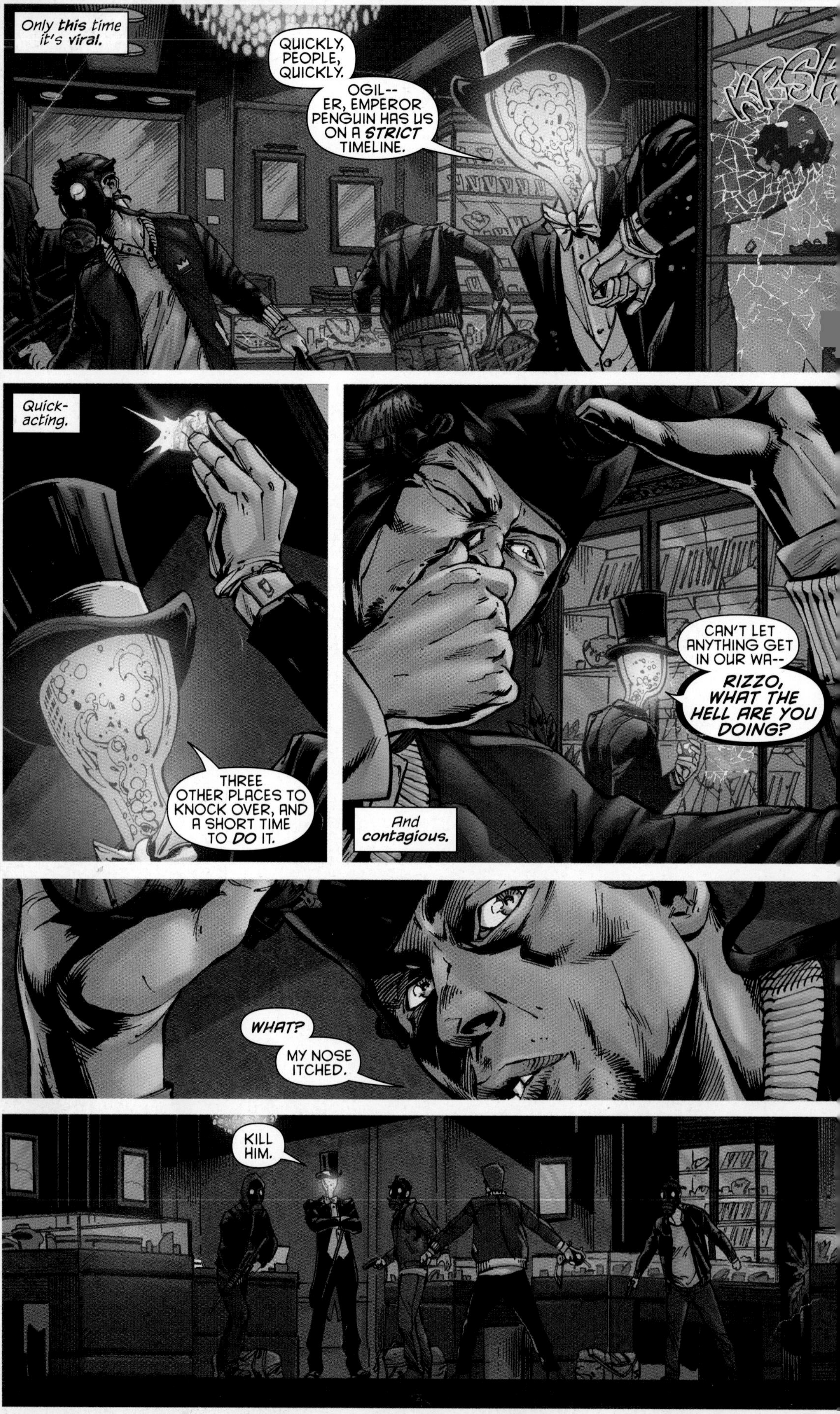
Only this time it's viral.
QUICKLY, PEOPLE, QUICKLY.
OGIL-- ER, EMPEROR PENGUIN HAS US ON A STRICT TIMELINE.
Quick-acting.
THREE OTHER PLACES TO KNOCK OVER, AND A SHORT TIME TO DO IT.
CAN'T LET ANYTHING GET IN OUR WA--
RIZZO, WHAT THE HELL ARE YOU DOING?
And contagious.
WHAT?
MY NOSE ITCHED.
KILL HIM.

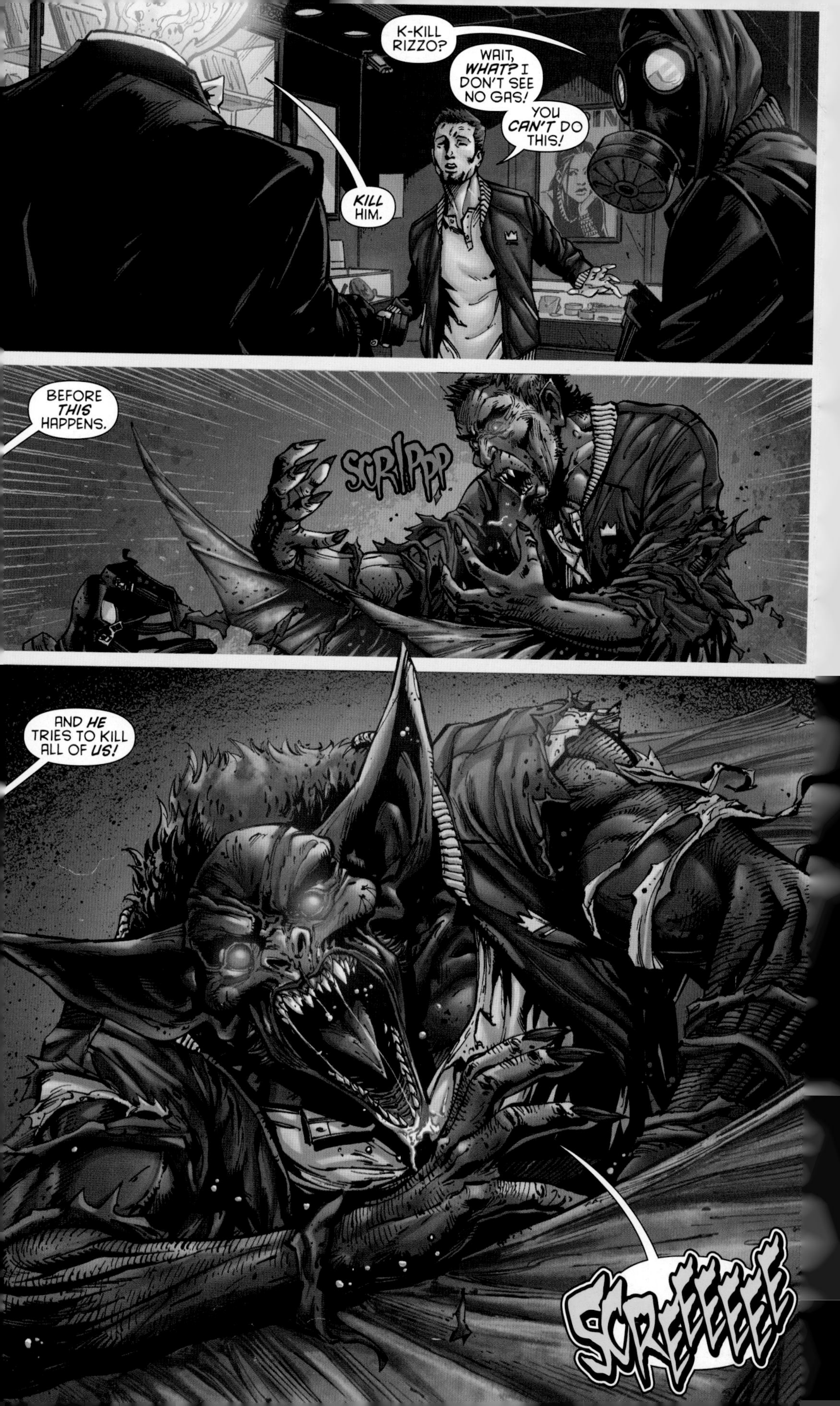
K-KILL RIZZO?
KILL HIM.
WAIT, WHAT? I DON'T SEE NO GAS!
YOU CAN'T DO THIS!
BEFORE THIS HAPPENS.
SCRIPPP
AND HE TRIES TO KILL ALL OF US!
SCREEEEEE

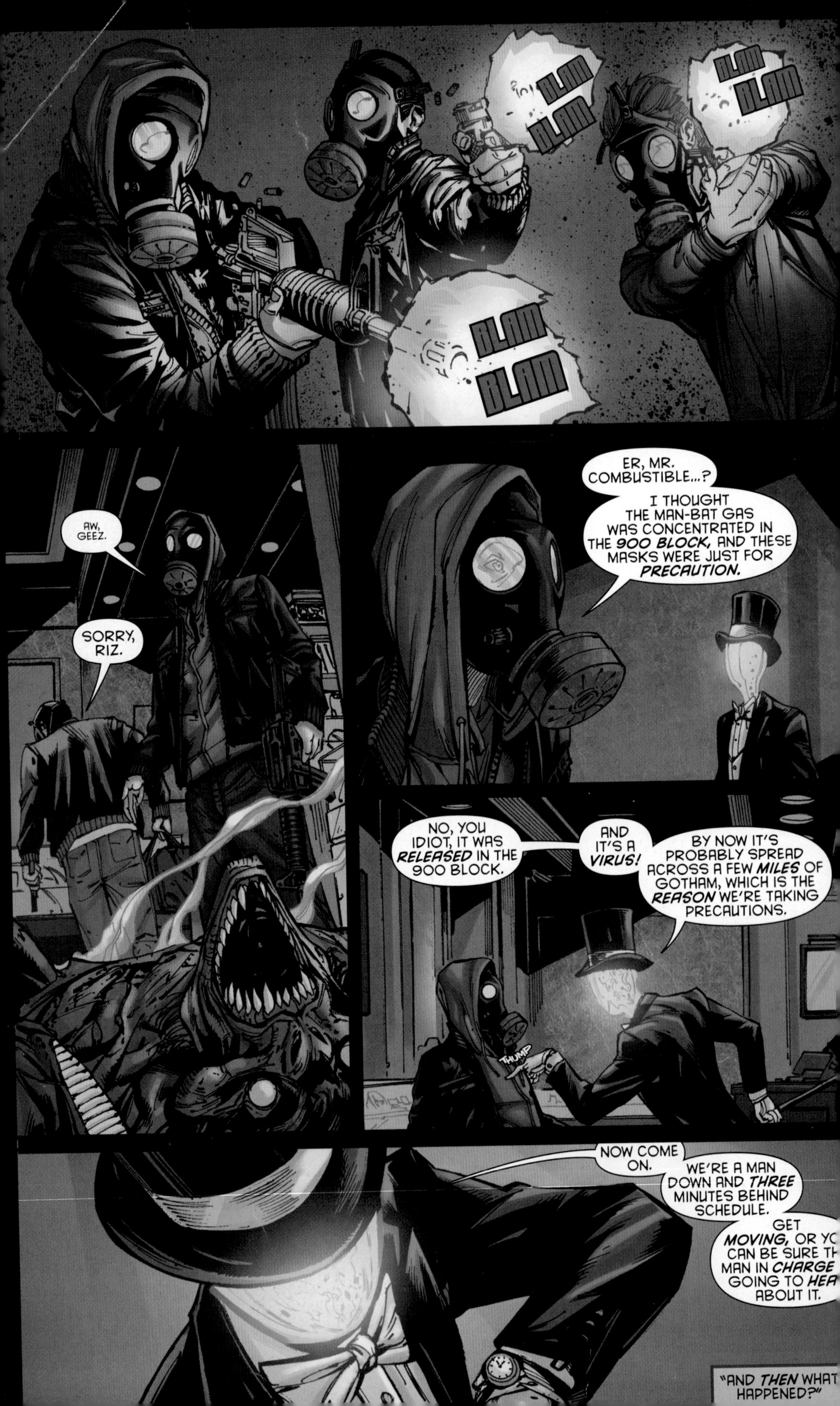
BLAM BLAM
BLAM BLAM
BLAM BLAM
AW, GEEZ.
SORRY, RIZ.
ER, MR. COMBUSTIBLE...?
I THOUGHT THE MAN-BAT GAS WAS CONCENTRATED IN THE 900 BLOCK, AND THESE MASKS WERE JUST FOR PRECAUTION.
NO, YOU IDIOT, IT WAS RELEASED IN THE 900 BLOCK.
AND IT'S A VIRUS!
BY NOW IT'S PROBABLY SPREAD ACROSS A FEW MILES OF GOTHAM, WHICH IS THE REASON WE'RE TAKING PRECAUTIONS.
THUMP
NOW COME ON.
WE'RE A MAN DOWN AND THREE MINUTES BEHIND SCHEDULE.
GET MOVING, OR YO CAN BE SURE TH MAN IN CHARGE GOING TO HEA ABOUT IT.
"AND THEN WHAT HAPPENED?"

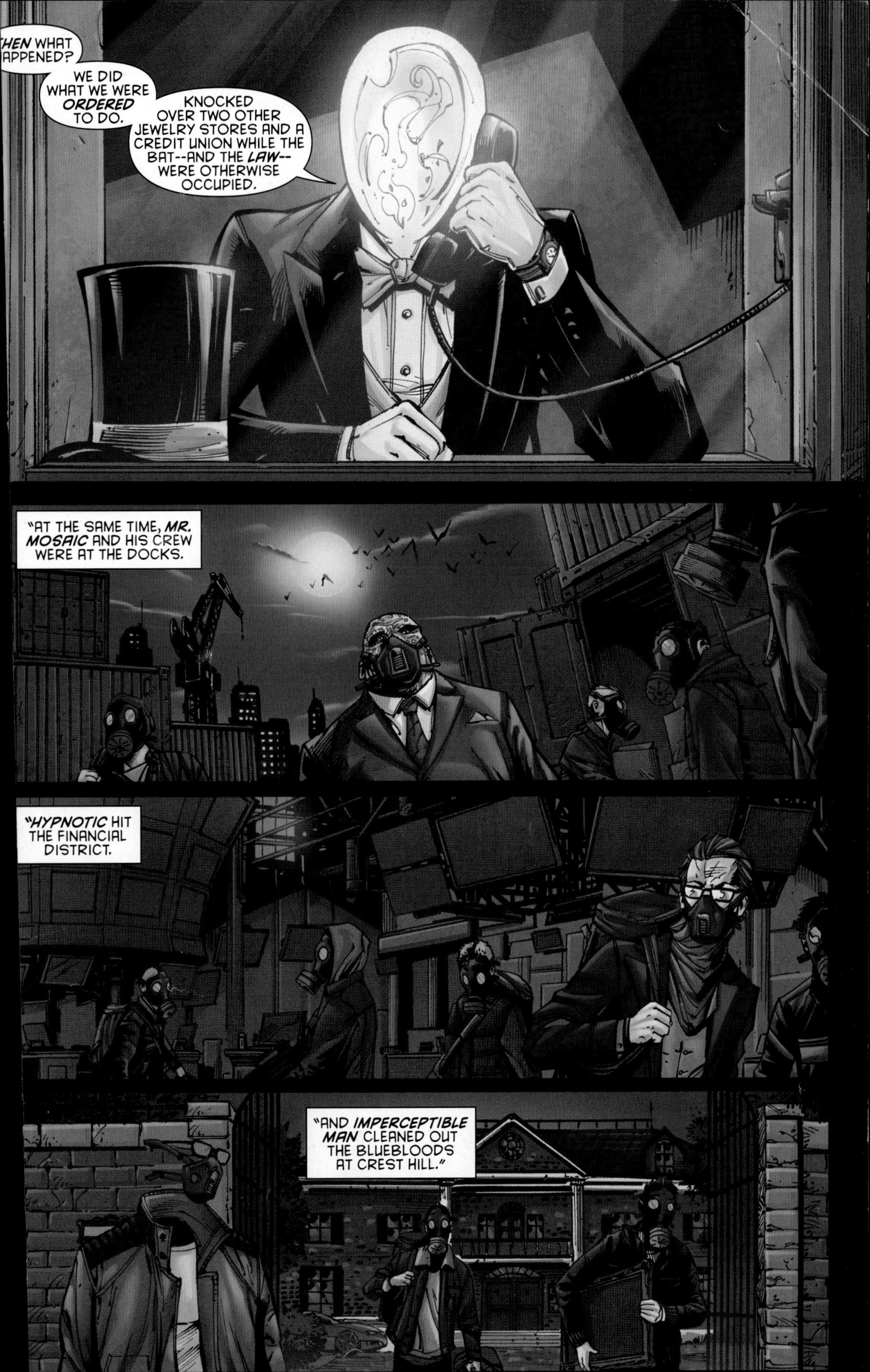
THEN WHAT HAPPENED?
WE DID WHAT WE WERE ORDERED TO DO.
KNOCKED OVER TWO OTHER JEWELRY STORES AND A CREDIT UNION WHILE THE BAT--AND THE LAW--WERE OTHERWISE OCCUPIED.
"AT THE SAME TIME, MR. MOSAIC AND HIS CREW WERE AT THE DOCKS.
"HYPNOTIC HIT THE FINANCIAL DISTRICT.
"AND IMPERCEPTIBLE MAN CLEANED OUT THE BLUEBLOODS AT CREST HILL."

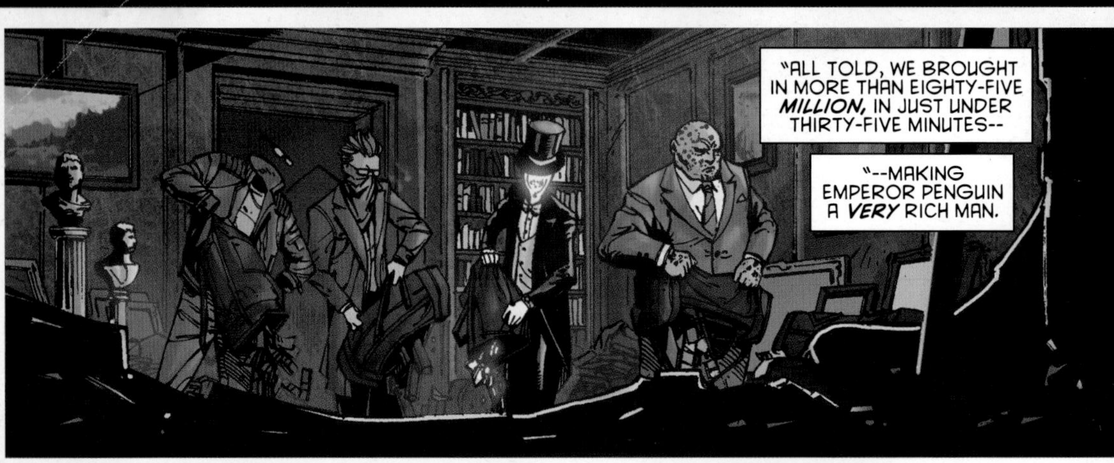
"ALL TOLD, WE BROUGHT IN MORE THAN EIGHTY-FIVE MILLION, IN JUST UNDER THIRTY-FIVE MINUTES--
"--MAKING EMPEROR PENGUIN A VERY RICH MAN.

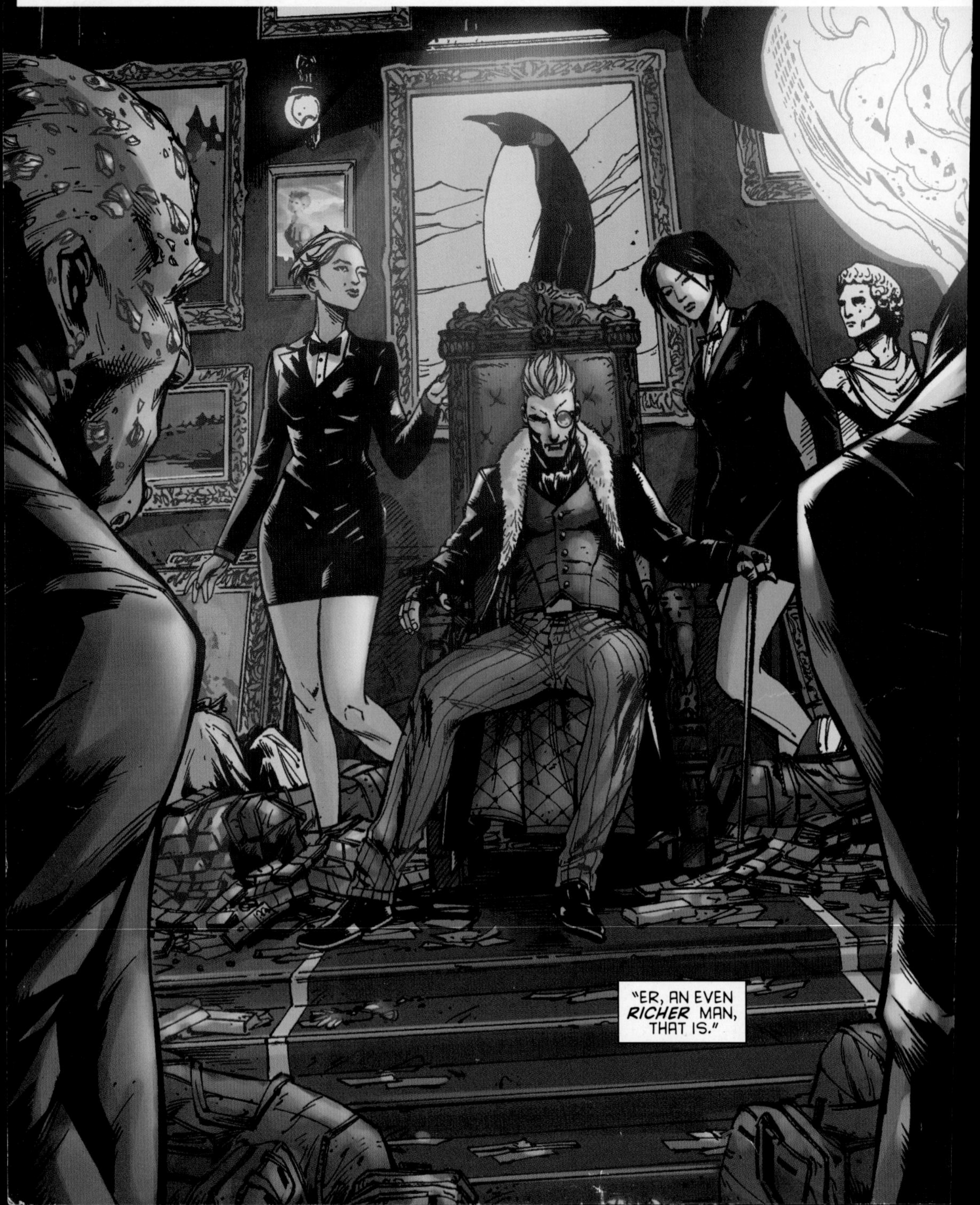
"ER, AN EVEN RICHER MAN, THAT IS."

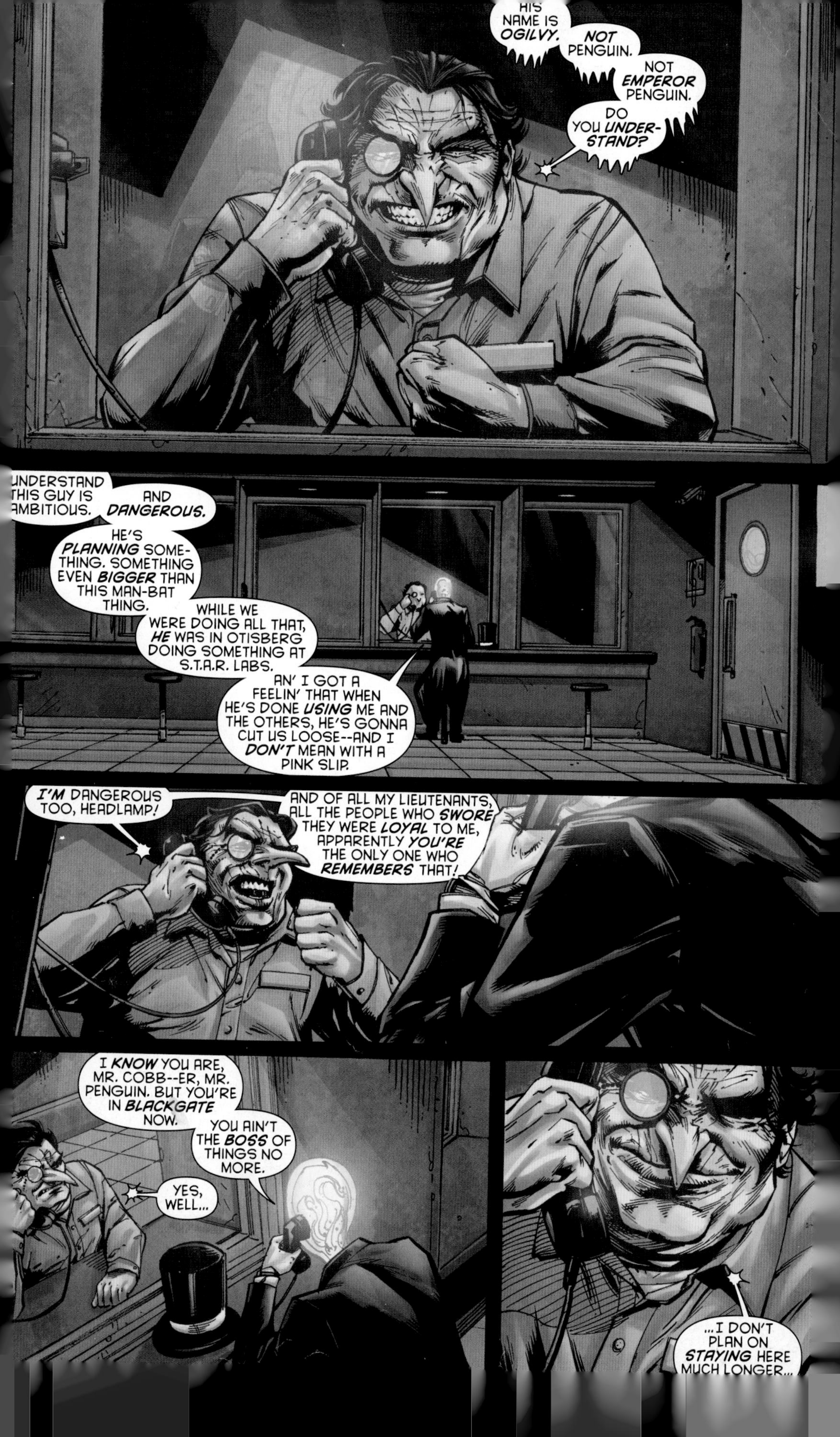

HIS NAME IS OGILVY.
NOT PENGUIN.
NOT EMPEROR PENGUIN.
DO YOU UNDER-STAND?
UNDERSTAND THIS GUY IS AMBITIOUS.
AND DANGEROUS.
HE'S PLANNING SOME-THING. SOMETHING EVEN BIGGER THAN THIS MAN-BAT THING.
WHILE WE WERE DOING ALL THAT, HE WAS IN OTISBERG DOING SOMETHING AT S.T.A.R. LABS.
AN' I GOT A FEELIN' THAT WHEN HE'S DONE USING ME AND THE OTHERS, HE'S GONNA CUT US LOOSE--AND I DON'T MEAN WITH A PINK SLIP.
I'M DANGEROUS TOO, HEADLAMP!
AND OF ALL MY LIEUTENANTS, ALL THE PEOPLE WHO SWORE THEY WERE LOYAL TO ME, APPARENTLY YOU'RE THE ONLY ONE WHO REMEMBERS THAT!
I KNOW YOU ARE, MR. COBB--ER, MR. PENGUIN. BUT YOU'RE IN BLACKGATE NOW.
YOU AIN'T THE BOSS OF THINGS NO MORE.
YES, WELL...
...I DON'T PLAN ON STAYING HERE MUCH LONGER...

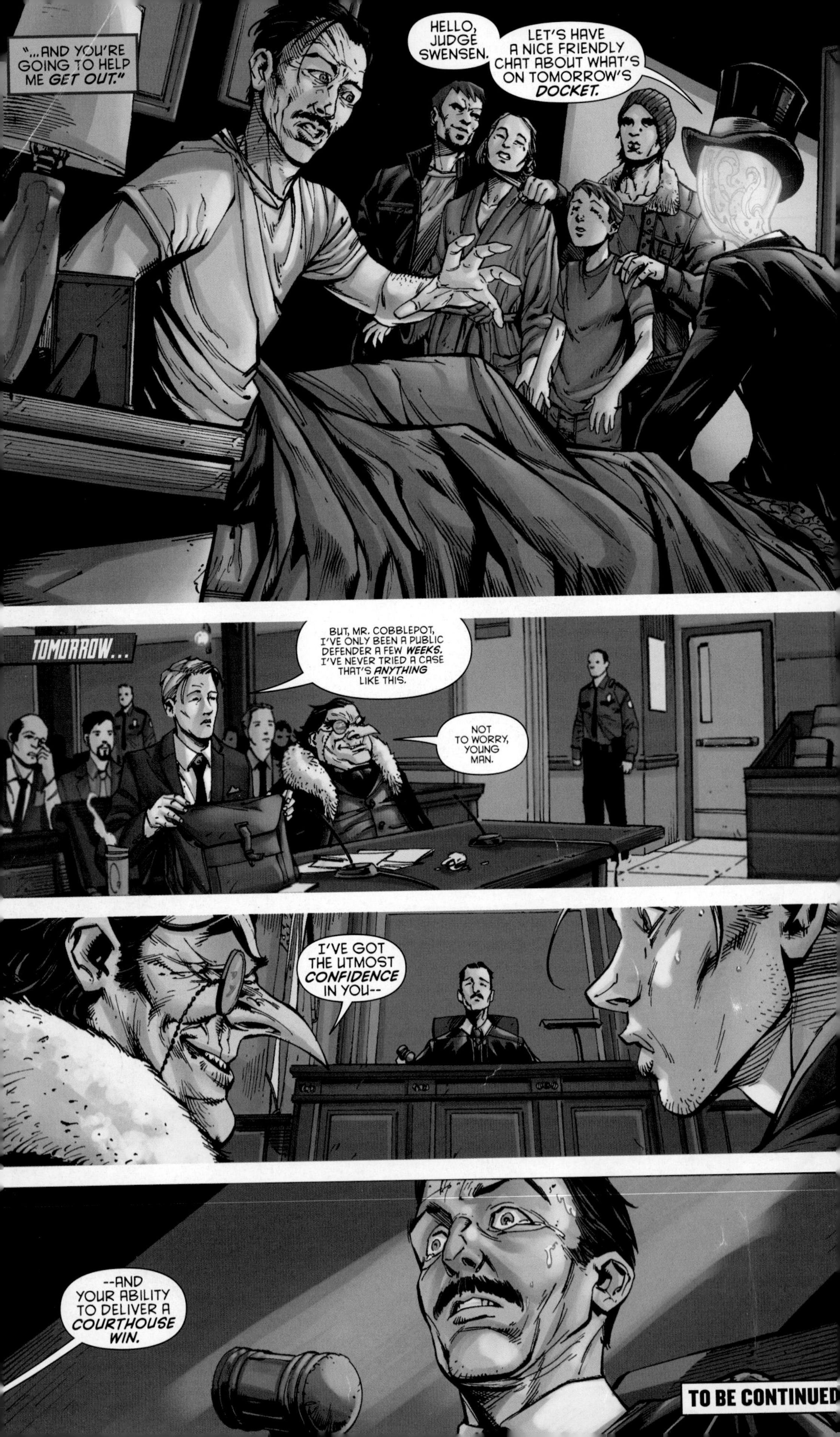
"...AND YOU'RE GOING TO HELP ME *GET OUT.*"
HELLO, JUDGE SWENSEN.
LET'S HAVE A NICE FRIENDLY CHAT ABOUT WHAT'S ON TOMORROW'S *DOCKET.*
TOMORROW...
BUT, MR. COBBLEPOT, I'VE ONLY BEEN A PUBLIC DEFENDER A FEW *WEEKS.* I'VE NEVER TRIED A CASE THAT'S *ANYTHING* LIKE THIS.
NOT TO WORRY, YOUNG MAN.
I'VE GOT THE UTMOST *CONFIDENCE* IN YOU--
--AND YOUR ABILITY TO DELIVER A *COURTHOUSE* WIN.
TO BE CONTINUED

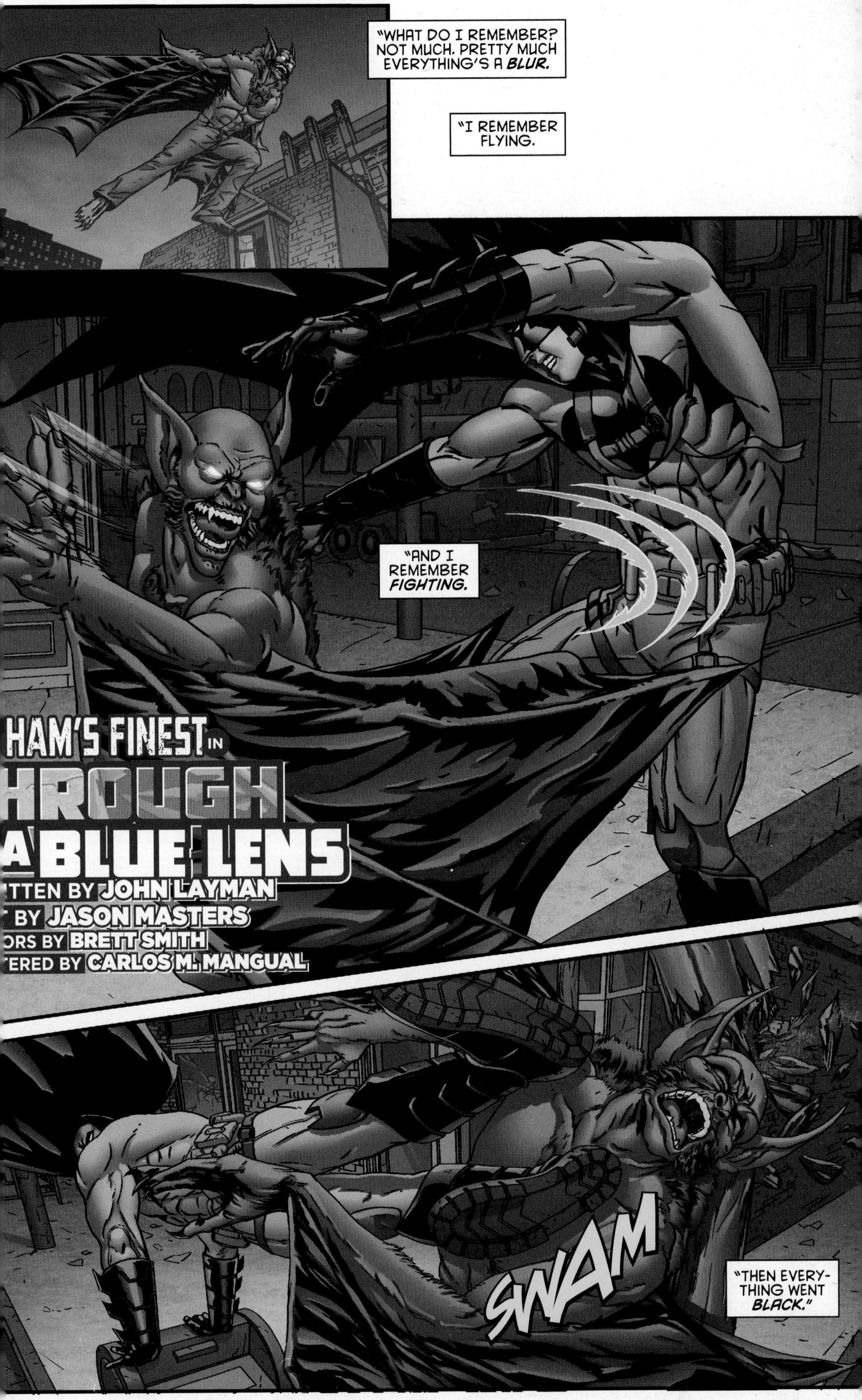
"WHAT DO I REMEMBER? NOT MUCH. PRETTY MUCH EVERYTHING'S A *BLUR.*
"I REMEMBER FLYING.
"AND I REMEMBER *FIGHTING.*
HAM'S FINEST IN
HROUGH A BLUE LENS
TTEN BY JOHN LAYMAN
BY JASON MASTERS
ORS BY BRETT SMITH
TERED BY CARLOS M. MANGUAL
SWAM
"THEN EVERY-THING WENT *BLACK.*"

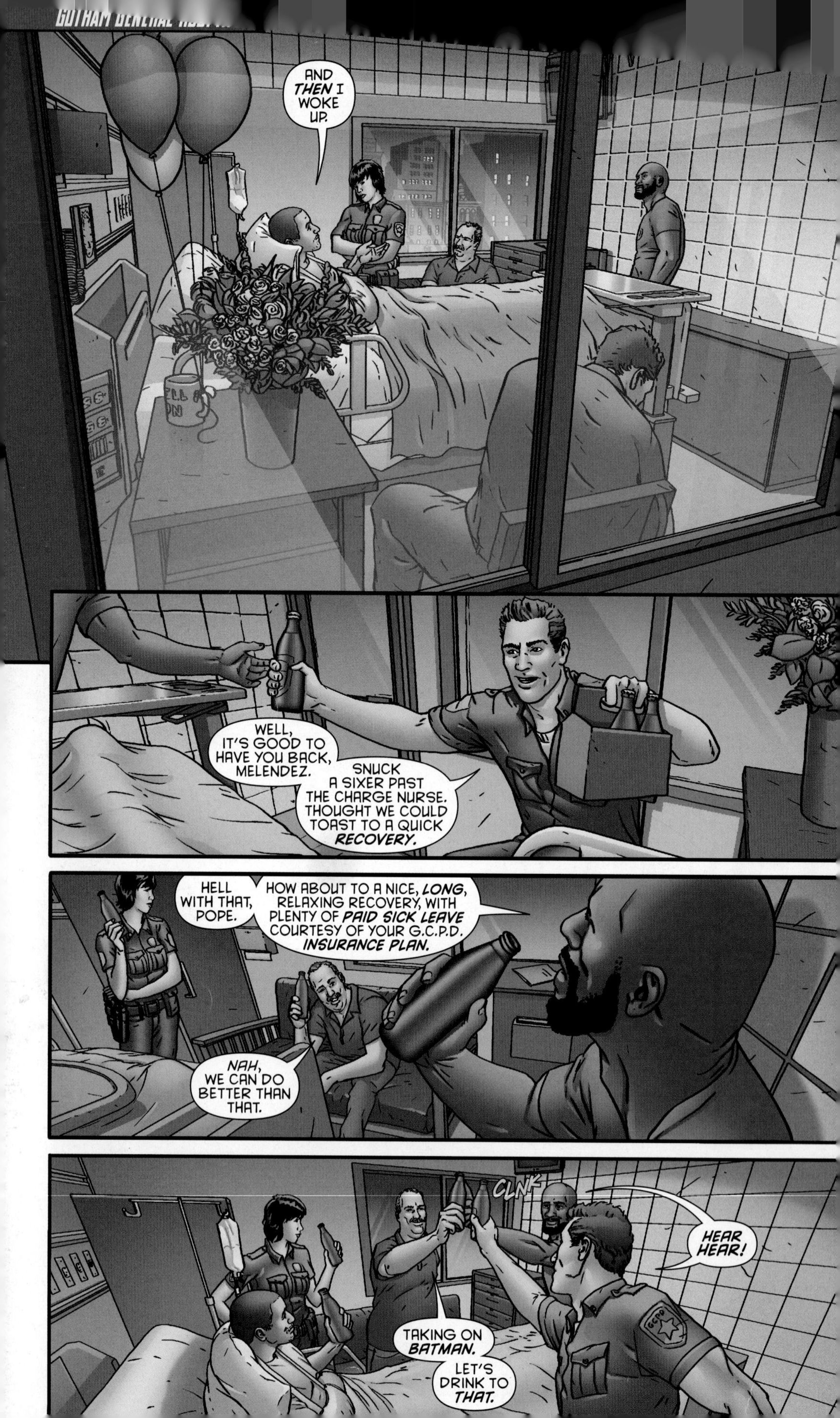
GOTHAM GENERAL
AND THEN I WOKE UP.
WELL, IT'S GOOD TO HAVE YOU BACK, MELENDEZ.
SNUCK A SIXER PAST THE CHARGE NURSE. THOUGHT WE COULD TOAST TO A QUICK RECOVERY.
HELL WITH THAT, POPE.
HOW ABOUT TO A NICE, LONG, RELAXING RECOVERY, WITH PLENTY OF PAID SICK LEAVE COURTESY OF YOUR G.C.P.D. INSURANCE PLAN.
NAH, WE CAN DO BETTER THAN THAT.
TAKING ON BATMAN.
LET'S DRINK TO THAT.
CLNK
HEAR HEAR!

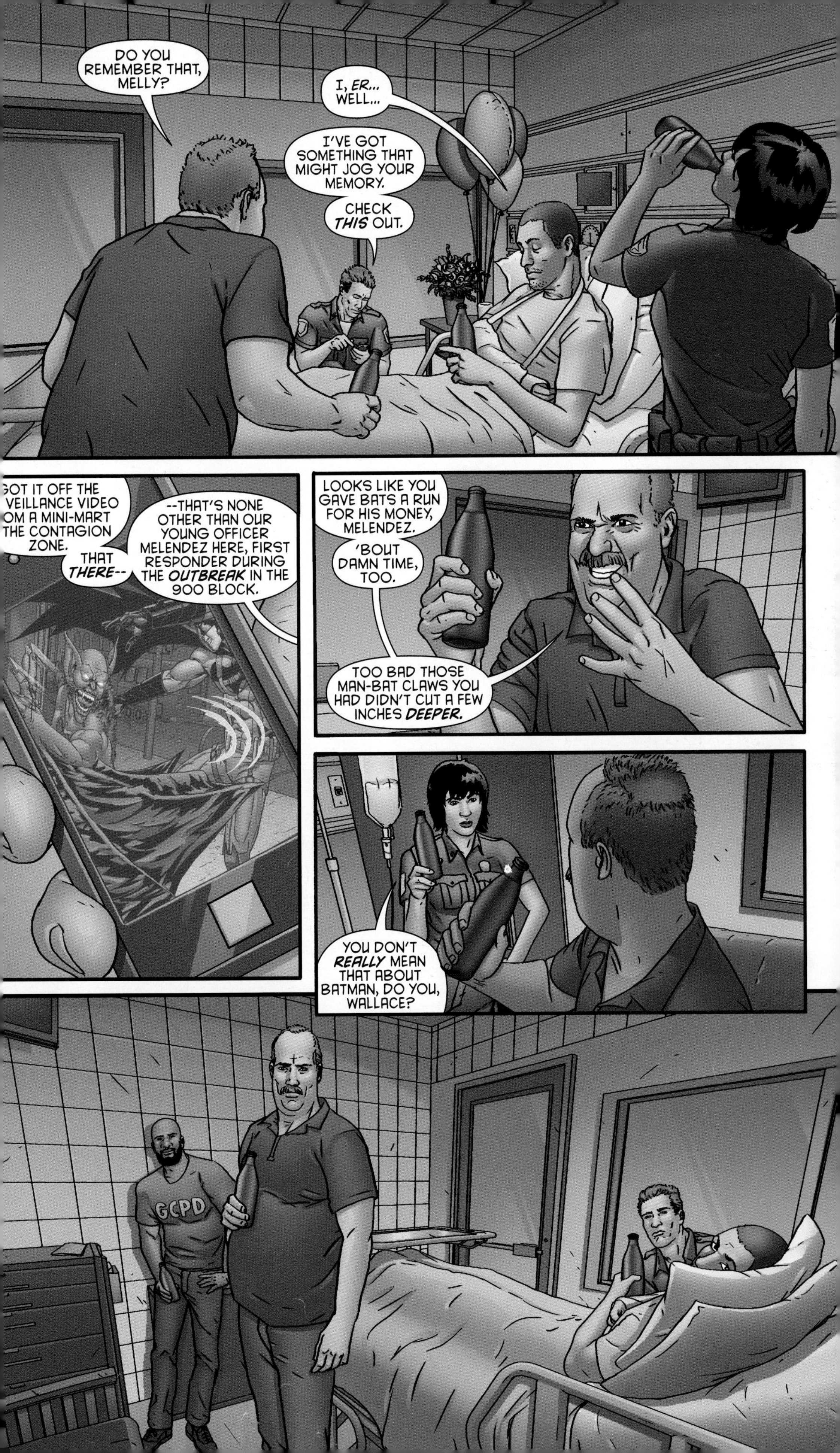
DO YOU REMEMBER THAT, MELLY?
I, ER... WELL...
I'VE GOT SOMETHING THAT MIGHT JOG YOUR MEMORY.
CHECK THIS OUT.
GOT IT OFF THE VEILLANCE VIDEO OM A MINI-MART THE CONTAGION ZONE.
THAT THERE--
--THAT'S NONE OTHER THAN OUR YOUNG OFFICER MELENDEZ HERE, FIRST RESPONDER DURING THE OUTBREAK IN THE 900 BLOCK.
LOOKS LIKE YOU GAVE BATS A RUN FOR HIS MONEY, MELENDEZ.
'BOUT DAMN TIME, TOO.
TOO BAD THOSE MAN-BAT CLAWS YOU HAD DIDN'T CUT A FEW INCHES DEEPER.
YOU DON'T REALLY MEAN THAT ABOUT BATMAN, DO YOU, WALLACE?
GCPD

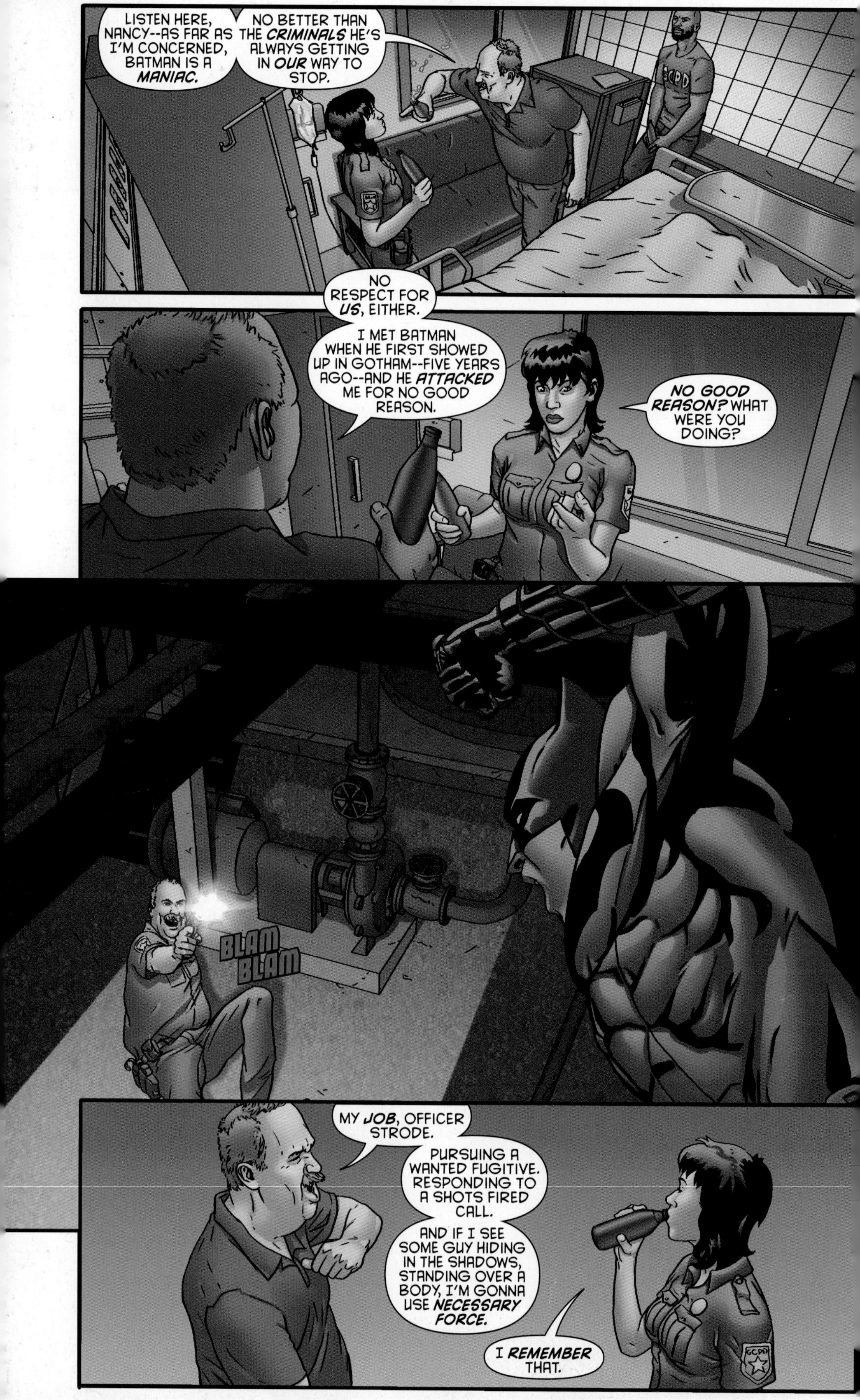
LISTEN HERE, NANCY--AS FAR AS I'M CONCERNED, BATMAN IS A MANIAC.
NO BETTER THAN THE CRIMINALS HE'S ALWAYS GETTING IN OUR WAY TO STOP.
NO RESPECT FOR US, EITHER.
I MET BATMAN WHEN HE FIRST SHOWED UP IN GOTHAM--FIVE YEARS AGO--AND HE ATTACKED ME FOR NO GOOD REASON.
NO GOOD REASON? WHAT WERE YOU DOING?
BLAM BLAM
MY JOB, OFFICER STRODE.
PURSUING A WANTED FUGITIVE. RESPONDING TO A SHOTS FIRED CALL.
AND IF I SEE SOME GUY HIDING IN THE SHADOWS, STANDING OVER A BODY, I'M GONNA USE NECESSARY FORCE.
I REMEMBER THAT.

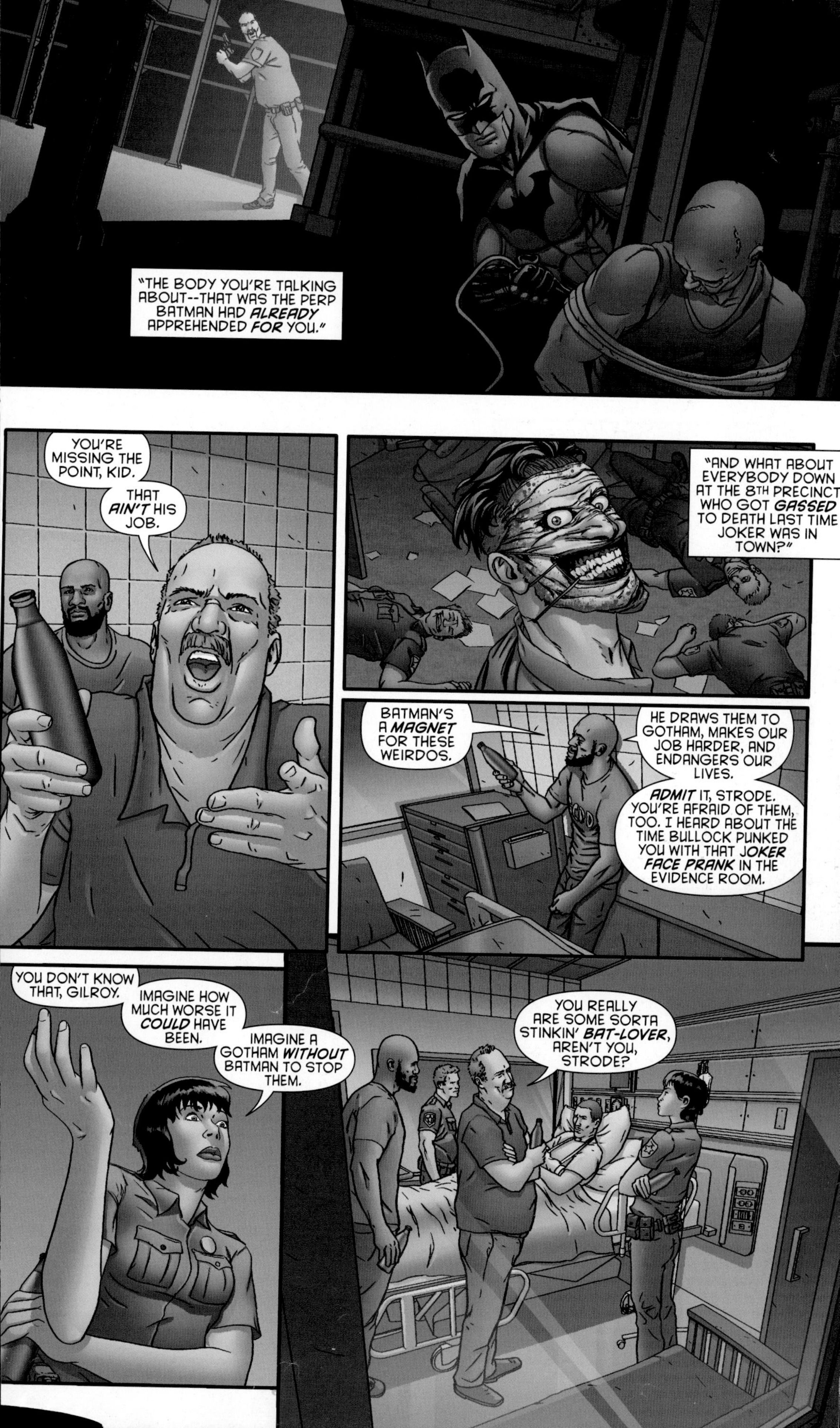

"THE BODY YOU'RE TALKING ABOUT--THAT WAS THE PERP BATMAN HAD ALREADY APPREHENDED FOR YOU."
YOU'RE MISSING THE POINT, KID.
THAT AIN'T HIS JOB.
"AND WHAT ABOUT EVERYBODY DOWN AT THE 8TH PRECINCT WHO GOT GASSED TO DEATH LAST TIME JOKER WAS IN TOWN?"
BATMAN'S A MAGNET FOR THESE WEIRDOS.
HE DRAWS THEM TO GOTHAM, MAKES OUR JOB HARDER, AND ENDANGERS OUR LIVES.
ADMIT IT, STRODE. YOU'RE AFRAID OF THEM, TOO. I HEARD ABOUT THE TIME BULLOCK PUNKED YOU WITH THAT JOKER FACE PRANK IN THE EVIDENCE ROOM.
YOU DON'T KNOW THAT, GILROY.
IMAGINE HOW MUCH WORSE IT COULD HAVE BEEN.
IMAGINE A GOTHAM WITHOUT BATMAN TO STOP THEM.
YOU REALLY ARE SOME SORTA STINKIN' BAT-LOVER, AREN'T YOU, STRODE?

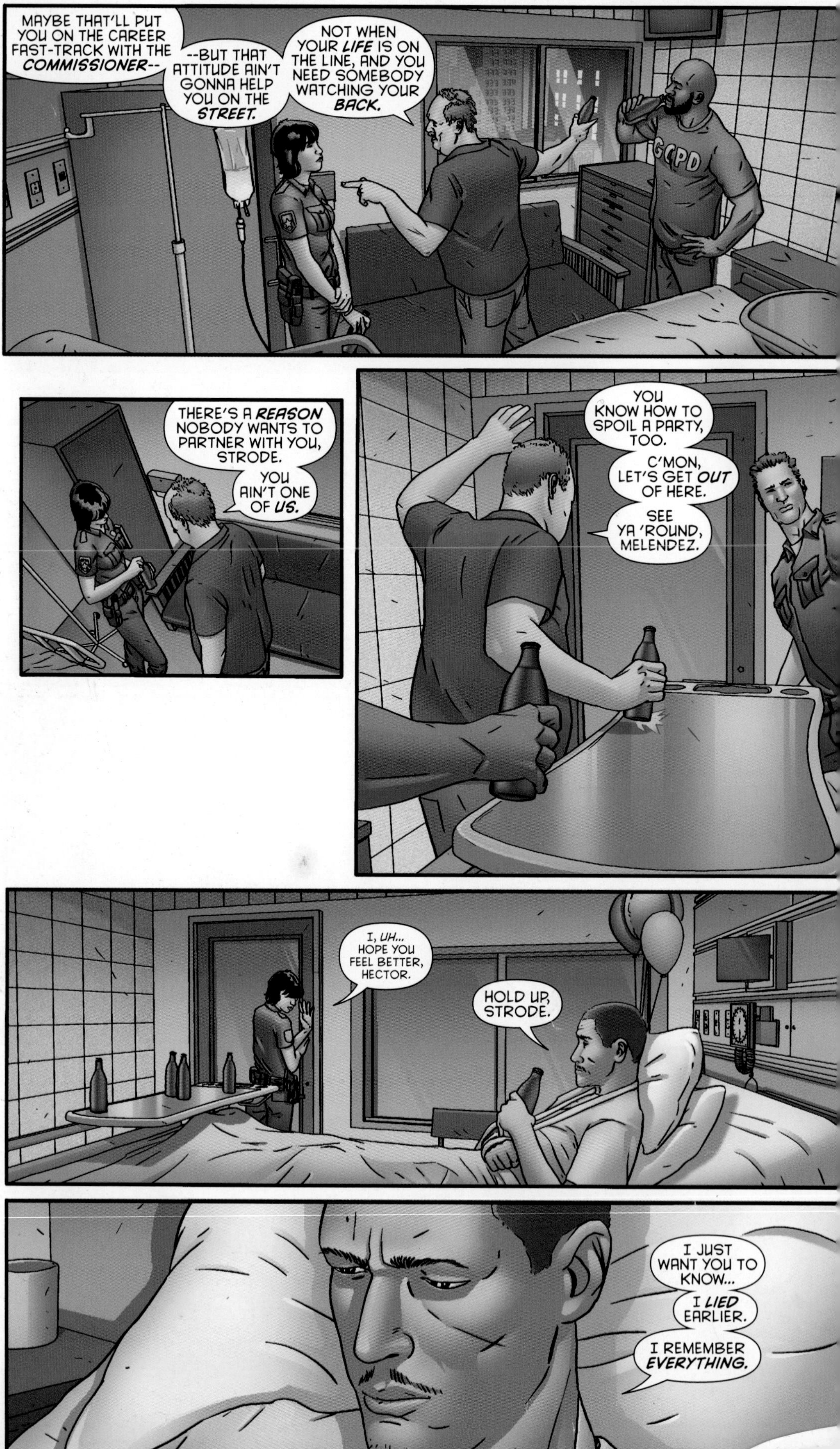
MAYBE THAT'LL PUT YOU ON THE CAREER FAST-TRACK WITH THE COMMISSIONER--
--BUT THAT ATTITUDE AIN'T GONNA HELP YOU ON THE STREET.
NOT WHEN YOUR LIFE IS ON THE LINE, AND YOU NEED SOMEBODY WATCHING YOUR BACK.
GCPD
THERE'S A REASON NOBODY WANTS TO PARTNER WITH YOU, STRODE.
YOU AIN'T ONE OF US.
YOU KNOW HOW TO SPOIL A PARTY, TOO.
C'MON, LET'S GET OUT OF HERE.
SEE YA 'ROUND, MELENDEZ.
I, UH... HOPE YOU FEEL BETTER, HECTOR.
HOLD UP, STRODE.
I JUST WANT YOU TO KNOW...
I LIED EARLIER.
I REMEMBER EVERYTHING.

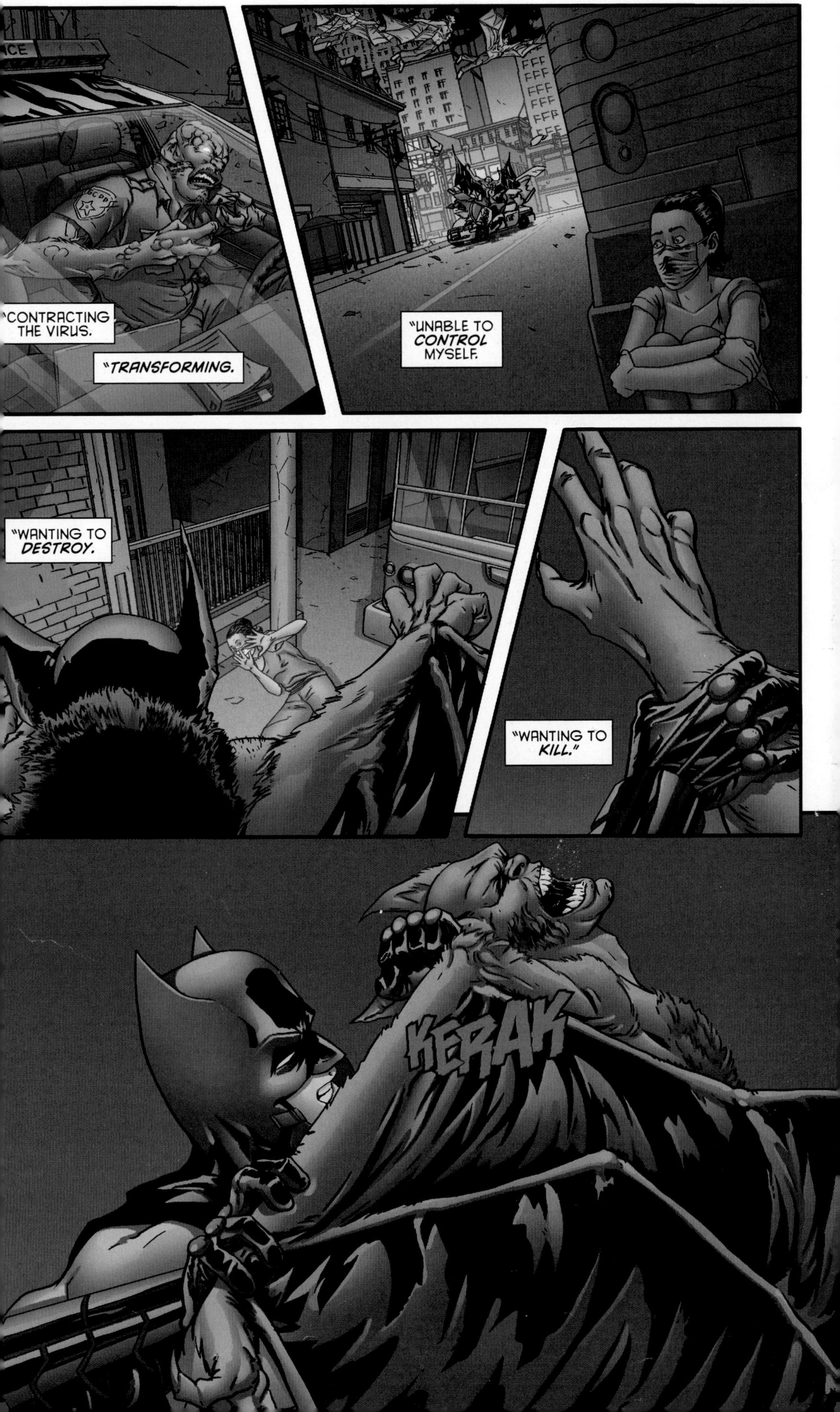
"CONTRACTING THE VIRUS.
"TRANSFORMING.
"UNABLE TO CONTROL MYSELF.
"WANTING TO DESTROY.
"WANTING TO KILL."
KERAK

THERE WAS ONE LADY... SHE HADN'T *CHANGED* YET, HADN'T CONTRACTED THE VIRUS--

--AND IF *BATMAN* HADN'T BEEN THERE TO *STOP* ME--

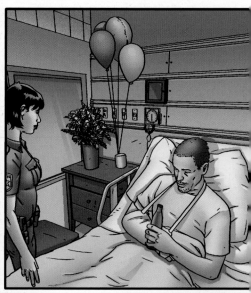

SOME OF THE *OTHERS*, THEY DON'T UNDERSTAND. AND MAYBE THEY NEVER WILL.

BUT WHEN I GET *OUT* OF HERE, STRODE, *I'D* BE WILLING TO PARTNER UP WITH YOU.

YOU MIGHT WANT TO RETHINK THAT. YOU HEARD WALLACE.

YOU PARTNER UP WITH *ME*, WHO'S GONNA WATCH *OUR* BACKS?

THAT ONE'S EASY, STRODE.

BATMAN.

EN

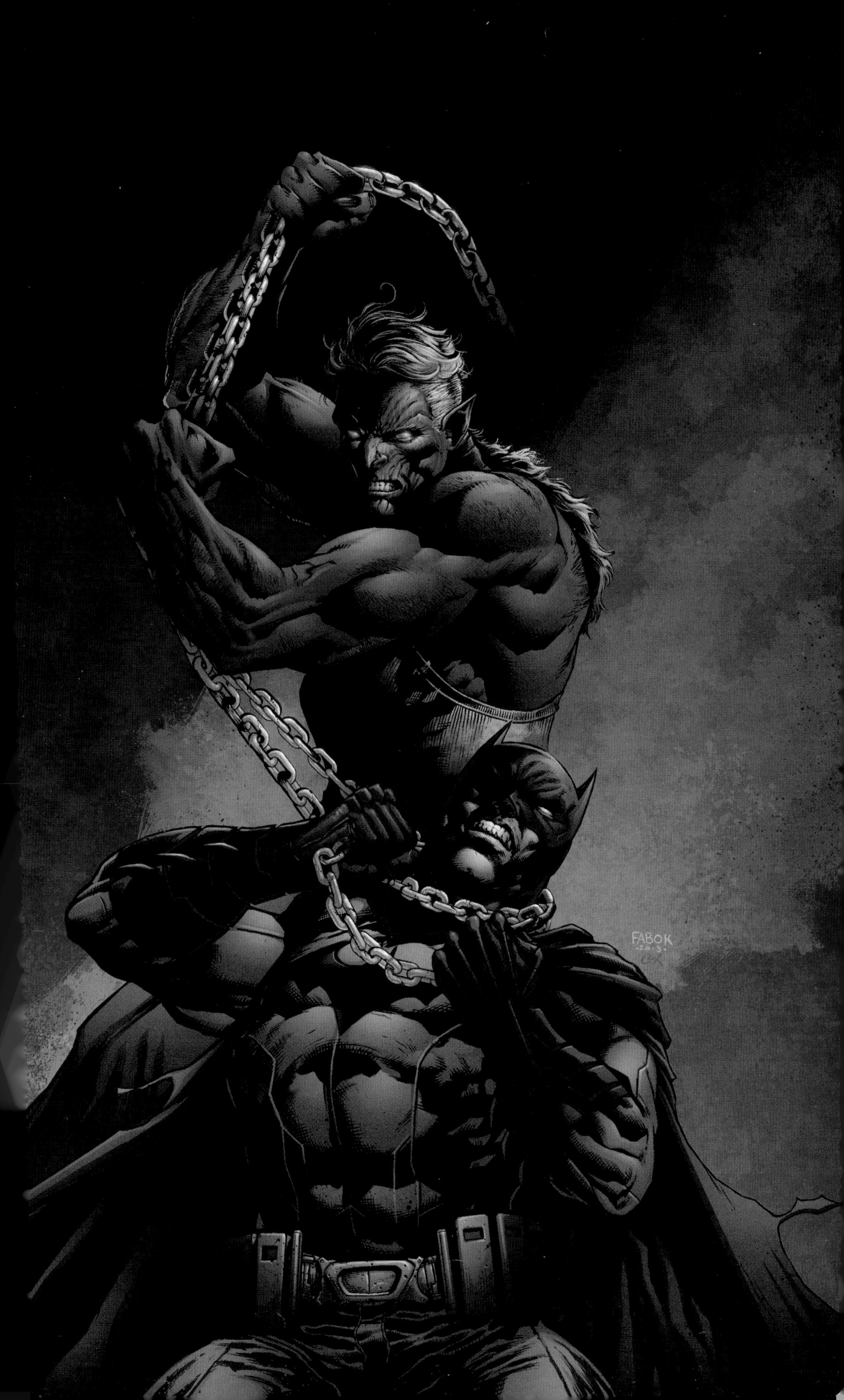
FABOK

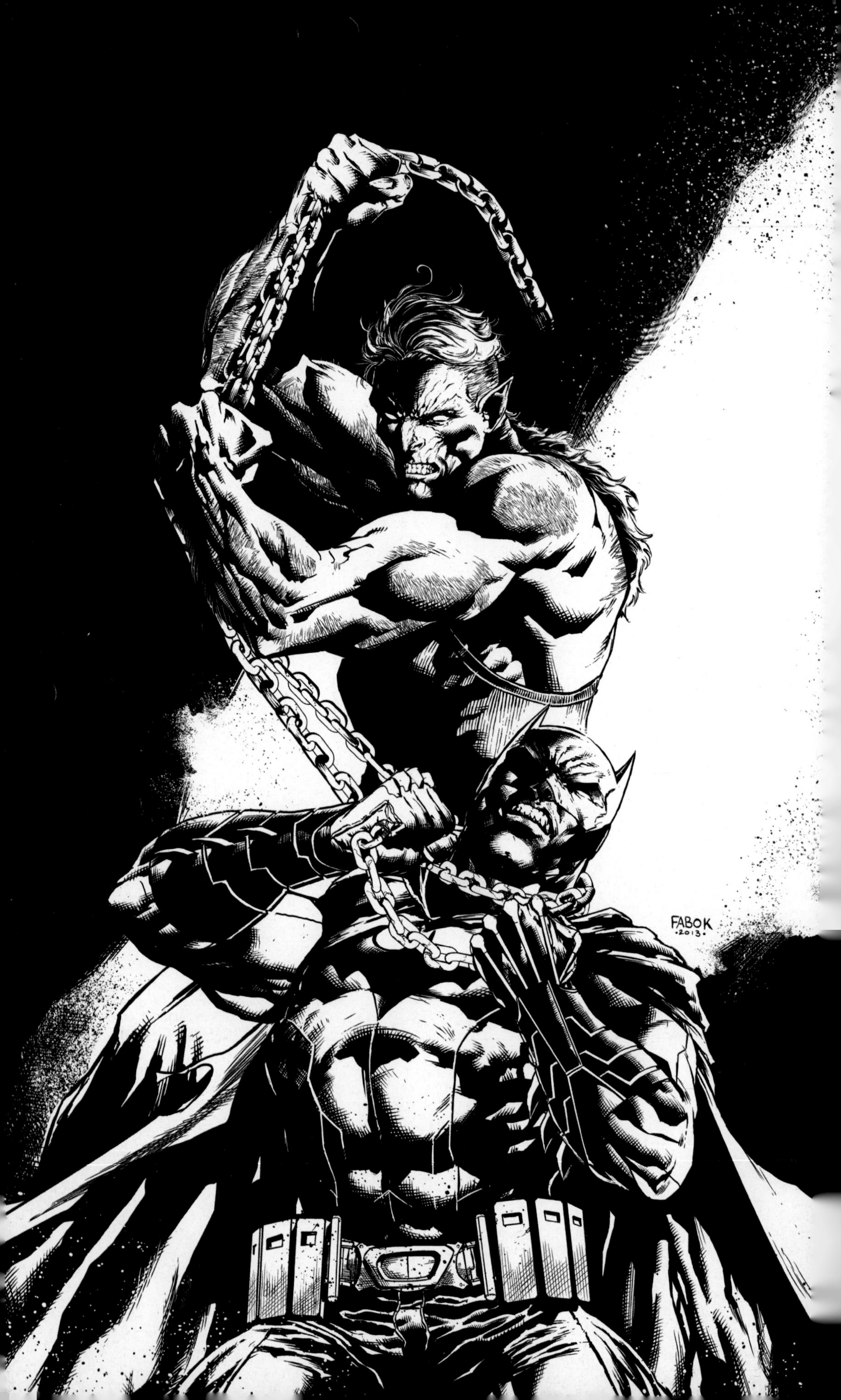
FABOK
·2013·

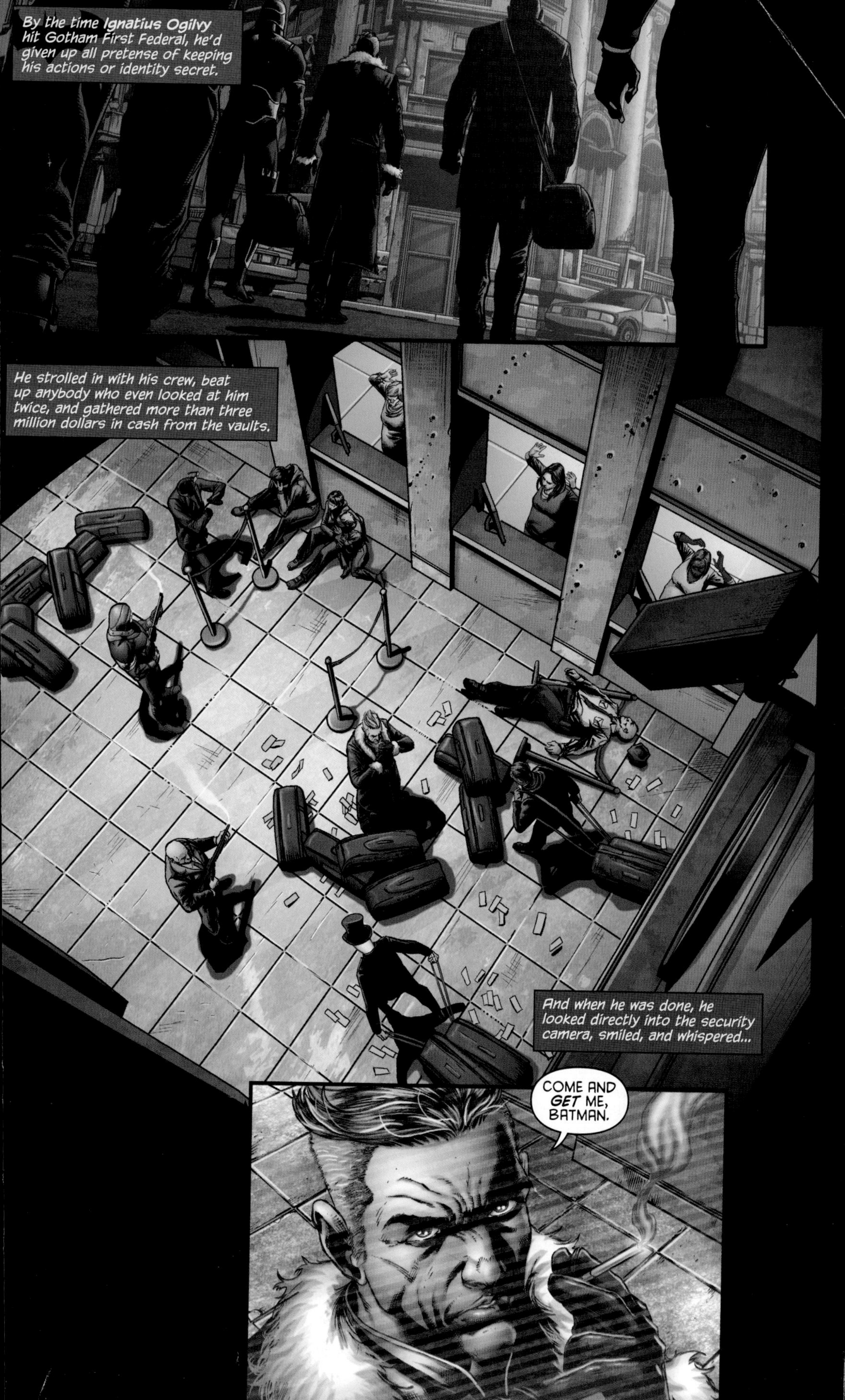
By the time Ignatius Ogilvy hit Gotham First Federal, he'd given up all pretense of keeping his actions or identity secret.
He strolled in with his crew, beat up anybody who even looked at him twice, and gathered more than three million dollars in cash from the vaults.
And when he was done, he looked directly into the security camera, smiled, and whispered...
COME AND GET ME, BATMAN.

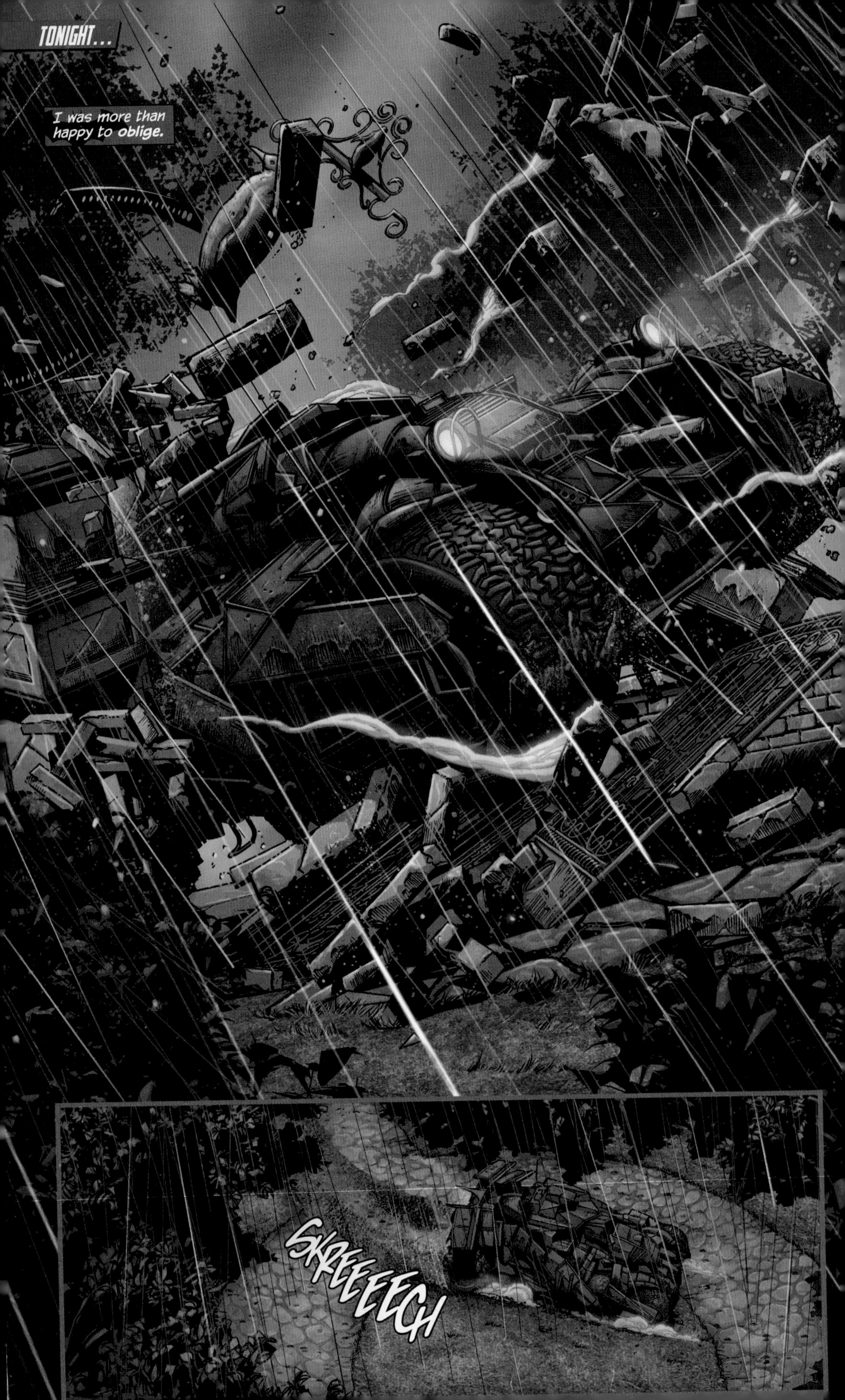
TONIGHT...
I was more than happy to oblige.
SKREEEECH

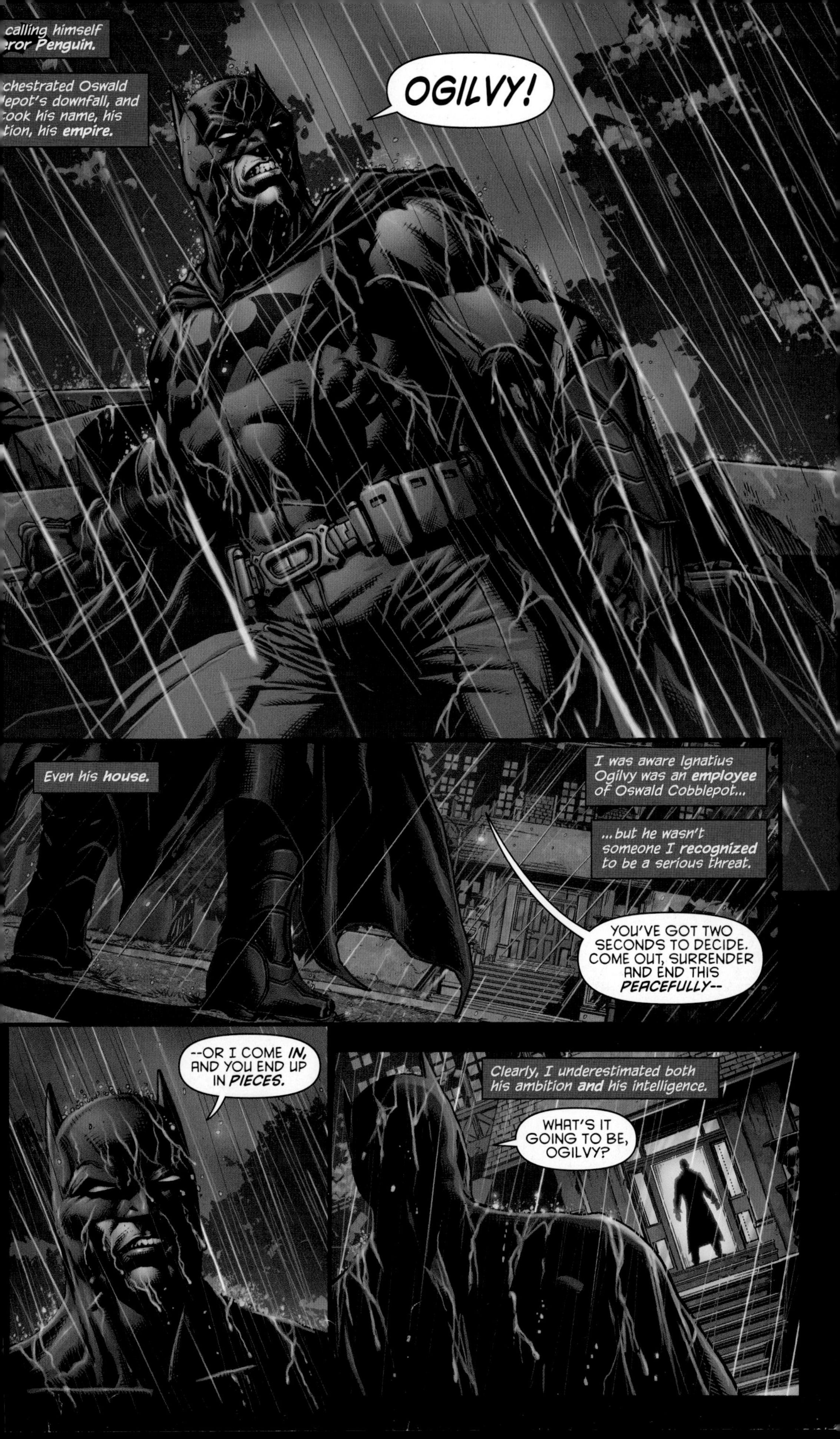

calling himself
eror Penguin.
chestrated Oswald
epot's downfall, and
ook his name, his
tion, his empire.
OGILVY!
Even his house.
I was aware Ignatius Ogilvy was an employee of Oswald Cobblepot...
...but he wasn't someone I recognized to be a serious threat.
YOU'VE GOT TWO SECONDS TO DECIDE. COME OUT, SURRENDER AND END THIS PEACEFULLY--
--OR I COME IN, AND YOU END UP IN PIECES.
Clearly, I underestimated both his ambition and his intelligence.
WHAT'S IT GOING TO BE, OGILVY?

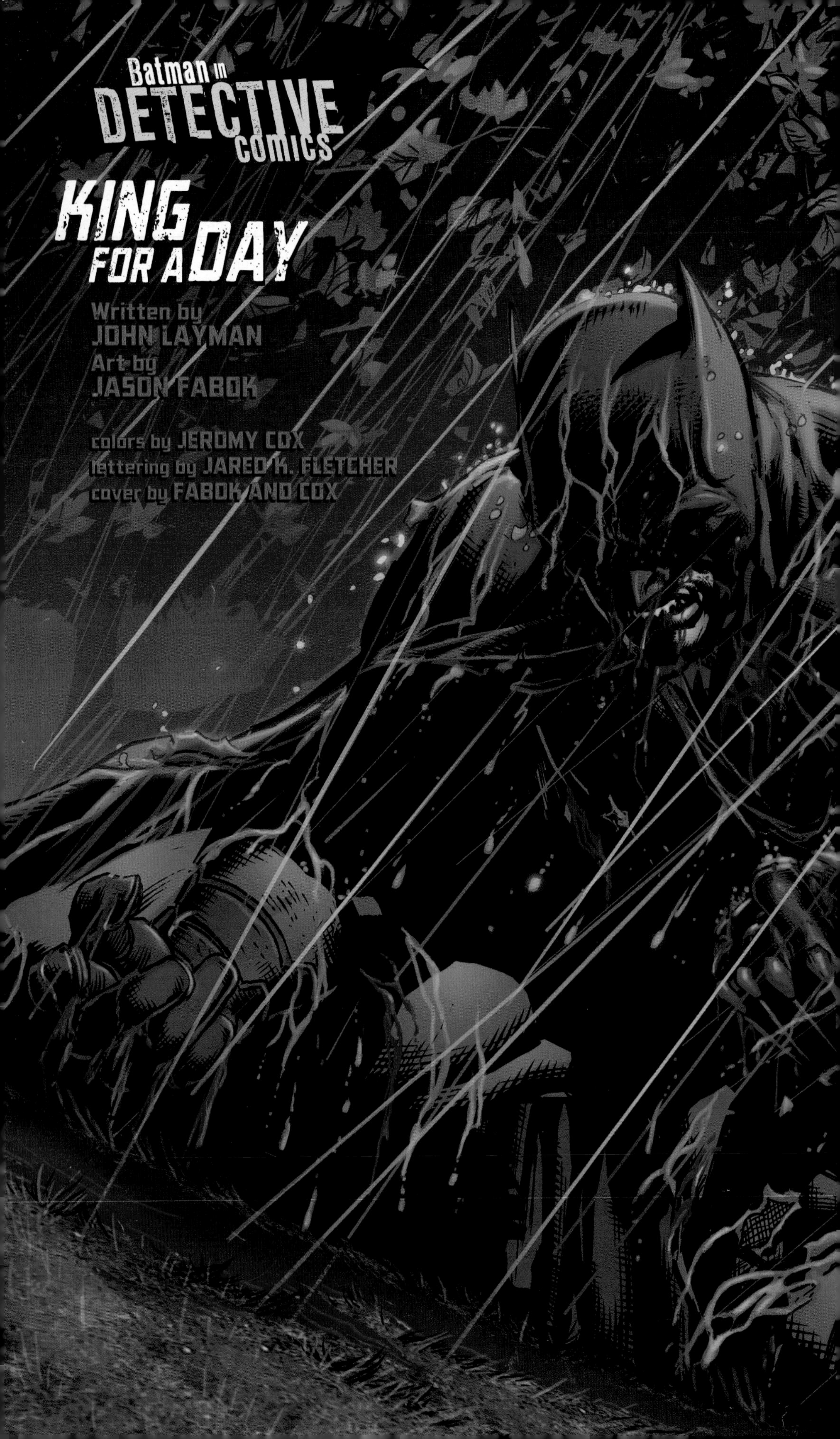
Batman in
DETECTIVE
comics
KING FOR A DAY
Written by
JOHN LAYMAN
Art by
JASON FABOK
colors by JEROMY COX
lettering by JARED K. FLETCHER
cover by FABOK AND COX

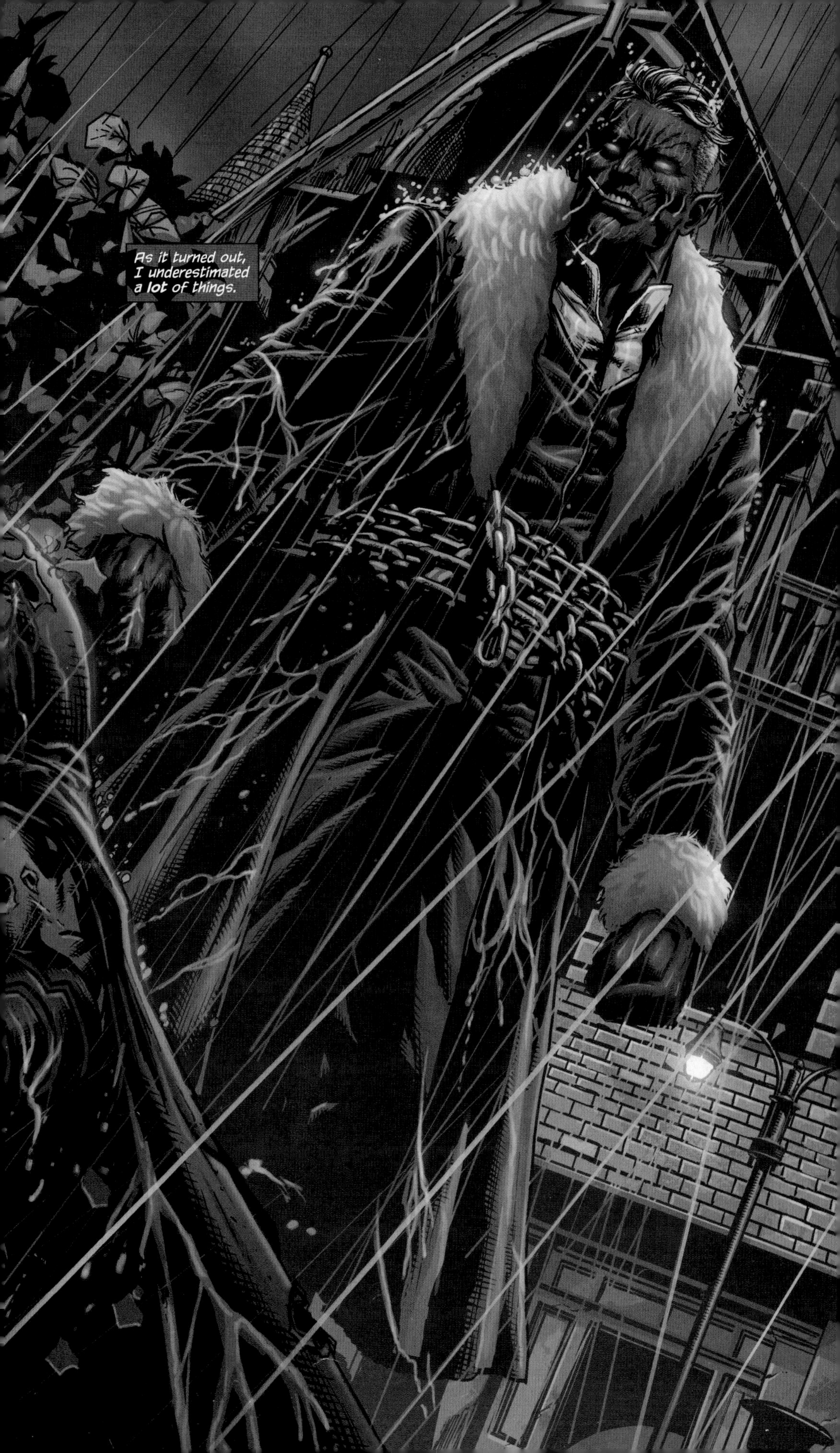
As it turned out, I underestimated a lot of things.

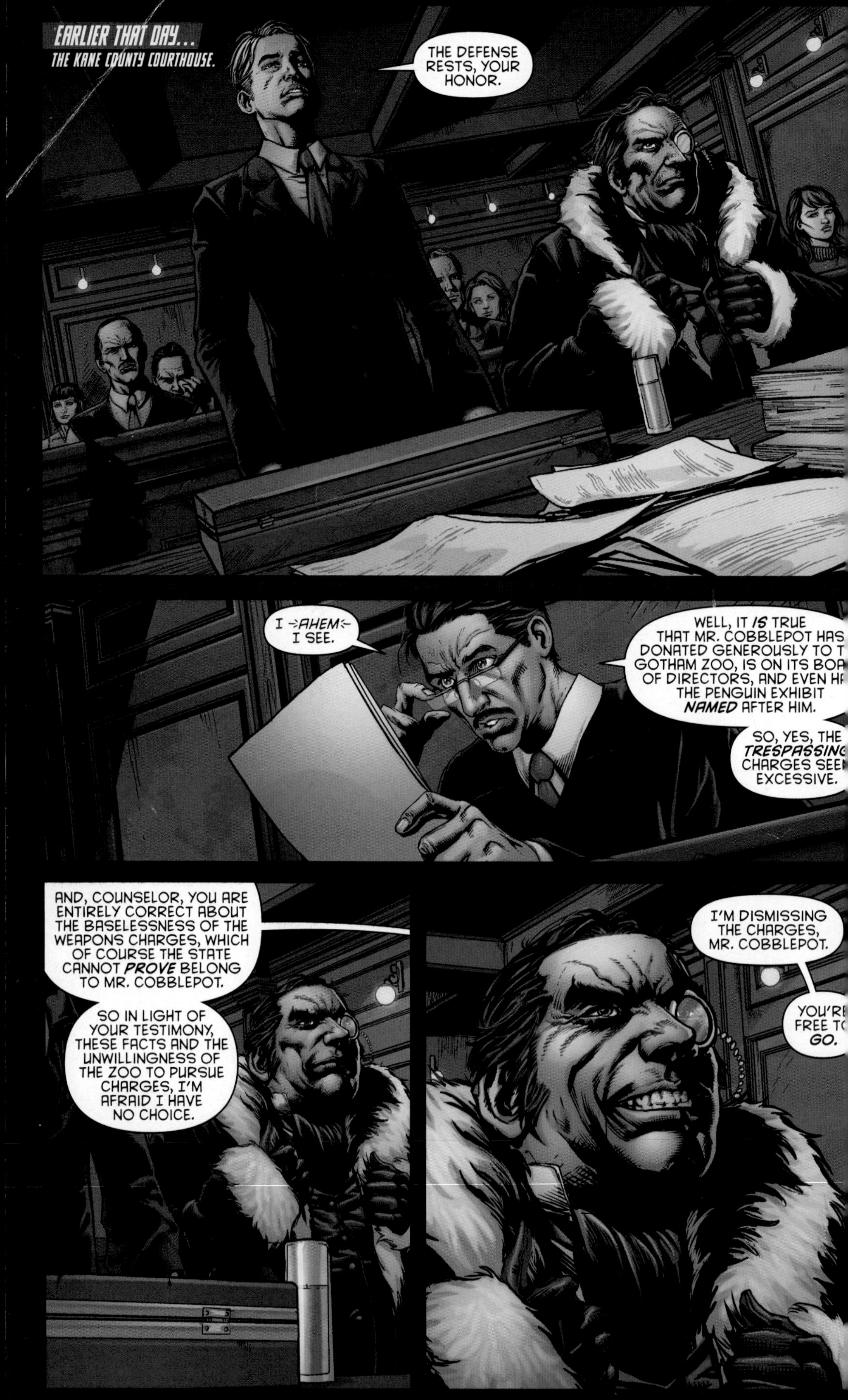
EARLIER THAT DAY...
THE KANE COUNTY COURTHOUSE.
THE DEFENSE RESTS, YOUR HONOR.
I -AHEM- I SEE.
WELL, IT IS TRUE THAT MR. COBBLEPOT HAS DONATED GENEROUSLY TO T GOTHAM ZOO, IS ON ITS BOA OF DIRECTORS, AND EVEN H THE PENGUIN EXHIBIT NAMED AFTER HIM.
SO, YES, THE TRESPASSIN CHARGES SEE EXCESSIVE.
AND, COUNSELOR, YOU ARE ENTIRELY CORRECT ABOUT THE BASELESSNESS OF THE WEAPONS CHARGES, WHICH OF COURSE THE STATE CANNOT PROVE BELONG TO MR. COBBLEPOT.
SO IN LIGHT OF YOUR TESTIMONY, THESE FACTS AND THE UNWILLINGNESS OF THE ZOO TO PURSUE CHARGES, I'M AFRAID I HAVE NO CHOICE.
I'M DISMISSING THE CHARGES, MR. COBBLEPOT.
YOU'R FREE T GO.

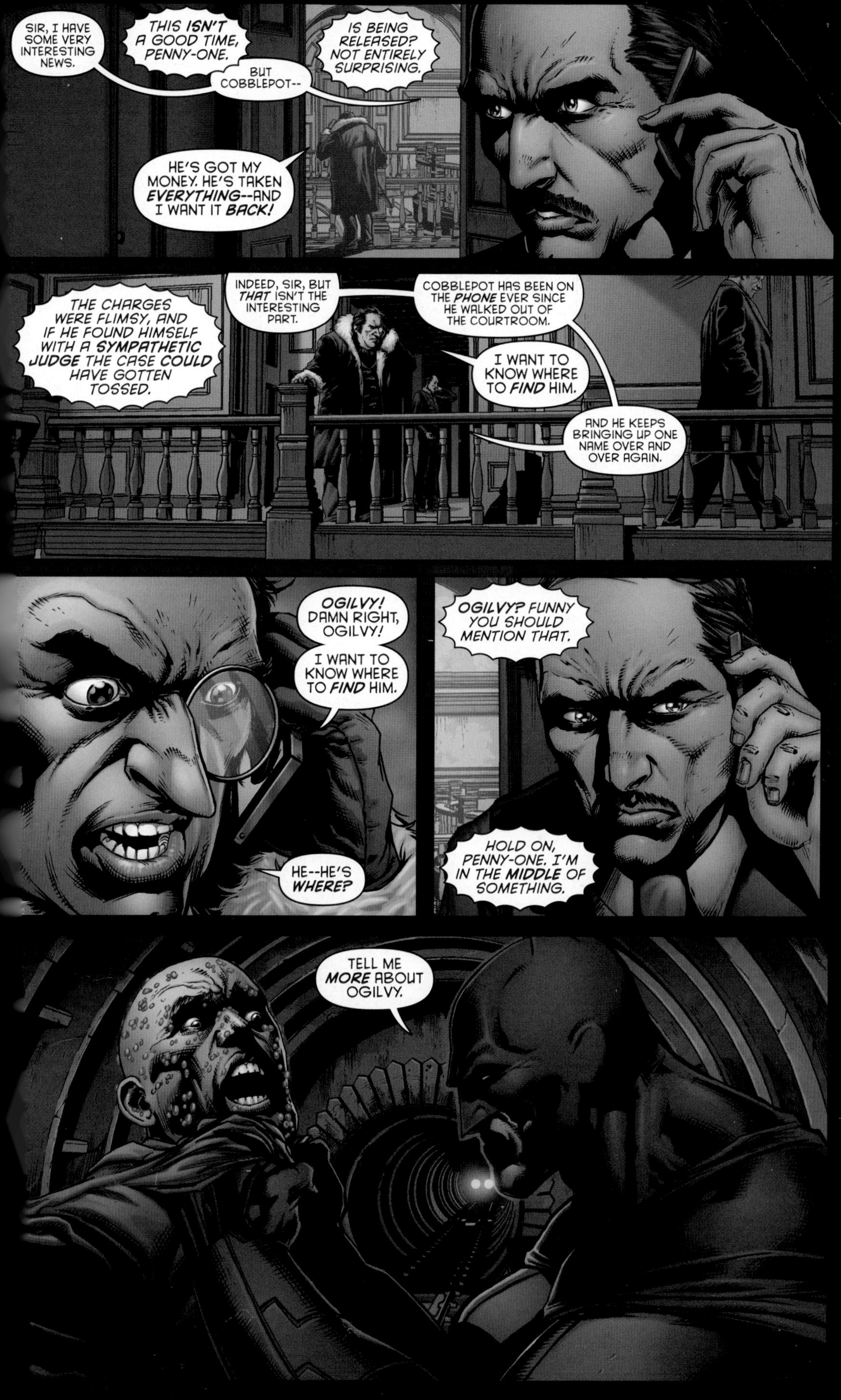
SIR, I HAVE SOME VERY INTERESTING NEWS.
THIS ISN'T A GOOD TIME, PENNY-ONE.
BUT COBBLEPOT--
IS BEING RELEASED? NOT ENTIRELY SURPRISING.
HE'S GOT MY MONEY. HE'S TAKEN EVERYTHING--AND I WANT IT BACK!
THE CHARGES WERE FLIMSY, AND IF HE FOUND HIMSELF WITH A SYMPATHETIC JUDGE THE CASE COULD HAVE GOTTEN TOSSED.
INDEED, SIR, BUT THAT ISN'T THE INTERESTING PART.
COBBLEPOT HAS BEEN ON THE PHONE EVER SINCE HE WALKED OUT OF THE COURTROOM.
I WANT TO KNOW WHERE TO FIND HIM.
AND HE KEEPS BRINGING UP ONE NAME OVER AND OVER AGAIN.
OGILVY! DAMN RIGHT, OGILVY!
I WANT TO KNOW WHERE TO FIND HIM.
HE--HE'S WHERE?
OGILVY? FUNNY YOU SHOULD MENTION THAT.
HOLD ON, PENNY-ONE. I'M IN THE MIDDLE OF SOMETHING.
TELL ME MORE ABOUT OGILVY.

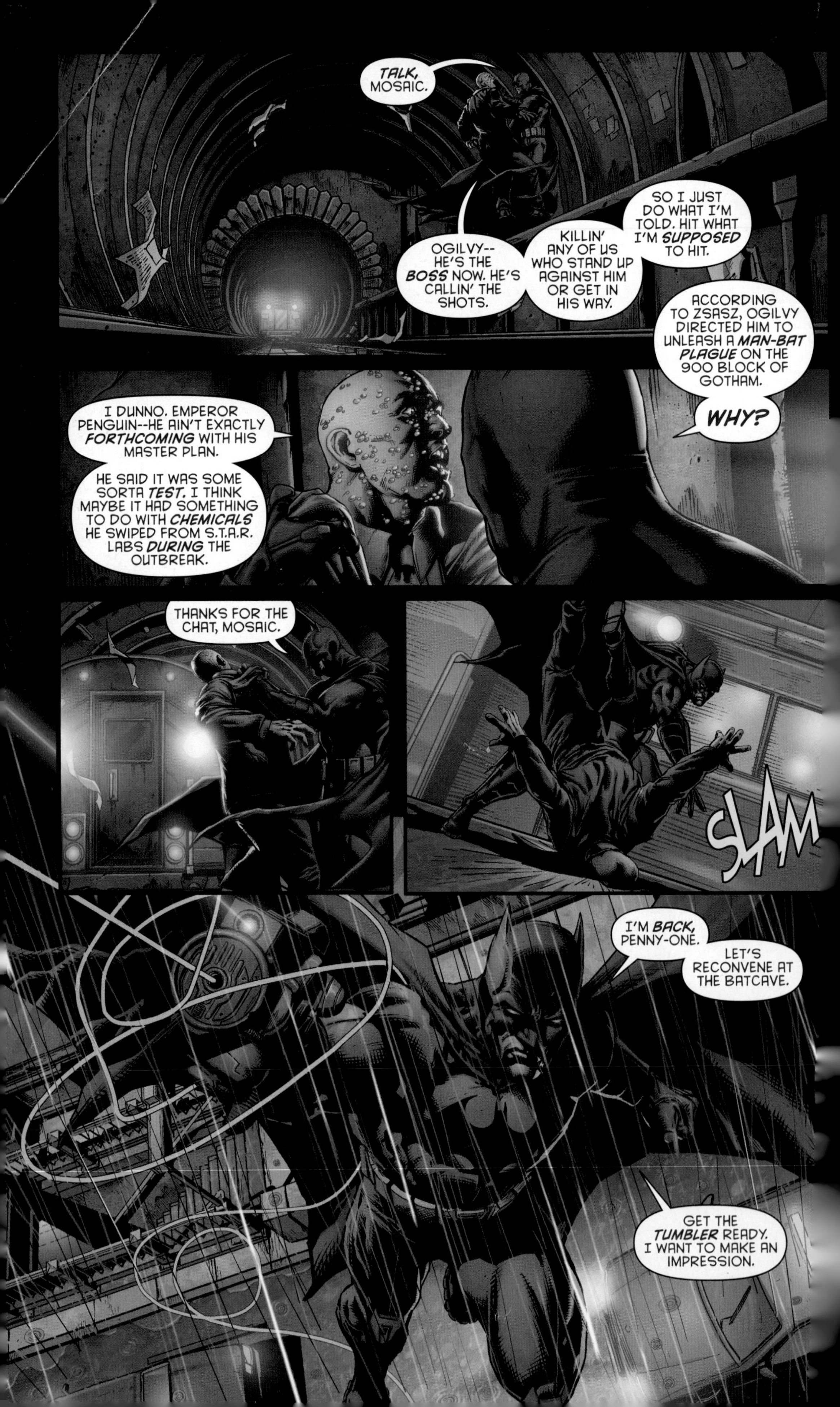
TALK, MOSAIC.
OGILVY--HE'S THE BOSS NOW. HE'S CALLIN' THE SHOTS.
KILLIN' ANY OF US WHO STAND UP AGAINST HIM OR GET IN HIS WAY.
SO I JUST DO WHAT I'M TOLD. HIT WHAT I'M SUPPOSED TO HIT.
ACCORDING TO ZSASZ, OGILVY DIRECTED HIM TO UNLEASH A MAN-BAT PLAGUE ON THE 900 BLOCK OF GOTHAM.
WHY?
I DUNNO. EMPEROR PENGUIN--HE AIN'T EXACTLY FORTHCOMING WITH HIS MASTER PLAN.
HE SAID IT WAS SOME SORTA TEST. I THINK MAYBE IT HAD SOMETHING TO DO WITH CHEMICALS HE SWIPED FROM S.T.A.R. LABS DURING THE OUTBREAK.
THANKS FOR THE CHAT, MOSAIC.
SLAM
I'M BACK, PENNY-ONE.
LET'S RECONVENE AT THE BATCAVE.
GET THE TUMBLER READY. I WANT TO MAKE AN IMPRESSION.

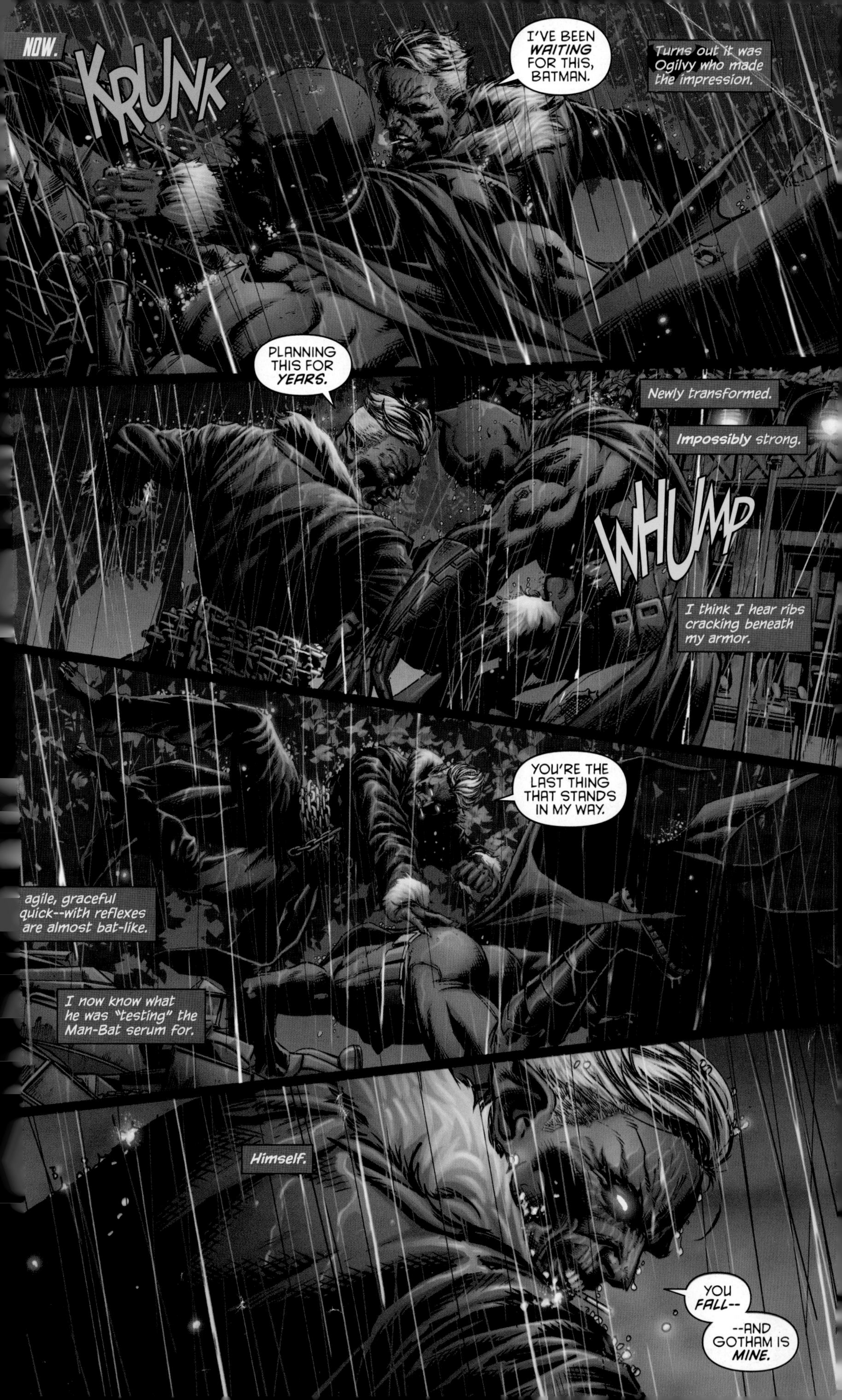

NOW.
KRUNK
I'VE BEEN WAITING FOR THIS, BATMAN.
Turns out it was Ogilvy who made the impression.
PLANNING THIS FOR YEARS.
Newly transformed.
Impossibly strong.
WHUMP
I think I hear ribs cracking beneath my armor.
YOU'RE THE LAST THING THAT STANDS IN MY WAY.
agile, graceful quick--with reflexes are almost bat-like.
I now know what he was "testing" the Man-Bat serum for.
Himself.
YOU FALL--
--AND GOTHAM IS MINE.

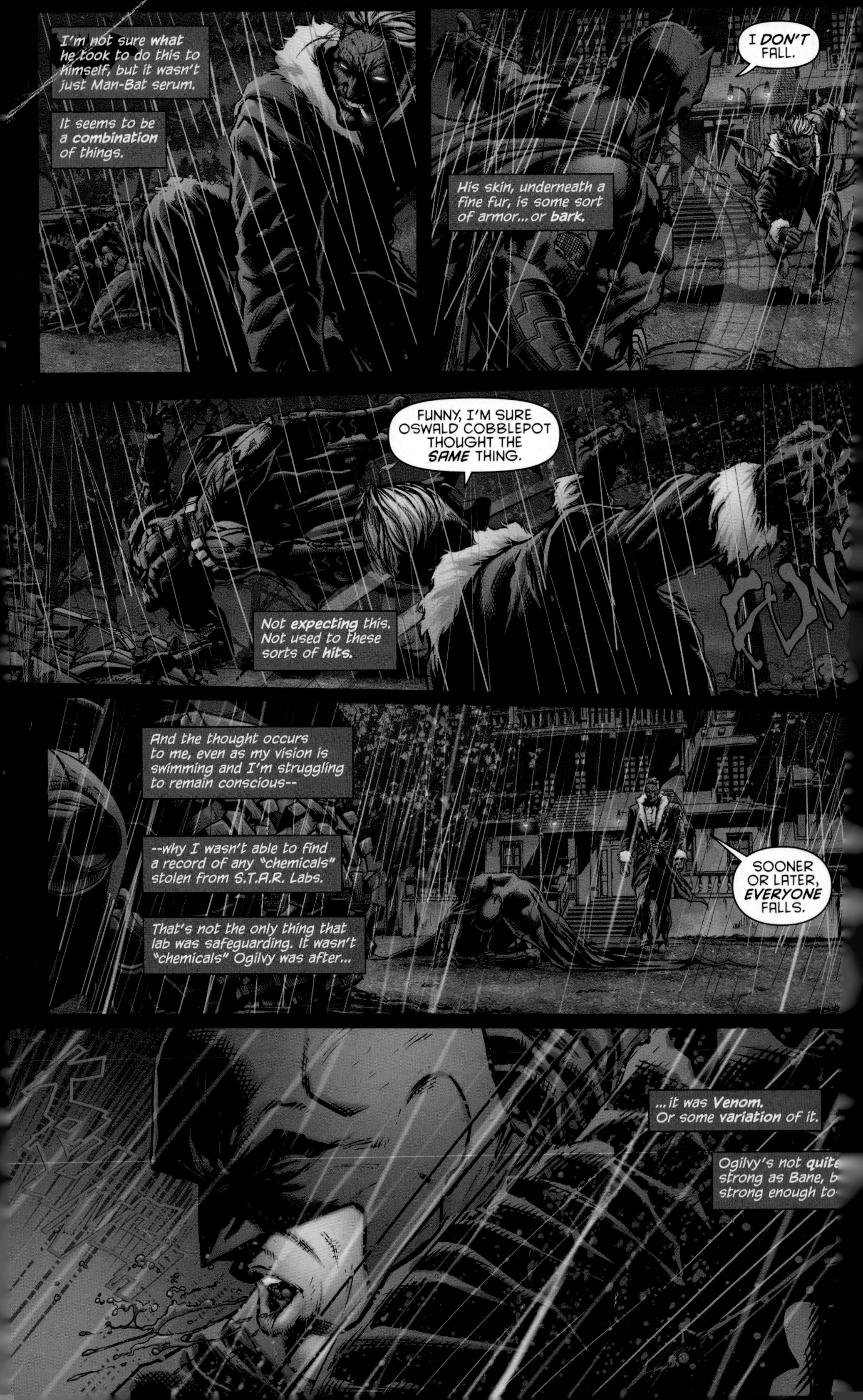

I'm not sure what he took to do this to himself, but it wasn't just Man-Bat serum.
It seems to be a combination of things.
I DON'T FALL.
His skin, underneath a fine fur, is some sort of armor...or bark.
FUNNY, I'M SURE OSWALD COBBLEPOT THOUGHT THE SAME THING.
Not expecting this. Not used to these sorts of hits.
And the thought occurs to me, even as my vision is swimming and I'm struggling to remain conscious--
--why I wasn't able to find a record of any "chemicals" stolen from S.T.A.R. Labs.
That's not the only thing that lab was safeguarding. It wasn't "chemicals" Ogilvy was after...
SOONER OR LATER, EVERYONE FALLS.
...it was Venom. Or some variation of it.
Ogilvy's not quite strong as Bane, b strong enough to

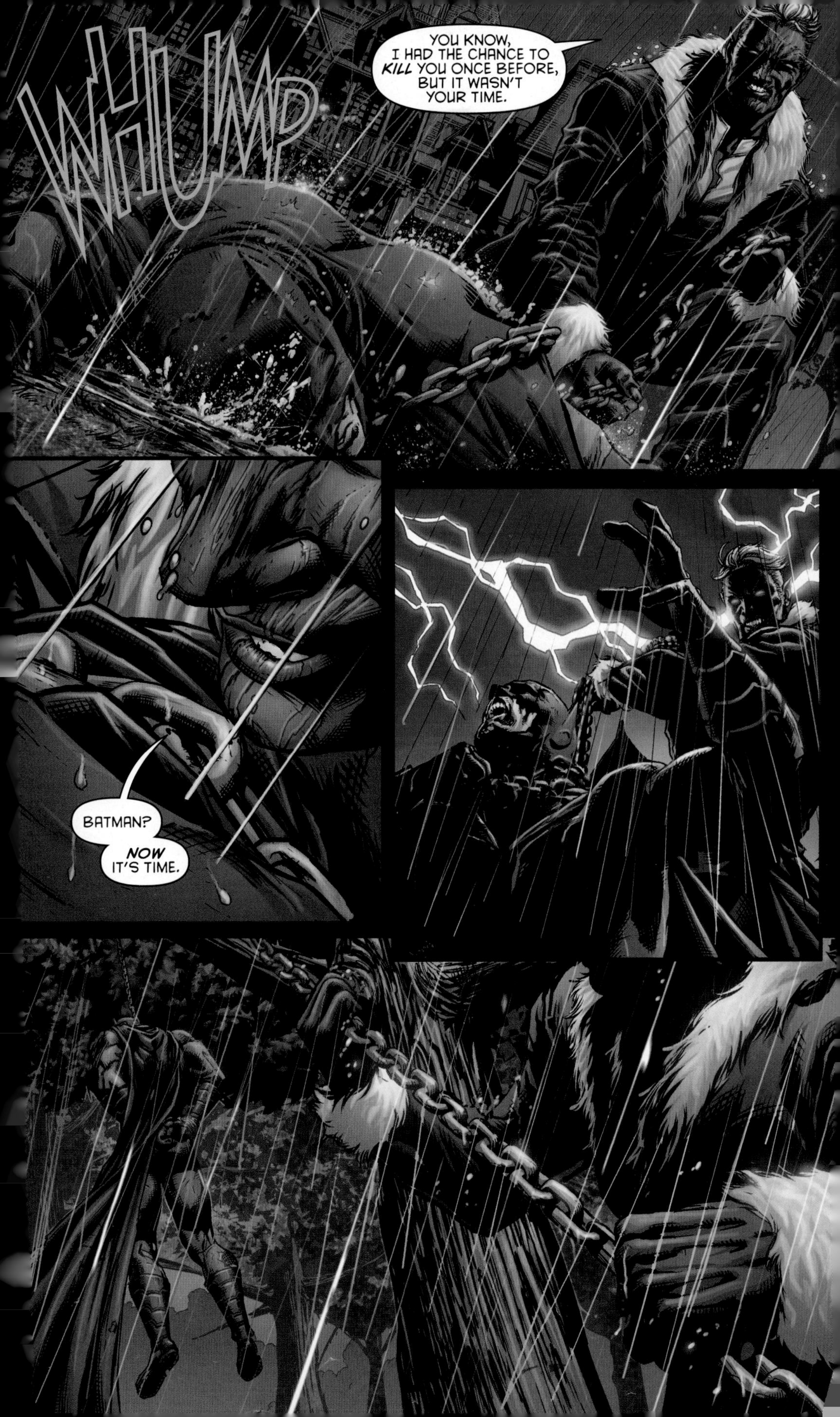
WHUMP
YOU KNOW, I HAD THE CHANCE TO KILL YOU ONCE BEFORE, BUT IT WASN'T YOUR TIME.
BATMAN?
NOW IT'S TIME.

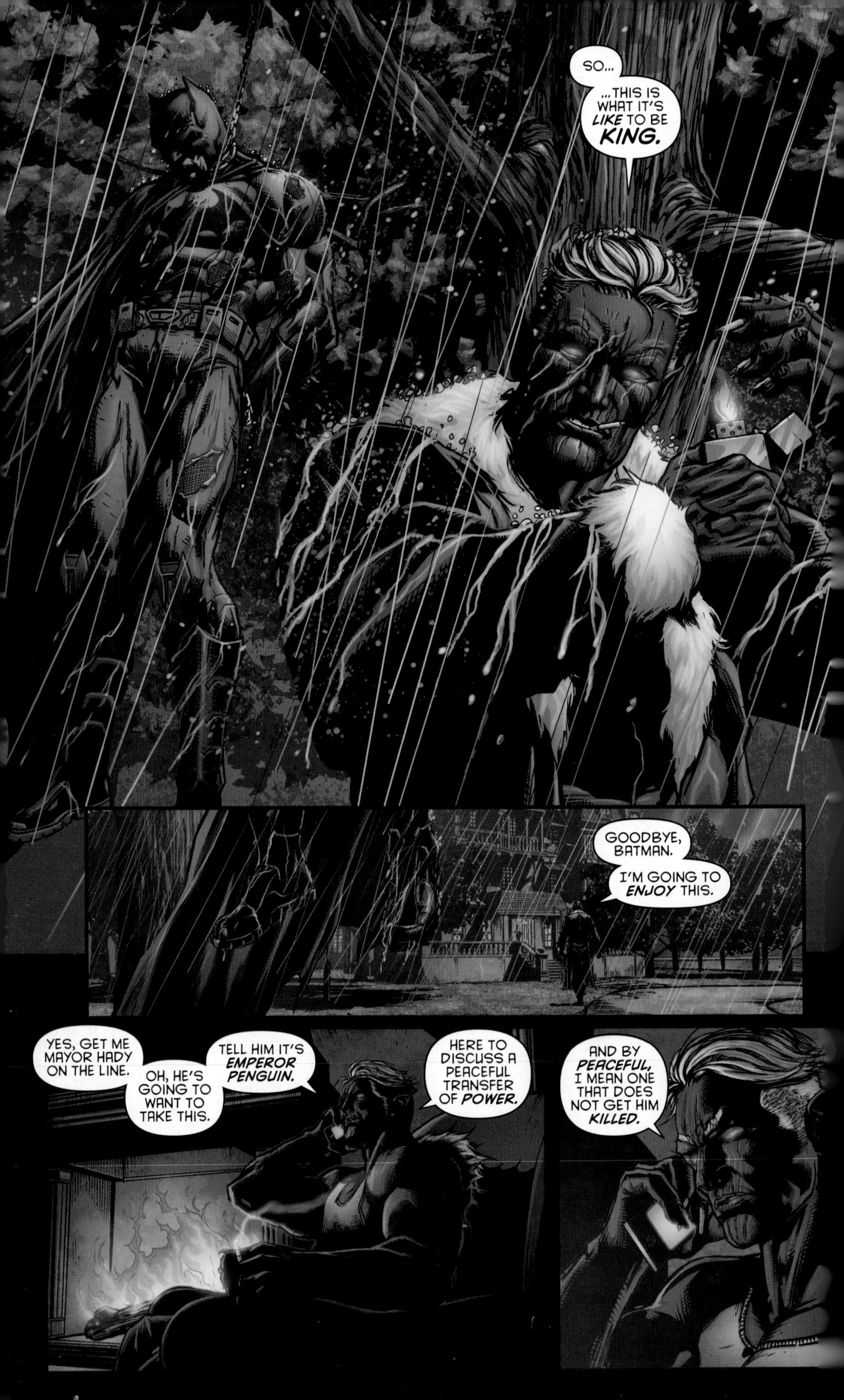
SO...
...THIS IS WHAT IT'S LIKE TO BE KING.
GOODBYE, BATMAN.
I'M GOING TO ENJOY THIS.
YES, GET ME MAYOR HADY ON THE LINE.
OH, HE'S GOING TO WANT TO TAKE THIS.
TELL HIM IT'S EMPEROR PENGUIN.
HERE TO DISCUSS A PEACEFUL TRANSFER OF POWER.
AND BY PEACEFUL, I MEAN ONE THAT DOES NOT GET HIM KILLED.

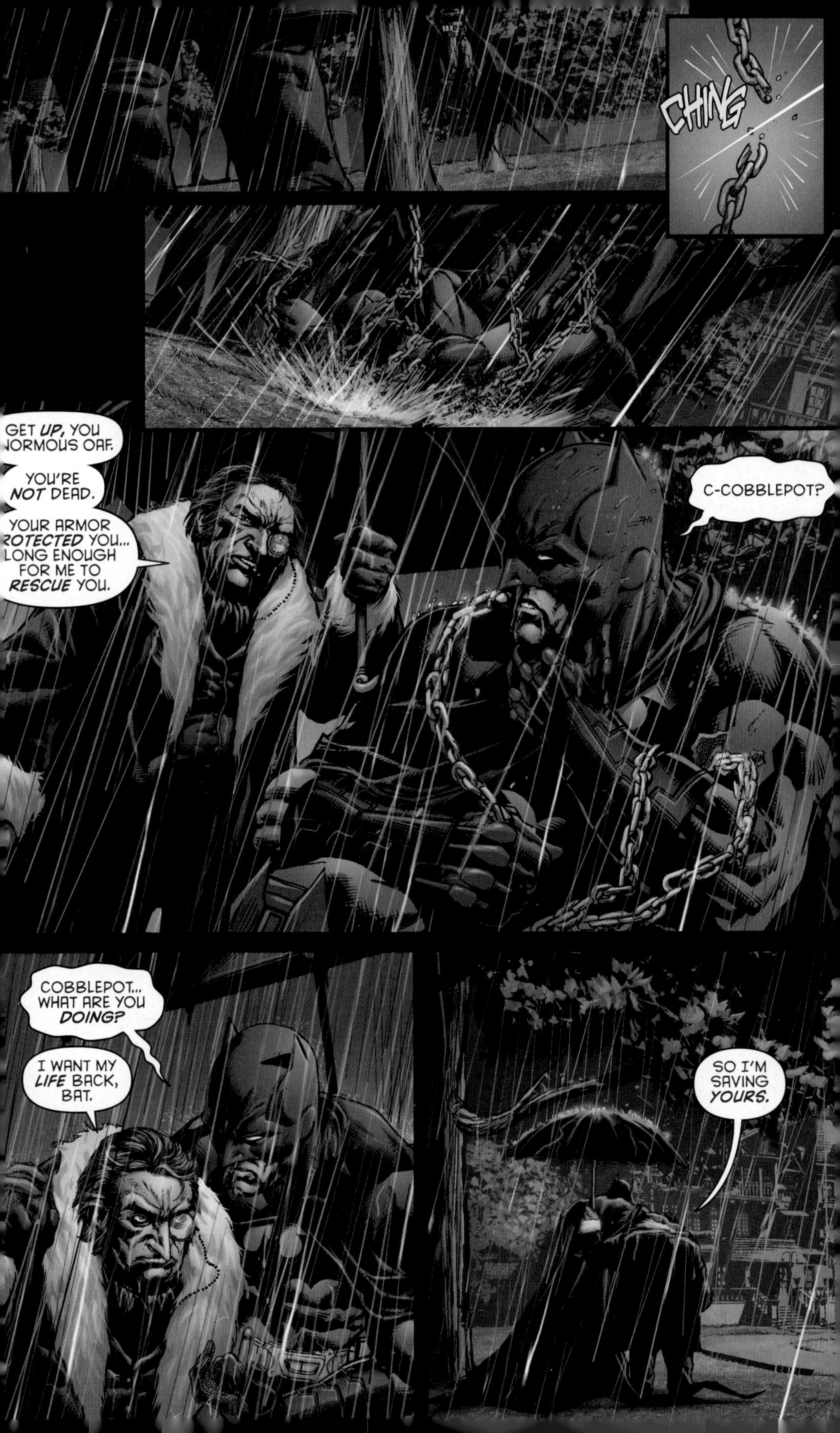
CHING
GET UP, YOU NORMOUS OAF.
YOU'RE NOT DEAD.
YOUR ARMOR ROTECTED YOU... LONG ENOUGH FOR ME TO RESCUE YOU.
C-COBBLEPOT?
COBBLEPOT... WHAT ARE YOU DOING?
I WANT MY LIFE BACK, BAT.
SO I'M SAVING YOURS.

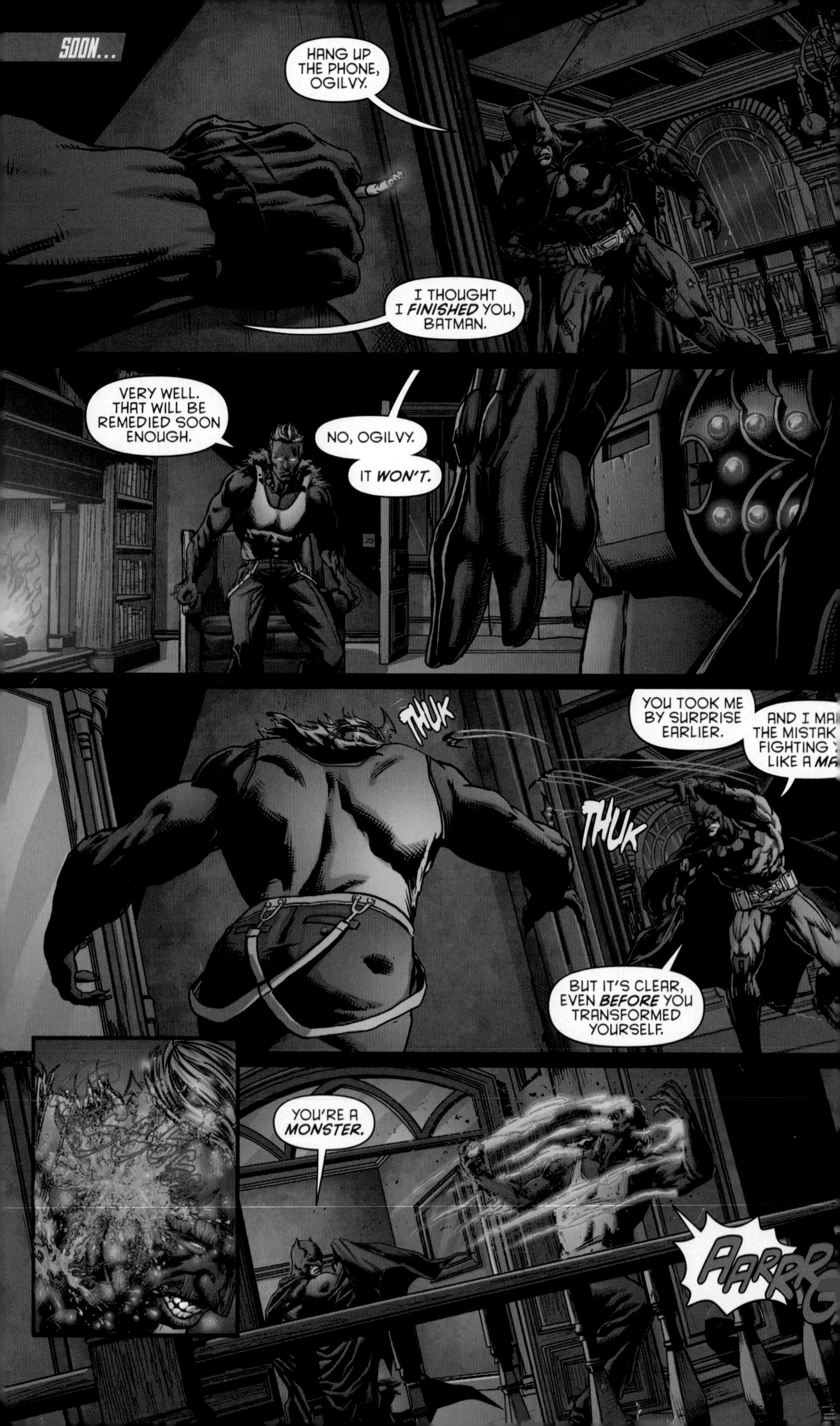
SOON...
HANG UP THE PHONE, OGILVY.
I THOUGHT I *FINISHED* YOU, BATMAN.
VERY WELL. THAT WILL BE REMEDIED SOON ENOUGH.
NO, OGILVY.
IT *WON'T.*
THUK
THUK
YOU TOOK ME BY SURPRISE EARLIER.
AND I MA THE MISTAK FIGHTING LIKE A MA
BUT IT'S CLEAR, EVEN *BEFORE* YOU TRANSFORMED YOURSELF.
YOU'RE A *MONSTER.*
AARRR

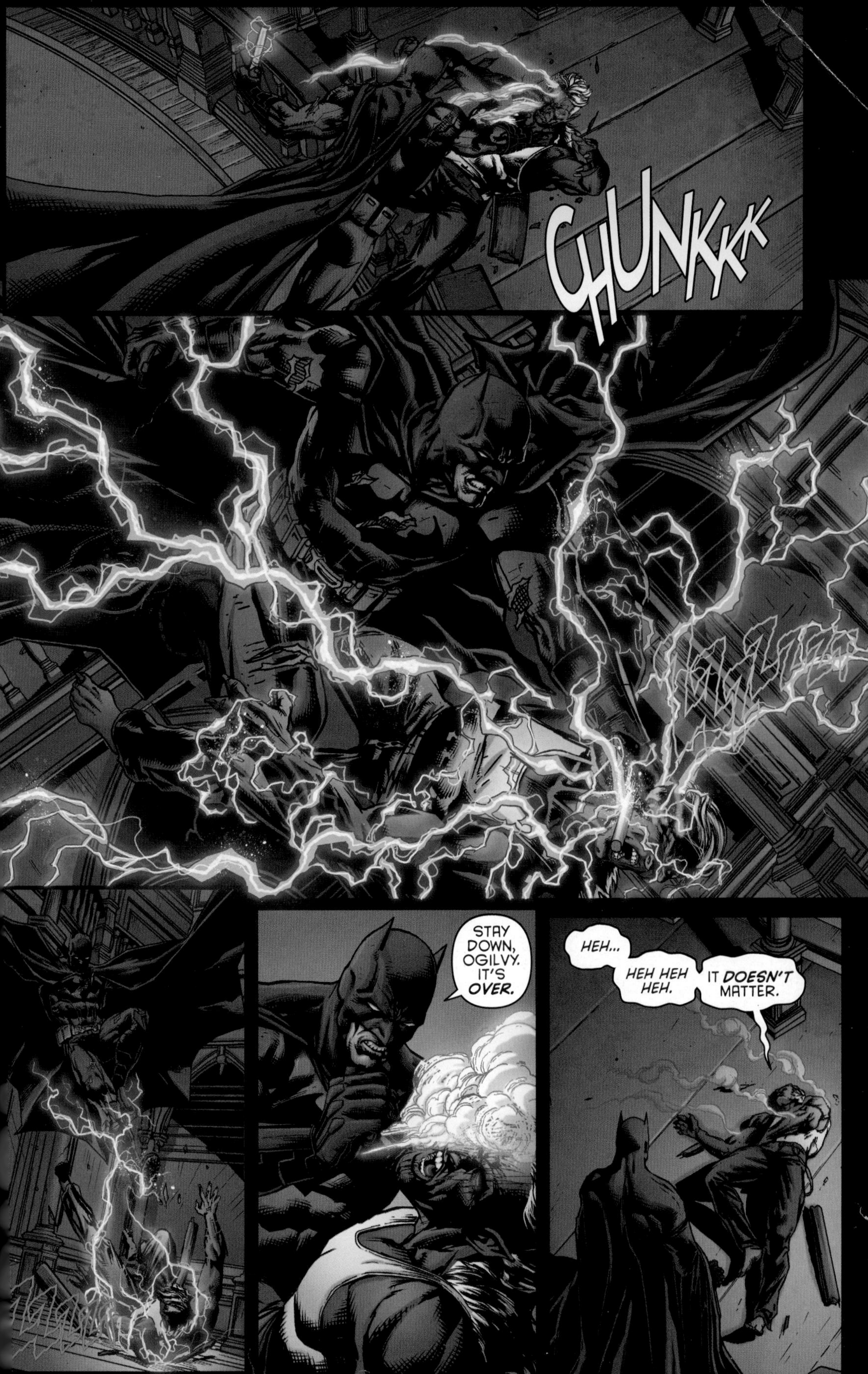
CHUNKKK
STAY DOWN, OGILVY. IT'S OVER.
HEH...
HEH HEH HEH.
IT DOESN'T MATTER.

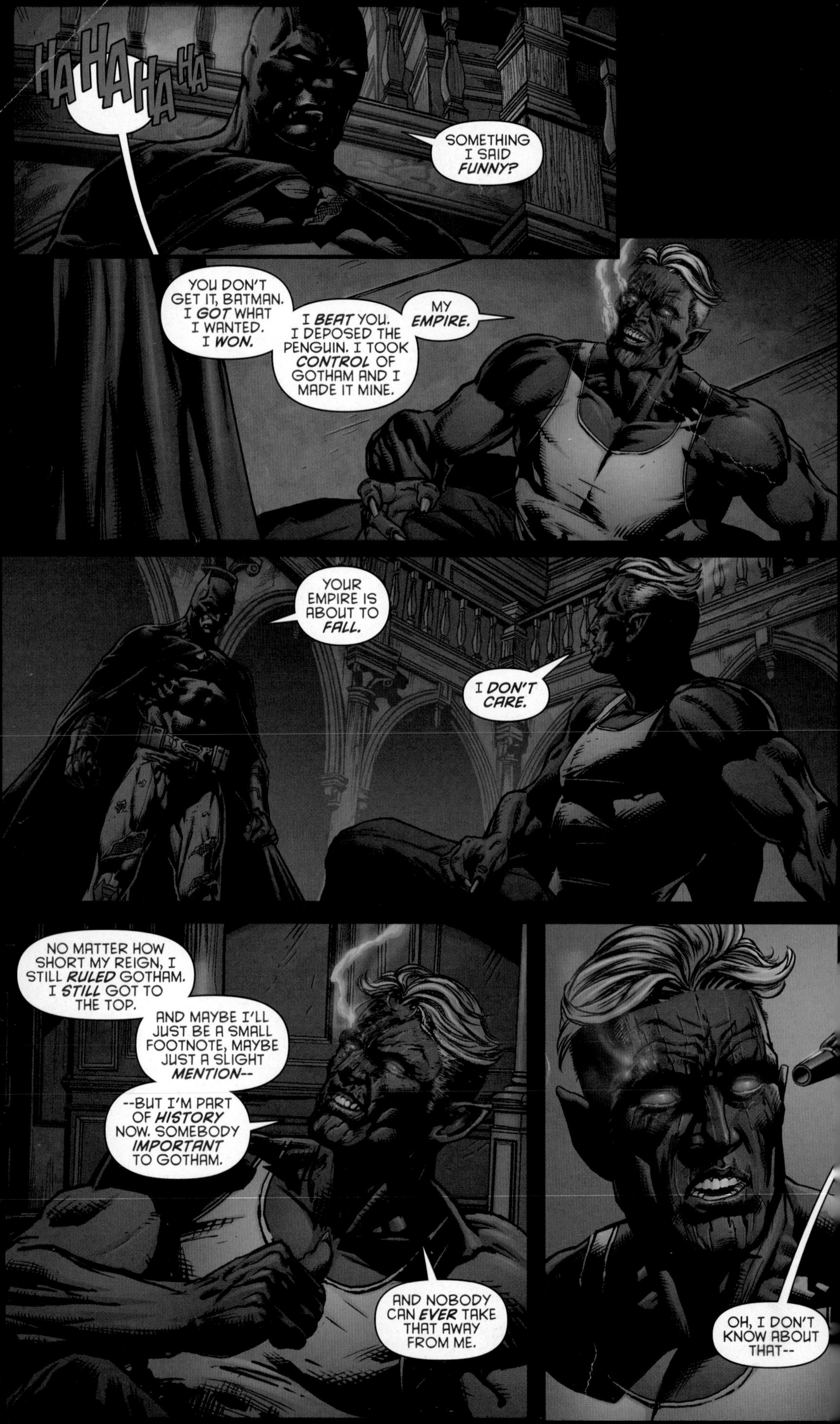
HA HA HA HA HA
SOMETHING I SAID FUNNY?
YOU DON'T GET IT, BATMAN. I GOT WHAT I WANTED. I WON.
I BEAT YOU. I DEPOSED THE PENGUIN. I TOOK CONTROL OF GOTHAM AND I MADE IT MINE.
MY EMPIRE.
YOUR EMPIRE IS ABOUT TO FALL.
I DON'T CARE.
NO MATTER HOW SHORT MY REIGN, I STILL RULED GOTHAM. I STILL GOT TO THE TOP.
AND MAYBE I'LL JUST BE A SMALL FOOTNOTE, MAYBE JUST A SLIGHT MENTION--
--BUT I'M PART OF HISTORY NOW. SOMEBODY IMPORTANT TO GOTHAM.
AND NOBODY CAN EVER TAKE THAT AWAY FROM ME.
OH, I DON'T KNOW ABOUT THAT--

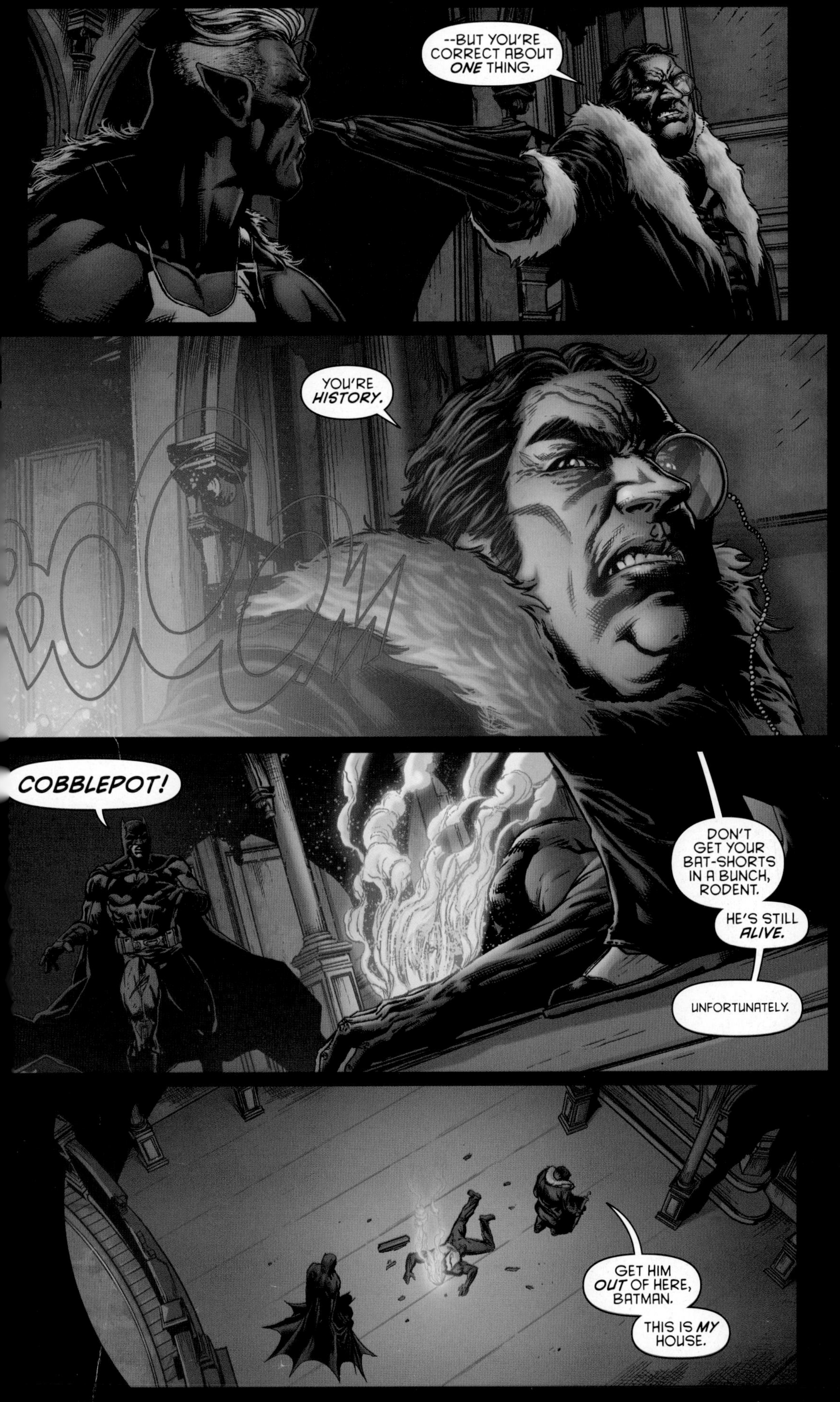
--BUT YOU'RE CORRECT ABOUT ONE THING.
YOU'RE HISTORY.
BOOOM
COBBLEPOT!
DON'T GET YOUR BAT-SHORTS IN A BUNCH, RODENT.
HE'S STILL ALIVE.
UNFORTUNATELY.
GET HIM OUT OF HERE, BATMAN.
THIS IS MY HOUSE.

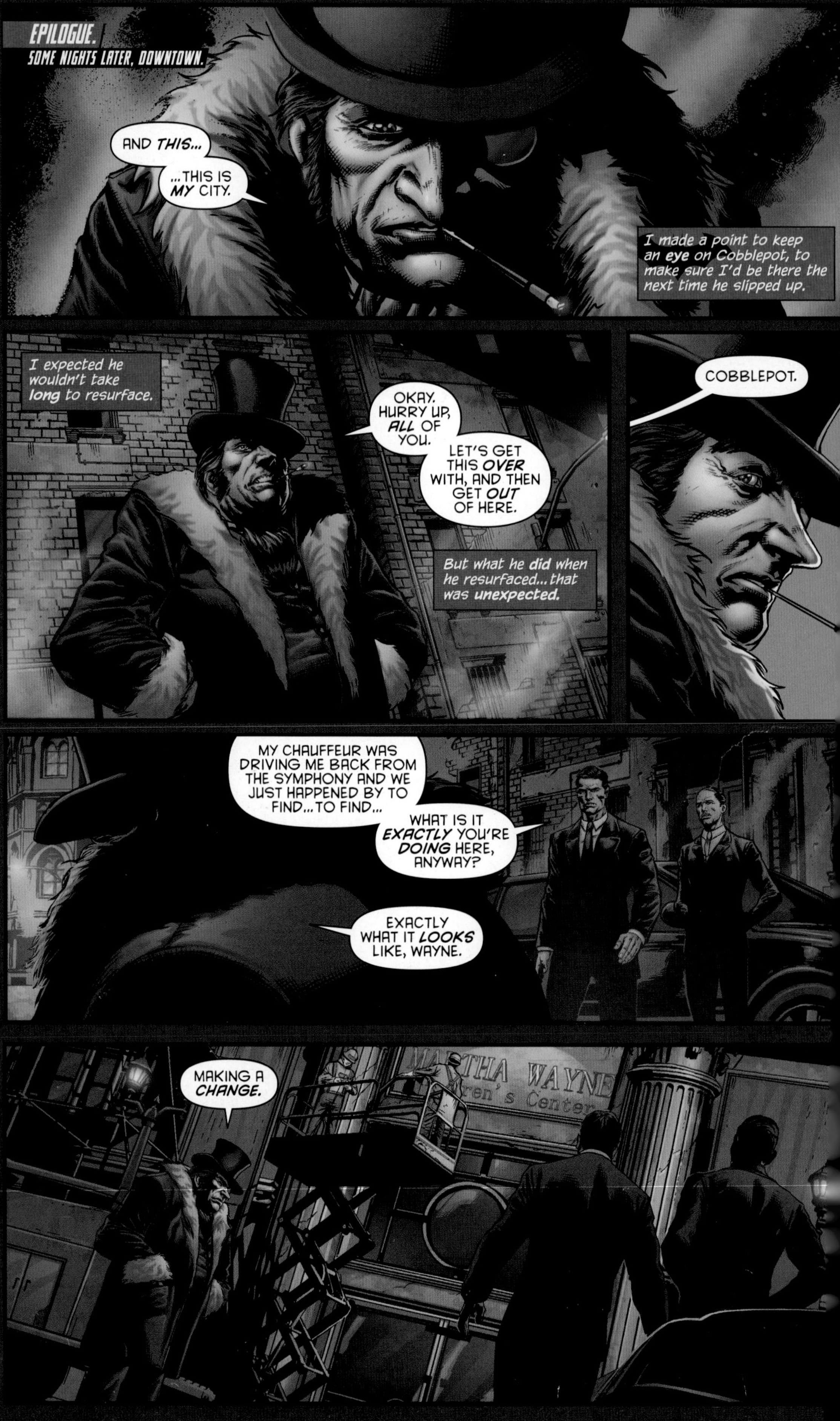
EPILOGUE.
SOME NIGHTS LATER, DOWNTOWN.
AND THIS...
...THIS IS MY CITY.
I made a point to keep an eye on Cobblepot, to make sure I'd be there the next time he slipped up.
I expected he wouldn't take long to resurface.
OKAY. HURRY UP, ALL OF YOU.
LET'S GET THIS OVER WITH, AND THEN GET OUT OF HERE.
But what he did when he resurfaced... that was unexpected.
COBBLEPOT.
MY CHAUFFEUR WAS DRIVING ME BACK FROM THE SYMPHONY AND WE JUST HAPPENED BY TO FIND... TO FIND...
WHAT IS IT EXACTLY YOU'RE DOING HERE, ANYWAY?
EXACTLY WHAT IT LOOKS LIKE, WAYNE.
MAKING A CHANGE.

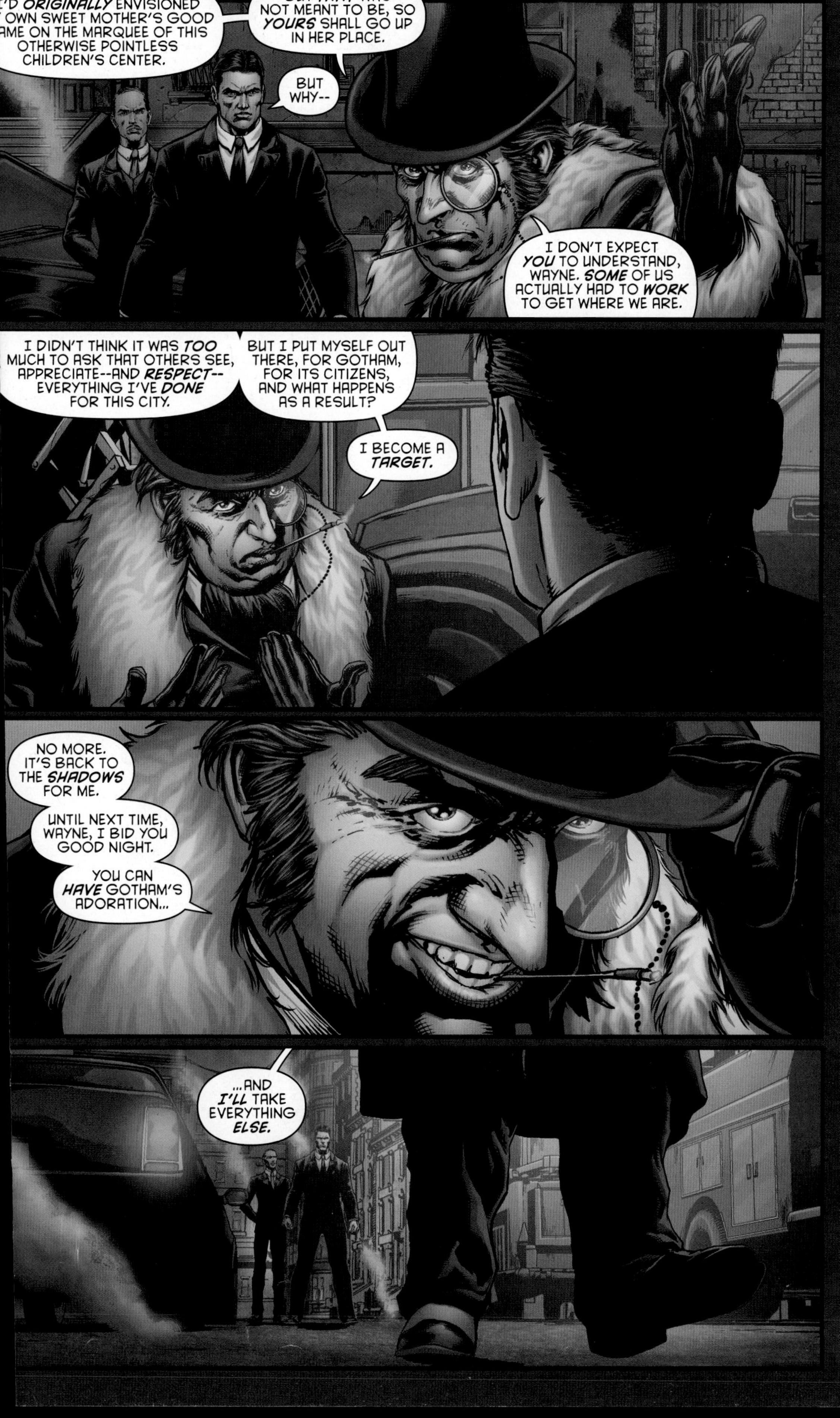

'D ORIGINALLY ENVISIONED OWN SWEET MOTHER'S GOOD AME ON THE MARQUEE OF THIS OTHERWISE POINTLESS CHILDREN'S CENTER.
NOT MEANT TO BE, SO YOURS SHALL GO UP IN HER PLACE.
BUT WHY--
I DON'T EXPECT YOU TO UNDERSTAND, WAYNE. SOME OF US ACTUALLY HAD TO WORK TO GET WHERE WE ARE.
I DIDN'T THINK IT WAS TOO MUCH TO ASK THAT OTHERS SEE, APPRECIATE--AND RESPECT--EVERYTHING I'VE DONE FOR THIS CITY.
BUT I PUT MYSELF OUT THERE, FOR GOTHAM, FOR ITS CITIZENS, AND WHAT HAPPENS AS A RESULT?
I BECOME A TARGET.
NO MORE. IT'S BACK TO THE SHADOWS FOR ME.
UNTIL NEXT TIME, WAYNE, I BID YOU GOOD NIGHT.
YOU CAN HAVE GOTHAM'S ADORATION...
...AND I'LL TAKE EVERYTHING ELSE.

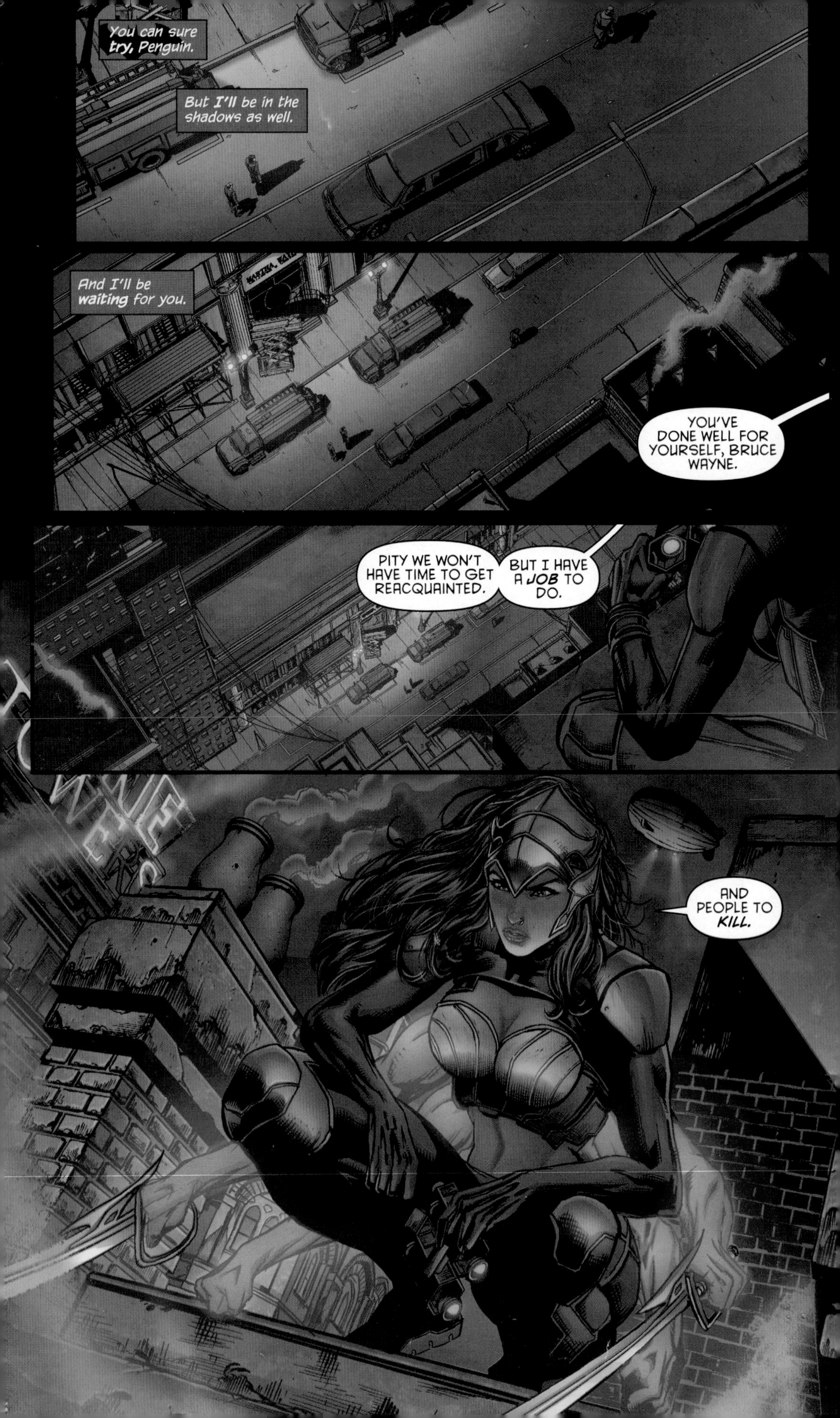

You can sure try, Penguin.
But I'll be in the shadows as well.
And I'll be waiting for you.
YOU'VE DONE WELL FOR YOURSELF, BRUCE WAYNE.
PITY WE WON'T HAVE TIME TO GET REACQUAINTED.
BUT I HAVE A JOB TO DO.
AND PEOPLE TO KILL.

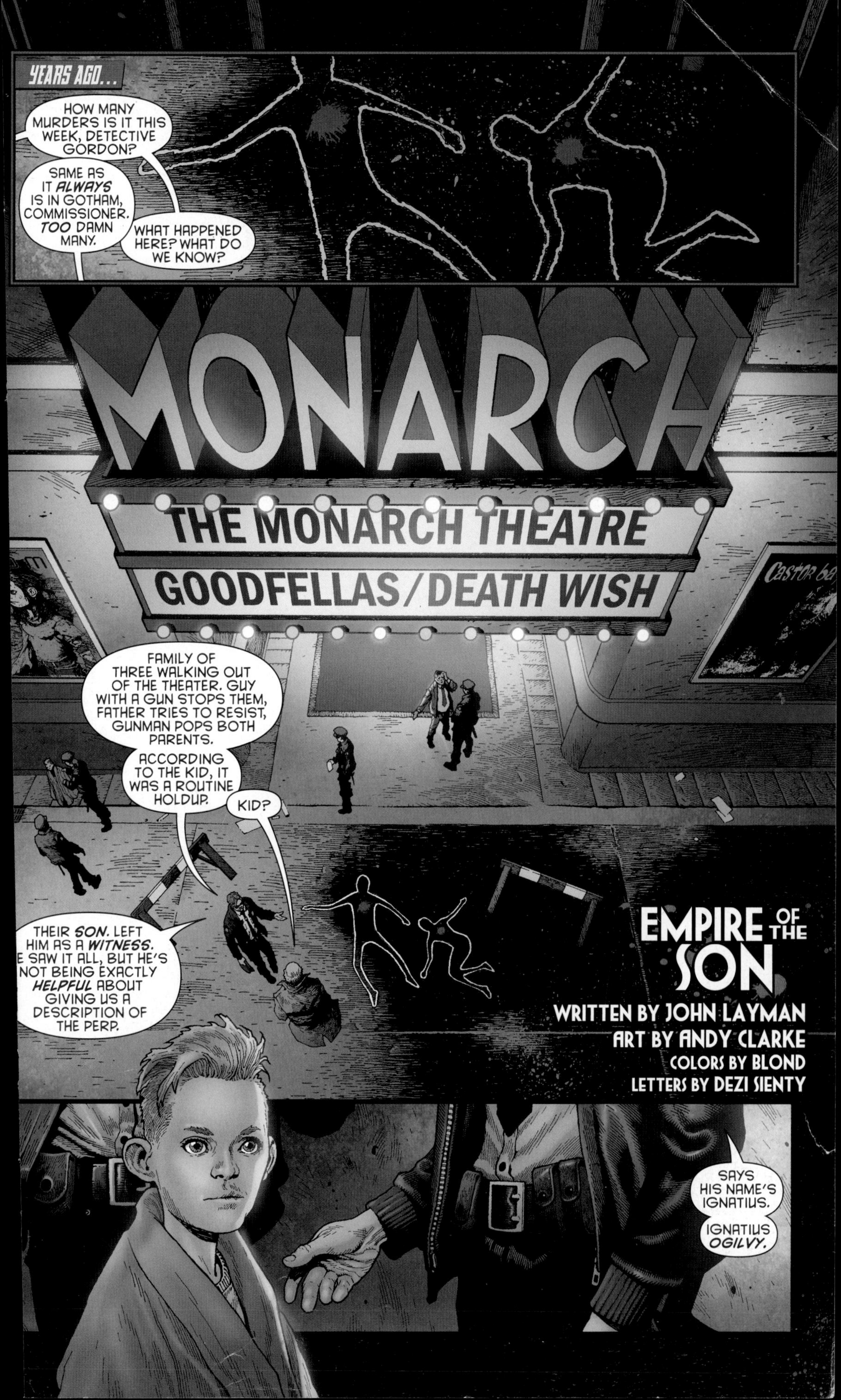
YEARS AGO...
HOW MANY MURDERS IS IT THIS WEEK, DETECTIVE GORDON?
SAME AS IT *ALWAYS* IS IN GOTHAM, COMMISSIONER. *TOO* DAMN MANY.
WHAT HAPPENED HERE? WHAT DO WE KNOW?
MONARCH
THE MONARCH THEATRE
GOODFELLAS/DEATH WISH
FAMILY OF THREE WALKING OUT OF THE THEATER. GUY WITH A GUN STOPS THEM, FATHER TRIES TO RESIST, GUNMAN POPS BOTH PARENTS.
ACCORDING TO THE KID, IT WAS A ROUTINE HOLDUP.
KID?
THEIR *SON*. LEFT HIM AS A *WITNESS*. E SAW IT ALL, BUT HE'S NOT BEING EXACTLY *HELPFUL* ABOUT GIVING US A DESCRIPTION OF THE PERP.
EMPIRE OF THE SON
WRITTEN BY JOHN LAYMAN
ART BY ANDY CLARKE
COLORS BY BLOND
LETTERS BY DEZI SIENTY
SAYS HIS NAME'S IGNATIUS.
IGNATIUS *OGILVY*.

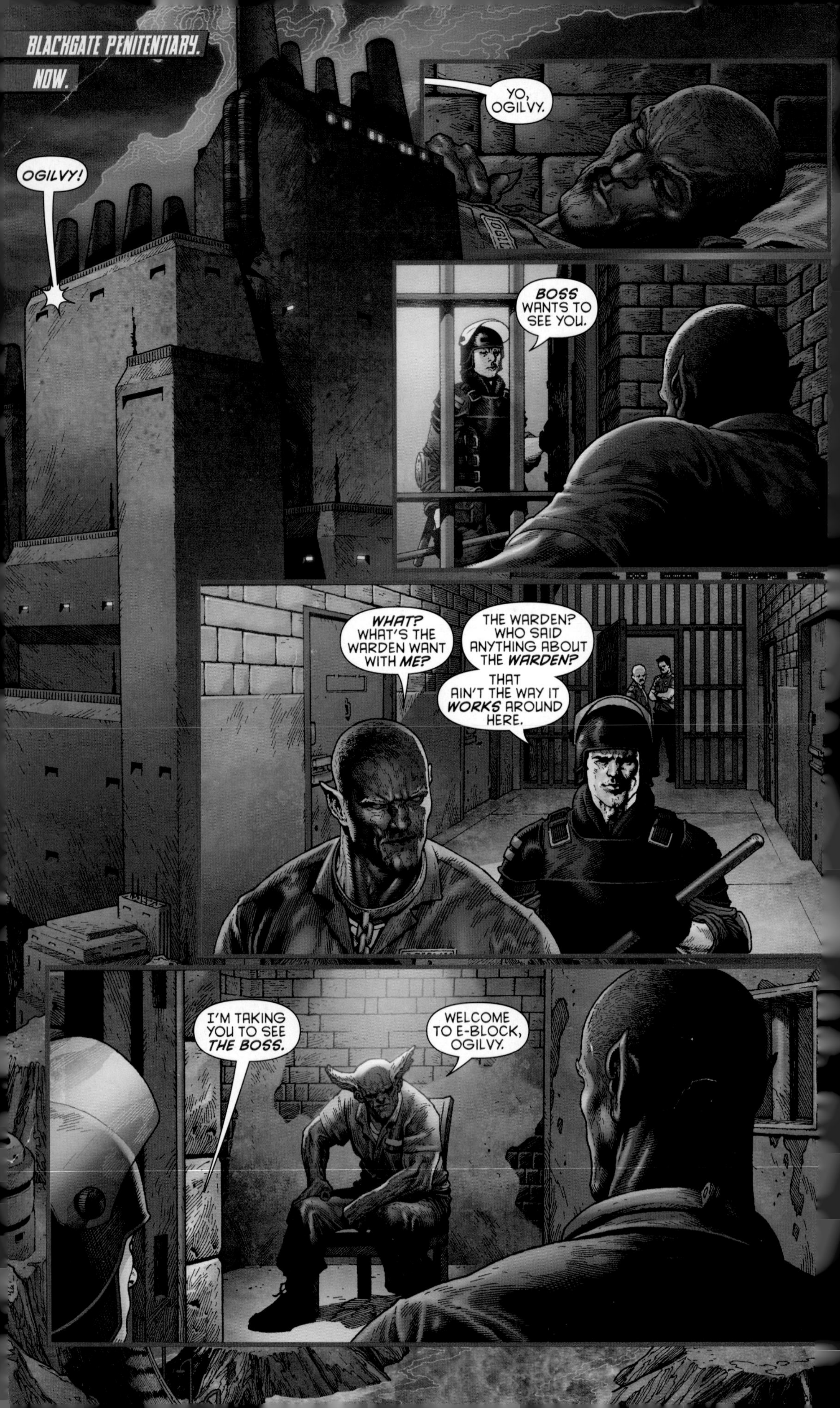
BLACKGATE PENITENTIARY.
NOW.
OGILVY!
YO, OGILVY.
BOSS WANTS TO SEE YOU.
WHAT? WHAT'S THE WARDEN WANT WITH ME?
THE WARDEN? WHO SAID ANYTHING ABOUT THE WARDEN?
THAT AIN'T THE WAY IT WORKS AROUND HERE.
I'M TAKING YOU TO SEE THE BOSS.
WELCOME TO E-BLOCK, OGILVY.

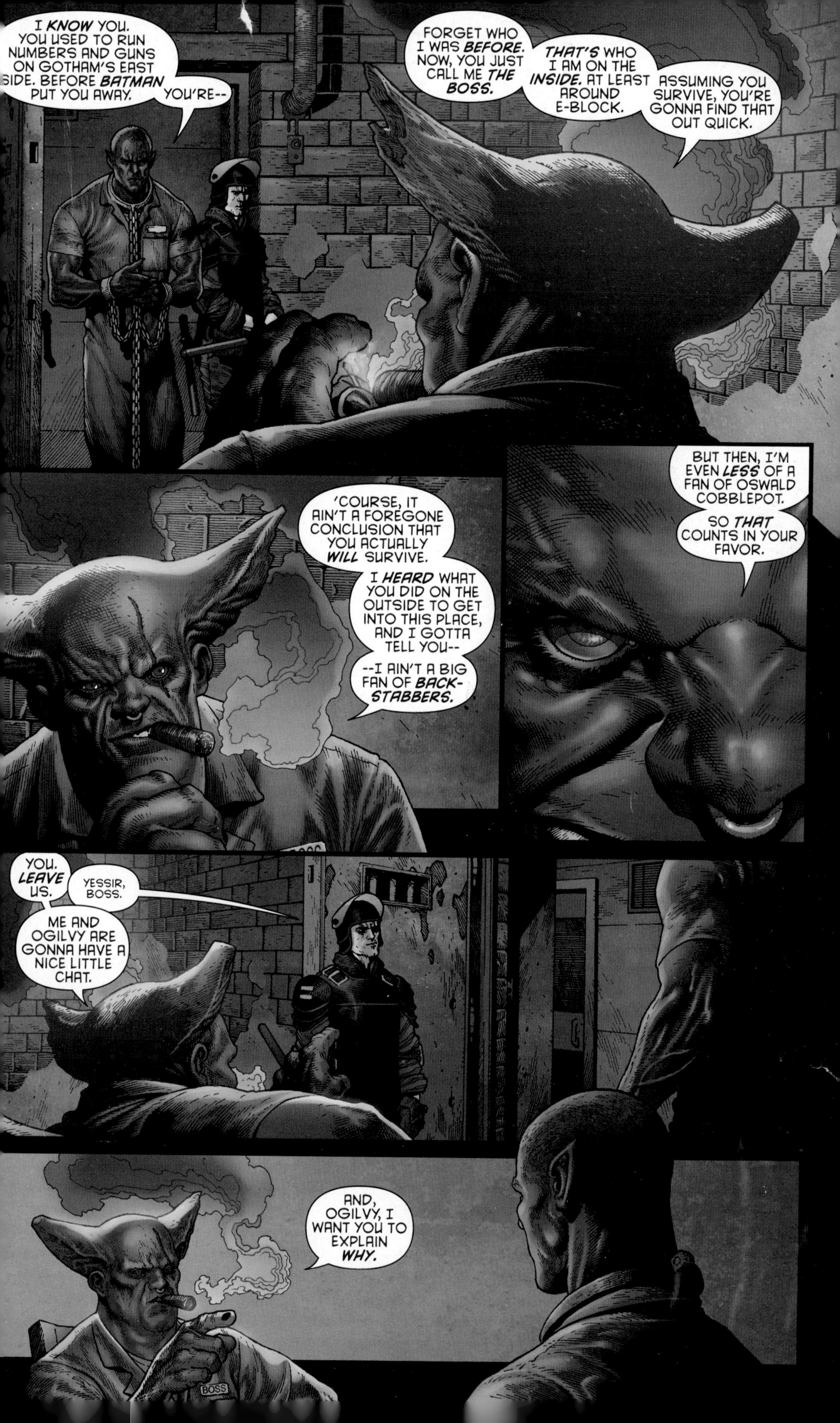
I KNOW YOU. YOU USED TO RUN NUMBERS AND GUNS ON GOTHAM'S EAST SIDE. BEFORE BATMAN PUT YOU AWAY.
YOU'RE--
FORGET WHO I WAS BEFORE. NOW, YOU JUST CALL ME THE BOSS.
THAT'S WHO I AM ON THE INSIDE. AT LEAST AROUND E-BLOCK.
ASSUMING YOU SURVIVE, YOU'RE GONNA FIND THAT OUT QUICK.
'COURSE, IT AIN'T A FOREGONE CONCLUSION THAT YOU ACTUALLY WILL SURVIVE.
I HEARD WHAT YOU DID ON THE OUTSIDE TO GET INTO THIS PLACE, AND I GOTTA TELL YOU--
--I AIN'T A BIG FAN OF BACK-STABBERS.
BUT THEN, I'M EVEN LESS OF A FAN OF OSWALD COBBLEPOT.
SO THAT COUNTS IN YOUR FAVOR.
YOU. LEAVE US.
YESSIR, BOSS.
ME AND OGILVY ARE GONNA HAVE A NICE LITTLE CHAT.
AND, OGILVY, I WANT YOU TO EXPLAIN WHY.
BOSS

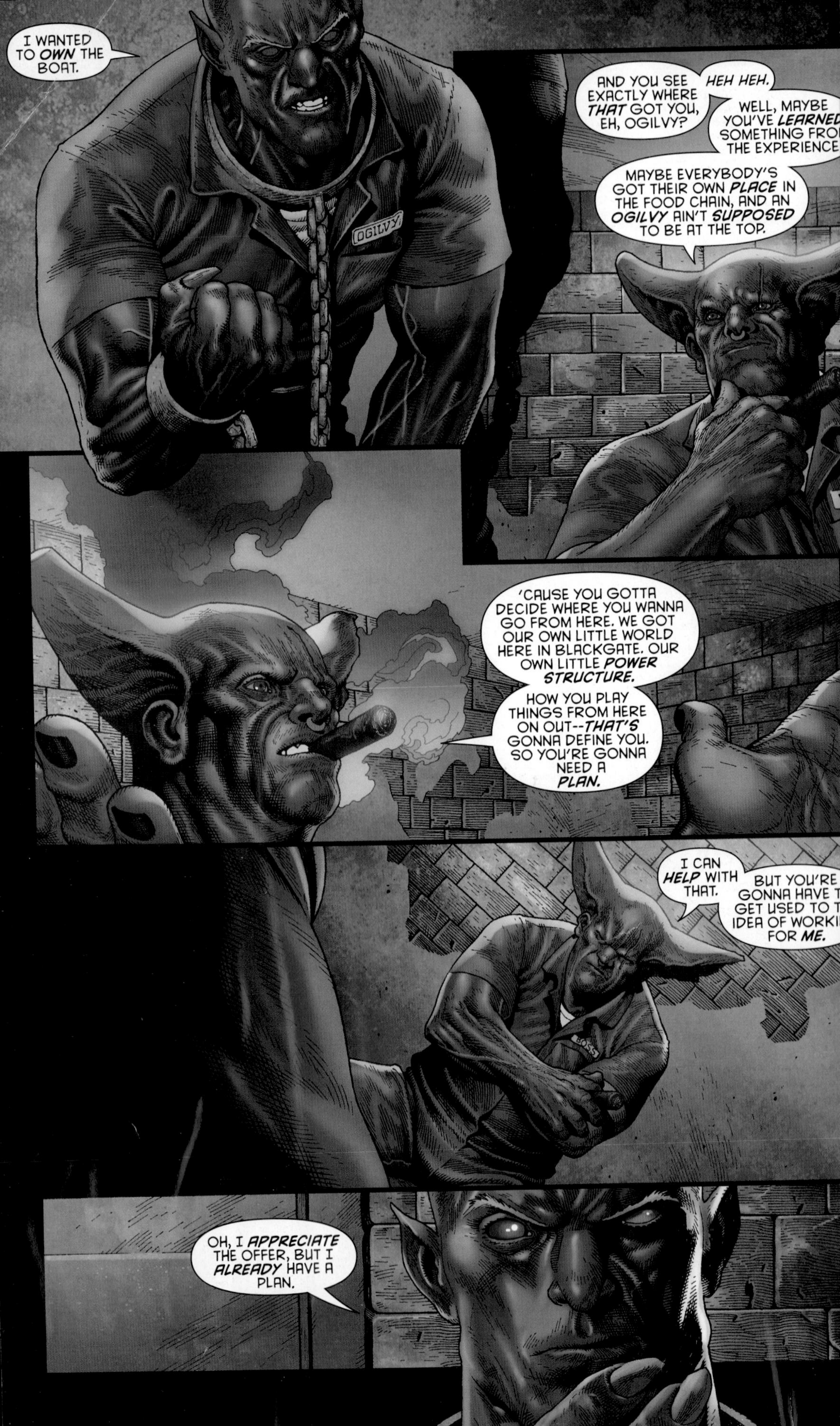
I WANTED TO **OWN** THE BOAT.
OGILVY
AND YOU SEE EXACTLY WHERE **THAT** GOT YOU, EH, OGILVY?
HEH HEH.
WELL, MAYBE YOU'VE ***LEARNED*** SOMETHING FROM THE EXPERIENCE.
MAYBE EVERYBODY'S GOT THEIR OWN ***PLACE*** IN THE FOOD CHAIN, AND AN ***OGILVY*** AIN'T ***SUPPOSED*** TO BE AT THE TOP.
'CAUSE YOU GOTTA DECIDE WHERE YOU WANNA GO FROM HERE. WE GOT OUR OWN LITTLE WORLD HERE IN BLACKGATE. OUR OWN LITTLE ***POWER STRUCTURE.***
HOW YOU PLAY THINGS FROM HERE ON OUT--***THAT'S*** GONNA DEFINE YOU. SO YOU'RE GONNA NEED A ***PLAN.***
I CAN ***HELP*** WITH THAT.
BUT YOU'RE GONNA HAVE TO GET USED TO THE IDEA OF WORKING FOR ***ME.***
OH, I ***APPRECIATE*** THE OFFER, BUT I ***ALREADY*** HAVE A PLAN.

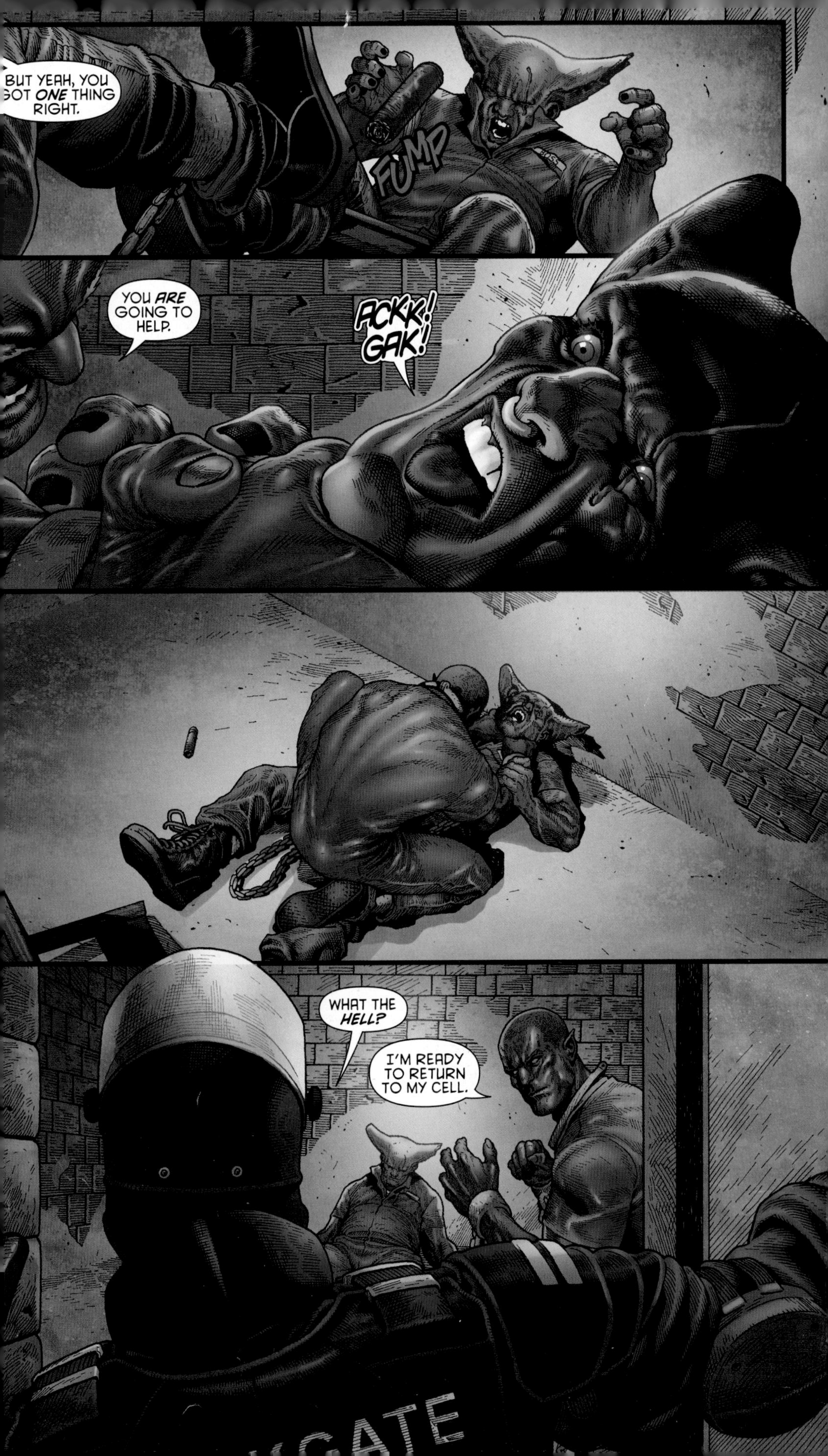

BUT YEAH, YOU GOT *ONE* THING RIGHT.
FUMP
YOU *ARE* GOING TO HELP.
ACKK! GAK!
WHAT THE *HELL?*
I'M READY TO RETURN TO MY CELL.

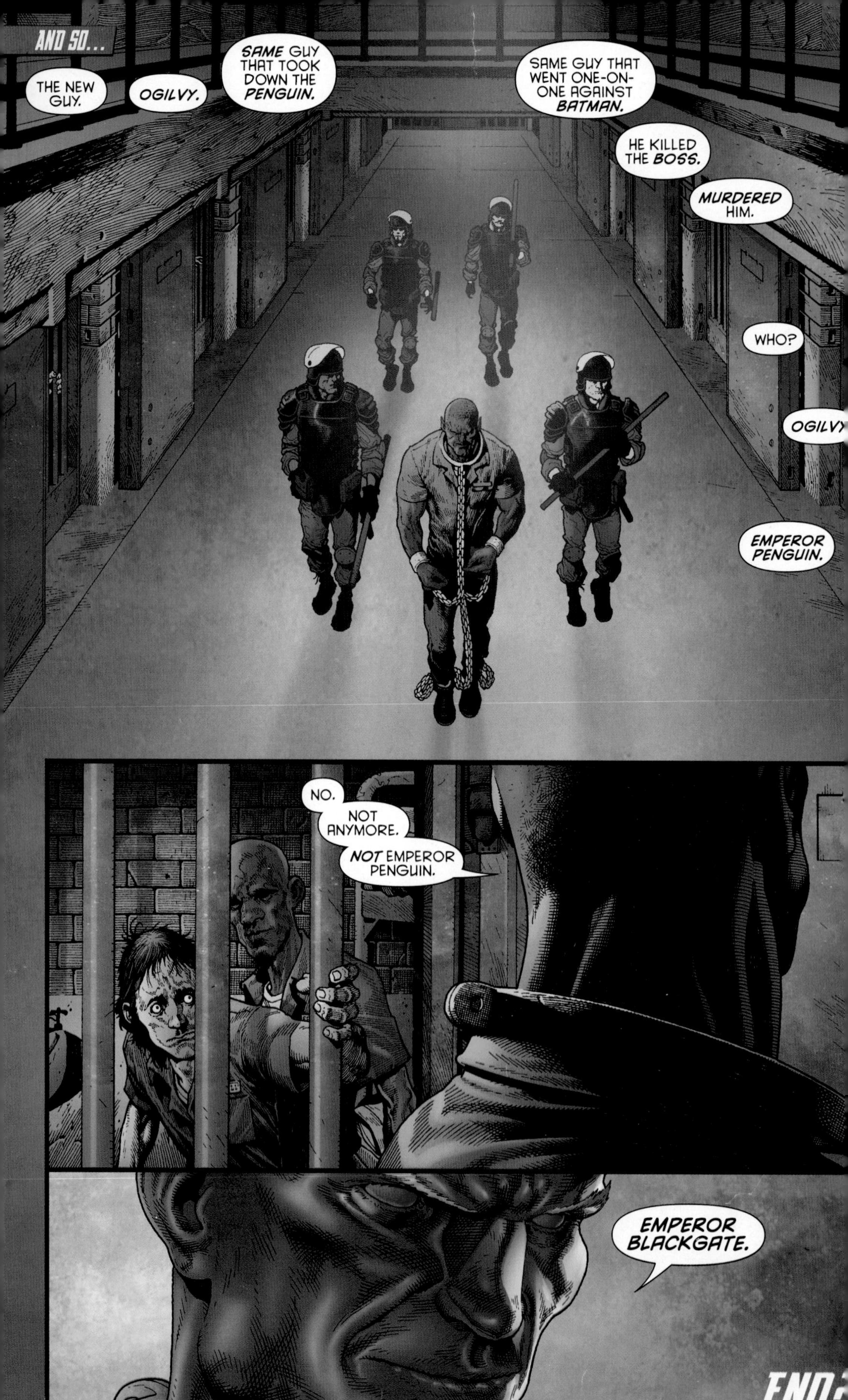
AND SO...
THE NEW GUY.
OGILVY.
SAME GUY THAT TOOK DOWN THE PENGUIN.
SAME GUY THAT WENT ONE-ON-ONE AGAINST BATMAN.
HE KILLED THE BOSS.
MURDERED HIM.
WHO?
EMPEROR PENGUIN.
NO.
NOT ANYMORE.
NOT EMPEROR PENGUIN.
EMPEROR BLACKGATE.
END?

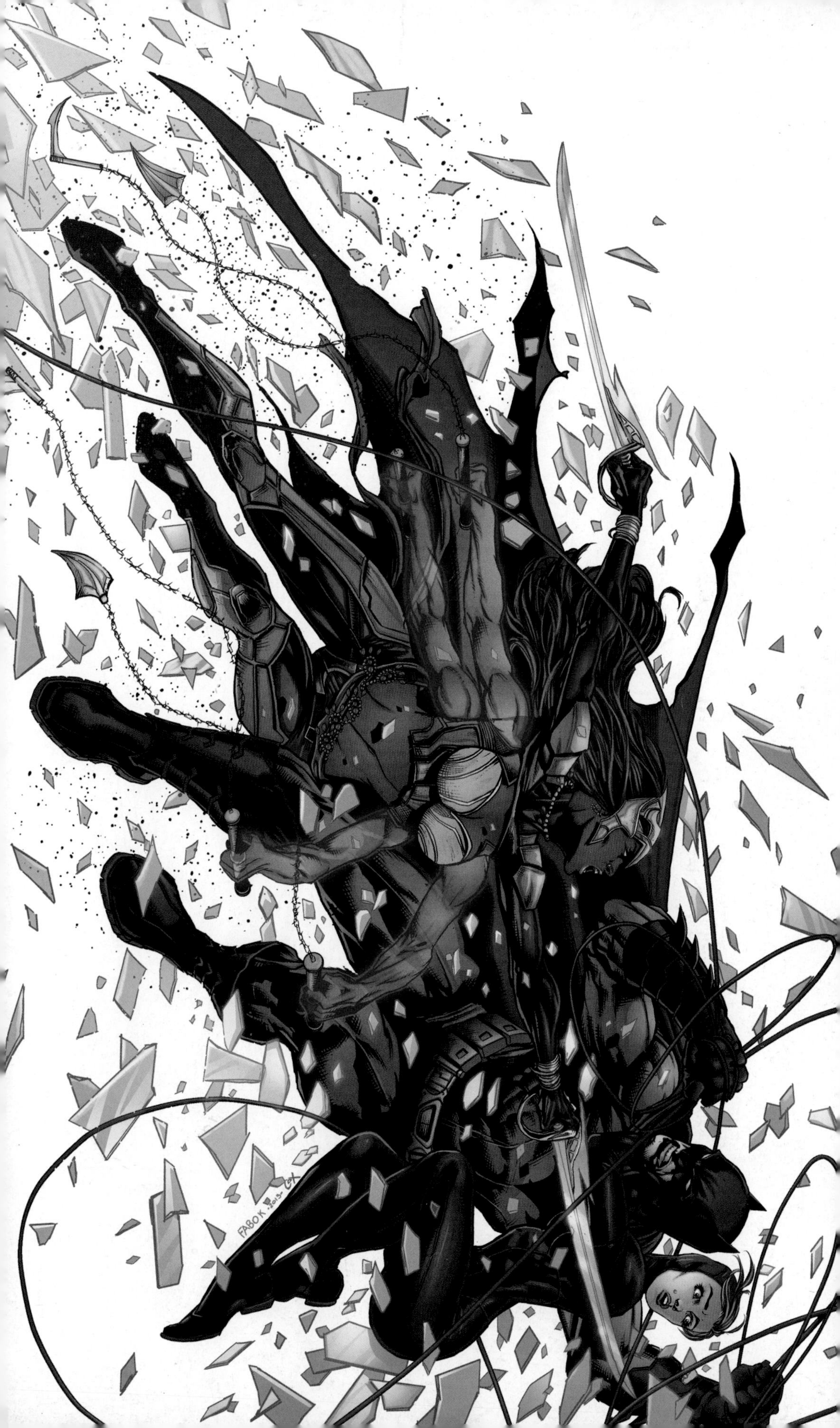
FABOK 2013

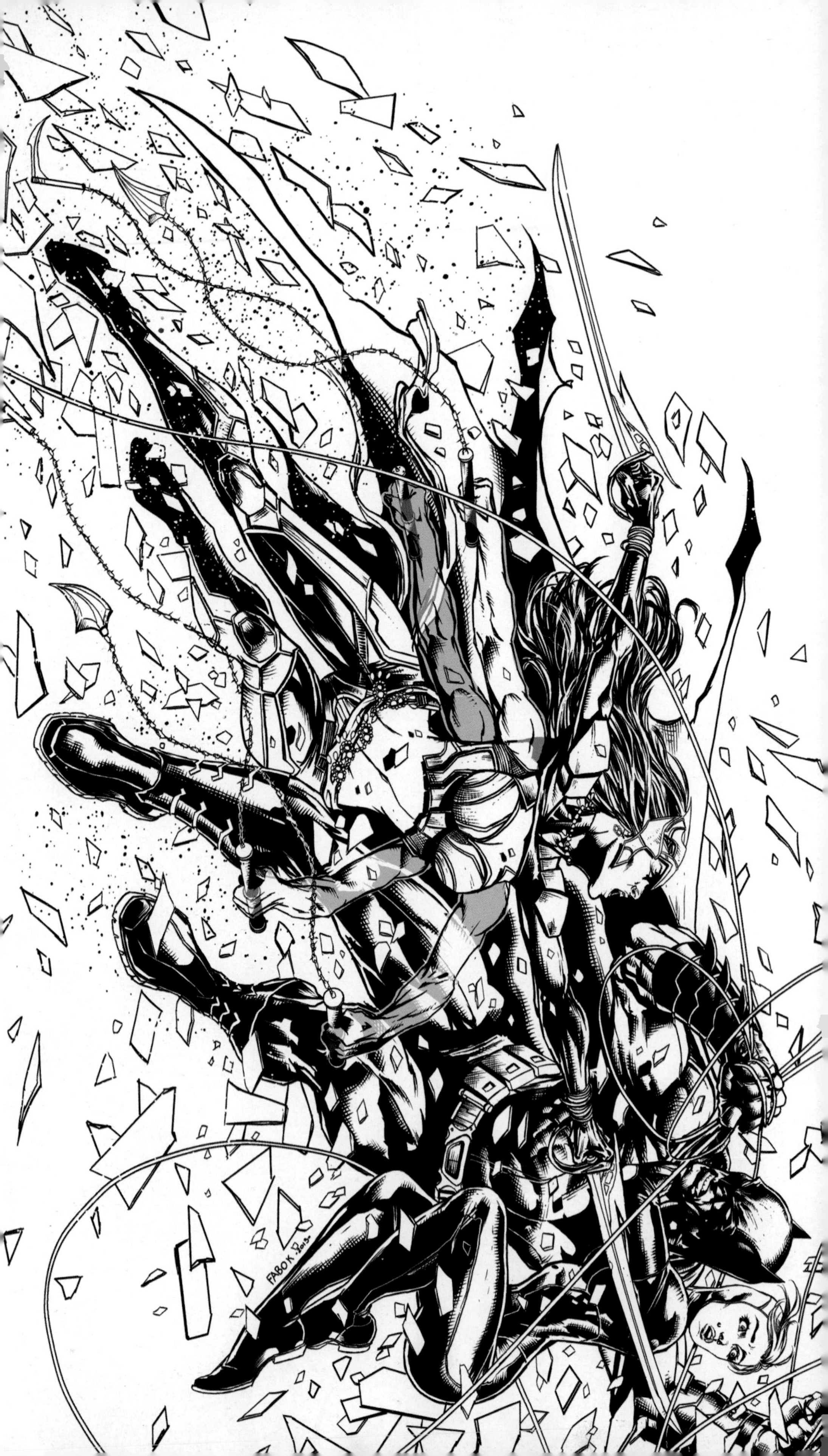

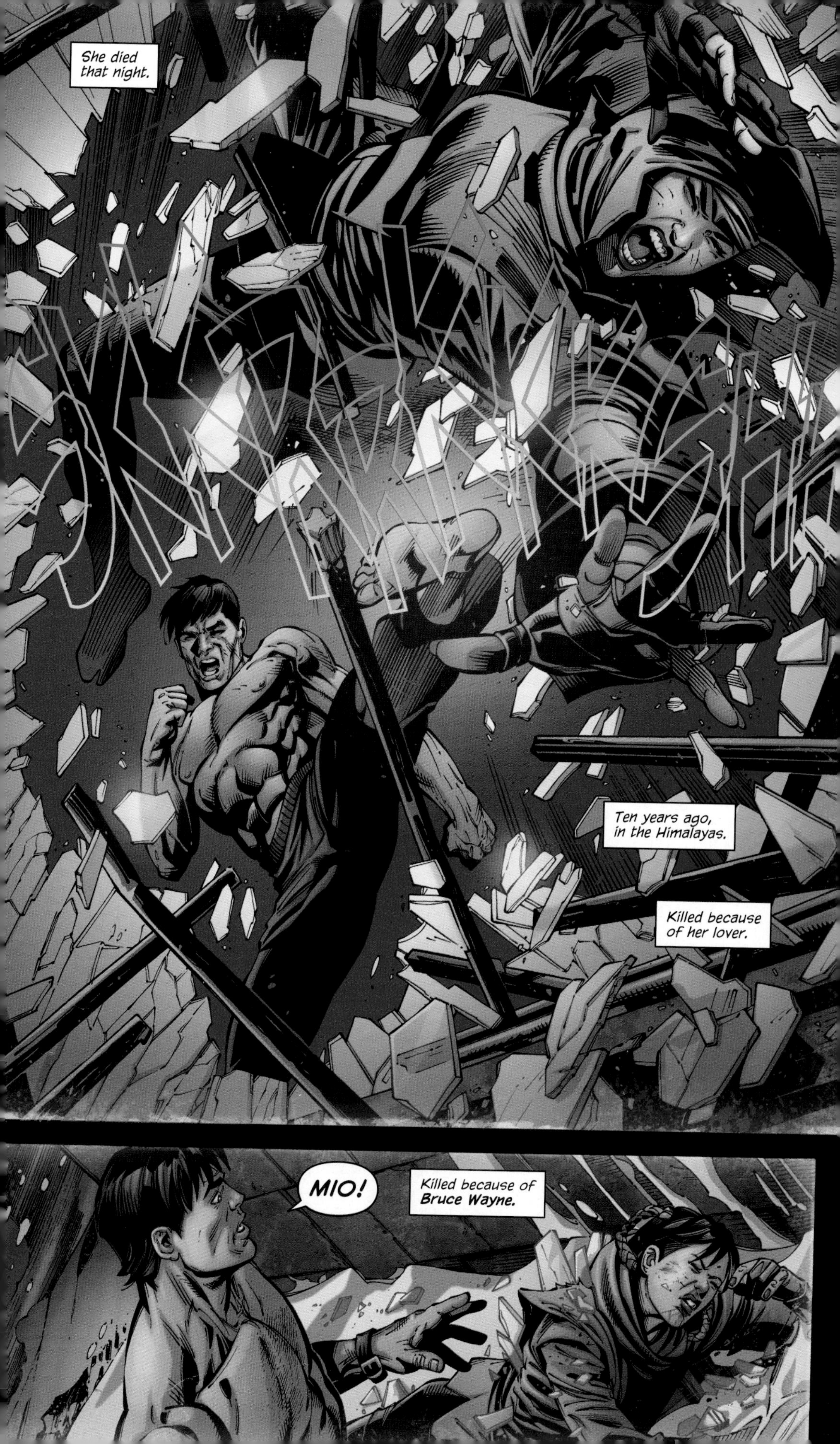
She died that night.
Ten years ago, in the Himalayas.
Killed because of her lover.
MIO!
Killed because of Bruce Wayne.

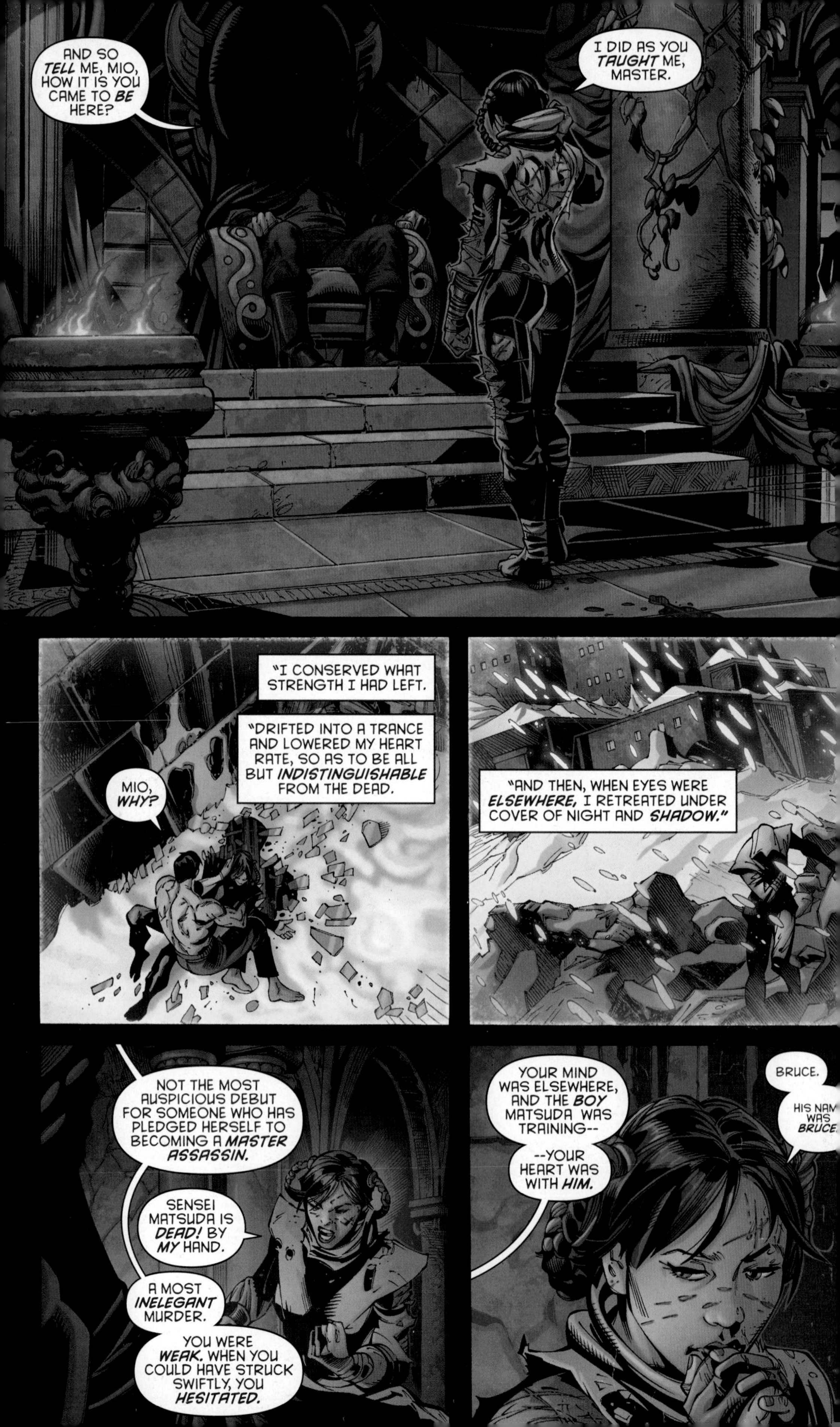
AND SO TELL ME, MIO, HOW IT IS YOU CAME TO BE HERE?
I DID AS YOU TAUGHT ME, MASTER.
"I CONSERVED WHAT STRENGTH I HAD LEFT.
"DRIFTED INTO A TRANCE AND LOWERED MY HEART RATE, SO AS TO BE ALL BUT INDISTINGUISHABLE FROM THE DEAD.
MIO, WHY?
"AND THEN, WHEN EYES WERE ELSEWHERE, I RETREATED UNDER COVER OF NIGHT AND SHADOW."
NOT THE MOST AUSPICIOUS DEBUT FOR SOMEONE WHO HAS PLEDGED HERSELF TO BECOMING A MASTER ASSASSIN.
SENSEI MATSUDA IS DEAD! BY MY HAND.
A MOST INELEGANT MURDER.
YOU WERE WEAK. WHEN YOU COULD HAVE STRUCK SWIFTLY, YOU HESITATED.
YOUR MIND WAS ELSEWHERE, AND THE BOY MATSUDA WAS TRAINING--
--YOUR HEART WAS WITH HIM.
BRUCE.

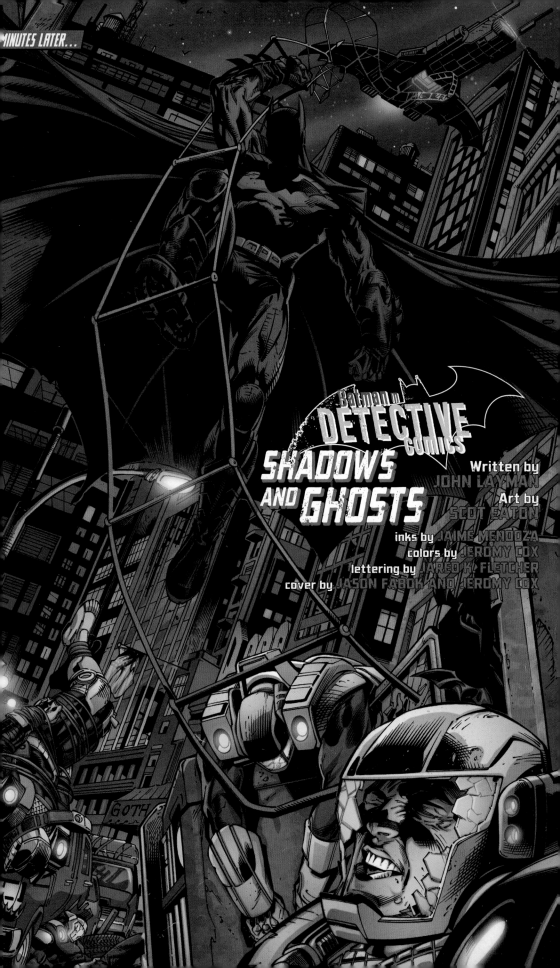

Batman in
DETECTIVE
comics
SHADOWS
AND GHOSTS

Written by
JOHN LAYMAN

Art by
SCOT EATON

inks by JAIME MENDOZA
colors by JEROMY COX
lettering by JARED K. FLETCHER
cover by JASON FABOK AND JEROMY COX

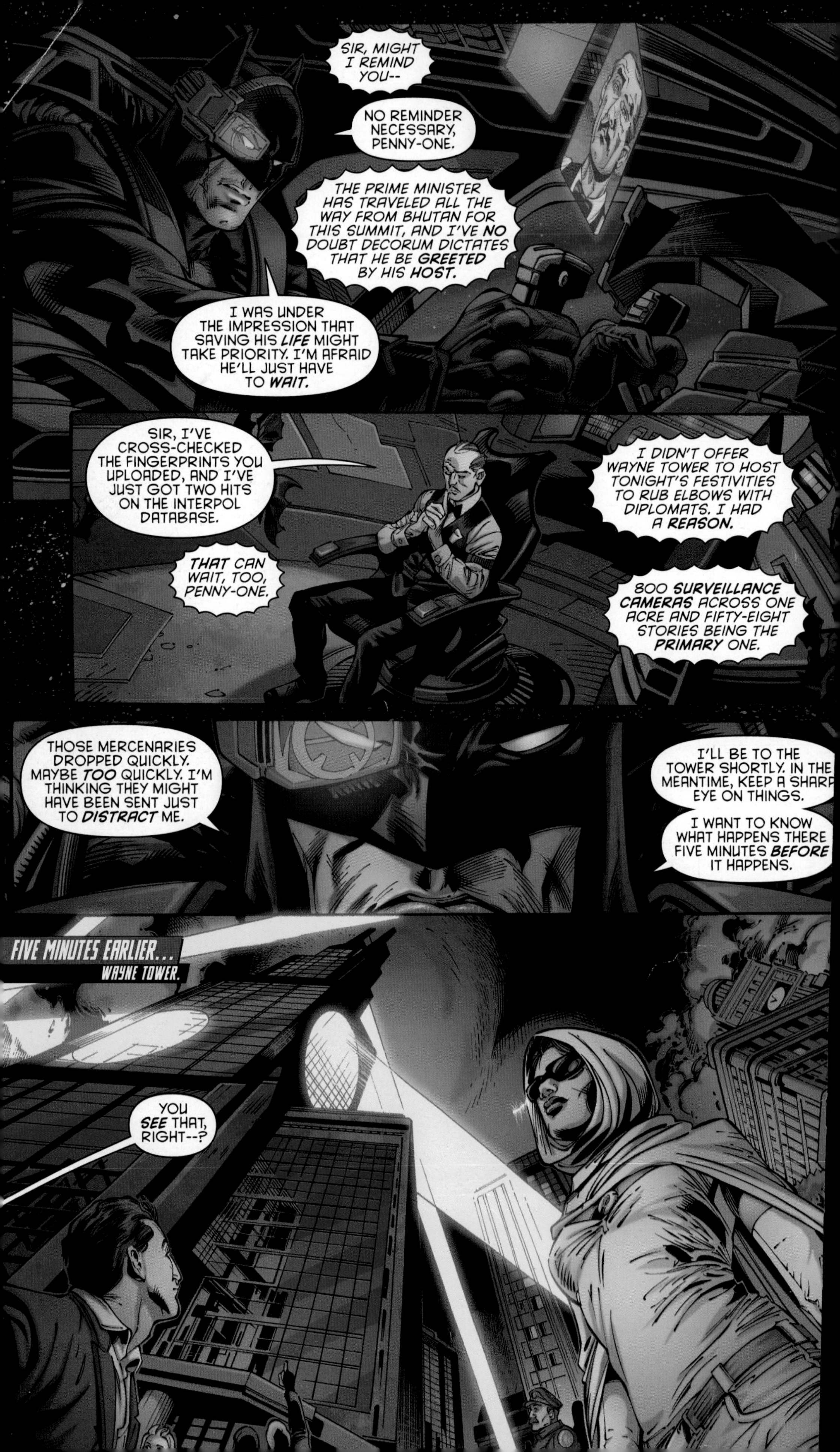
SIR, MIGHT I REMIND YOU--
NO REMINDER NECESSARY, PENNY-ONE.
THE PRIME MINISTER HAS TRAVELED ALL THE WAY FROM BHUTAN FOR THIS SUMMIT, AND I'VE NO DOUBT DECORUM DICTATES THAT HE BE GREETED BY HIS HOST.
I WAS UNDER THE IMPRESSION THAT SAVING HIS LIFE MIGHT TAKE PRIORITY. I'M AFRAID HE'LL JUST HAVE TO WAIT.
SIR, I'VE CROSS-CHECKED THE FINGERPRINTS YOU UPLOADED, AND I'VE JUST GOT TWO HITS ON THE INTERPOL DATABASE.
THAT CAN WAIT, TOO, PENNY-ONE.
I DIDN'T OFFER WAYNE TOWER TO HOST TONIGHT'S FESTIVITIES TO RUB ELBOWS WITH DIPLOMATS. I HAD A REASON.
800 SURVEILLANCE CAMERAS ACROSS ONE ACRE AND FIFTY-EIGHT STORIES BEING THE PRIMARY ONE.
THOSE MERCENARIES DROPPED QUICKLY. MAYBE TOO QUICKLY. I'M THINKING THEY MIGHT HAVE BEEN SENT JUST TO DISTRACT ME.
I'LL BE TO THE TOWER SHORTLY. IN THE MEANTIME, KEEP A SHARP EYE ON THINGS.
I WANT TO KNOW WHAT HAPPENS THERE FIVE MINUTES BEFORE IT HAPPENS.
FIVE MINUTES EARLIER...
WAYNE TOWER.
YOU SEE THAT, RIGHT--?

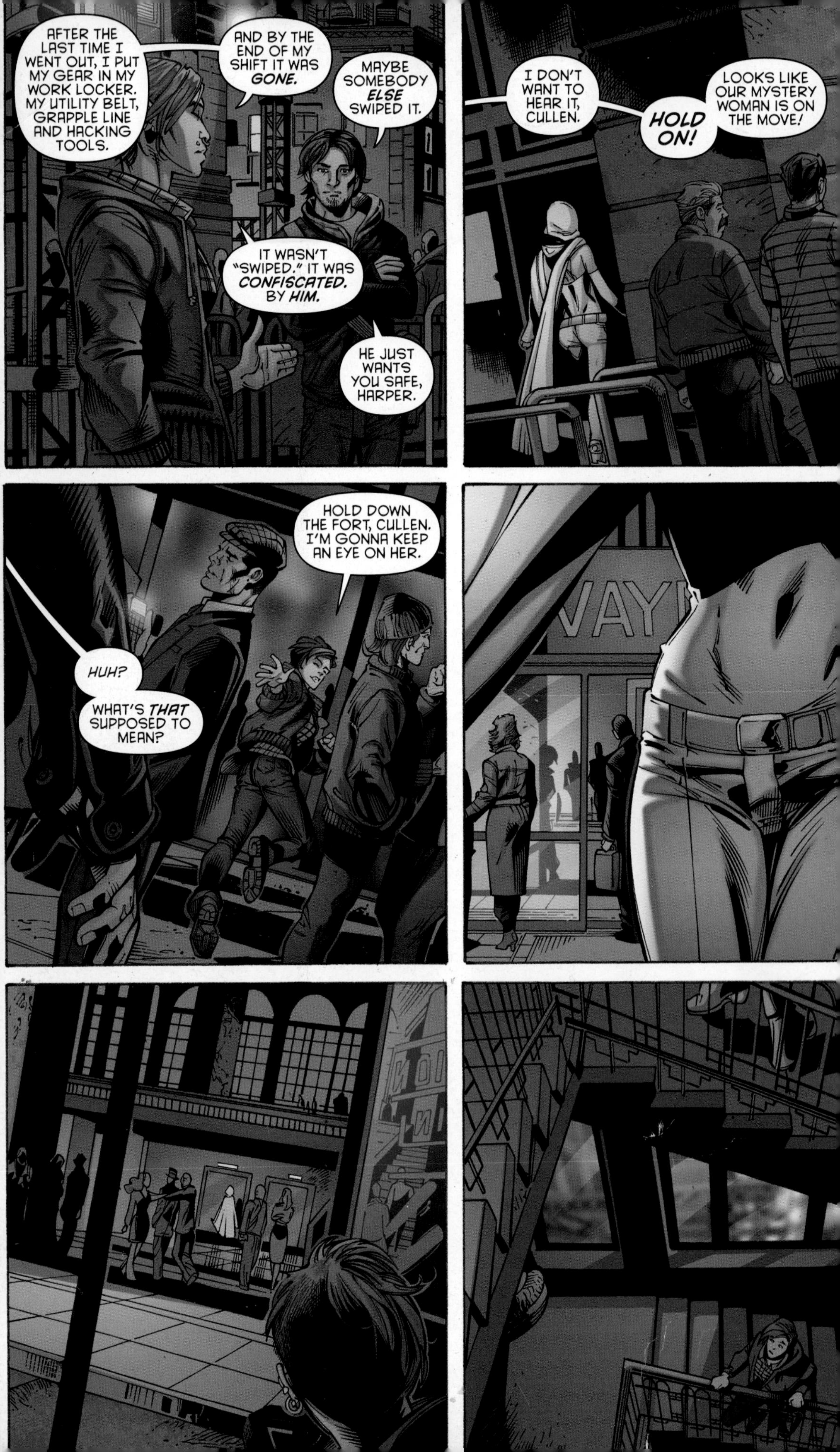
AFTER THE LAST TIME I WENT OUT, I PUT MY GEAR IN MY WORK LOCKER. MY UTILITY BELT, GRAPPLE LINE AND HACKING TOOLS.
AND BY THE END OF MY SHIFT IT WAS *GONE.*
MAYBE SOMEBODY *ELSE* SWIPED IT.
IT WASN'T "SWIPED." IT WAS *CONFISCATED.* BY *HIM.*
HE JUST WANTS YOU SAFE, HARPER.
I DON'T WANT TO HEAR IT, CULLEN.
HOLD ON!
LOOKS LIKE OUR MYSTERY WOMAN IS ON THE MOVE!
HOLD DOWN THE FORT, CULLEN. I'M GONNA KEEP AN EYE ON HER.
HUH?
WHAT'S *THAT* SUPPOSED TO MEAN?

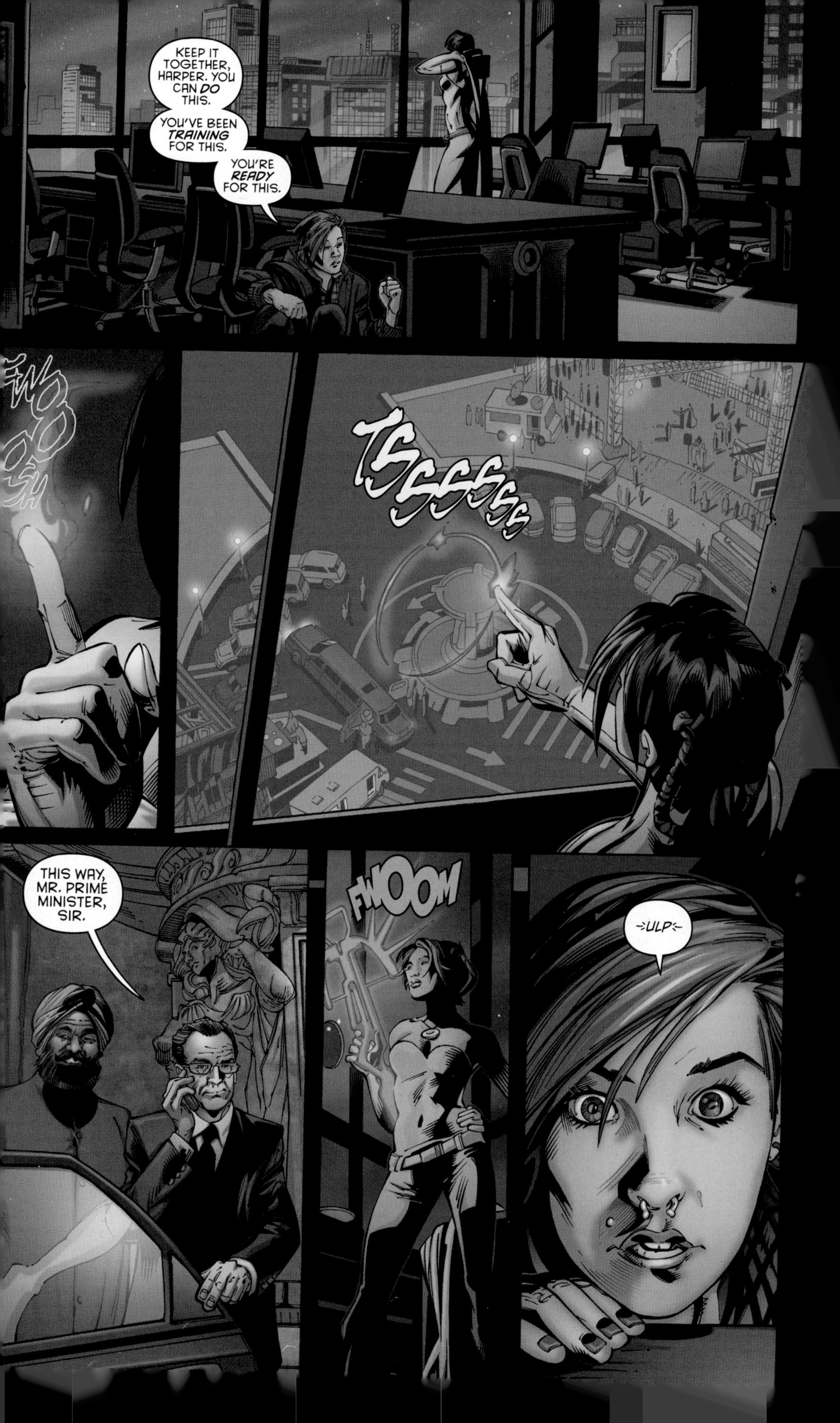

KEEP IT TOGETHER, HARPER. YOU CAN *DO* THIS.
YOU'VE BEEN *TRAINING* FOR THIS.
YOU'RE *READY* FOR THIS.
TSSSSSS
THIS WAY, MR. PRIME MINISTER, SIR.
FWOOM
-ULP-

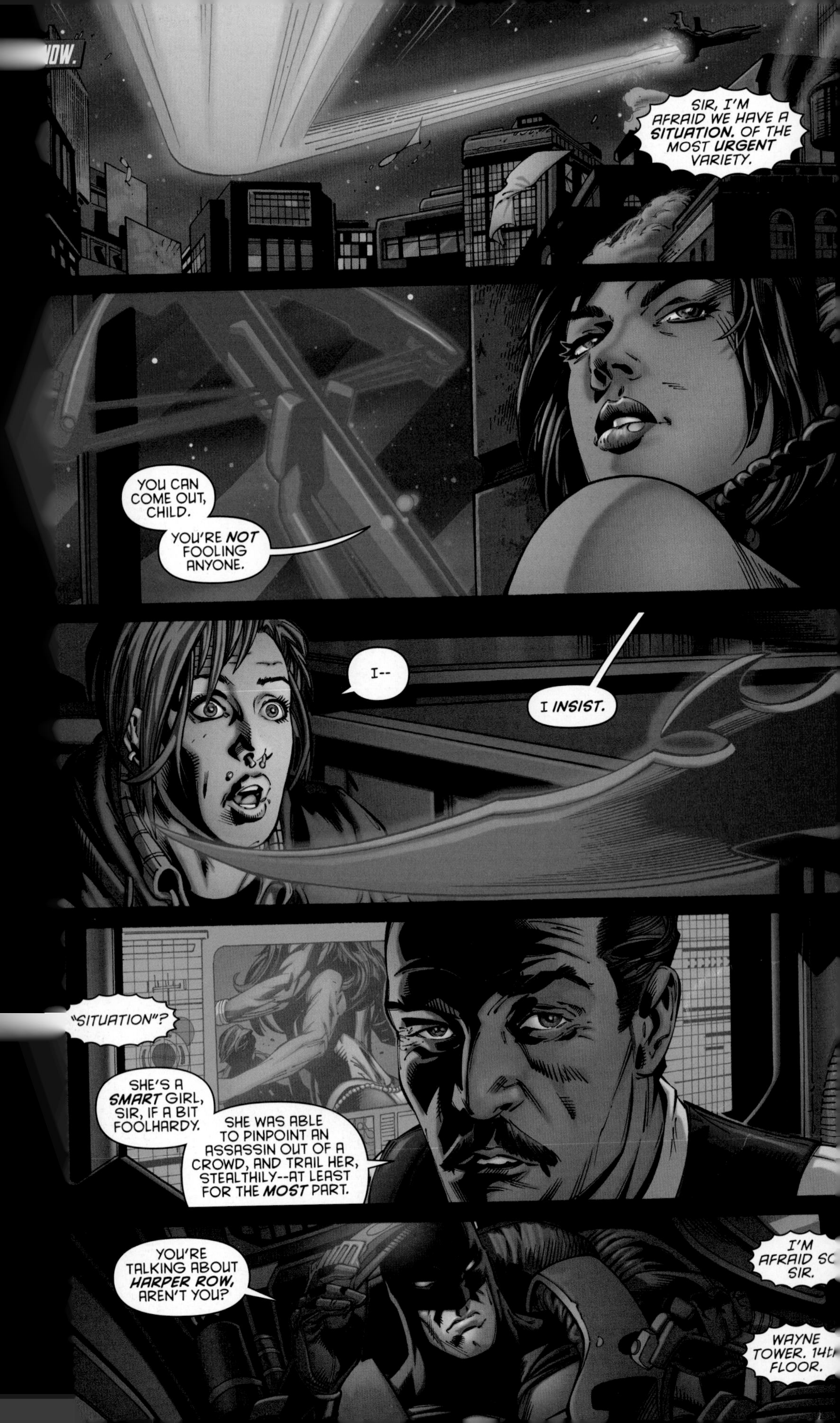
NOW.
SIR, I'M AFRAID WE HAVE A SITUATION. OF THE MOST URGENT VARIETY.
YOU CAN COME OUT, CHILD.
YOU'RE NOT FOOLING ANYONE.
I--
I INSIST.
"SITUATION"?
SHE'S A SMART GIRL, SIR, IF A BIT FOOLHARDY.
SHE WAS ABLE TO PINPOINT AN ASSASSIN OUT OF A CROWD, AND TRAIL HER, STEALTHILY--AT LEAST FOR THE MOST PART.
YOU'RE TALKING ABOUT HARPER ROW, AREN'T YOU?
I'M AFRAID SO, SIR.
WAYNE TOWER. 14th FLOOR.

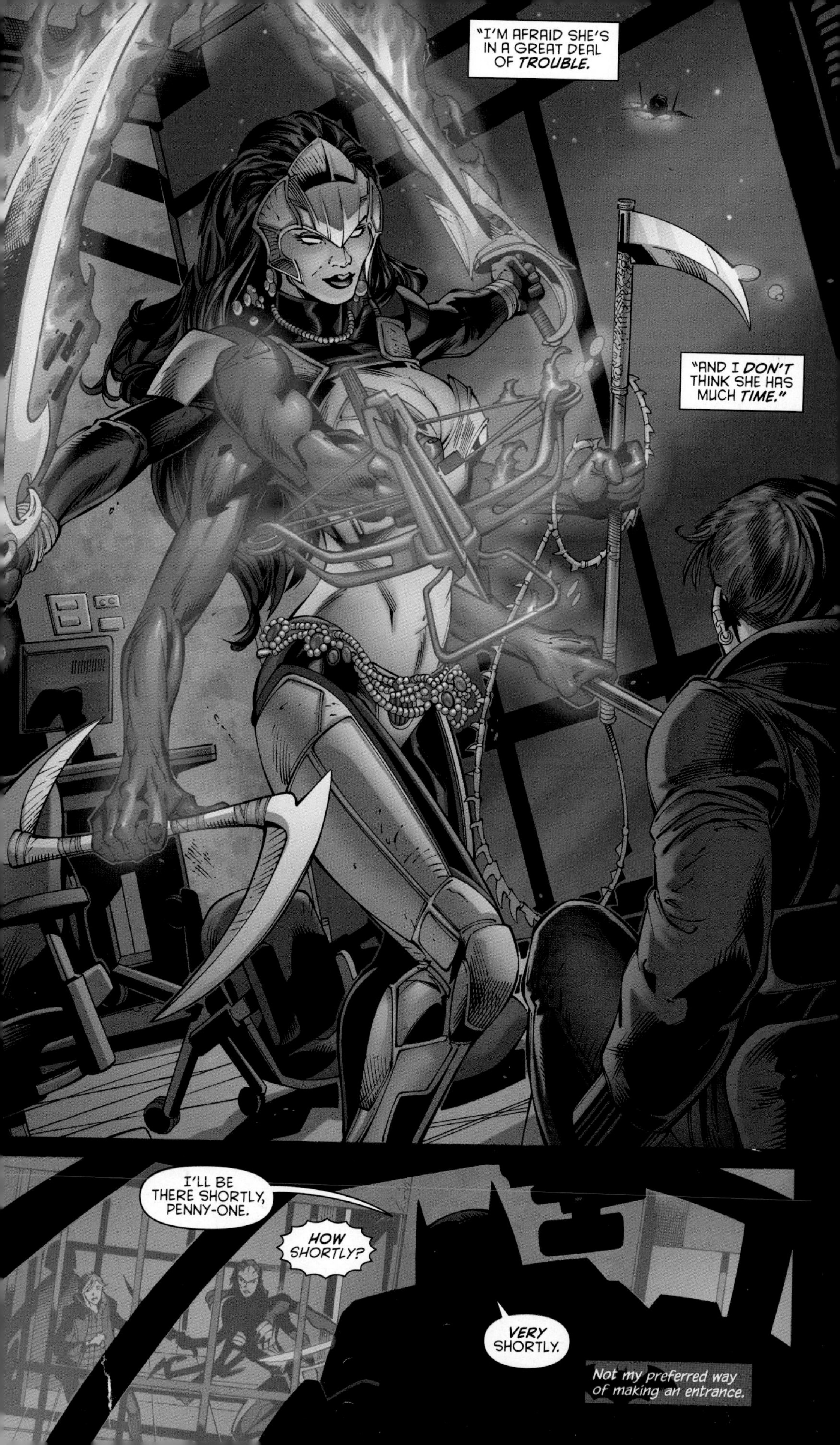
"I'M AFRAID SHE'S IN A GREAT DEAL OF TROUBLE.
"AND I DON'T THINK SHE HAS MUCH TIME."
I'LL BE THERE SHORTLY, PENNY-ONE.
HOW SHORTLY?
VERY SHORTLY.
Not my preferred way of making an entrance.

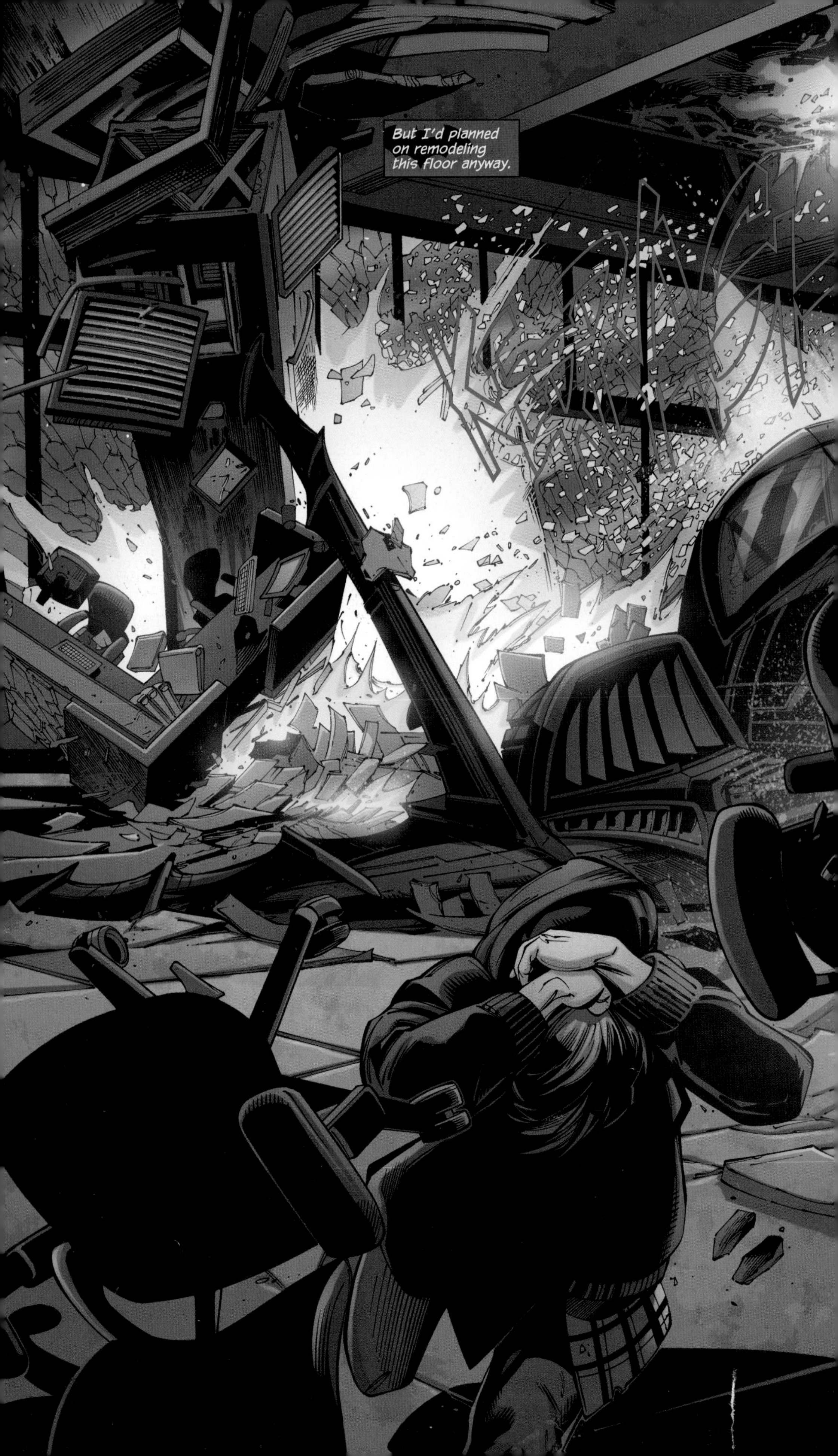
But I'd planned on remodeling this floor anyway.

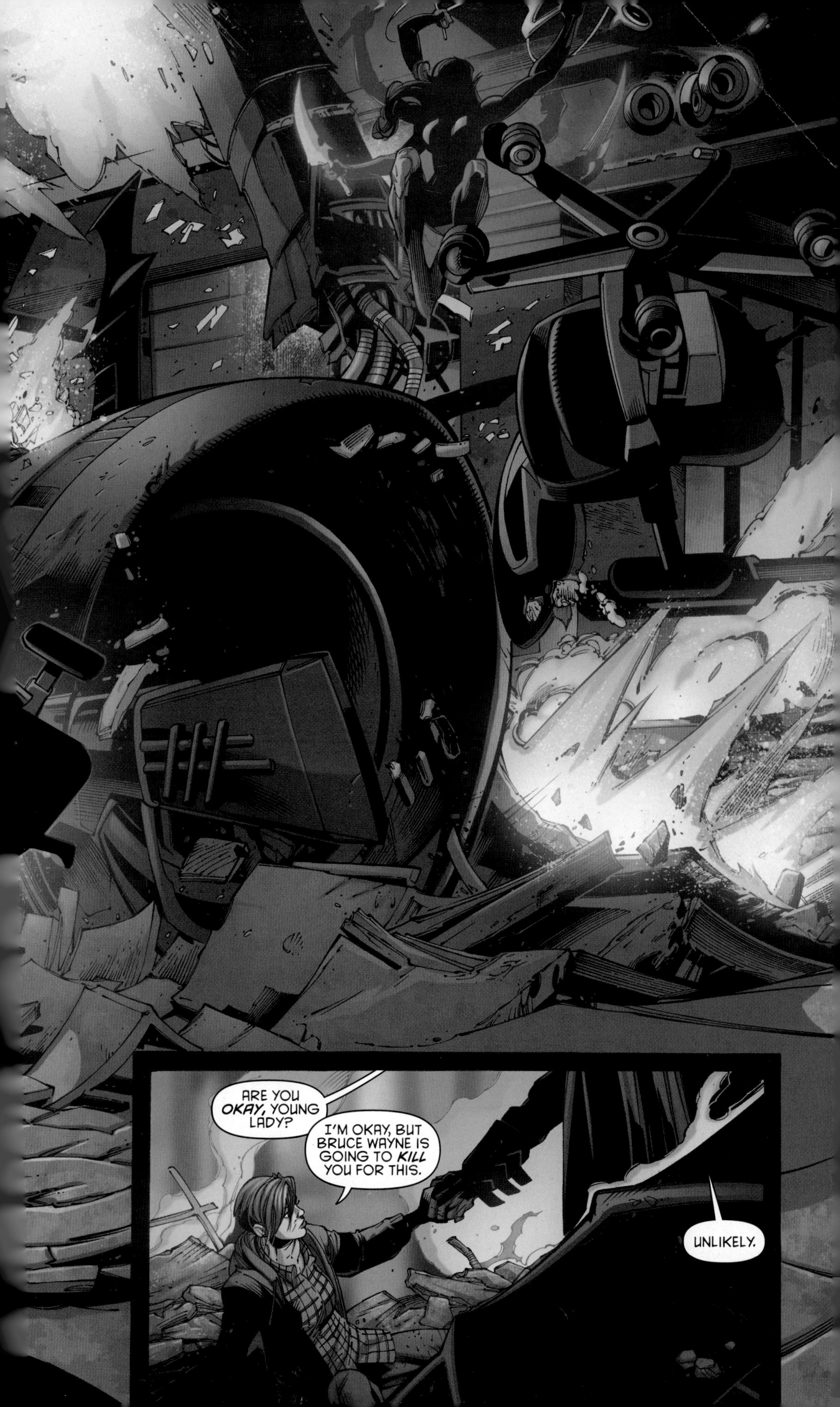
ARE YOU OKAY, YOUNG LADY?
I'M OKAY, BUT BRUCE WAYNE IS GOING TO KILL YOU FOR THIS.
UNLIKELY.

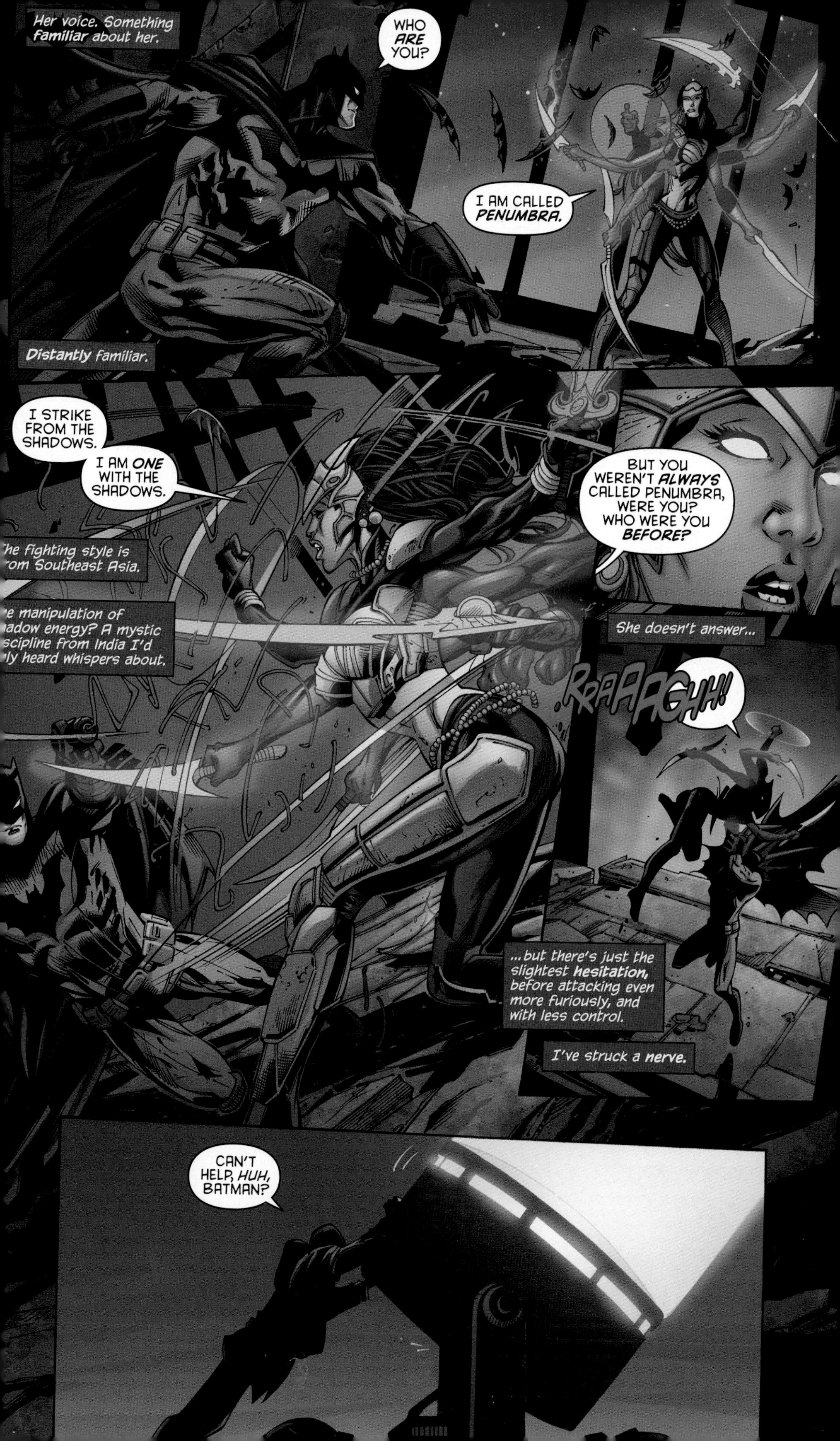
Her voice. Something familiar about her.
WHO ARE YOU?
I AM CALLED PENUMBRA.
Distantly familiar.
I STRIKE FROM THE SHADOWS.
I AM ONE WITH THE SHADOWS.
BUT YOU WEREN'T ALWAYS CALLED PENUMBRA, WERE YOU? WHO WERE YOU BEFORE?
he fighting style is rom Southeast Asia.
e manipulation of adow energy? A mystic scipline from India I'd ly heard whispers about.
She doesn't answer...
RRAAAAGHH!
...but there's just the slightest hesitation, before attacking even more furiously, and with less control.
I've struck a nerve.
CAN'T HELP, HUH, BATMAN?

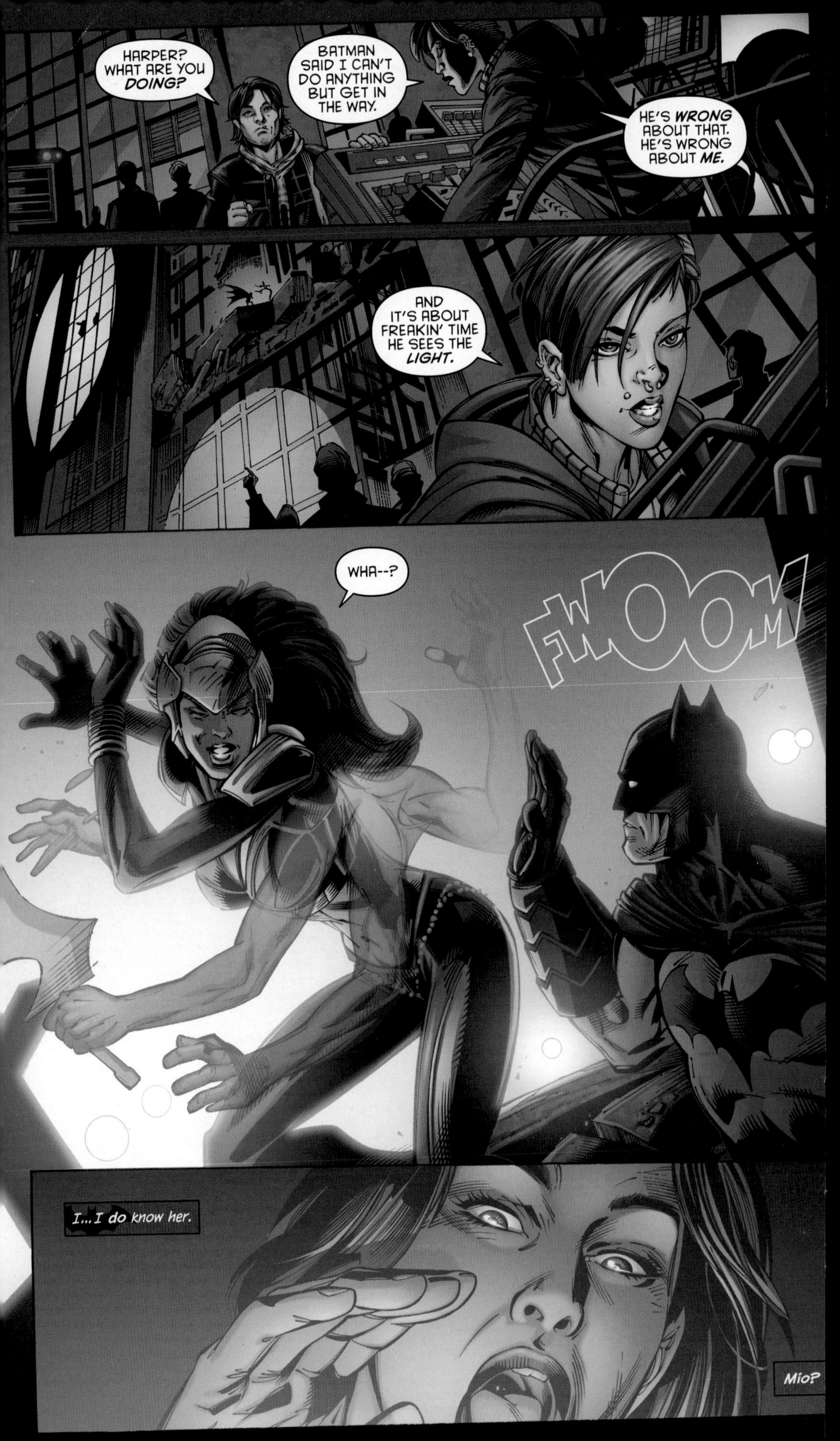
HARPER? WHAT ARE YOU *DOING?*
BATMAN SAID I CAN'T DO ANYTHING BUT GET IN THE WAY.
HE'S *WRONG* ABOUT THAT. HE'S WRONG ABOUT *ME.*
AND IT'S ABOUT FREAKIN' TIME HE SEES THE *LIGHT.*
WHA--?
FWOOM
I...I do know her.
Mio?

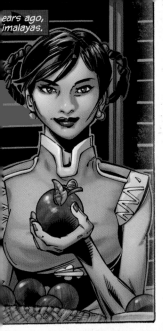

ears ago,
imalayas.

I remember a girl who worked for the local sword vendor, with a bright smile, a quick laugh and a mischievous streak.

Seems like a *lifetime* ago.

Staring up at the clouds, sharing our secrets, sharing our dreams.

MIO... YOU'RE *ALIVE?!*

I wonder how much *she* remembers of that time.

MIO... THAT WAS MY *NAME*, ONCE.

course, her *biggest*
ret she never told me.

I refuse to
eve *everything*
told me was a lie.

THIS *ISN'T* YOU, MIO. NOT IN YOUR HEART. YOU DON'T *HAVE* TO BE A KILLER.

Y-YOU *KNOW* ME?

BUT WHY... W-WHY DO YOU STILL *BELIEVE*... IN ME?

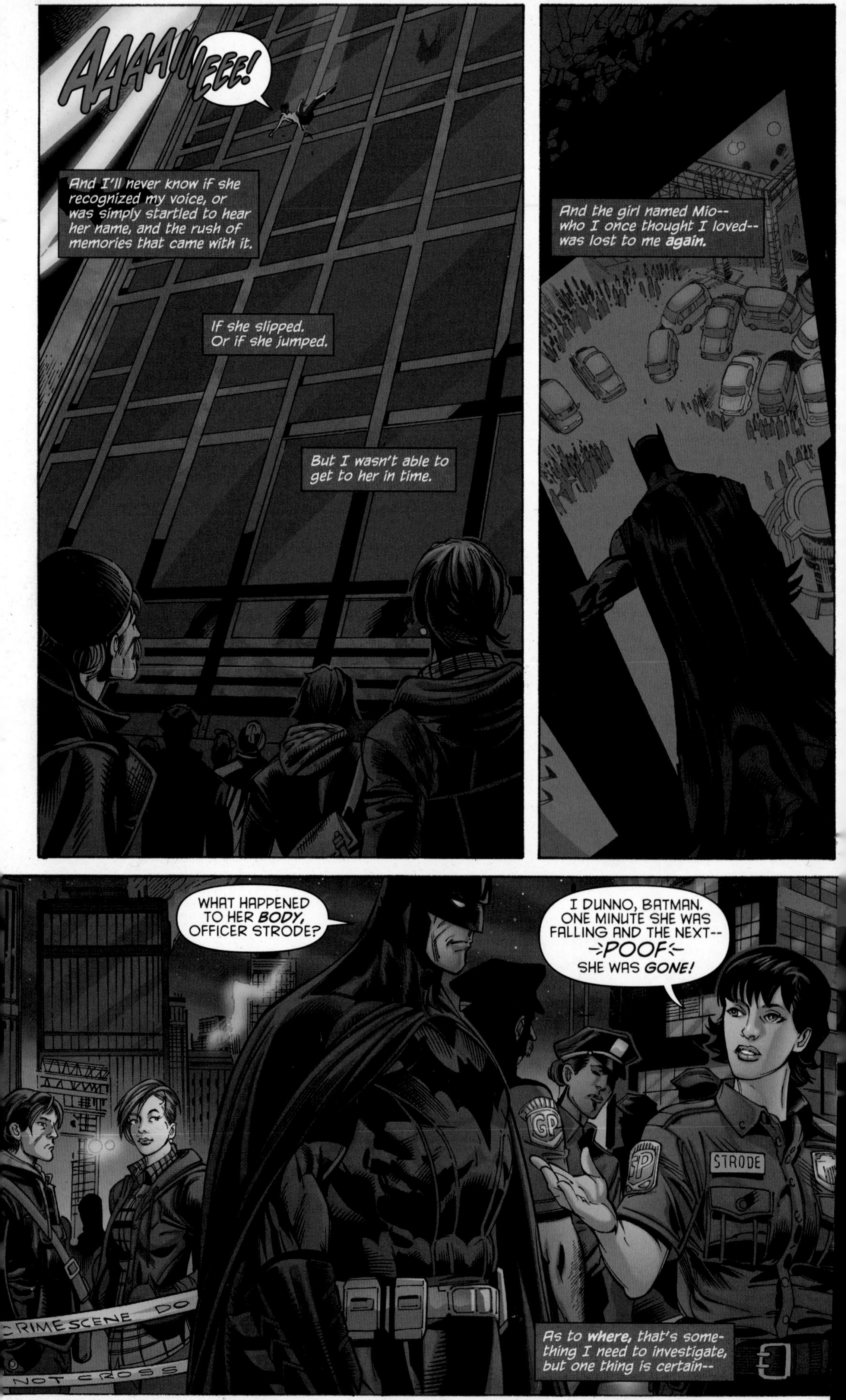
AAAAIIIEEE!
And I'll never know if she recognized my voice, or was simply startled to hear her name, and the rush of memories that came with it.
If she slipped. Or if she jumped.
But I wasn't able to get to her in time.
And the girl named Mio-- who I once thought I loved-- was lost to me again.
WHAT HAPPENED TO HER BODY, OFFICER STRODE?
I DUNNO, BATMAN. ONE MINUTE SHE WAS FALLING AND THE NEXT-- POOF SHE WAS GONE!
STRODE
CRIME SCENE DO
NOT CROSS
As to where, that's something I need to investigate, but one thing is certain--

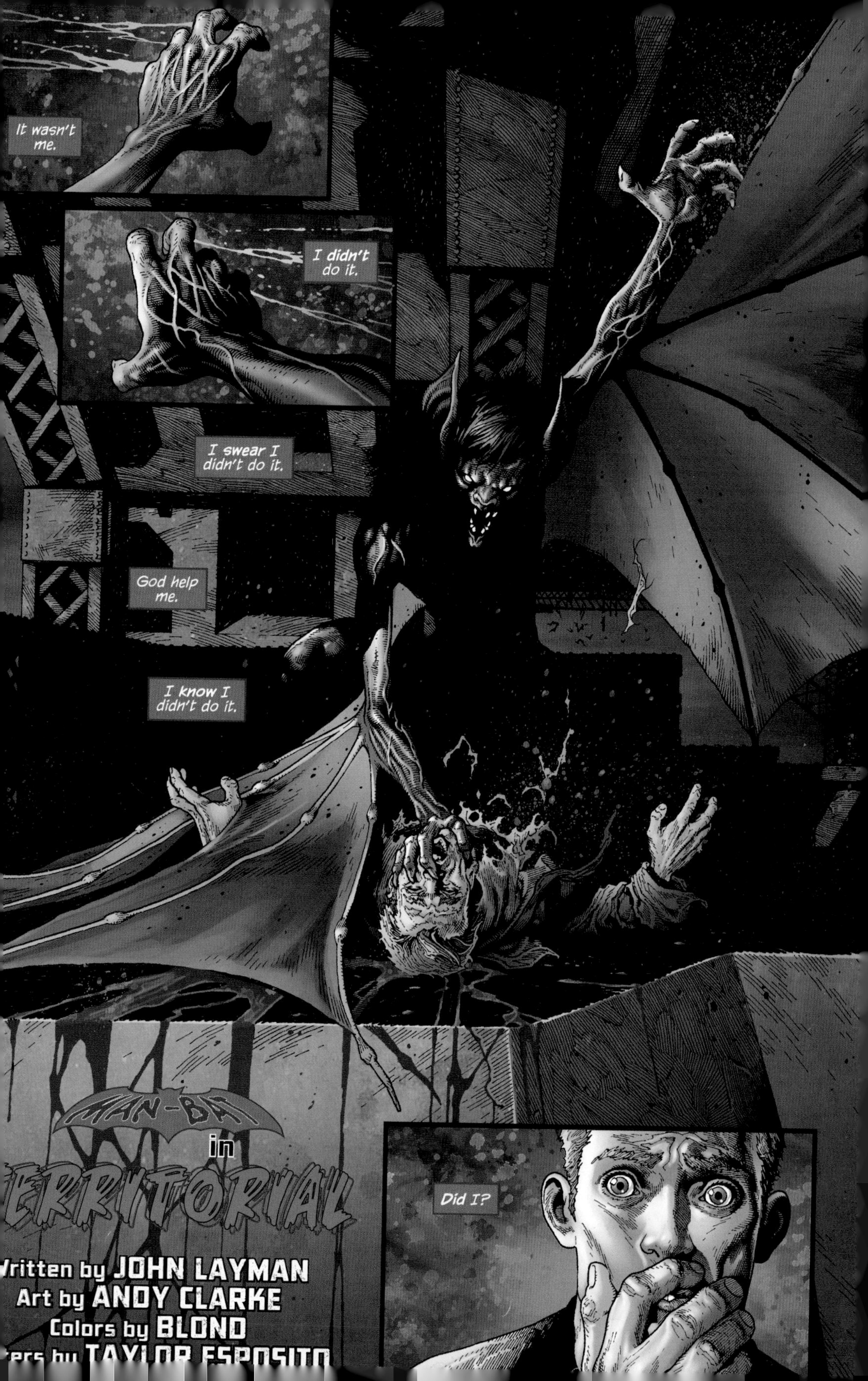
It wasn't me.
I didn't do it.
I swear I didn't do it.
God help me.
I know I didn't do it.
Did I?
MAN-BAT
in
ERRITORIAL
ritten by JOHN LAYMAN
Art by ANDY CLARKE
Colors by BLOND
ers by TAYLOR ESPOSITO

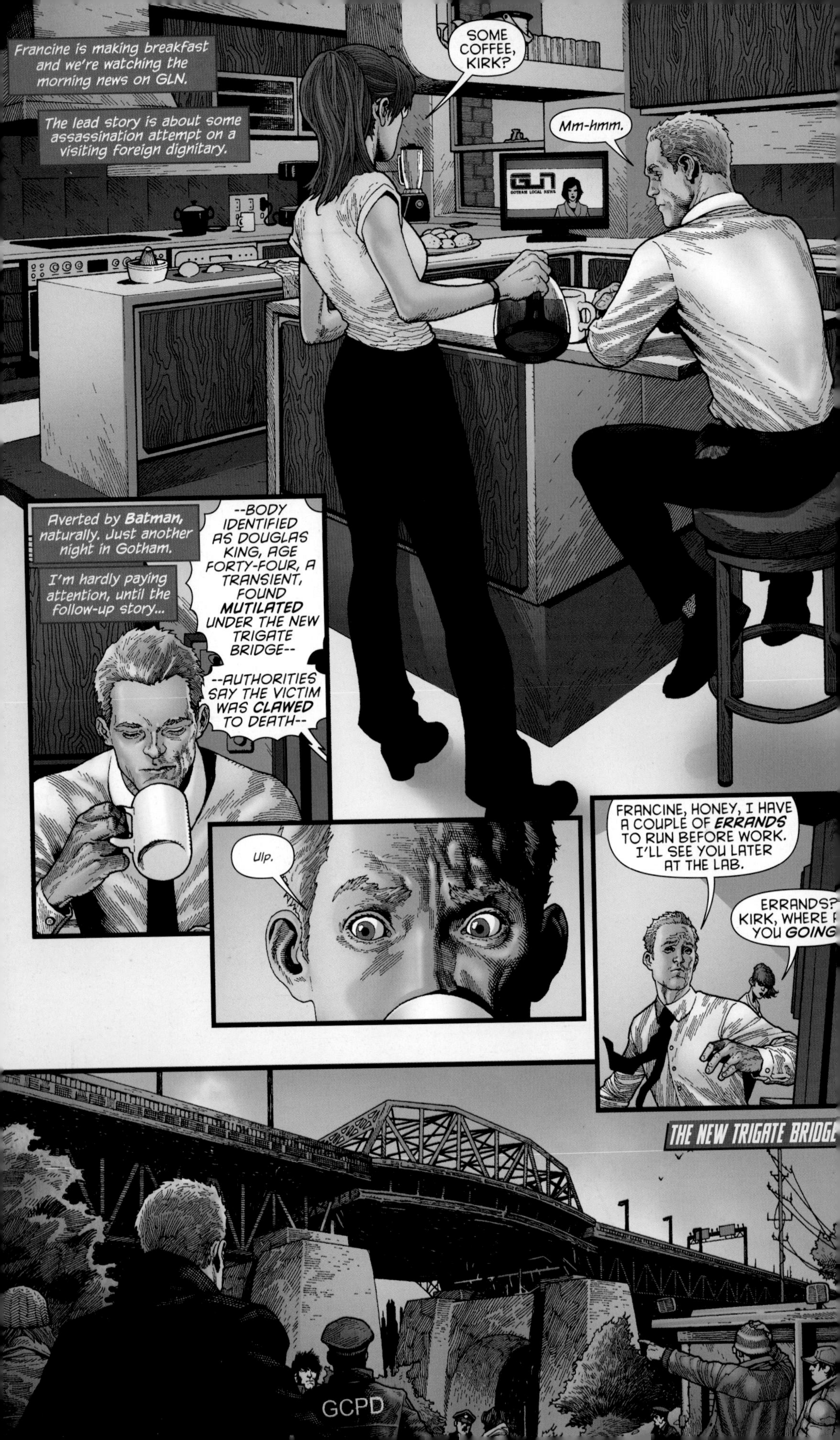
Francine is making breakfast and we're watching the morning news on GLN.
The lead story is about some assassination attempt on a visiting foreign dignitary.
SOME COFFEE, KIRK?
Mm-hmm.
Averted by Batman, naturally. Just another night in Gotham.
I'm hardly paying attention, until the follow-up story...
--BODY IDENTIFIED AS DOUGLAS KING, AGE FORTY-FOUR, A TRANSIENT, FOUND MUTILATED UNDER THE NEW TRIGATE BRIDGE--
--AUTHORITIES SAY THE VICTIM WAS CLAWED TO DEATH--
Ulp.
FRANCINE, HONEY, I HAVE A COUPLE OF ERRANDS TO RUN BEFORE WORK. I'LL SEE YOU LATER AT THE LAB.
ERRANDS? KIRK, WHERE
YOU GOING
THE NEW TRIGATE BRIDGE
GCPD

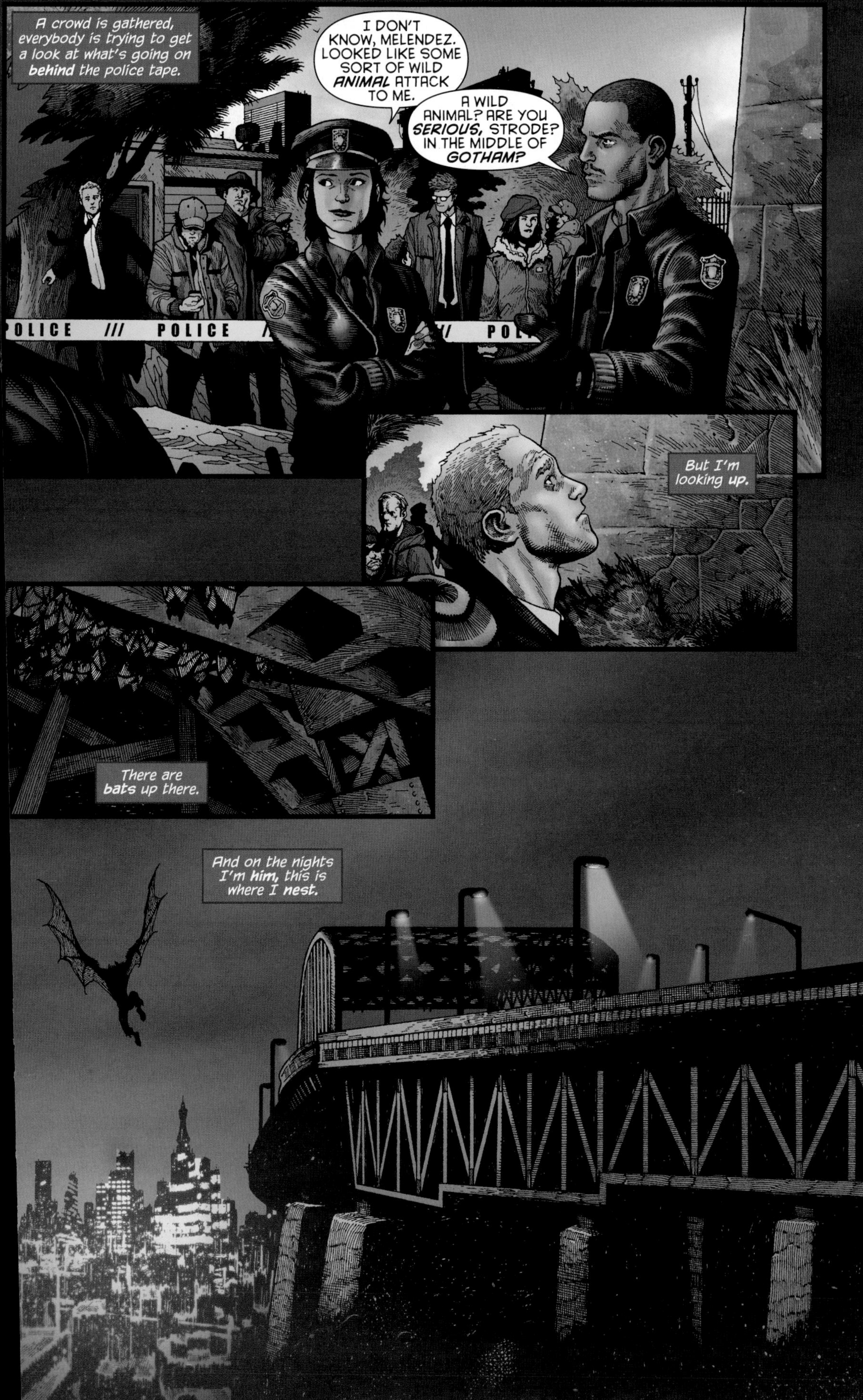
A crowd is gathered, everybody is trying to get a look at what's going on behind the police tape.
I DON'T KNOW, MELENDEZ. LOOKED LIKE SOME SORT OF WILD ANIMAL ATTACK TO ME.
A WILD ANIMAL? ARE YOU SERIOUS, STRODE? IN THE MIDDLE OF GOTHAM?
POLICE /// POLICE
But I'm looking up.
There are bats up there.
And on the nights I'm him, this is where I nest.

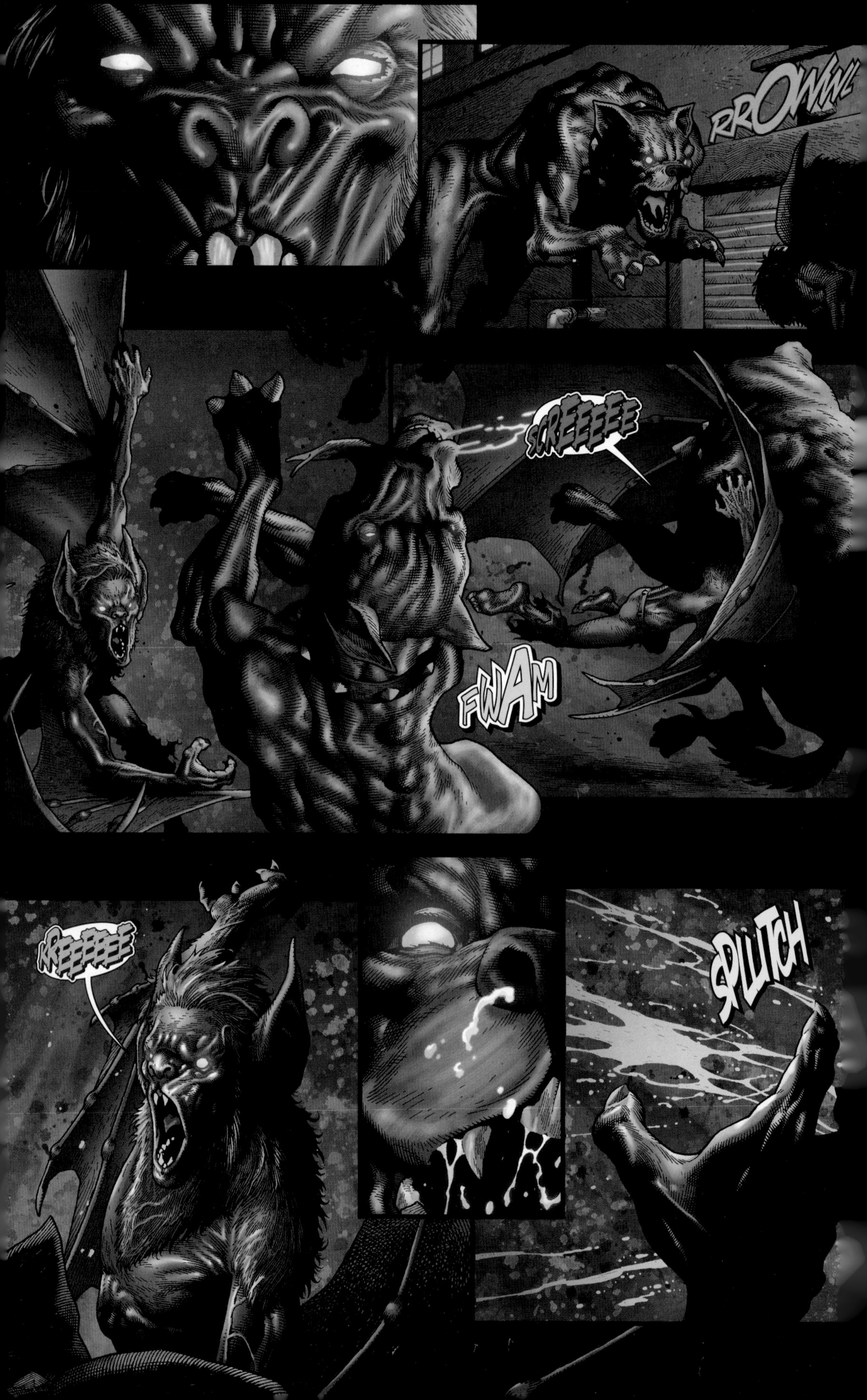

RROWWL
SCREEEEEE
FWAM
KREEEEEE
SPLUTCH

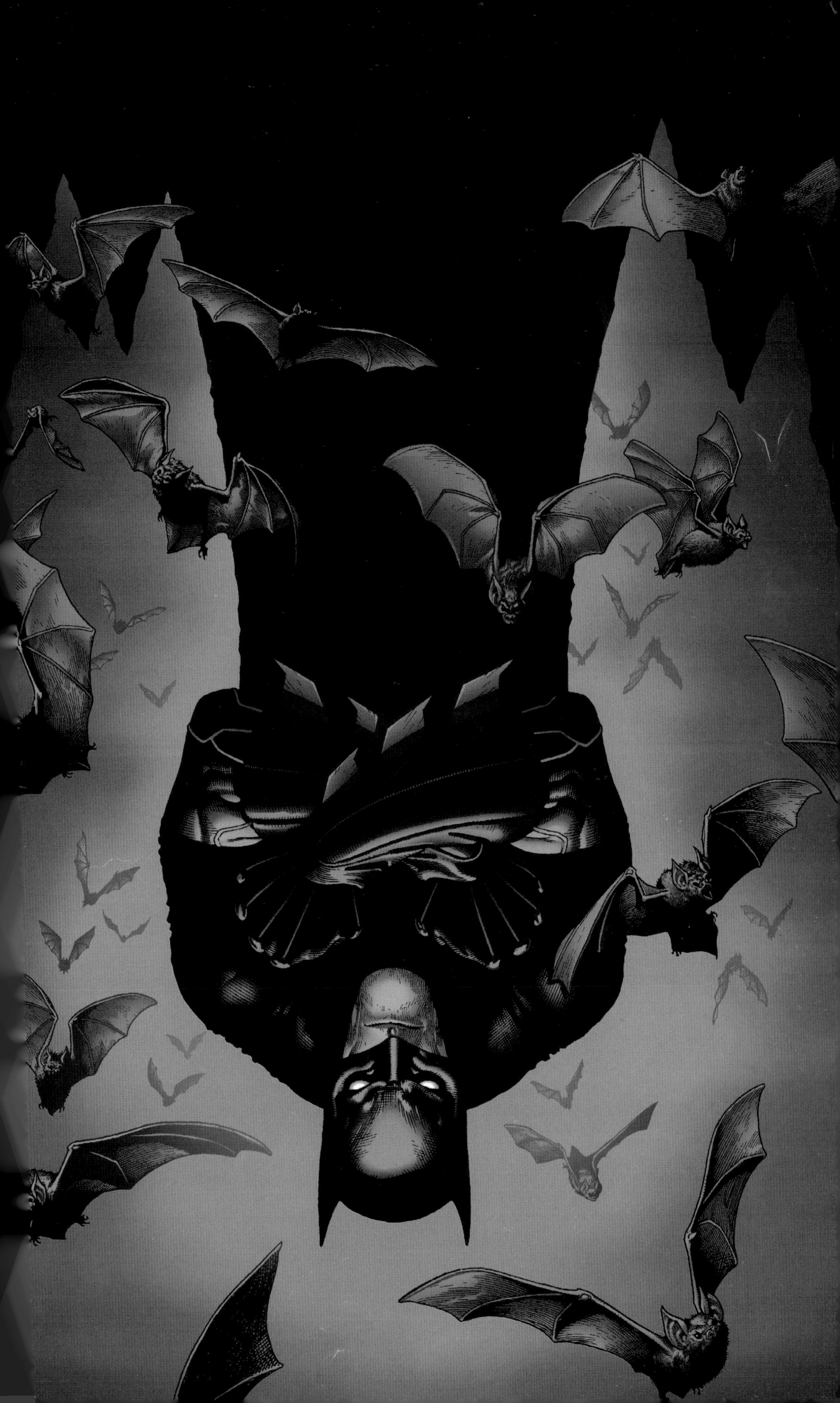

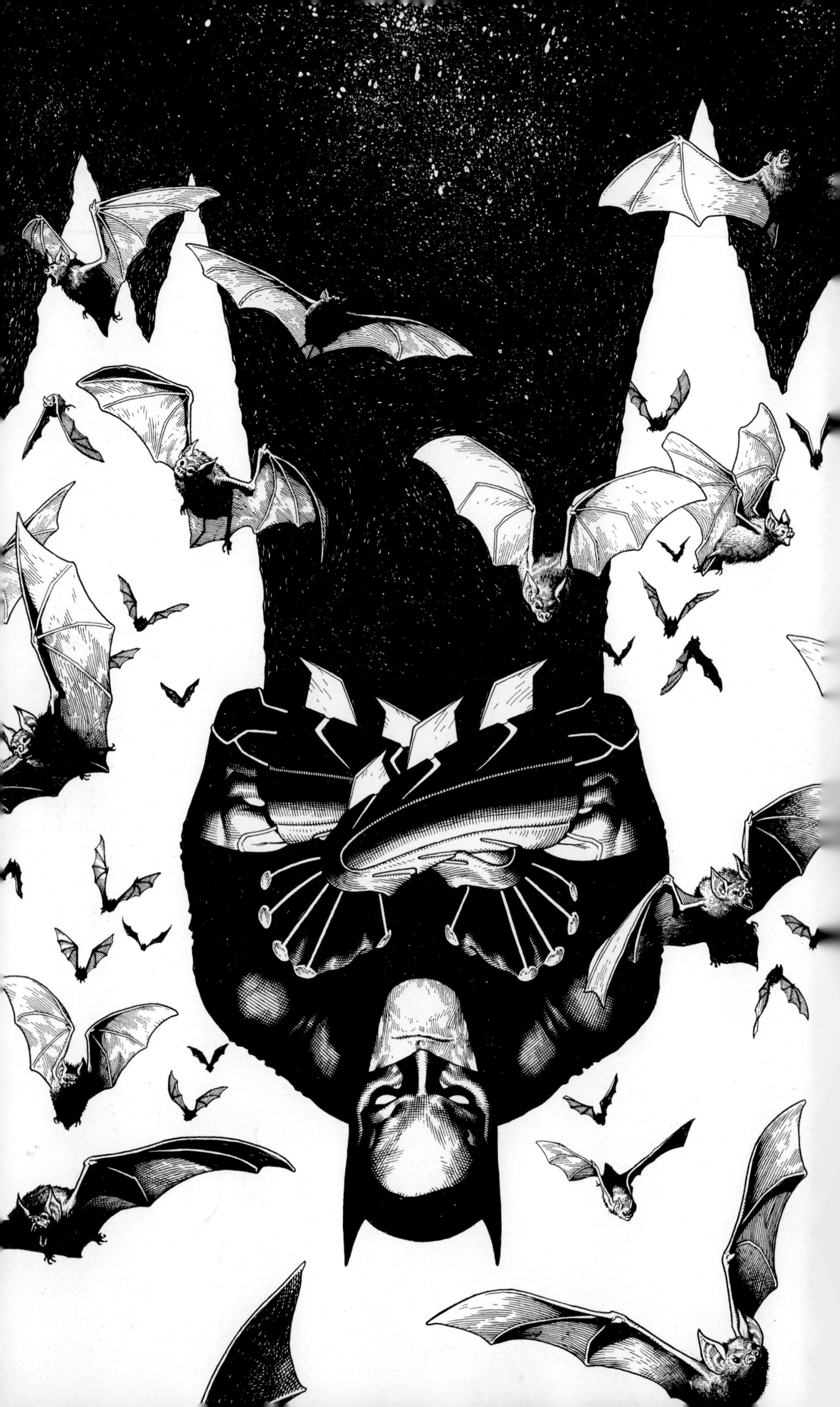

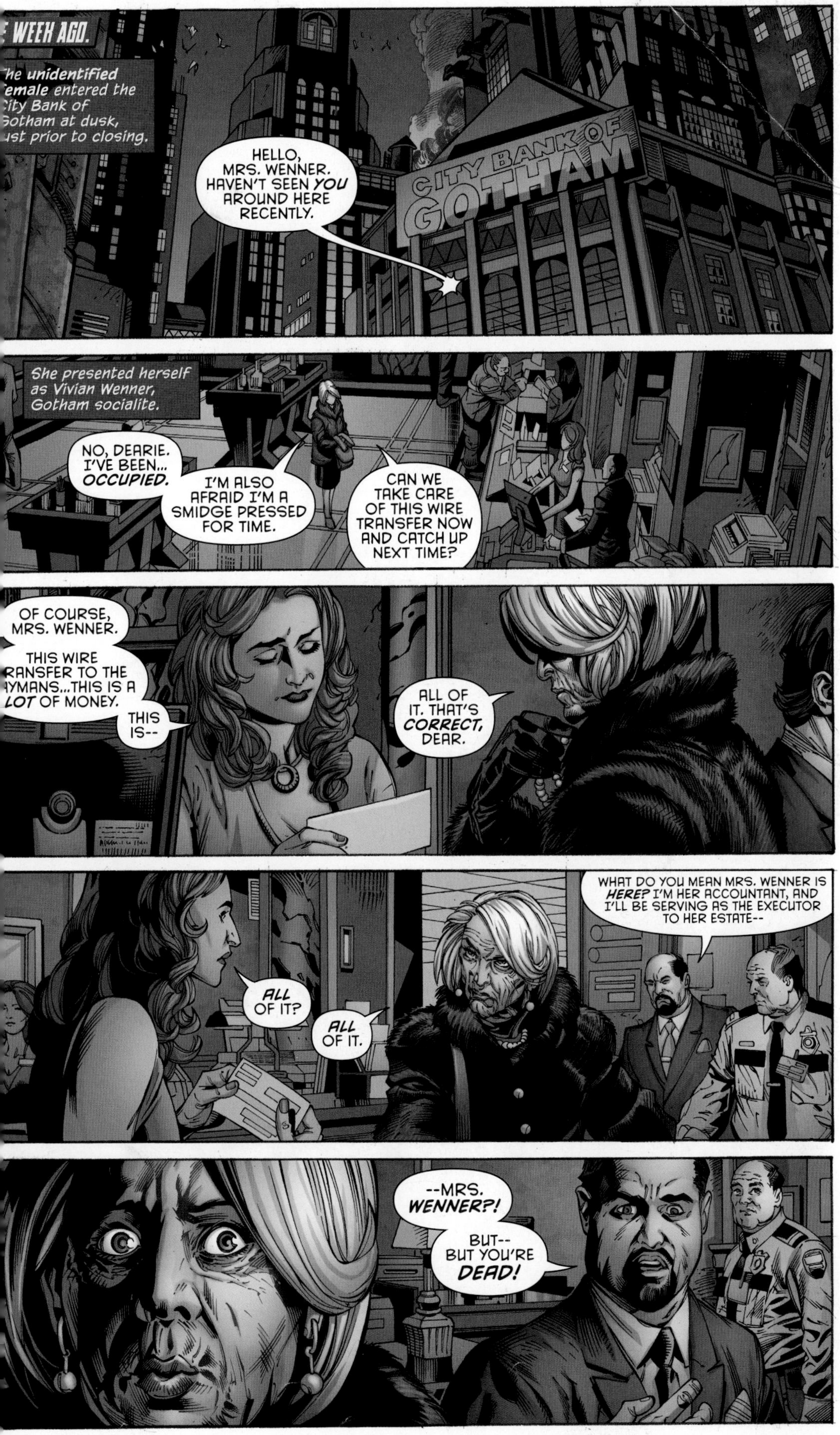
E WEEK AGO.
he unidentified emale entered the ity Bank of otham at dusk, ust prior to closing.
CITY BANK OF GOTHAM
HELLO, MRS. WENNER. HAVEN'T SEEN YOU AROUND HERE RECENTLY.
She presented herself as Vivian Wenner, Gotham socialite.
NO, DEARIE. I'VE BEEN... OCCUPIED.
I'M ALSO AFRAID I'M A SMIDGE PRESSED FOR TIME.
CAN WE TAKE CARE OF THIS WIRE TRANSFER NOW AND CATCH UP NEXT TIME?
OF COURSE, MRS. WENNER.
THIS WIRE RANSFER TO THE YMANS...THIS IS A LOT OF MONEY.
THIS IS--
ALL OF IT. THAT'S CORRECT, DEAR.
ALL OF IT?
ALL OF IT.
WHAT DO YOU MEAN MRS. WENNER IS HERE? I'M HER ACCOUNTANT, AND I'LL BE SERVING AS THE EXECUTOR TO HER ESTATE--
--MRS. WENNER?!
BUT-- BUT YOU'RE DEAD!

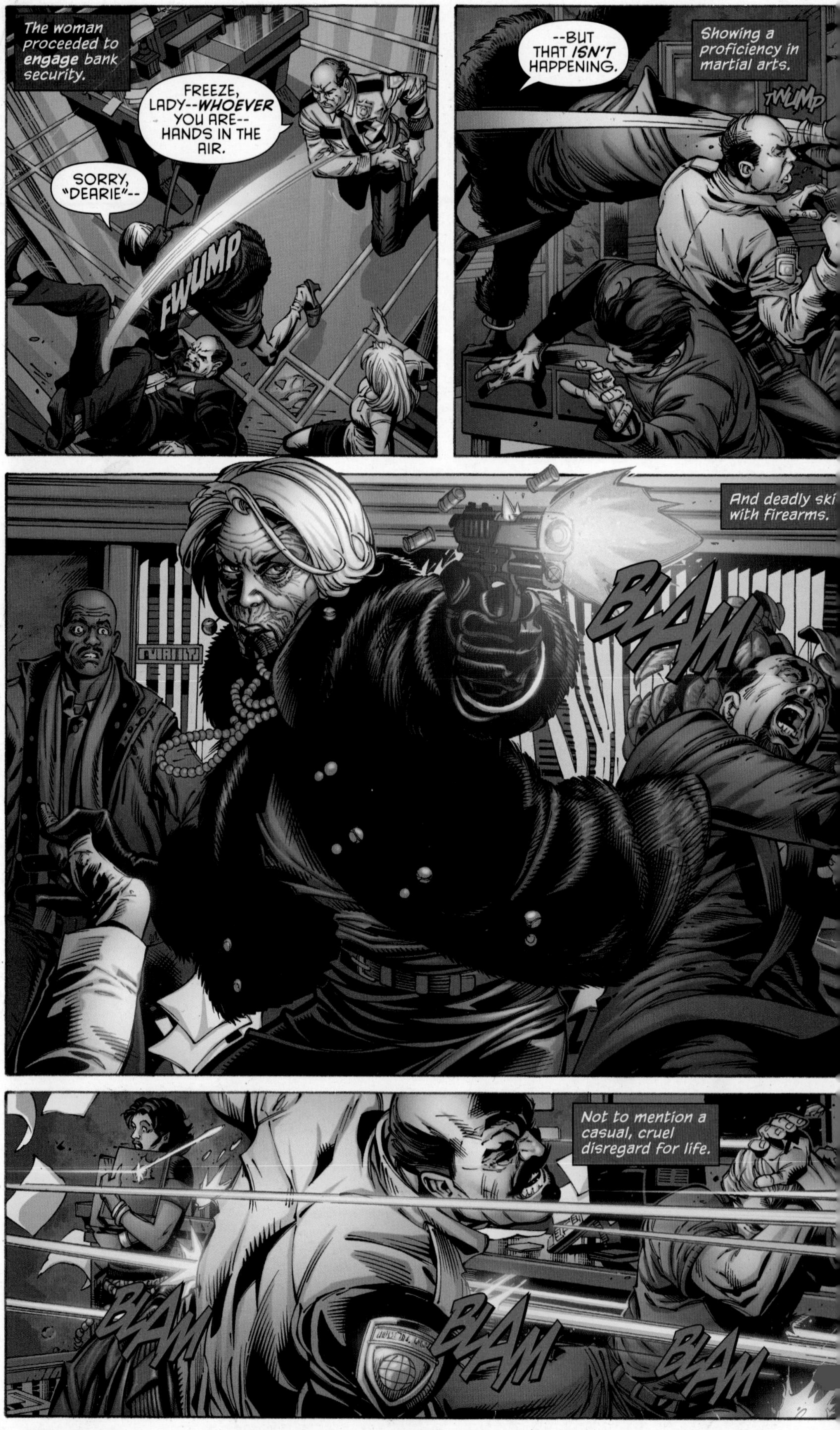
The woman proceeded to engage bank security.
FREEZE, LADY--WHOEVER YOU ARE--HANDS IN THE AIR.
SORRY, "DEARIE"--
FWUMP
--BUT THAT ISN'T HAPPENING.
Showing a proficiency in martial arts.
TWUMP
And deadly ski with firearms.
BLAM
Not to mention a casual, cruel disregard for life.
BLAM
BLAM
BLAM

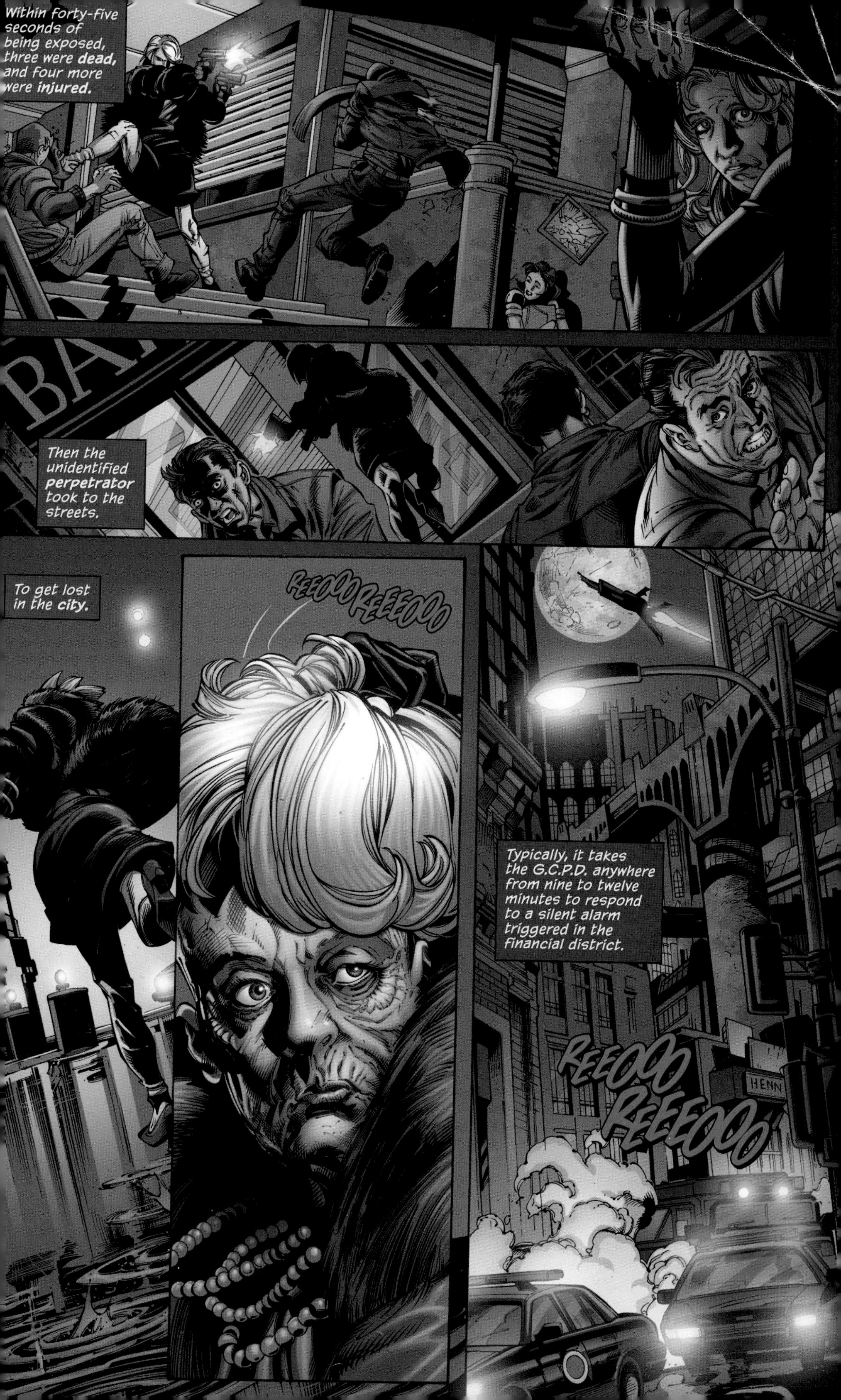
Within forty-five seconds of being exposed, three were dead, and four more were injured.
Then the unidentified perpetrator took to the streets.
To get lost in the city.
REEOOO REEEOOO
Typically, it takes the G.C.P.D. anywhere from nine to twelve minutes to respond to a silent alarm triggered in the financial district.
HENN
REEOOO REEEOOO

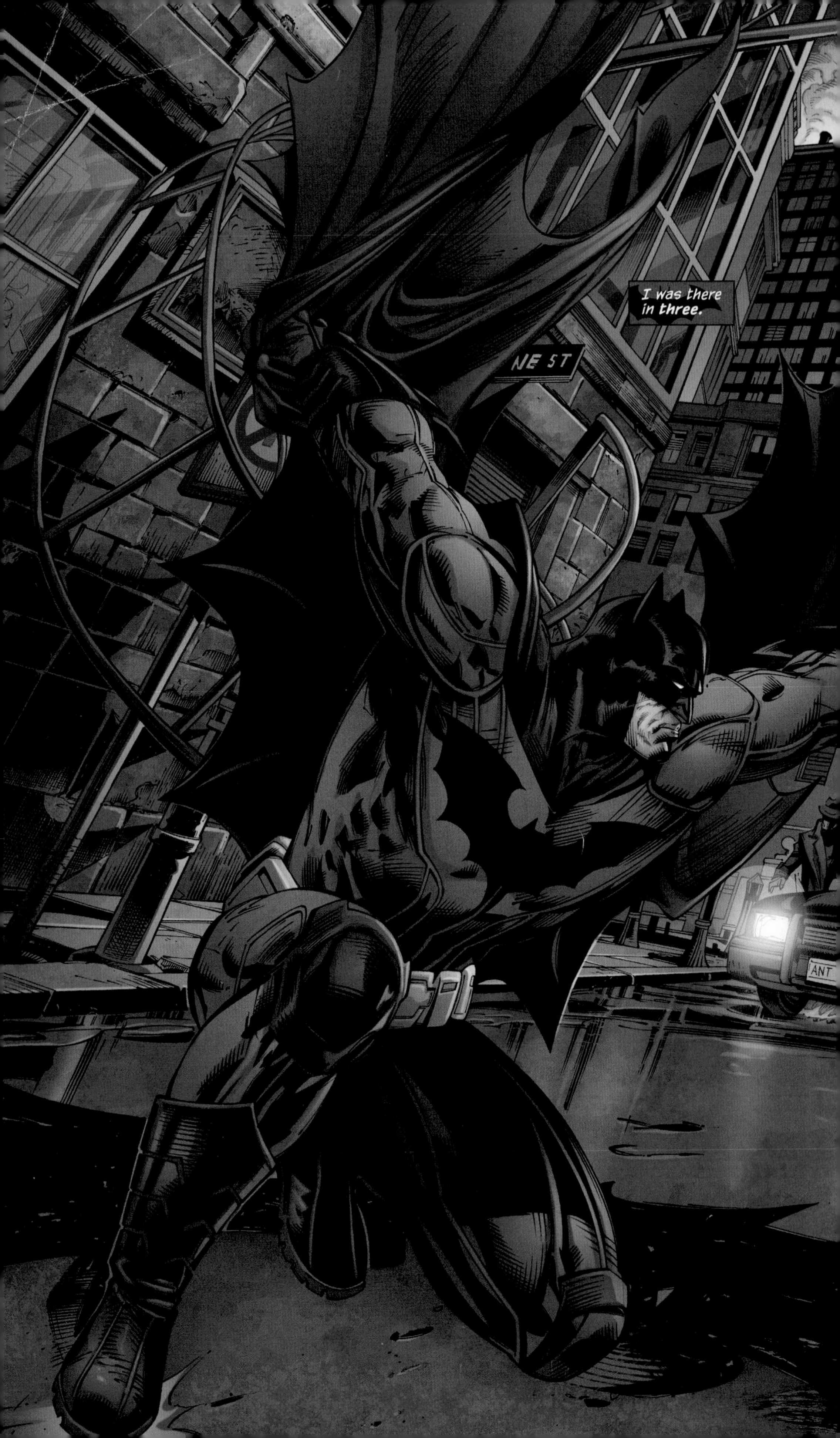
I was there in three.
NE ST
ANT

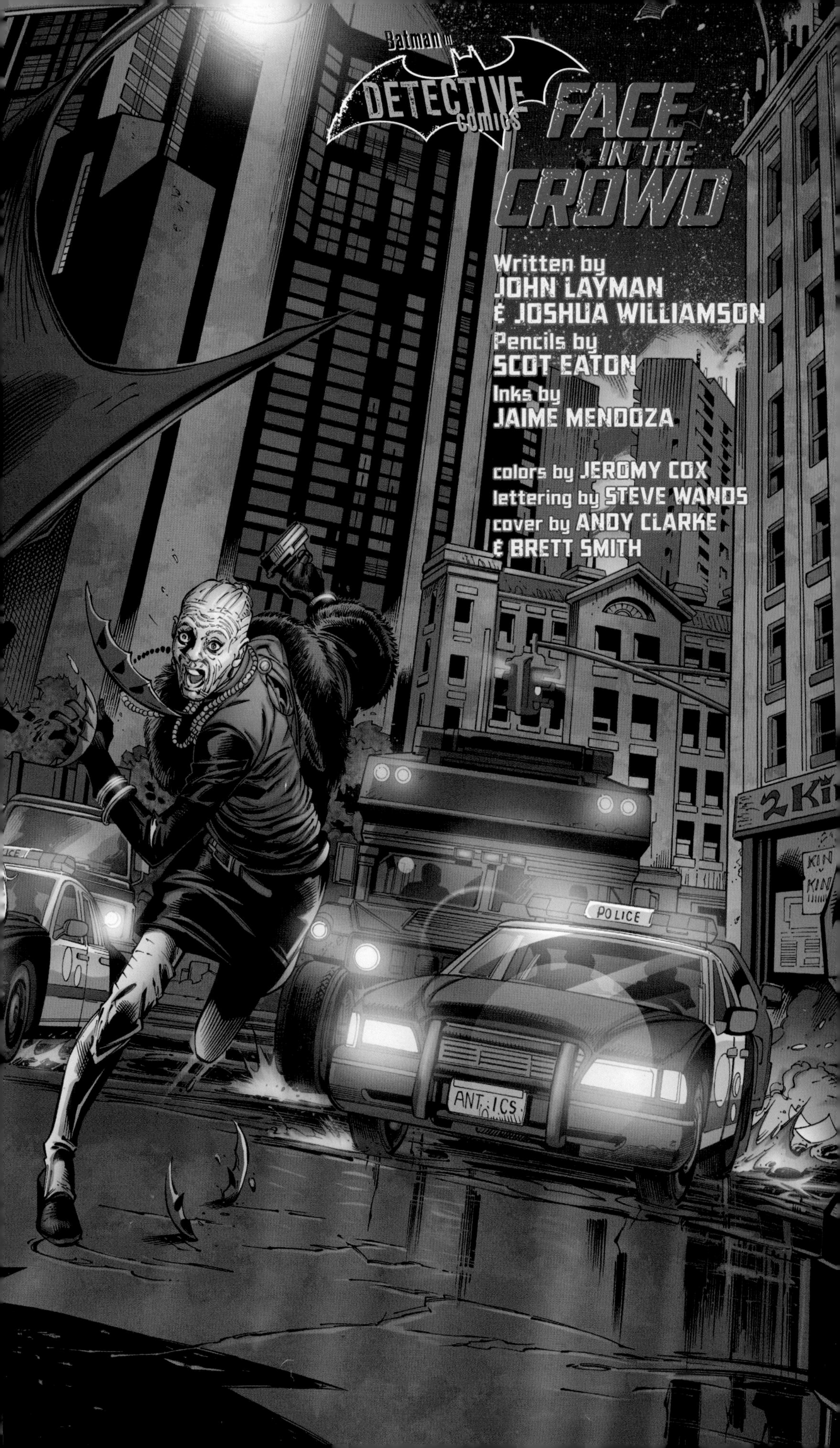
Batman in
DETECTIVE comics
FACE IN THE CROWD
Written by
JOHN LAYMAN
& JOSHUA WILLIAMSON
Pencils by
SCOT EATON
Inks by
JAIME MENDOZA
colors by JEROMY COX
lettering by STEVE WANDS
cover by ANDY CLARKE
& BRETT SMITH
POLICE
ANT.ICS

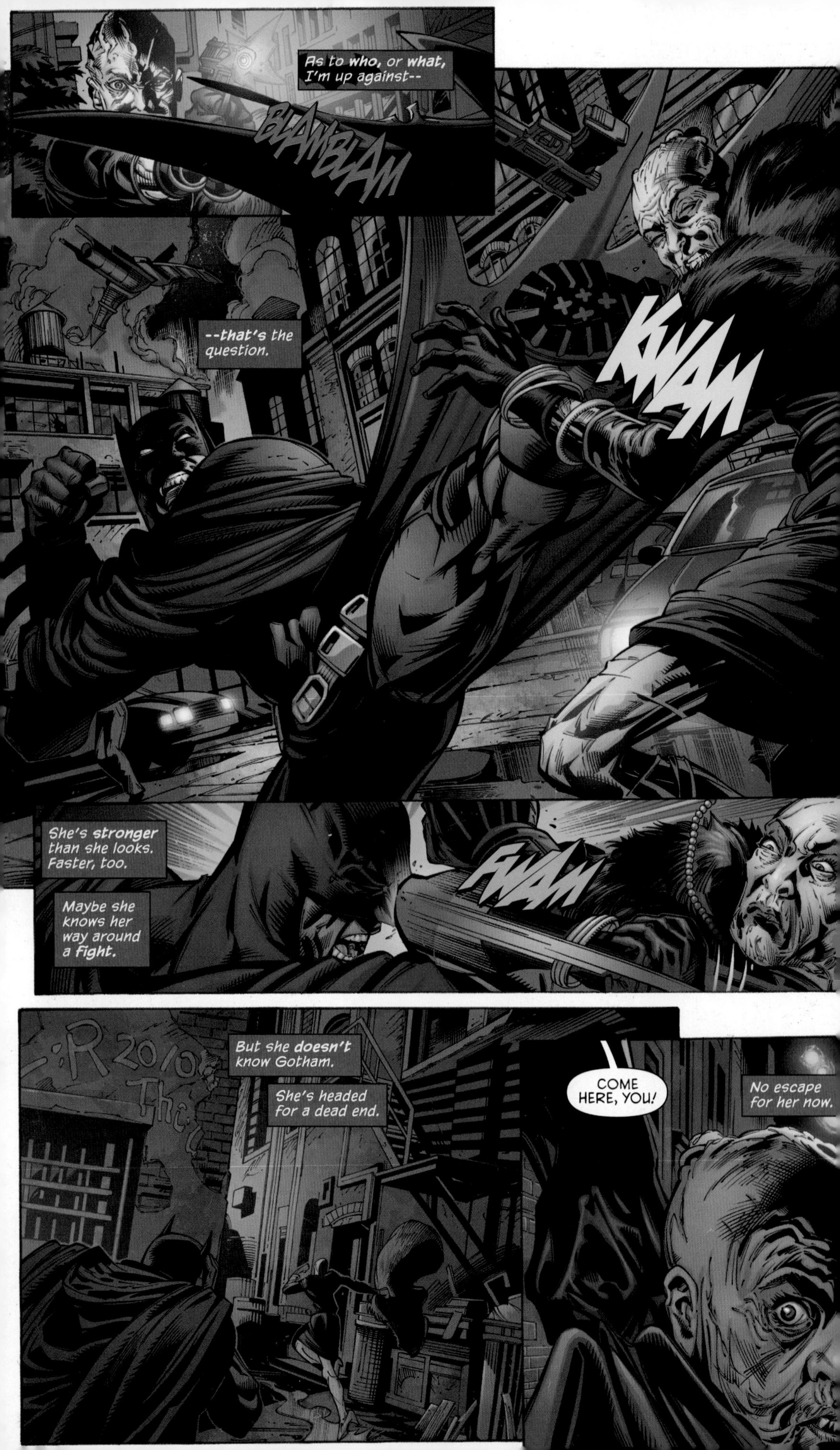
As to who, or what, I'm up against--
BLAMBLAM
--that's the question.
KWAM
She's stronger than she looks. Faster, too.
Maybe she knows her way around a fight.
FWAM
But she doesn't know Gotham.
She's headed for a dead end.
COME HERE, YOU!
No escape for her now.

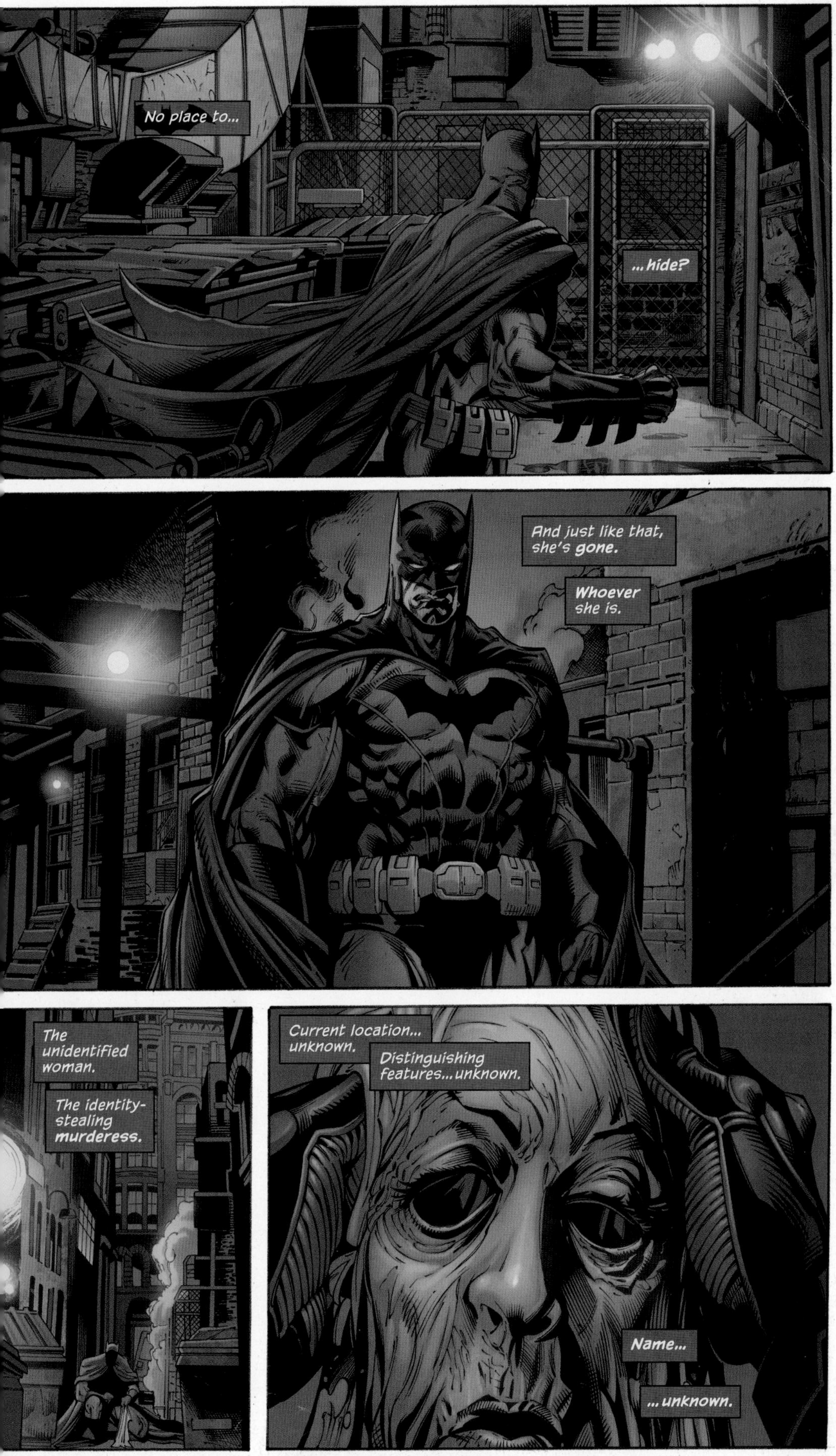
No place to...
...hide?
And just like that, she's **gone.**
Whoever she is.
The unidentified woman.
The identity-stealing **murderess.**
Current location... unknown.
Distinguishing features... unknown.
Name...
...unknown.

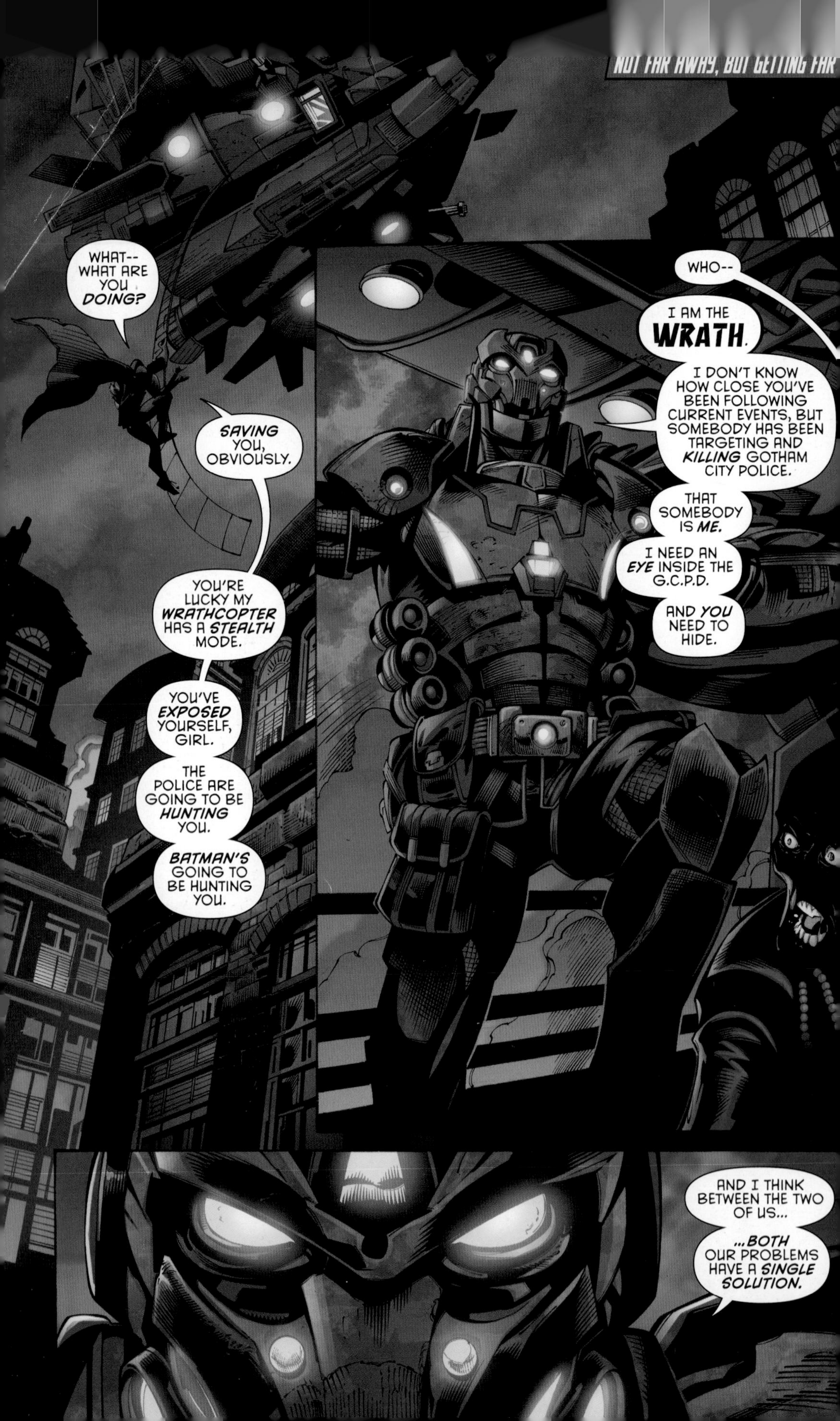
NOT FAR AWAY, BUT GETTING FAR
WHAT-- WHAT ARE YOU DOING?
SAVING YOU, OBVIOUSLY.
YOU'RE LUCKY MY WRATHCOPTER HAS A STEALTH MODE.
YOU'VE EXPOSED YOURSELF, GIRL.
THE POLICE ARE GOING TO BE HUNTING YOU.
BATMAN'S GOING TO BE HUNTING YOU.
WHO--
I AM THE WRATH.
I DON'T KNOW HOW CLOSE YOU'VE BEEN FOLLOWING CURRENT EVENTS, BUT SOMEBODY HAS BEEN TARGETING AND KILLING GOTHAM CITY POLICE.
THAT SOMEBODY IS ME.
I NEED AN EYE INSIDE THE G.C.P.D.
AND YOU NEED TO HIDE.
AND I THINK BETWEEN THE TWO OF US...
...BOTH OUR PROBLEMS HAVE A SINGLE SOLUTION.

OFFICERS DISCOVERED *THIS* WHILE CANVASSING THE PROSINSKI/McMAHON SCENE.

I'VE GOT *LIEUTENANT BULLOCK* TAKING POINT ON *THIS* INVESTIGATION.

LIEUTENANT.

BATMAN.

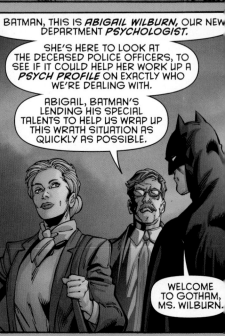

BATMAN, THIS IS *ABIGAIL WILBURN,* OUR NEW DEPARTMENT *PSYCHOLOGIST.*

SHE'S HERE TO LOOK AT THE DECEASED POLICE OFFICERS, TO SEE IF IT COULD HELP HER WORK UP A *PSYCH PROFILE* ON EXACTLY WHO WE'RE DEALING WITH.

ABIGAIL, BATMAN'S LENDING HIS SPECIAL TALENTS TO HELP US WRAP UP THIS WRATH SITUATION AS QUICKLY AS POSSIBLE.

WELCOME TO GOTHAM, MS. WILBURN.

AN' *I* BEEN SHOWIN' ABBY HERE AROUND, HELPIN' HER LEARN THE ROPES BACK AT THE STATION.

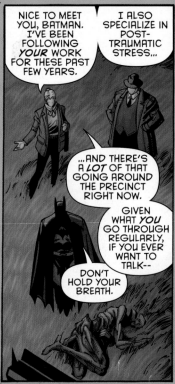

NICE TO MEET YOU, BATMAN. I'VE BEEN FOLLOWING *YOUR* WORK FOR THESE PAST FEW YEARS.

I ALSO SPECIALIZE IN POST-TRAUMATIC STRESS...

...AND THERE'S A *LOT* OF THAT GOING AROUND THE PRECINCT RIGHT NOW.

GIVEN WHAT *YOU* GO THROUGH REGULARLY, IF YOU EVER WANT TO TALK--

DON'T HOLD YOUR BREATH.

LET'S GET TO *BUSINESS,* COMMISSIONER.

WHAT DO WE KNOW ABOUT THE *JANE DOE?*

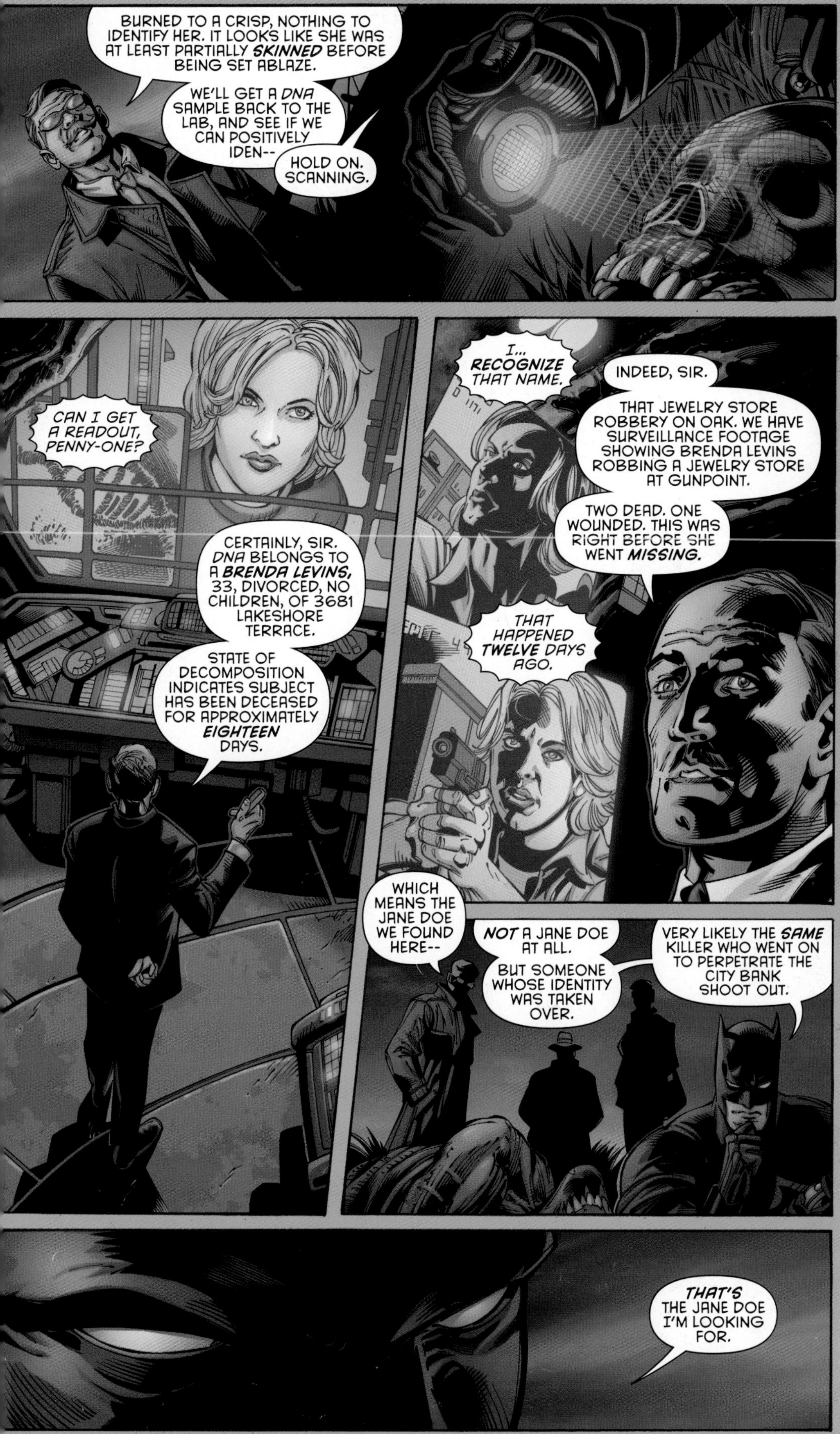
BURNED TO A CRISP, NOTHING TO IDENTIFY HER. IT LOOKS LIKE SHE WAS AT LEAST PARTIALLY *SKINNED* BEFORE BEING SET ABLAZE.
WE'LL GET A *DNA* SAMPLE BACK TO THE LAB, AND SEE IF WE CAN POSITIVELY IDEN--
HOLD ON. SCANNING.
CAN I GET A READOUT, PENNY-ONE?
CERTAINLY, SIR. *DNA* BELONGS TO A ***BRENDA LEVINS,*** 33, DIVORCED, NO CHILDREN, OF 3681 LAKESHORE TERRACE.
STATE OF DECOMPOSITION INDICATES SUBJECT HAS BEEN DECEASED FOR APPROXIMATELY ***EIGHTEEN*** DAYS.
I... ***RECOGNIZE*** THAT NAME.
INDEED, SIR.
THAT JEWELRY STORE ROBBERY ON OAK. WE HAVE SURVEILLANCE FOOTAGE SHOWING BRENDA LEVINS ROBBING A JEWELRY STORE AT GUNPOINT.
TWO DEAD. ONE WOUNDED. THIS WAS RIGHT BEFORE SHE WENT ***MISSING.***
THAT HAPPENED ***TWELVE*** DAYS AGO.
WHICH MEANS THE JANE DOE WE FOUND HERE--
NOT A JANE DOE AT ALL.
BUT SOMEONE WHOSE IDENTITY WAS TAKEN OVER.
VERY LIKELY THE ***SAME*** KILLER WHO WENT ON TO PERPETRATE THE CITY BANK SHOOT OUT.
THAT'S THE JANE DOE I'M LOOKING FOR.

...what I find is *far worse.*

SOON...

WE GOT IT COVERED FROM HERE, BATS.

SEE TO IT OFFICER BROOKINGS GETS THE *HELP* HE NEEDS.

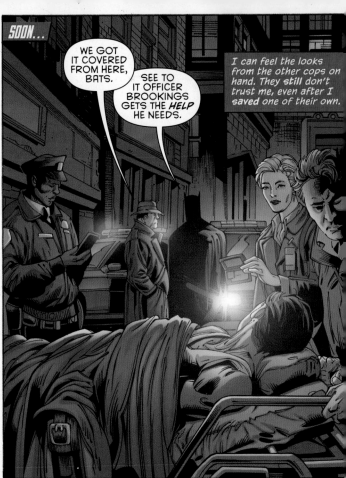

I can feel the looks from the other cops on hand. They still don't trust me, even after I saved one of their own.

CITY OF GOTHAM POLICE

18   BROOKINGS

TRUST IS IN SHORT SUPPLY AMONG THE G.C.P.D.--IT'S BEEN REPLACED BY FEAR.

YOU *KNOW* HIM?

NOT WELL.

LOST HIS PARTNER TO *WRATH* A FEW D AGO. HIS PART *BEFORE* THAT L THE LAST TIME *J* WENT ALL NUTS THE CITY.

Harvey Bullock look different *from the time I've seen him.*

Paying a little more attention to his hygie *than I'm used to.*

YOU MIGHT WANT TO TALK TO ABBY.

DR. WILBURN, I MEAN.

*He's actually wearing...*cologne?

And I think I know *why.*

SHE SPENT SOME TIME *COUNSELING* BROOKINGS.

I'VE BEEN TALKING TO AS MANY G.C.P.D. OFFICERS AFFECTED BY THESE TRAGEDIES AS I CAN, BATMAN.

EN I LAST TALKED
BROOKINGS, HE
IBITED NO SIGNS
THE PARANOIA AND
USIONAL THINKING
THAT EMERGED
WITH HIS
BREAKDOWN.

I don't mention to her I already *knew* Wilburn counseled Brookings.

Or that I knew she also talked to Nancy Strode, *another* officer who came perilously close to crossing the line recently, almost shooting one of Wrath's accomplices in cold blood.

AND AS FAR AS OUR *JANE DOE* KILLER IS CONCERNED, I'VE WORKED UP A PSYCHIATRIC PROFILE.

IT'S ON THIS FLASH-DRIVE.

GCPD

NKS, BUT
I PREFER
DO MY
OWN--

IT'S NOT ABOUT THE *MONEY*, BATMAN.

IT'S ABOUT THE *LIVES* SHE'S STEALING.

SHE'LL STAY *CLOSE* TO THOSE LIVES. SHE CAN'T LIVE WITHOUT THEM.

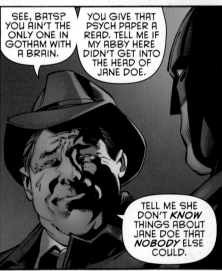

SEE, BATS? YOU AIN'T THE ONLY ONE IN GOTHAM WITH A BRAIN.

YOU GIVE THAT PSYCH PAPER A READ. TELL ME IF MY ABBY HERE DIDN'T GET INTO THE HEAD OF JANE DOE.

TELL ME SHE DON'T *KNOW* THINGS ABOUT JANE DOE THAT *NOBODY* ELSE COULD.

And maybe the psychiatric profile will prove *equally* useful getting into the head of the person who *wrote* it.

OKAY, LIEUTENANT. I'LL *DO* THAT.

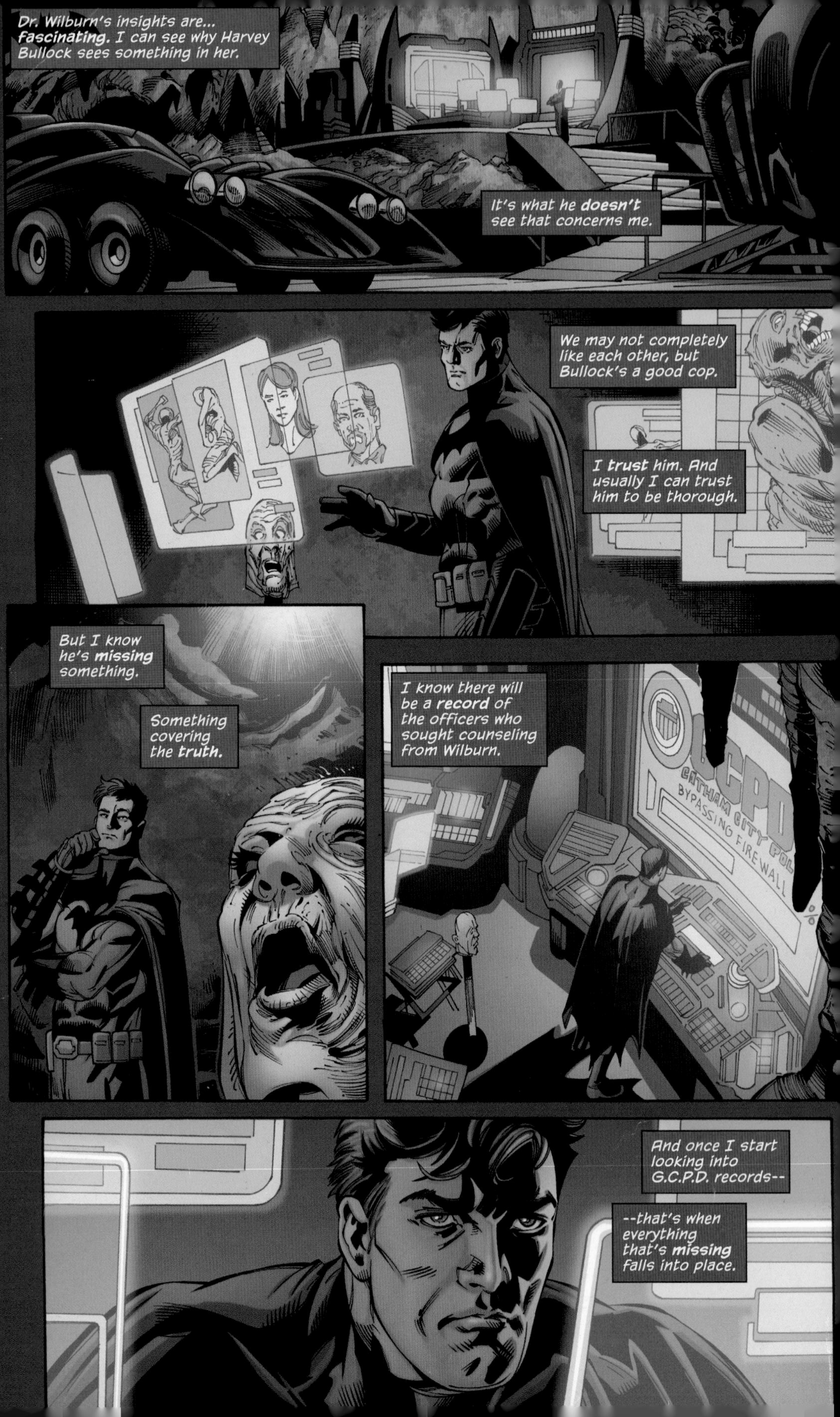
Dr. Wilburn's insights are... **fascinating.** I can see why Harvey Bullock sees something in her.
It's what he **doesn't** see that concerns me.
We may not completely like each other, but Bullock's a good cop.
I **trust** him. And usually I can trust him to be thorough.
But I know he's **missing** something.
Something covering the **truth.**
I know there will be a **record** of the officers who sought counseling from Wilburn.
GCPD
GOTHAM CITY PO
BYPASSING FIREWALL
And once I start looking into G.C.P.D. records--
--that's when everything that's **missing** falls into place.

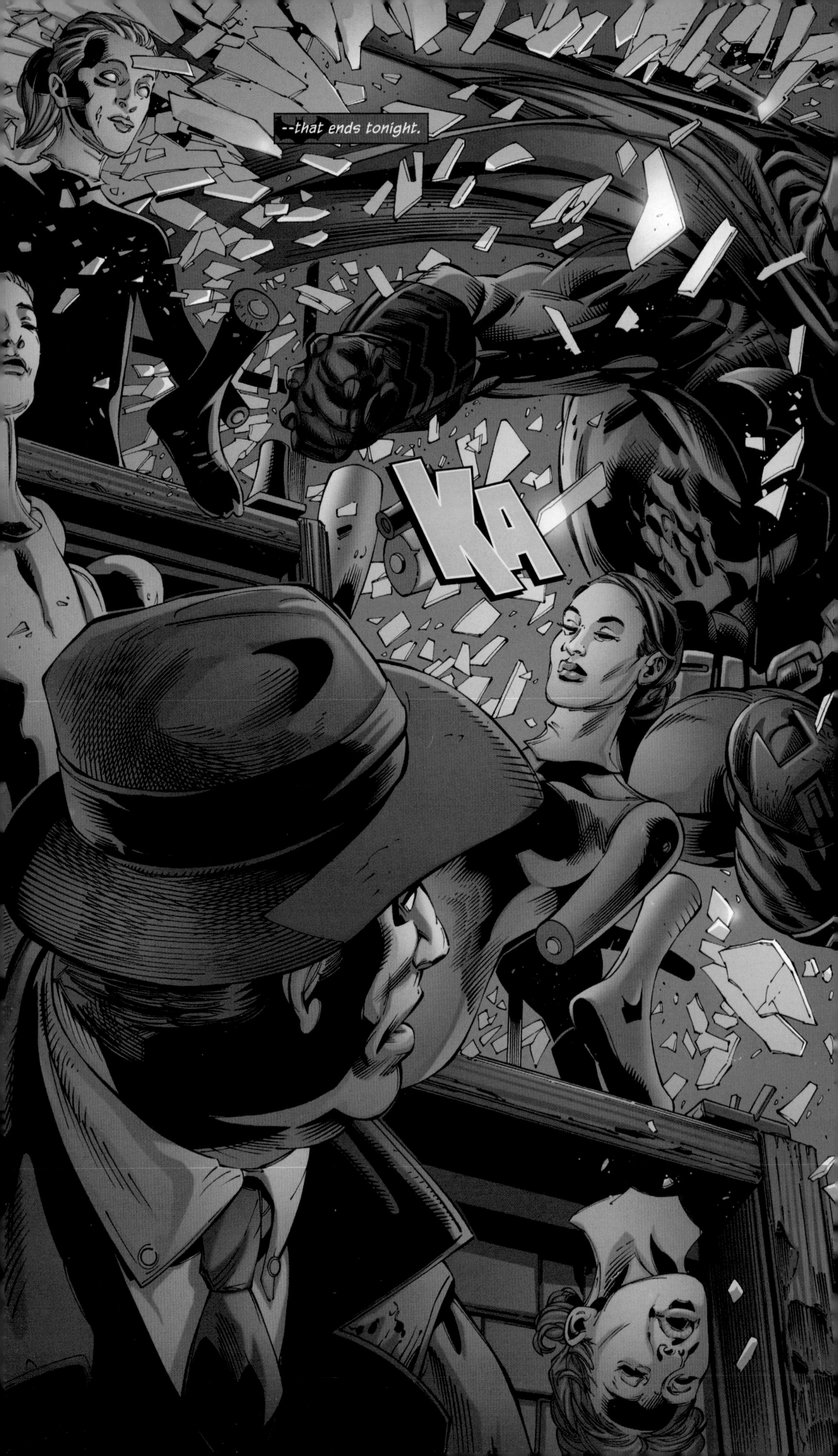
--that ends tonight.
KA

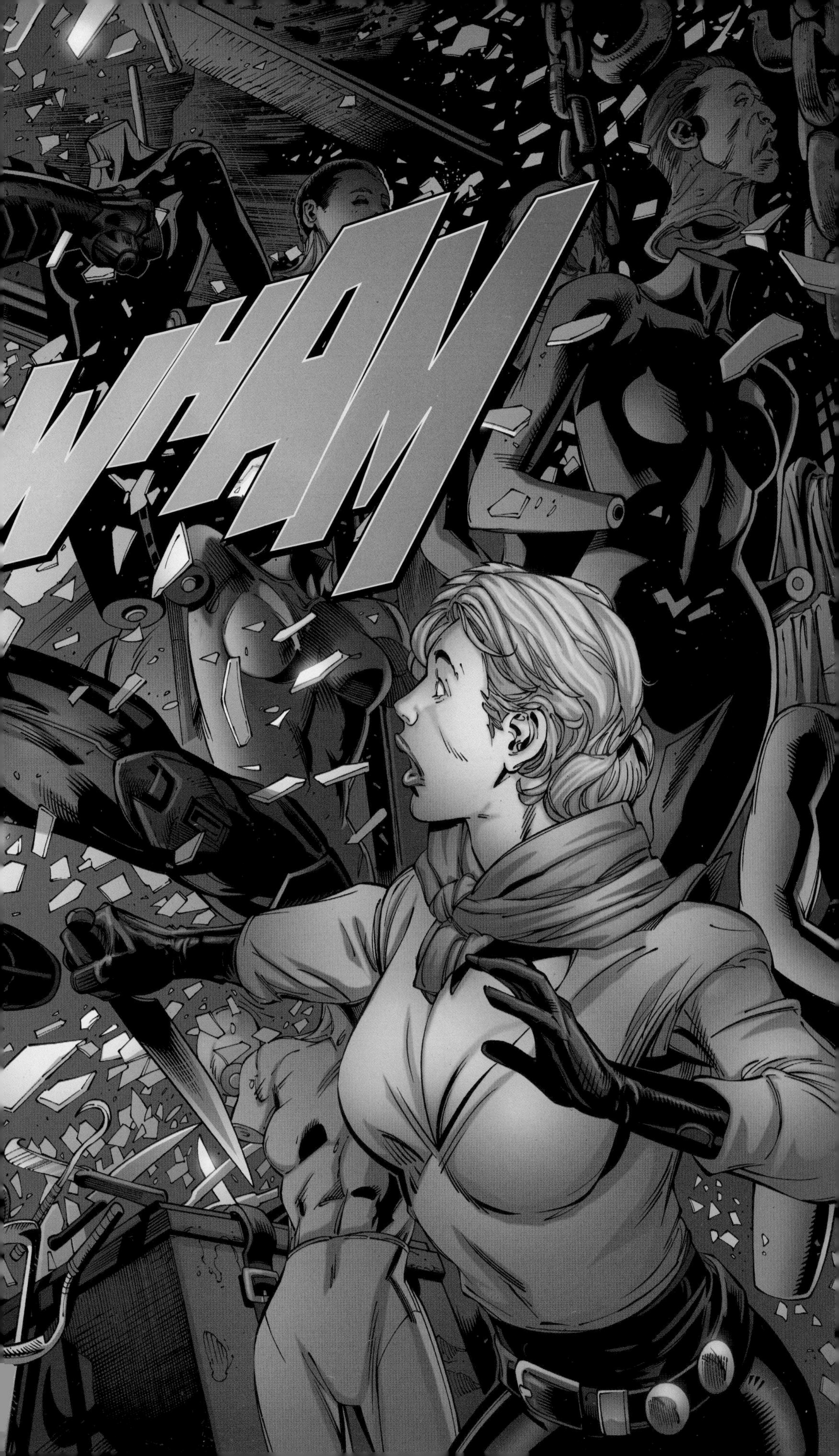
WHAM

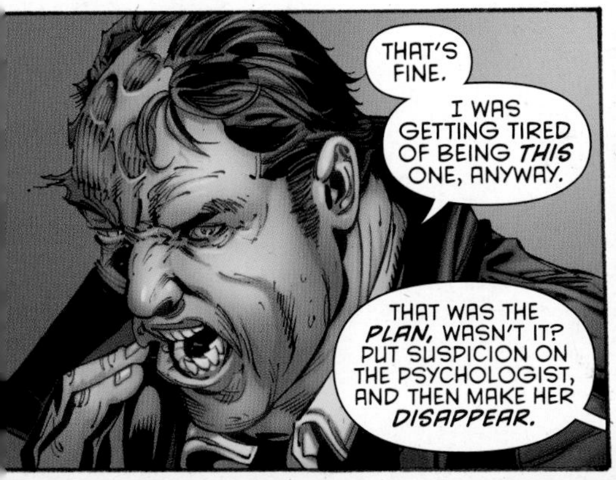
THAT'S FINE.
I WAS GETTING TIRED OF BEING *THIS* ONE, ANYWAY.
THAT WAS THE *PLAN,* WASN'T IT? PUT SUSPICION ON THE PSYCHOLOGIST, AND THEN MAKE HER *DISAPPEAR.*

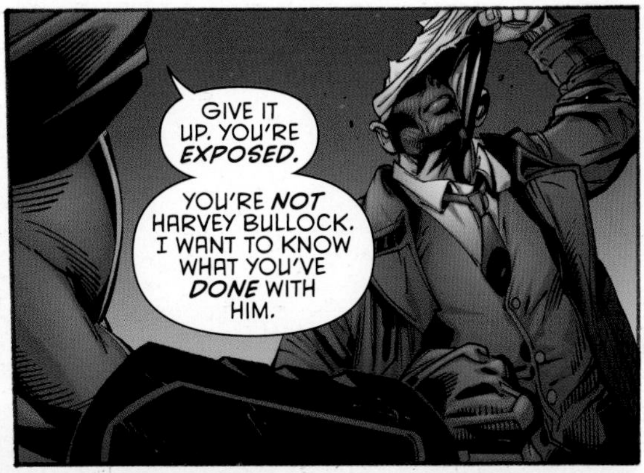
GIVE IT UP. YOU'RE *EXPOSED.*
YOU'RE *NOT* HARVEY BULLOCK. I WANT TO KNOW WHAT YOU'VE *DONE* WITH HIM.

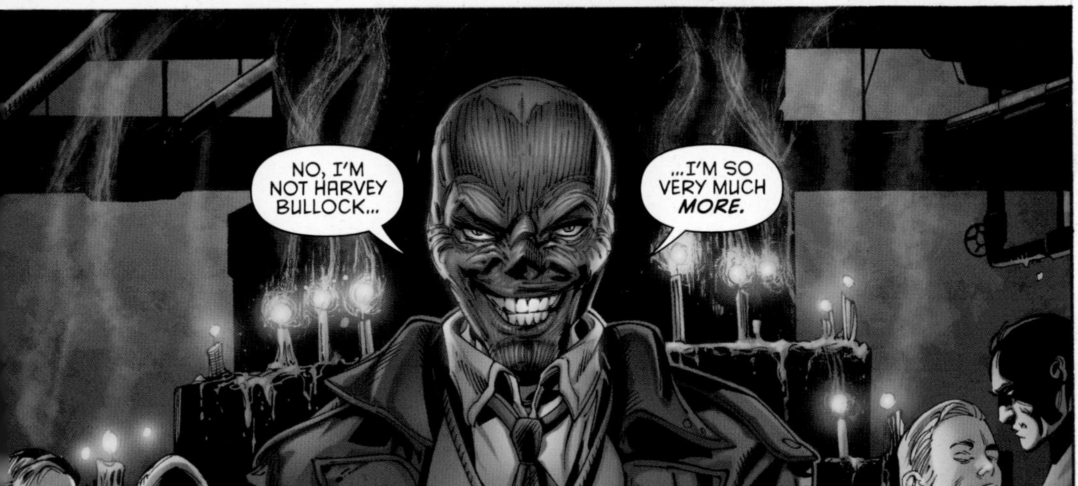
NO, I'M NOT HARVEY BULLOCK...
...I'M SO VERY MUCH *MORE.*

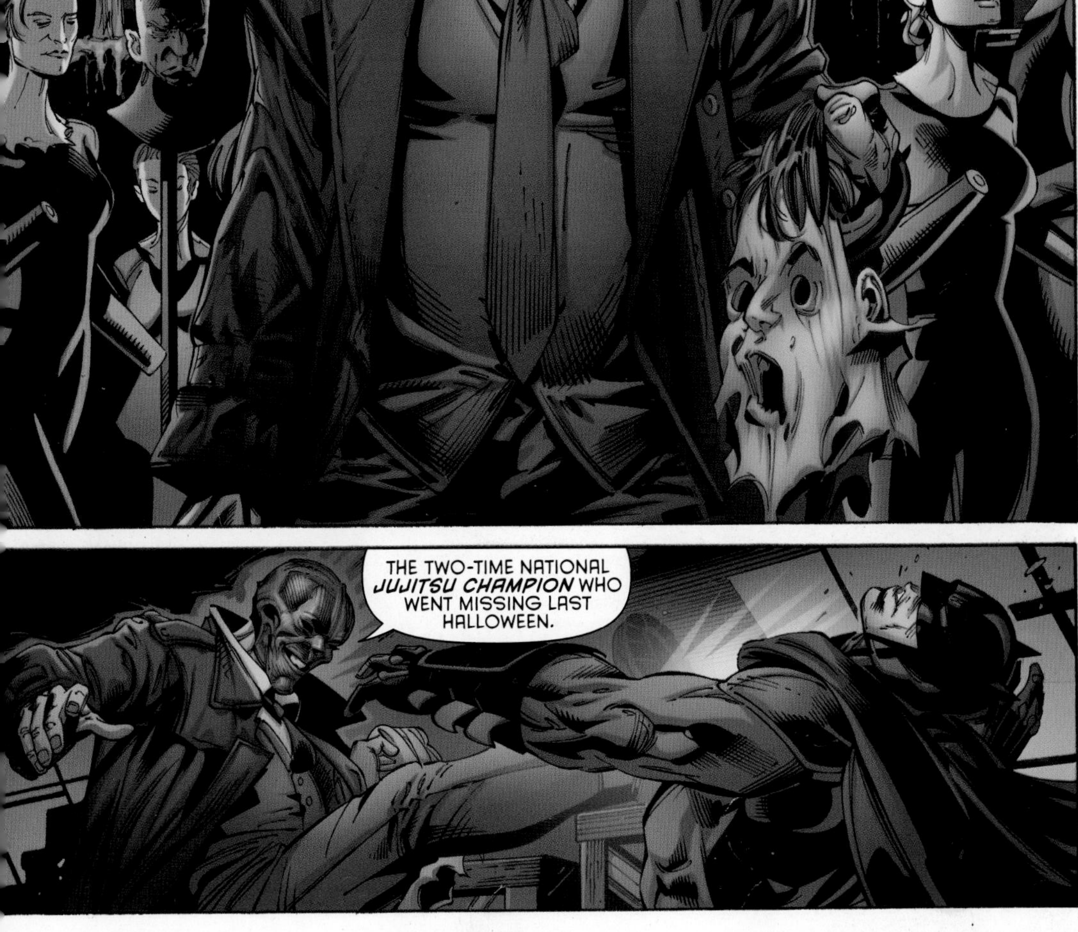
THE TWO-TIME NATIONAL *JUJITSU CHAMPION* WHO WENT MISSING LAST HALLOWEEN.

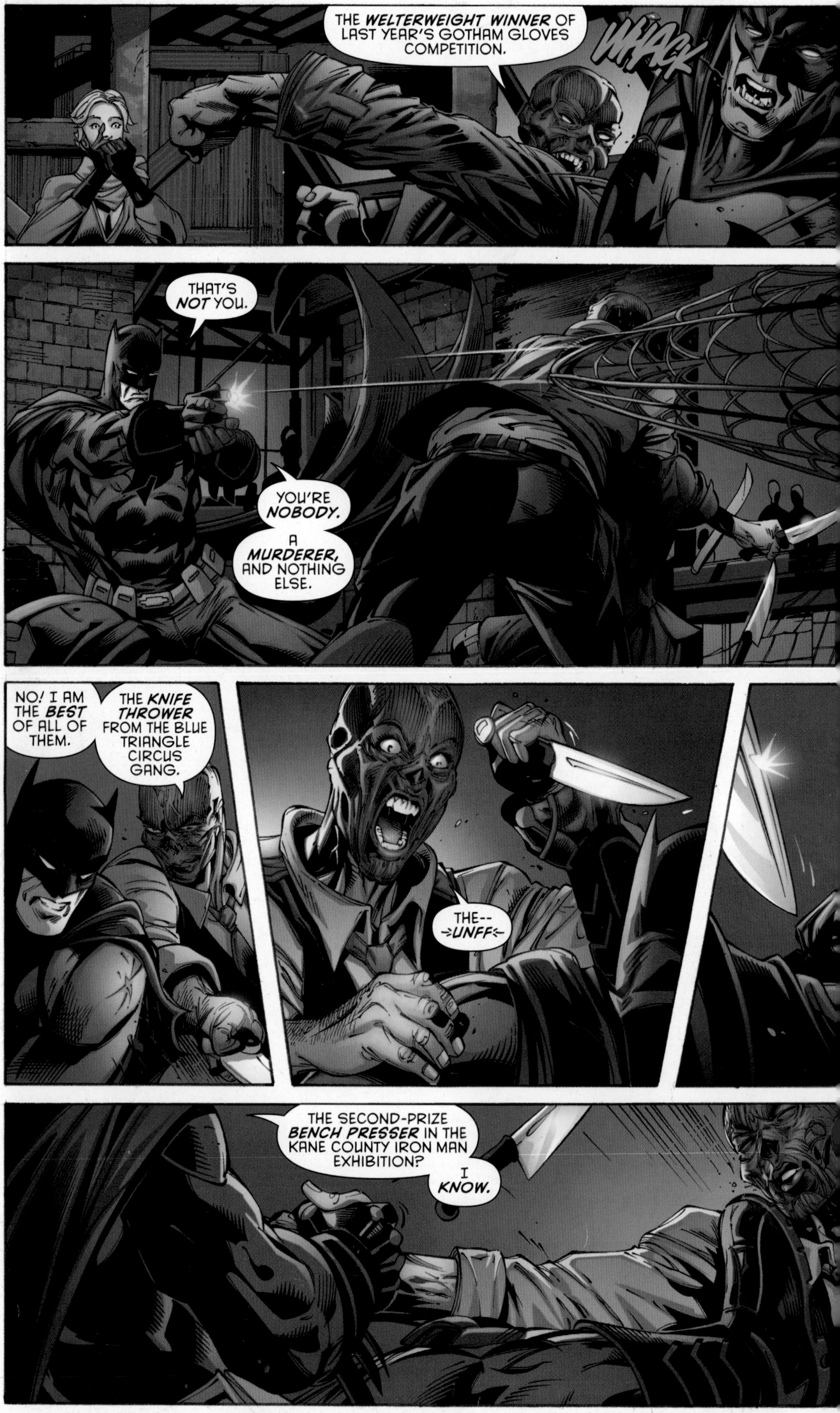
THE WELTERWEIGHT WINNER OF LAST YEAR'S GOTHAM GLOVES COMPETITION.
WHACK
THAT'S NOT YOU.
YOU'RE NOBODY.
A MURDERER, AND NOTHING ELSE.
NO! I AM THE BEST OF ALL OF THEM.
THE KNIFE THROWER FROM THE BLUE TRIANGLE CIRCUS GANG.
THE--
UNFF
THE SECOND-PRIZE BENCH PRESSER IN THE KANE COUNTY IRON MAN EXHIBITION?
I KNOW.

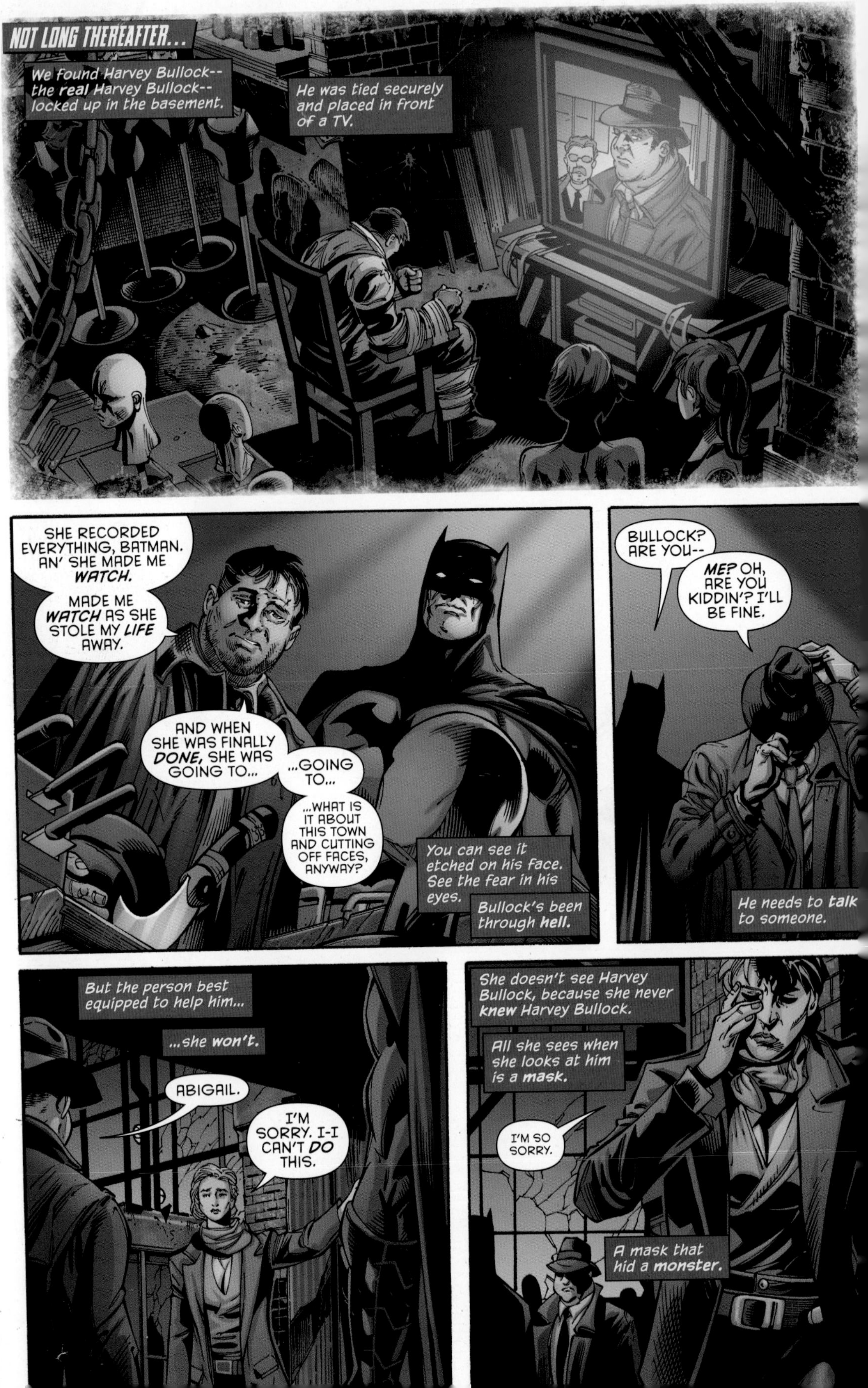
NOT LONG THEREAFTER...
We found Harvey Bullock--the real Harvey Bullock--locked up in the basement.
He was tied securely and placed in front of a TV.
SHE RECORDED EVERYTHING, BATMAN. AN' SHE MADE ME WATCH.
MADE ME WATCH AS SHE STOLE MY LIFE AWAY.
AND WHEN SHE WAS FINALLY DONE, SHE WAS GOING TO...
...GOING TO...
...WHAT IS IT ABOUT THIS TOWN AND CUTTING OFF FACES, ANYWAY?
You can see it etched on his face. See the fear in his eyes.
Bullock's been through hell.
BULLOCK? ARE YOU--
ME? OH, ARE YOU KIDDIN'? I'LL BE FINE.
He needs to talk to someone.
But the person best equipped to help him...
...she won't.
ABIGAIL.
I'M SORRY. I-I CAN'T DO THIS.
She doesn't see Harvey Bullock, because she never knew Harvey Bullock.
All she sees when she looks at him is a mask.
I'M SO SORRY.
A mask that hid a monster.

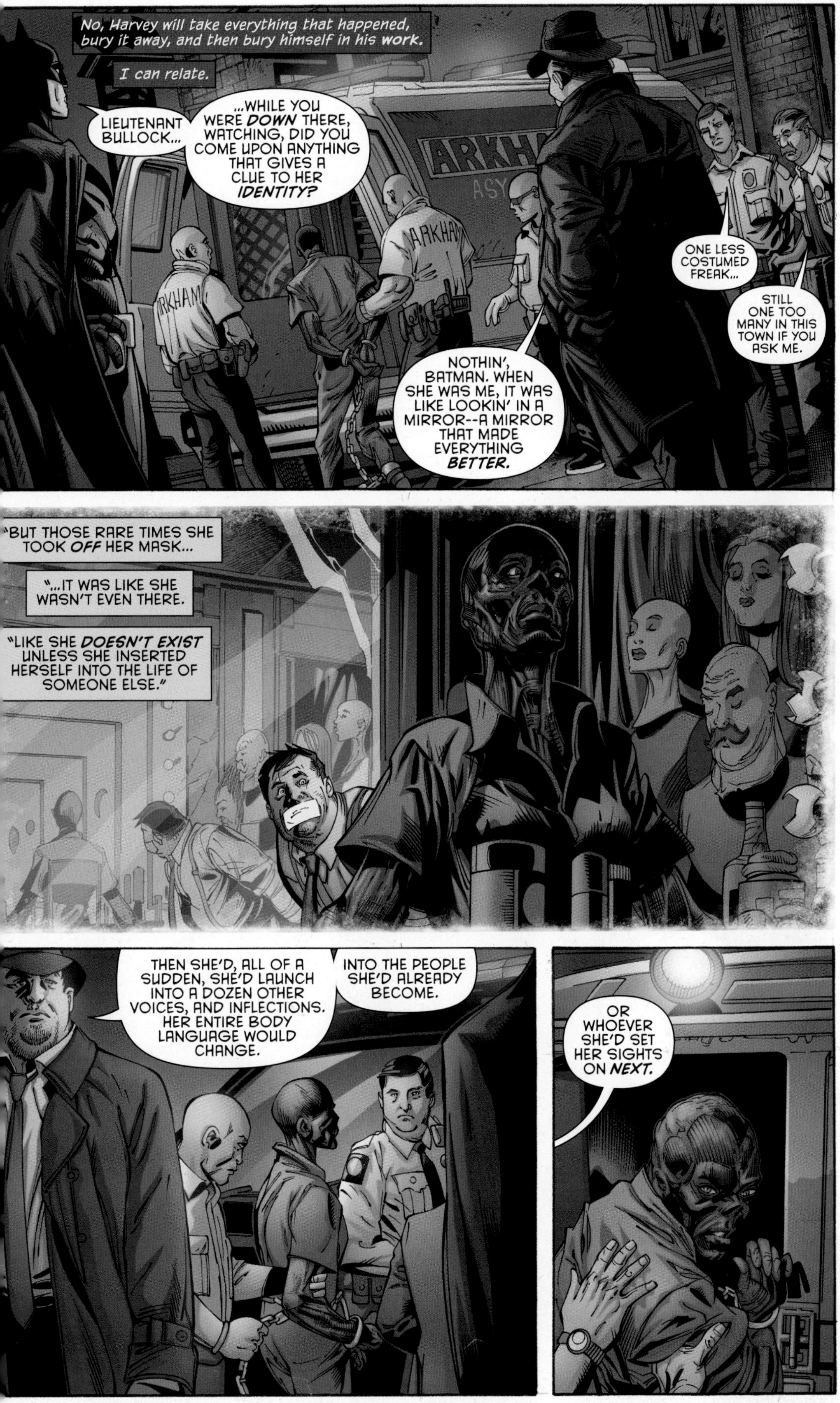

No, Harvey will take everything that happened, bury it away, and then bury himself in his work.
I can relate.
LIEUTENANT BULLOCK...
...WHILE YOU WERE DOWN THERE, WATCHING, DID YOU COME UPON ANYTHING THAT GIVES A CLUE TO HER IDENTITY?
ARKHAM
ASY
ARKHAM
ARKHAM
ONE LESS COSTUMED FREAK...
STILL ONE TOO MANY IN THIS TOWN IF YOU ASK ME.
NOTHIN', BATMAN. WHEN SHE WAS ME, IT WAS LIKE LOOKIN' IN A MIRROR--A MIRROR THAT MADE EVERYTHING BETTER.
"BUT THOSE RARE TIMES SHE TOOK OFF HER MASK...
"...IT WAS LIKE SHE WASN'T EVEN THERE.
"LIKE SHE DOESN'T EXIST UNLESS SHE INSERTED HERSELF INTO THE LIFE OF SOMEONE ELSE."
THEN SHE'D, ALL OF A SUDDEN, SHE'D LAUNCH INTO A DOZEN OTHER VOICES, AND INFLECTIONS. HER ENTIRE BODY LANGUAGE WOULD CHANGE.
INTO THE PEOPLE SHE'D ALREADY BECOME.
OR WHOEVER SHE'D SET HER SIGHTS ON NEXT.

IT DOESN'T MATTER.

ALL THAT MATTERS IS ANOTHER *LUNATIC* IS OFF THE STREETS OF GOTHAM, AND LOCKED AWAY INTO ARKHAM WHERE SHE CAN NO LONGER DO ANY HARM.

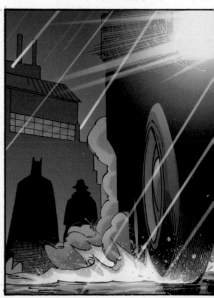

IT DOESN'T MATTER.

ALL THAT MATTERS IS ANOTHER *LUNATIC* IS OFF THE STREETS OF GOTHAM, AND LOCKED AWAY INTO ARKHAM WHERE SHE CAN NO LONGER DO ANY HARM.

THE END

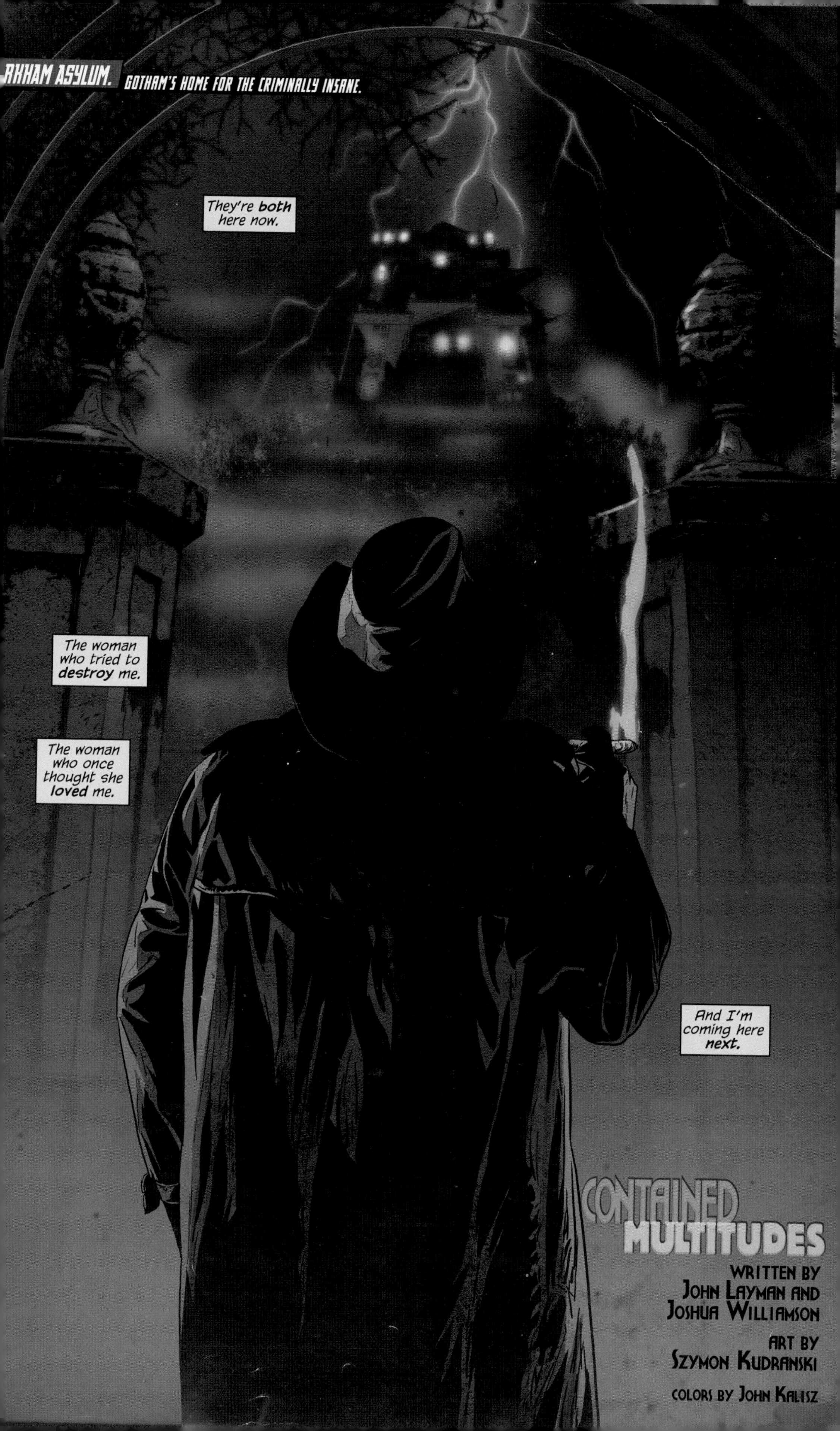

RKHAM ASYLUM. GOTHAM'S HOME FOR THE CRIMINALLY INSANE.
They're both here now.
The woman who tried to destroy me.
The woman who once thought she loved me.
And I'm coming here next.
CONTAINED MULTITUDES
WRITTEN BY JOHN LAYMAN AND JOSHUA WILLIAMSON
ART BY SZYMON KUDRANSKI
COLORS BY JOHN KALISZ

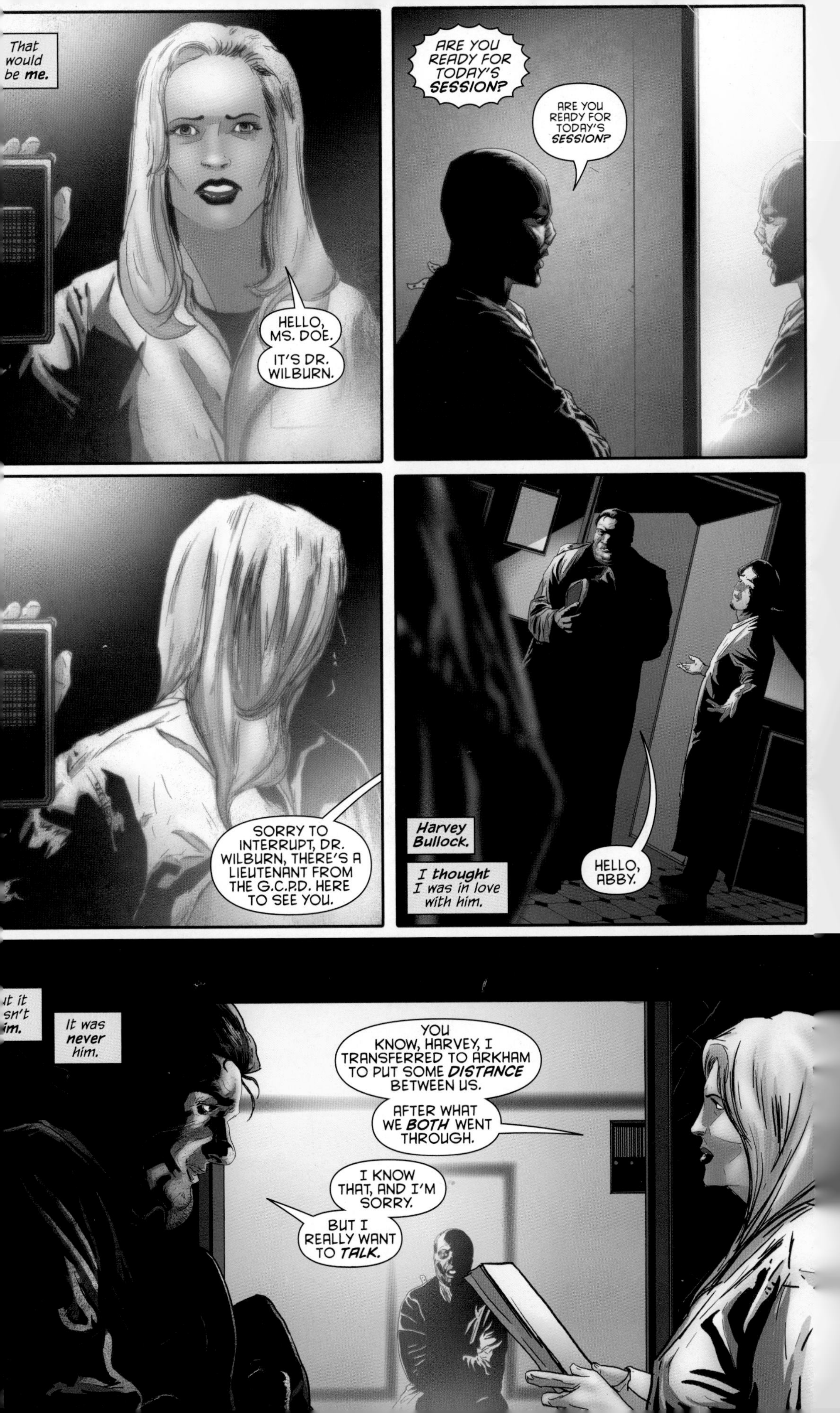

That would be *me.*
HELLO, MS. DOE.
IT'S DR. WILBURN.
ARE YOU READY FOR TODAY'S *SESSION?*
ARE YOU READY FOR TODAY'S *SESSION?*
SORRY TO INTERRUPT, DR. WILBURN, THERE'S A LIEUTENANT FROM THE G.C.P.D. HERE TO SEE YOU.
Harvey Bullock.
I thought I was in love with him.
HELLO, ABBY.
t it sn't *im.*
It was *never* him.
YOU KNOW, HARVEY, I TRANSFERRED TO ARKHAM TO PUT SOME *DISTANCE* BETWEEN US.
AFTER WHAT WE *BOTH* WENT THROUGH.
I KNOW THAT, AND I'M SORRY.
BUT I REALLY WANT TO *TALK.*

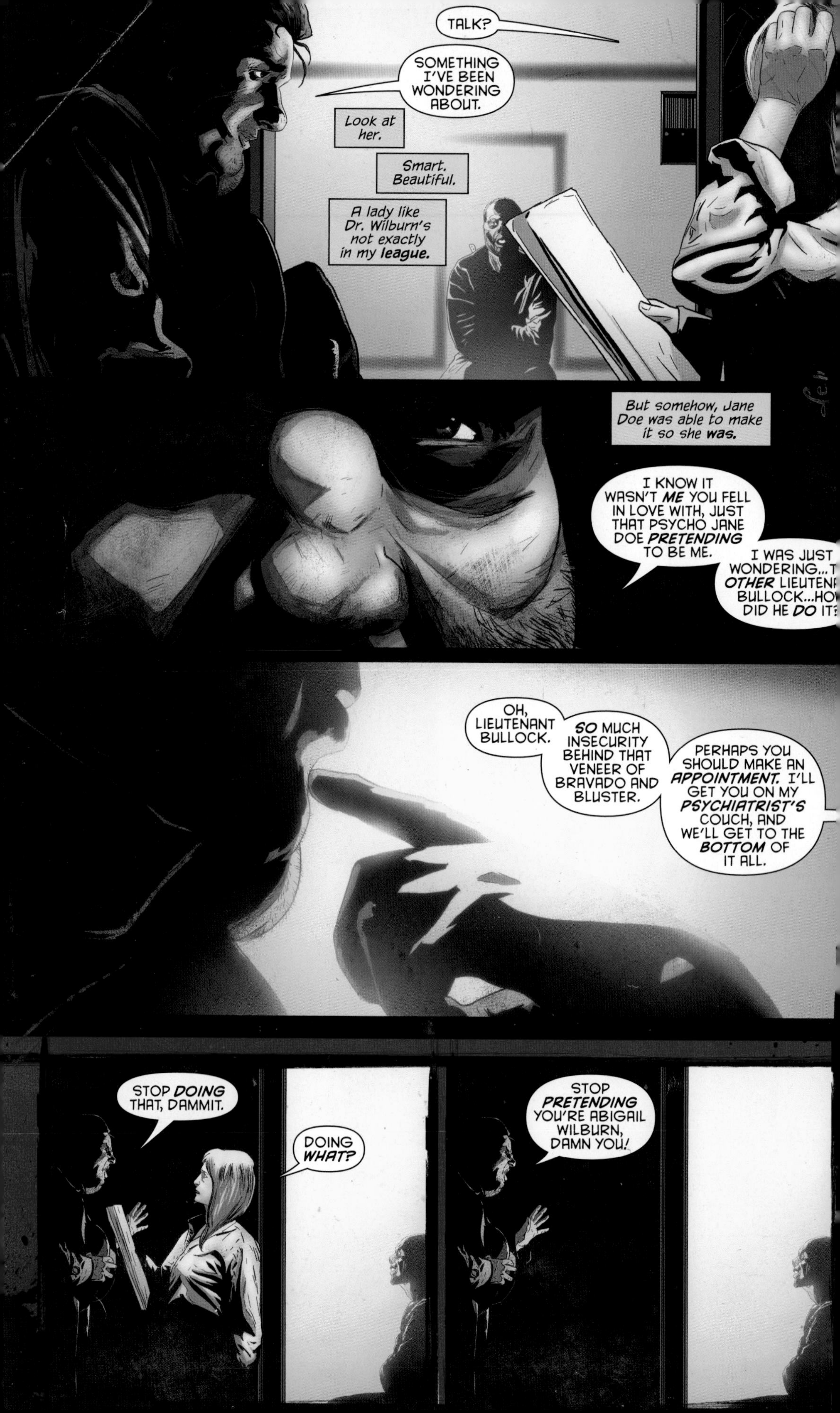
TALK?
SOMETHING I'VE BEEN WONDERING ABOUT.
Look at her.
Smart. Beautiful.
A lady like Dr. Wilburn's not exactly in my **league.**
But somehow, Jane Doe was able to make it so she **was.**
I KNOW IT WASN'T ***ME*** YOU FELL IN LOVE WITH, JUST THAT PSYCHO JANE DOE ***PRETENDING*** TO BE ME.
I WAS JUST WONDERING... ***OTHER*** BULLOCK... DID HE ***DO*** IT
OH, LIEUTENANT BULLOCK.
SO MUCH INSECURITY BEHIND THAT VENEER OF BRAVADO AND BLUSTER.
PERHAPS YOU SHOULD MAKE AN ***APPOINTMENT.*** I'LL GET YOU ON MY ***PSYCHIATRIST'S*** COUCH, AND WE'LL GET TO THE ***BOTTOM*** OF IT ALL.
STOP ***DOING*** THAT, DAMMIT.
DOING ***WHAT?***
STOP ***PRETENDING*** YOU'RE ABIGAIL WILBURN, DAMN YOU!

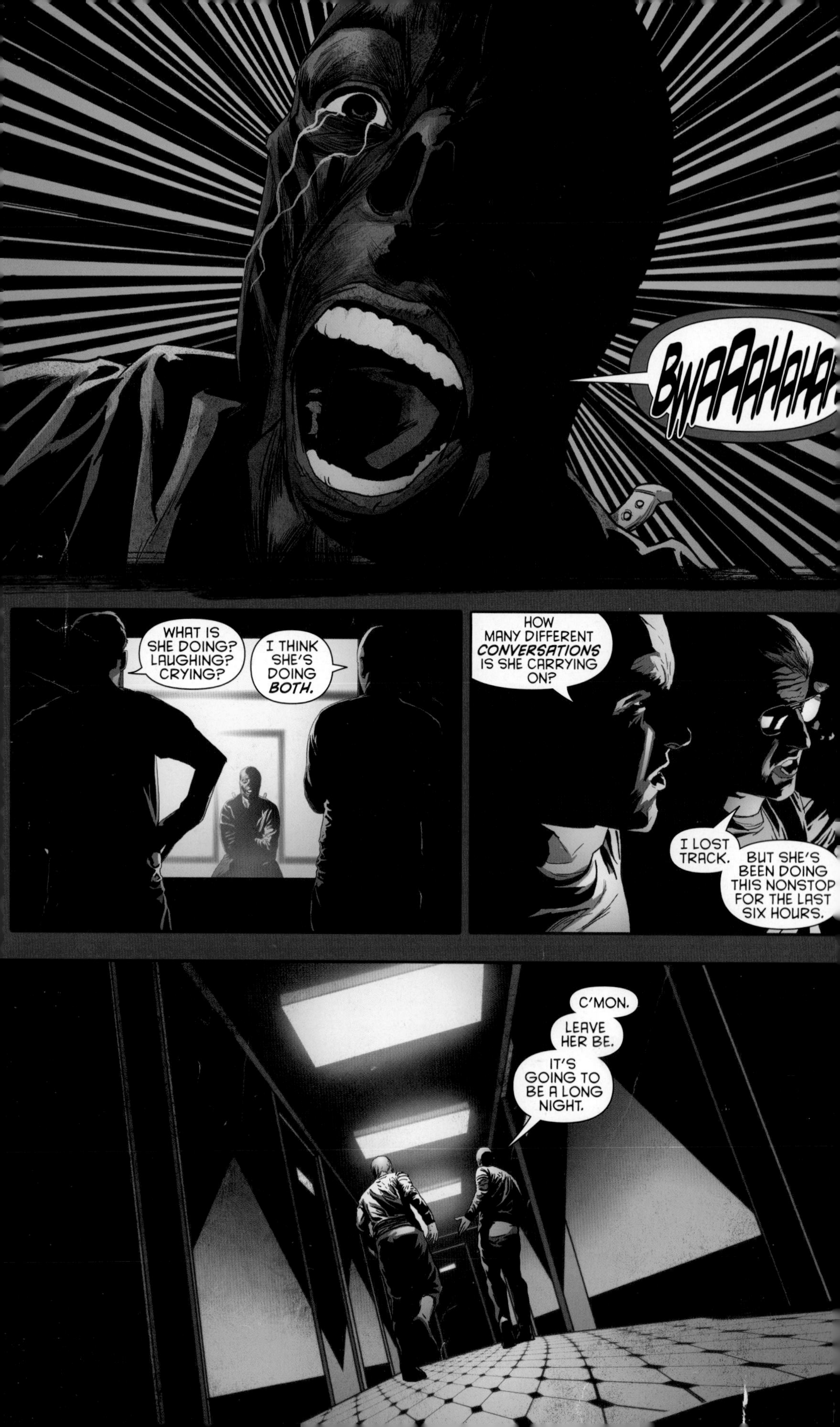
BWAAAHAHA!
WHAT IS SHE DOING? LAUGHING? CRYING?
I THINK SHE'S DOING BOTH.
HOW MANY DIFFERENT CONVERSATIONS IS SHE CARRYING ON?
I LOST TRACK.
BUT SHE'S BEEN DOING THIS NONSTOP FOR THE LAST SIX HOURS.
C'MON.
LEAVE HER BE.
IT'S GOING TO BE A LONG NIGHT.

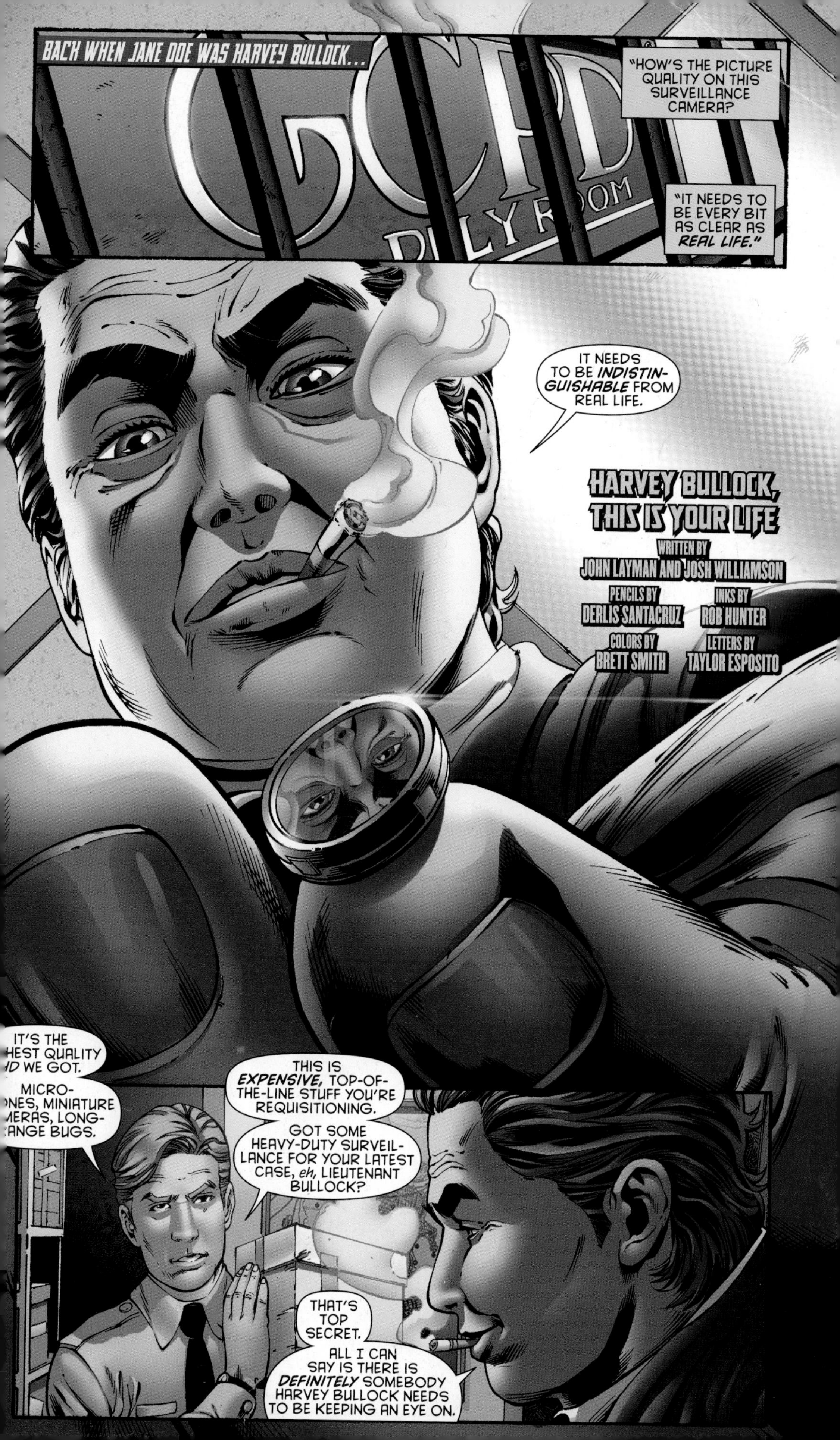

BACK WHEN JANE DOE WAS HARVEY BULLOCK...
GCPD
"HOW'S THE PICTURE QUALITY ON THIS SURVEILLANCE CAMERA?
"IT NEEDS TO BE EVERY BIT AS CLEAR AS *REAL LIFE.*"
IT NEEDS TO BE *INDISTIN-GUISHABLE* FROM REAL LIFE.
HARVEY BULLOCK, THIS IS YOUR LIFE
WRITTEN BY JOHN LAYMAN AND JOSH WILLIAMSON
PENCILS BY DERLIS SANTACRUZ
INKS BY ROB HUNTER
COLORS BY BRETT SMITH
LETTERS BY TAYLOR ESPOSITO
IT'S THE HEST QUALITY ND WE GOT.
MICRO-ONES, MINIATURE MERAS, LONG-ANGE BUGS.
THIS IS *EXPENSIVE,* TOP-OF-THE-LINE STUFF YOU'RE REQUISITIONING.
GOT SOME HEAVY-DUTY SURVEIL-LANCE FOR YOUR LATEST CASE, *eh,* LIEUTENANT BULLOCK?
THAT'S TOP SECRET.
ALL I CAN SAY IS THERE IS *DEFINITELY* SOMEBODY HARVEY BULLOCK NEEDS TO BE KEEPING AN EYE ON.

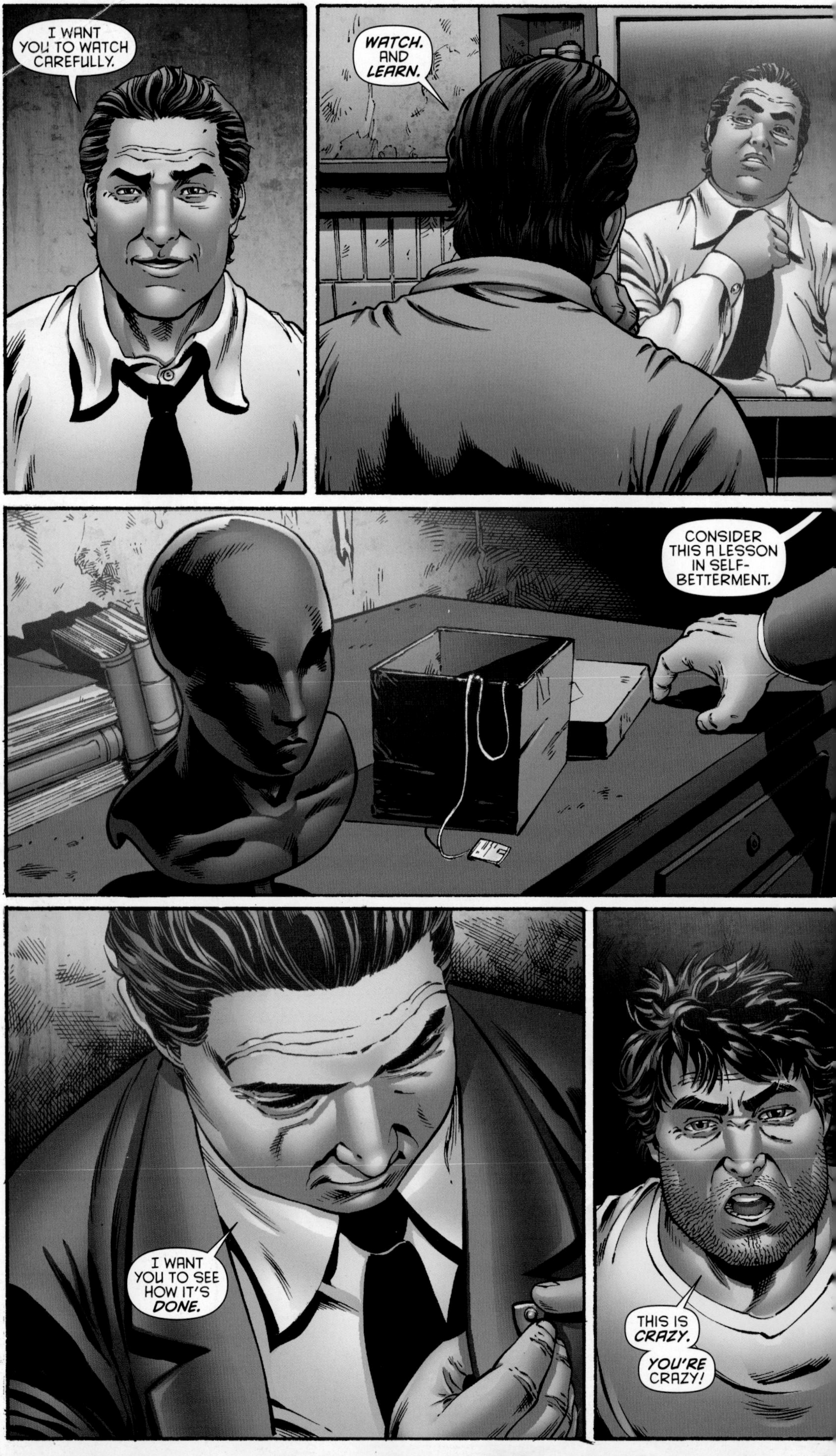
I WANT YOU TO WATCH CAREFULLY.
WATCH. AND LEARN.
CONSIDER THIS A LESSON IN SELF-BETTERMENT.
I WANT YOU TO SEE HOW IT'S DONE.
THIS IS CRAZY.
YOU'RE CRAZY!

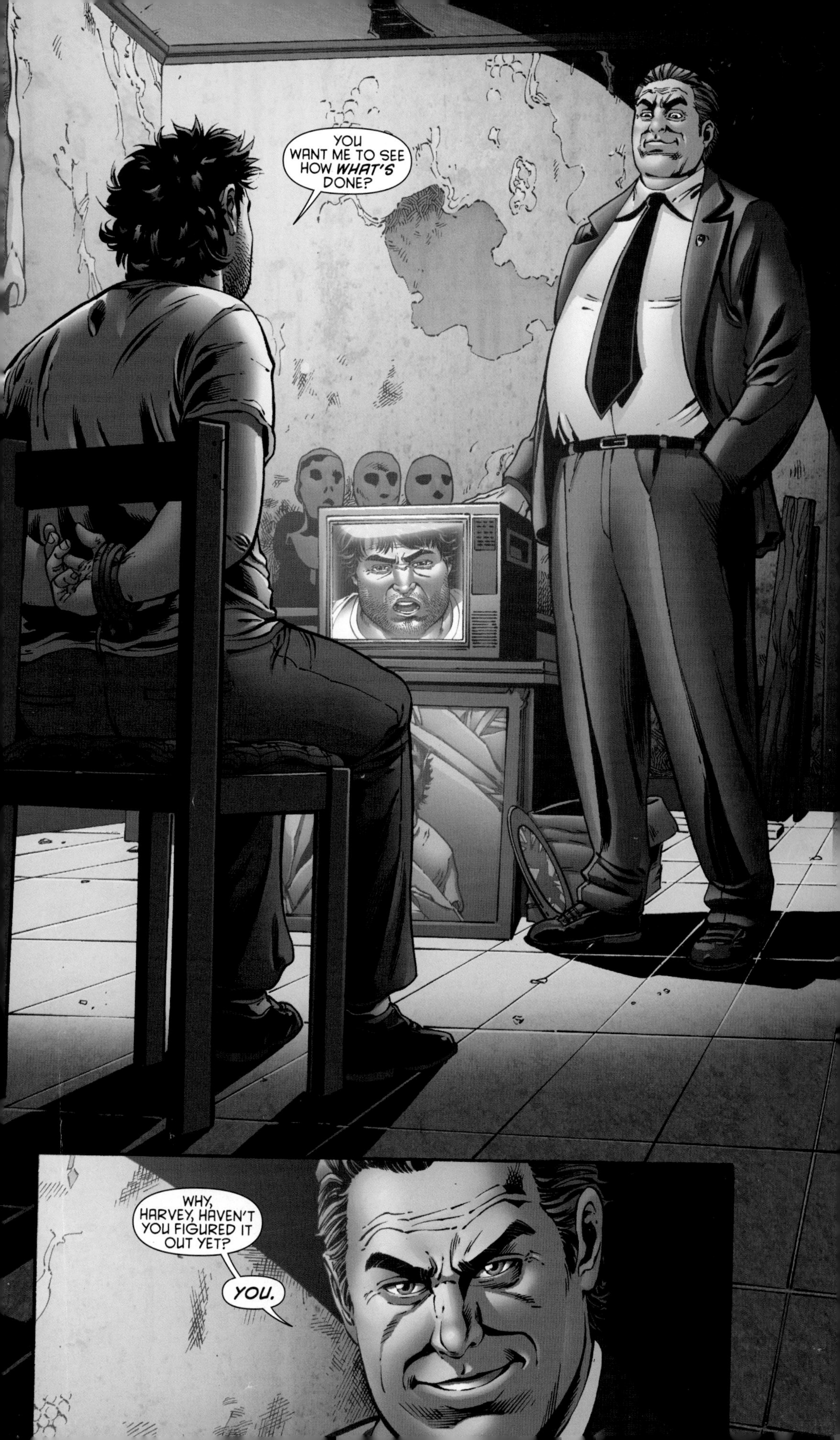
YOU WANT ME TO SEE HOW WHAT'S DONE?
WHY, HARVEY, HAVEN'T YOU FIGURED IT OUT YET?
YOU.

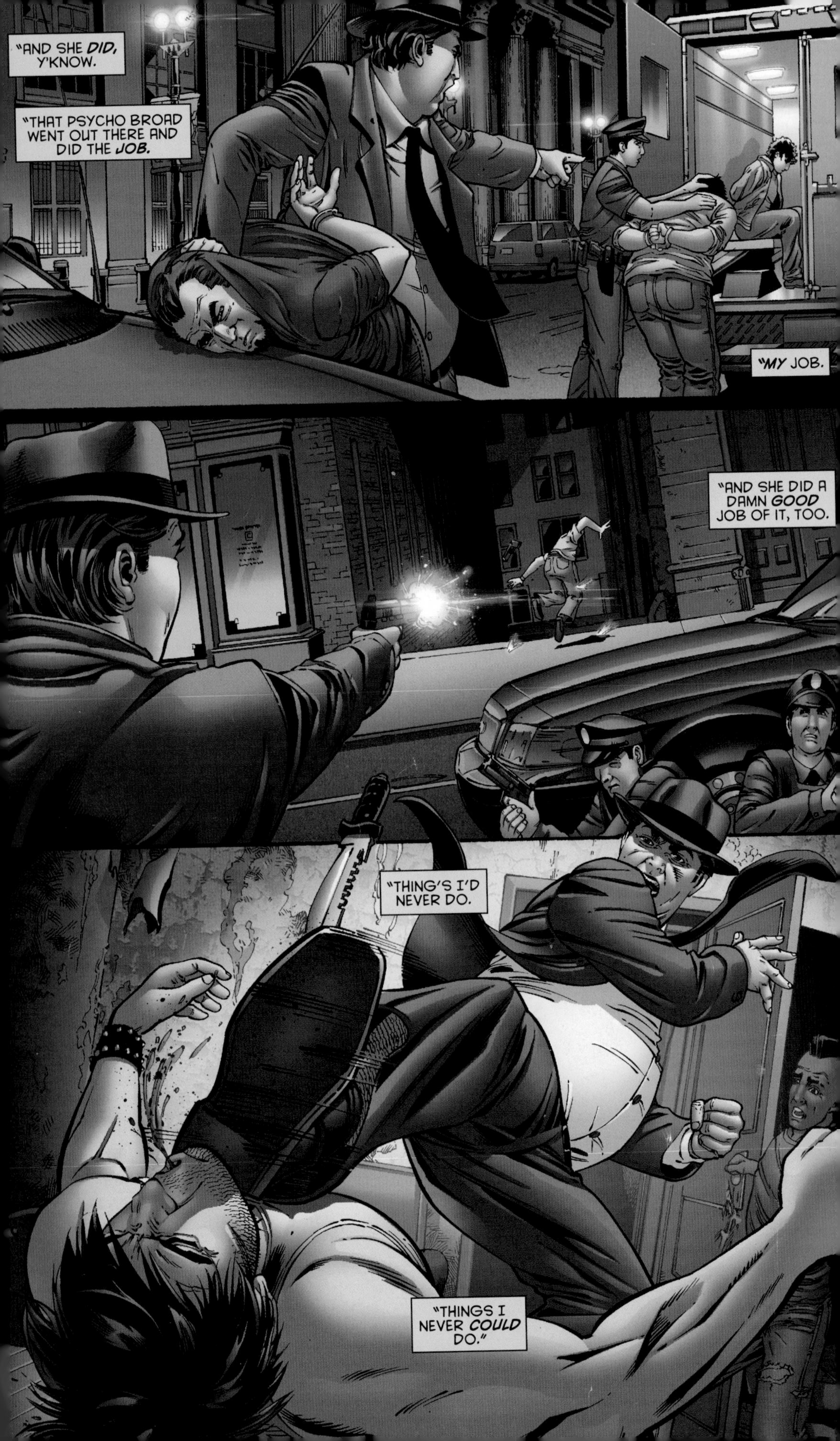
"AND SHE *DID,* Y'KNOW.
"THAT PSYCHO BROAD WENT OUT THERE AND DID THE *JOB.*
"*MY* JOB.
"AND SHE DID A DAMN *GOOD* JOB OF IT, TOO.
"THING'S I'D NEVER DO.
"THINGS I NEVER *COULD* DO."

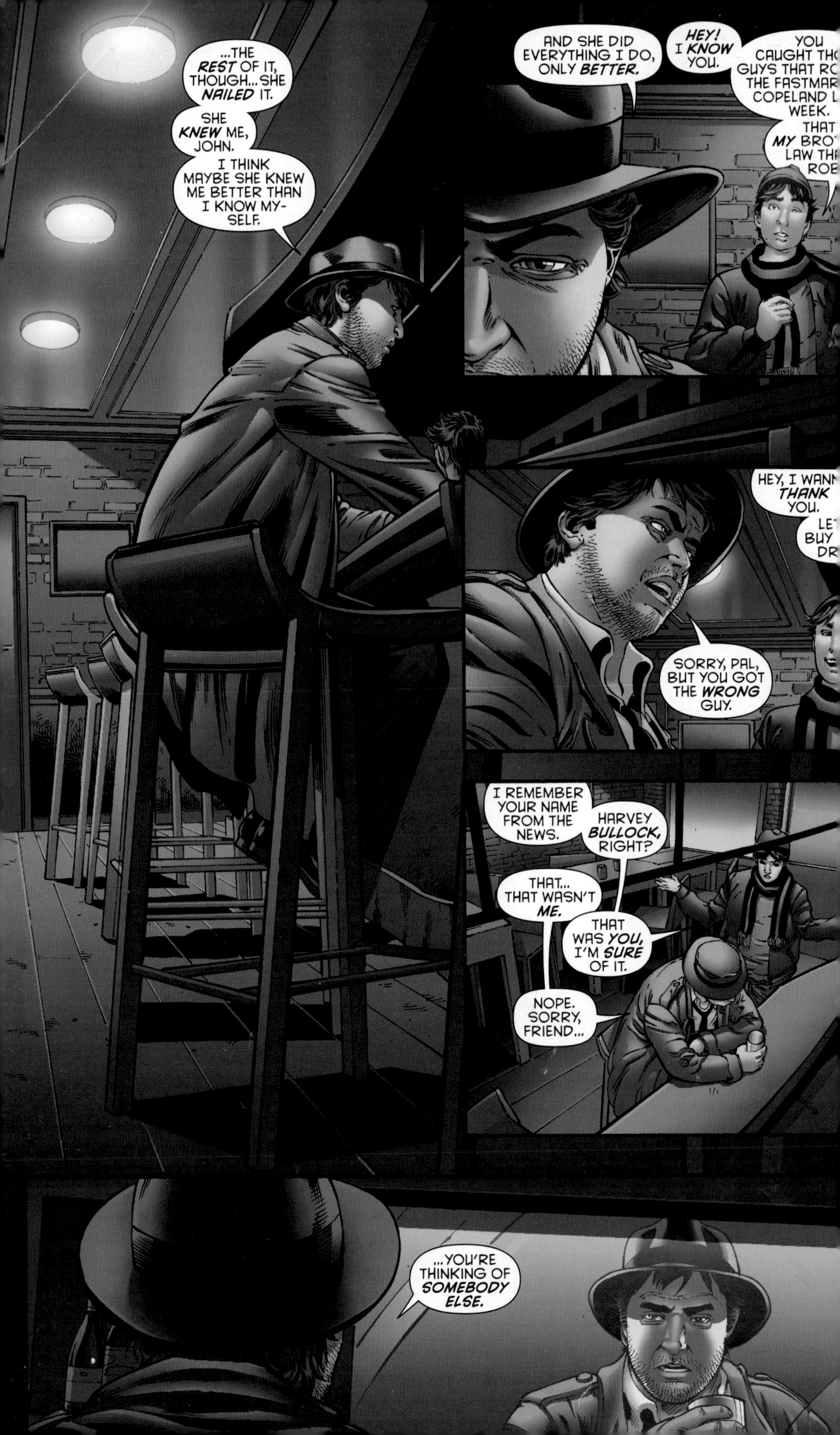
...THE REST OF IT, THOUGH... SHE NAILED IT.
SHE KNEW ME, JOHN.
I THINK MAYBE SHE KNEW ME BETTER THAN I KNOW MY-SELF.
AND SHE DID EVERYTHING I DO, ONLY BETTER.
HEY! I KNOW YOU.
YOU CAUGHT THO GUYS THAT RO THE FASTMAR COPELAND L WEEK.
THAT MY BRO LAW TH ROB
HEY, I WANN THANK YOU.
LE BUY DR
SORRY, PAL, BUT YOU GOT THE WRONG GUY.
I REMEMBER YOUR NAME FROM THE NEWS.
HARVEY BULLOCK, RIGHT?
THAT... THAT WASN'T ME.
THAT WAS YOU, I'M SURE OF IT.
NOPE. SORRY, FRIEND...
...YOU'RE THINKING OF SOMEBODY ELSE.

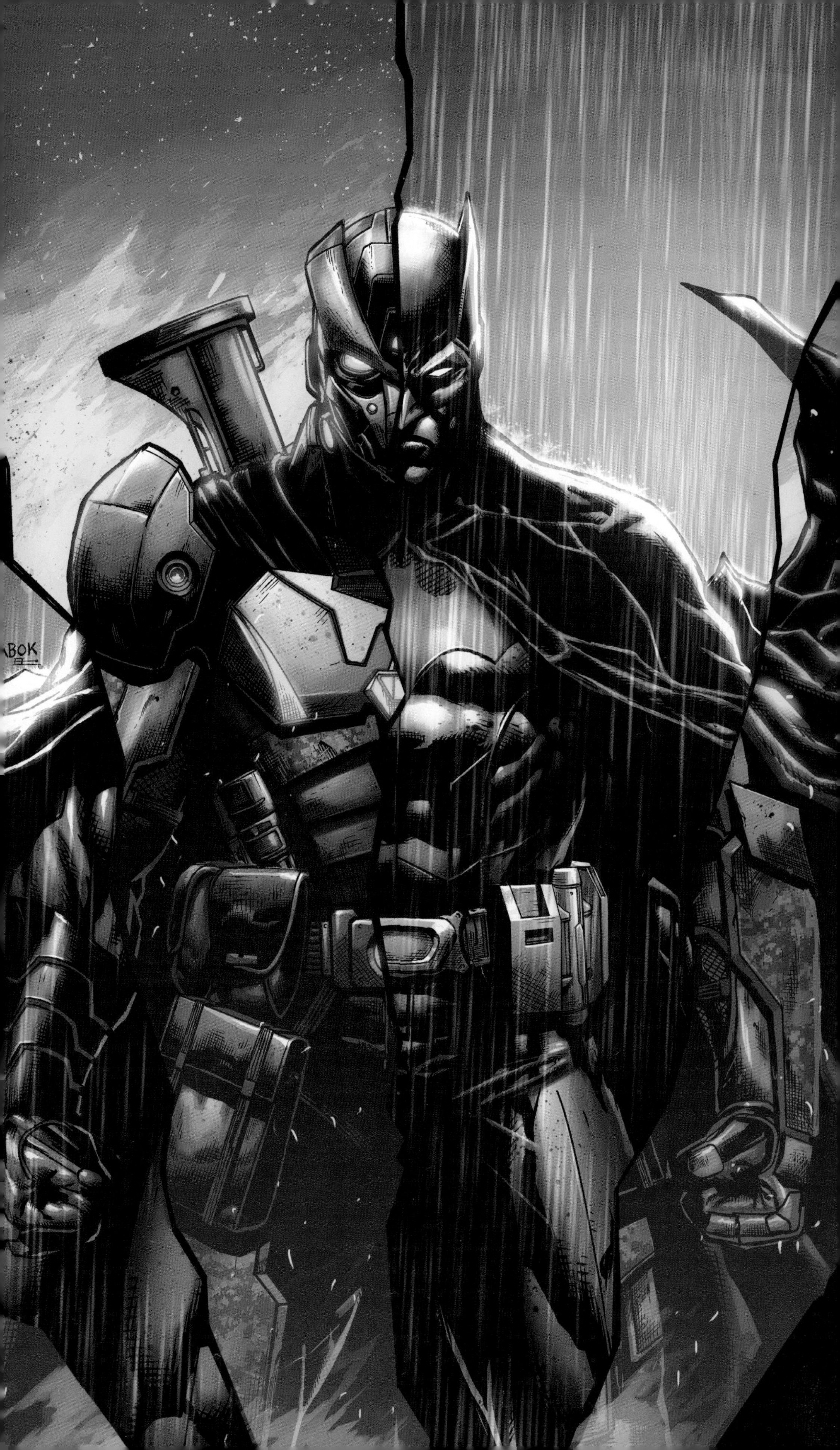

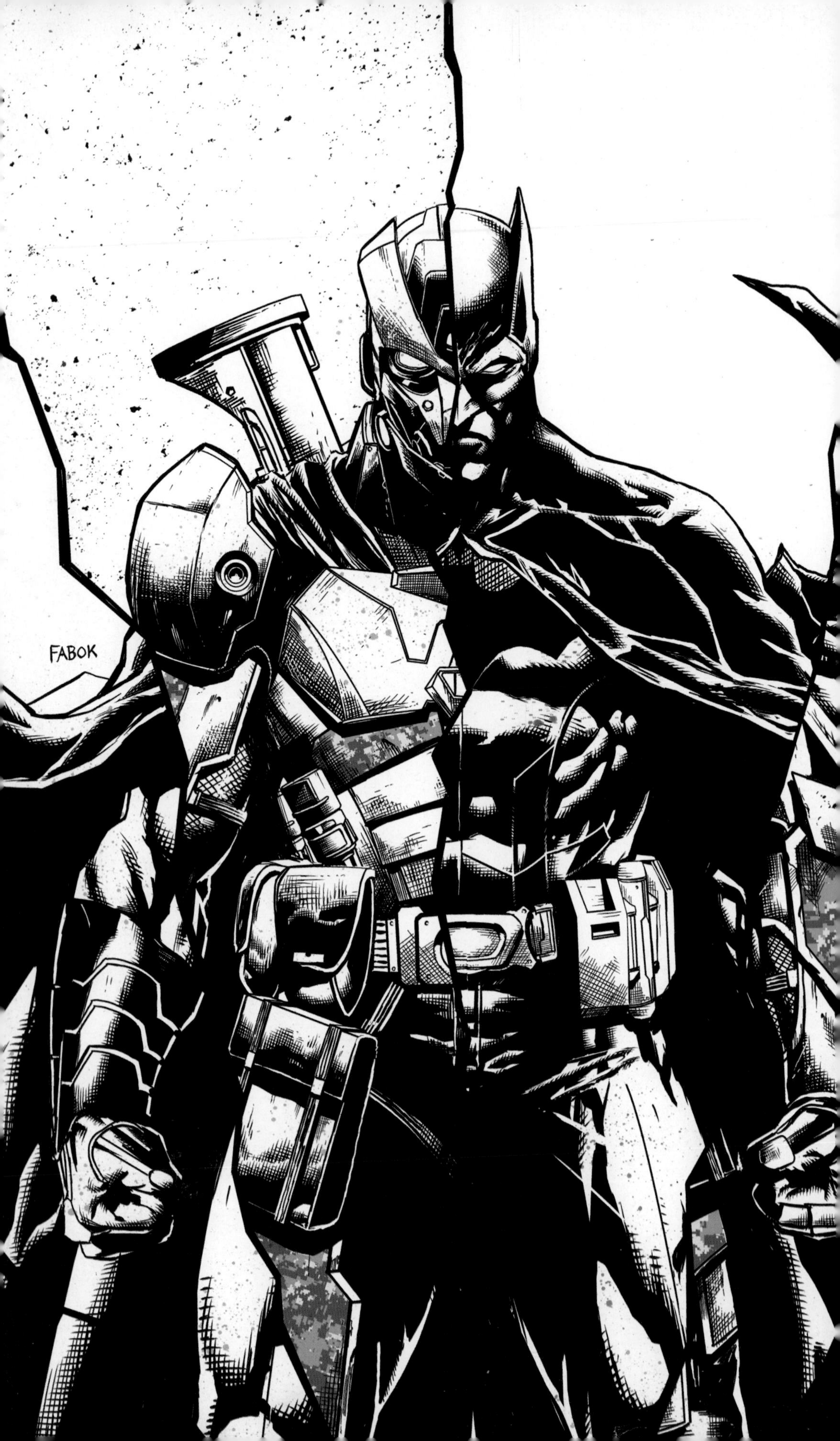
FABOK

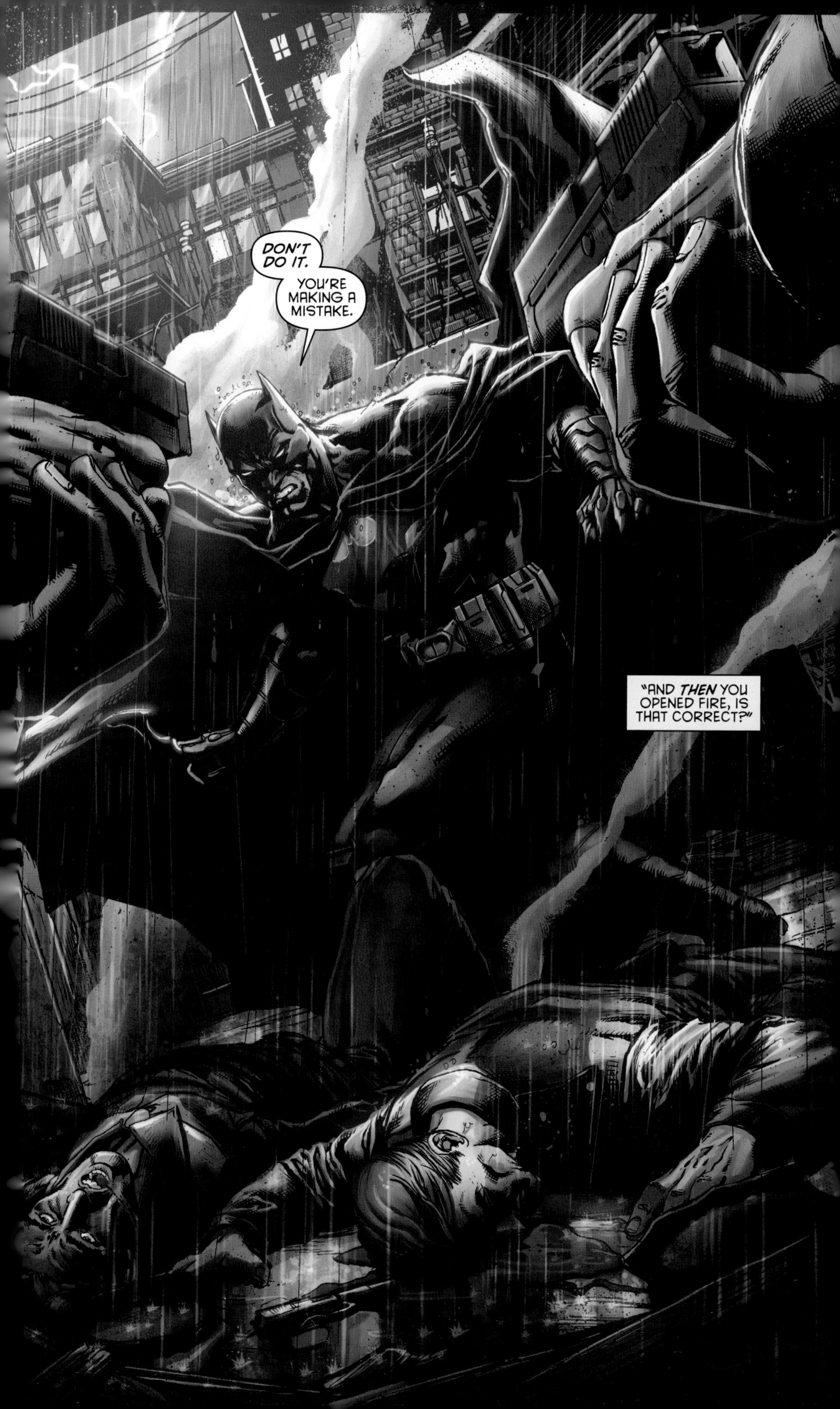
DON'T DO IT.
YOU'RE MAKING A MISTAKE.
"AND THEN YOU OPENED FIRE, IS THAT CORRECT?"

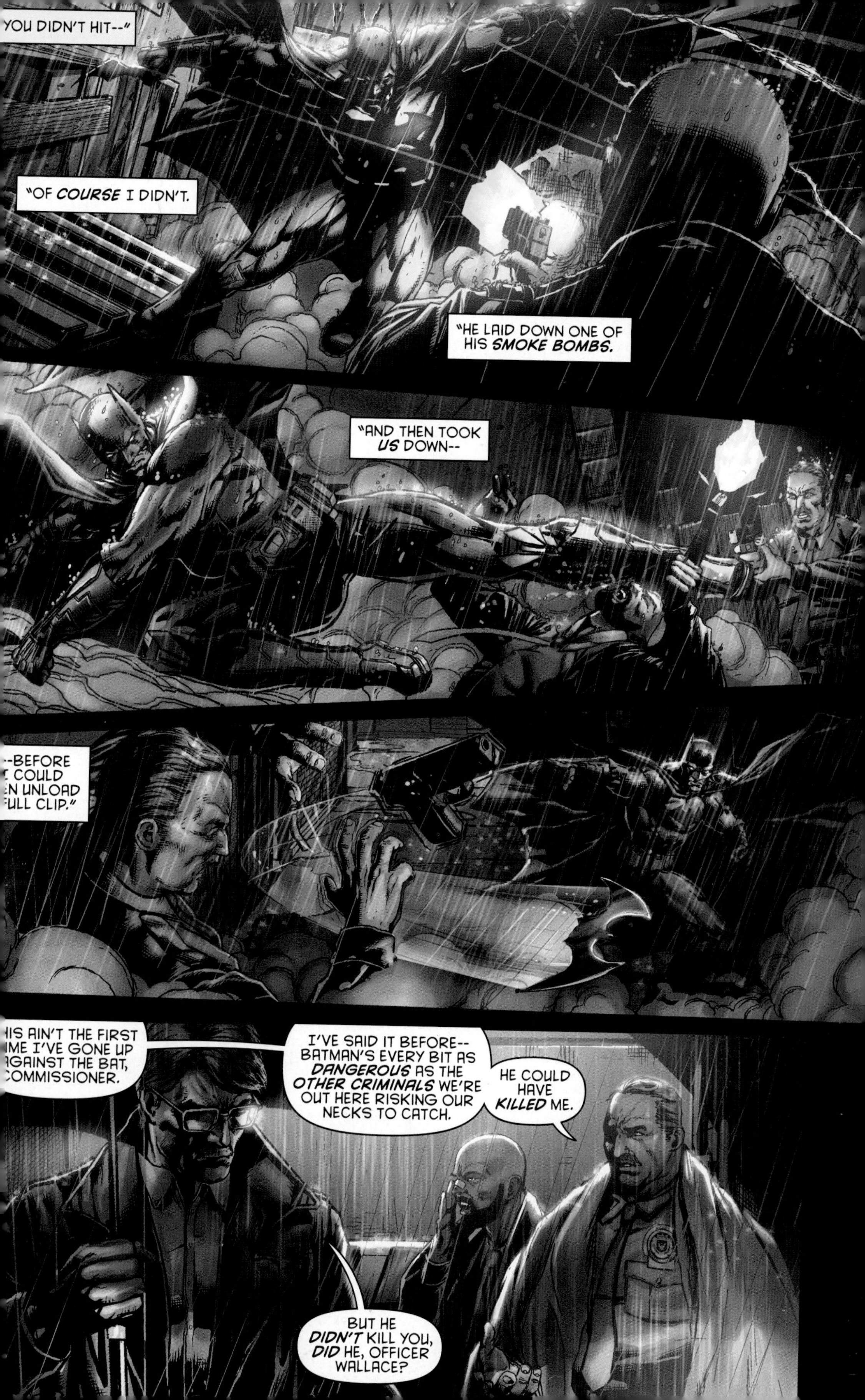

YOU DIDN'T HIT--"
"OF COURSE I DIDN'T.
"HE LAID DOWN ONE OF HIS SMOKE BOMBS.
"AND THEN TOOK US DOWN--
--BEFORE
COULD
N UNLOAD
ULL CLIP."
IS AIN'T THE FIRST
ME I'VE GONE UP
AGAINST THE BAT,
COMMISSIONER.
I'VE SAID IT BEFORE-- BATMAN'S EVERY BIT AS DANGEROUS AS THE OTHER CRIMINALS WE'RE OUT HERE RISKING OUR NECKS TO CATCH.
HE COULD HAVE KILLED ME.
BUT HE DIDN'T KILL YOU, DID HE, OFFICER WALLACE?

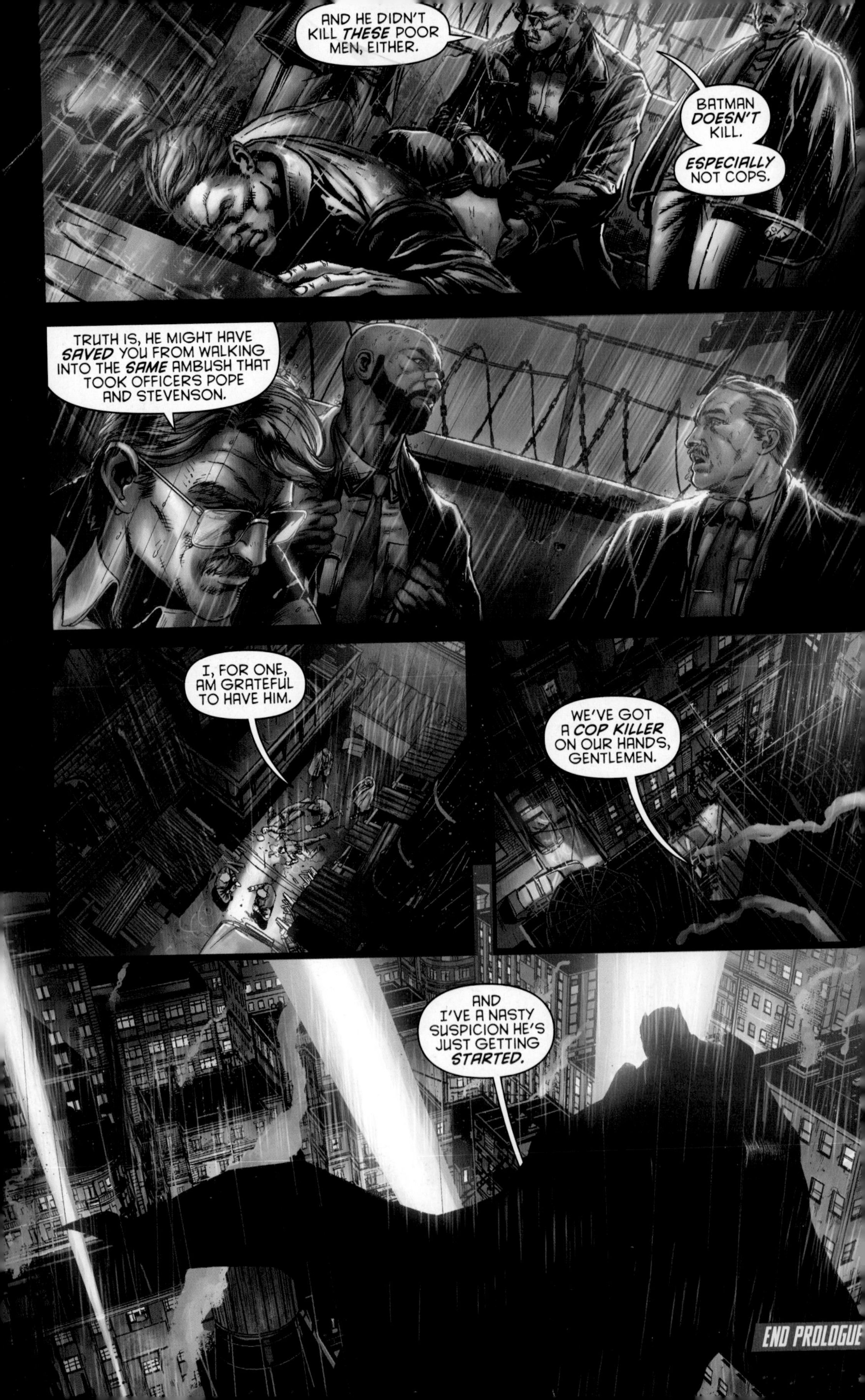
AND HE DIDN'T KILL *THESE* POOR MEN, EITHER.
BATMAN *DOESN'T* KILL.
ESPECIALLY NOT COPS.
TRUTH IS, HE MIGHT HAVE *SAVED* YOU FROM WALKING INTO THE *SAME* AMBUSH THAT TOOK OFFICERS POPE AND STEVENSON.
I, FOR ONE, AM GRATEFUL TO HAVE HIM.
WE'VE GOT A *COP KILLER* ON OUR HANDS, GENTLEMEN.
AND I'VE A NASTY SUSPICION HE'S JUST GETTING *STARTED.*
END PROLOGUE

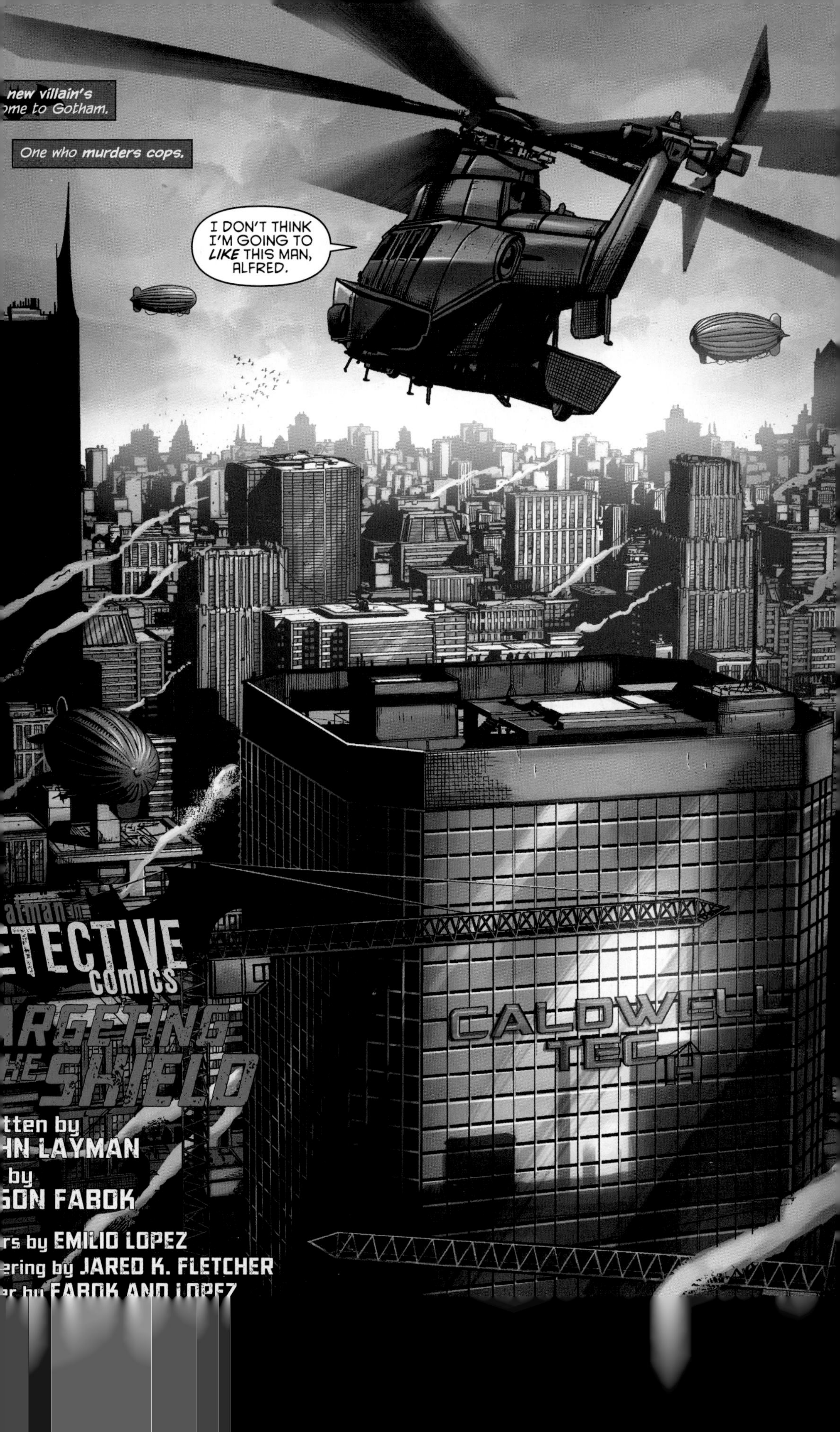
new villain's
ome to Gotham.
One who murders cops.
I DON'T THINK I'M GOING TO LIKE THIS MAN, ALFRED.
CALDWELL TEC
ETECTIVE
COMICS
ARGETING
HE SHIELD
tten by
HN LAYMAN
by
SON FABOK
rs by EMILIO LOPEZ
ering by JARED K. FLETCHER

The killer struck again just past midnight.

BUDDA
BUDDA
BUDDA
BUDDA

Ambushed and murdered Officers Bradley and Parker.

Strode and Melendez, two of the more *intelligent* officers on the G.C.P.D., were nearby. They'd been patrolling in tandem with Bradley and Parker to better protect one another.

BUDDA
BUDDA
BUDDA
BUDDA

For all the good it did them.

VRRRRRMM

GUNKK

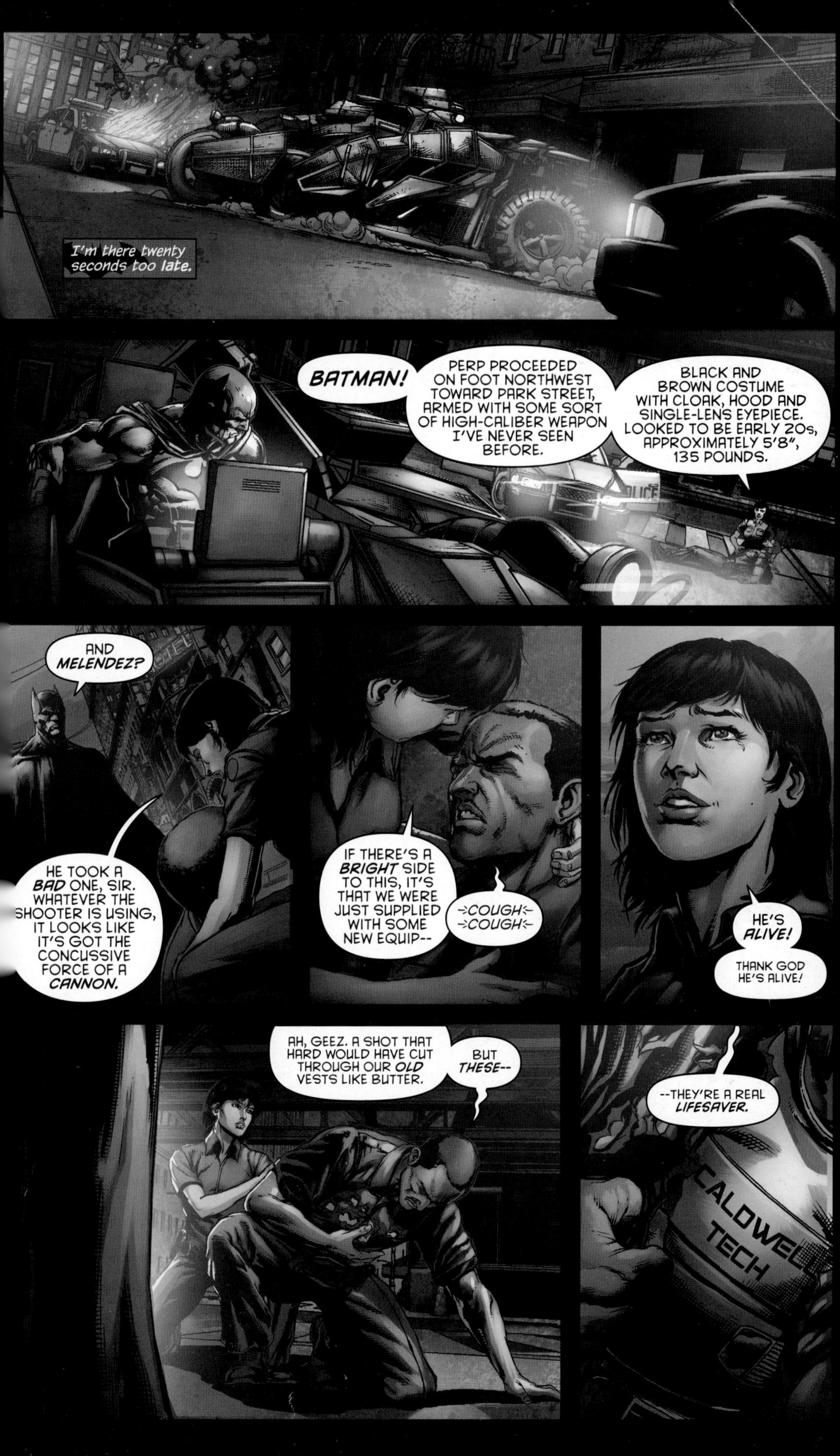
I'm there twenty seconds too late.
BATMAN!
PERP PROCEEDED ON FOOT NORTHWEST TOWARD PARK STREET, ARMED WITH SOME SORT OF HIGH-CALIBER WEAPON I'VE NEVER SEEN BEFORE.
BLACK AND BROWN COSTUME WITH CLOAK, HOOD AND SINGLE-LENS EYEPIECE. LOOKED TO BE EARLY 20s, APPROXIMATELY 5'8", 135 POUNDS.
AND MELENDEZ?
HE TOOK A BAD ONE, SIR. WHATEVER THE SHOOTER IS USING, IT LOOKS LIKE IT'S GOT THE CONCUSSIVE FORCE OF A CANNON.
IF THERE'S A BRIGHT SIDE TO THIS, IT'S THAT WE WERE JUST SUPPLIED WITH SOME NEW EQUIP--
COUGH COUGH
HE'S ALIVE!
THANK GOD HE'S ALIVE!
AH, GEEZ. A SHOT THAT HARD WOULD HAVE CUT THROUGH OUR OLD VESTS LIKE BUTTER.
BUT THESE--
--THEY'RE A REAL LIFESAVER.
CALDWELL TECH

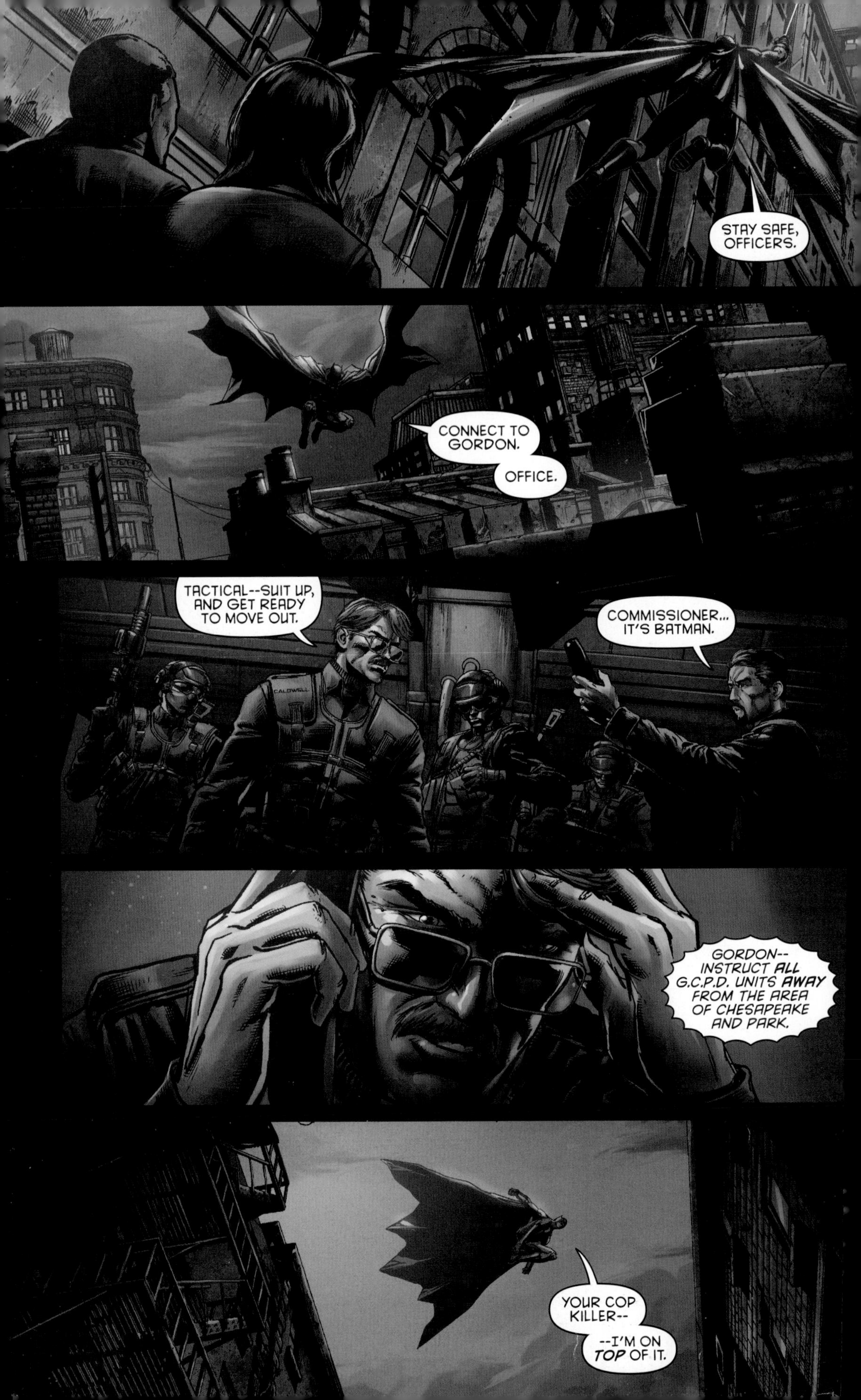
STAY SAFE, OFFICERS.
CONNECT TO GORDON.
OFFICE.
TACTICAL--SUIT UP, AND GET READY TO MOVE OUT.
COMMISSIONER... IT'S BATMAN.
CALDWELL
GORDON-- INSTRUCT ALL G.C.P.D. UNITS AWAY FROM THE AREA OF CHESAPEAKE AND PARK.
YOUR COP KILLER--
--I'M ON TOP OF IT.

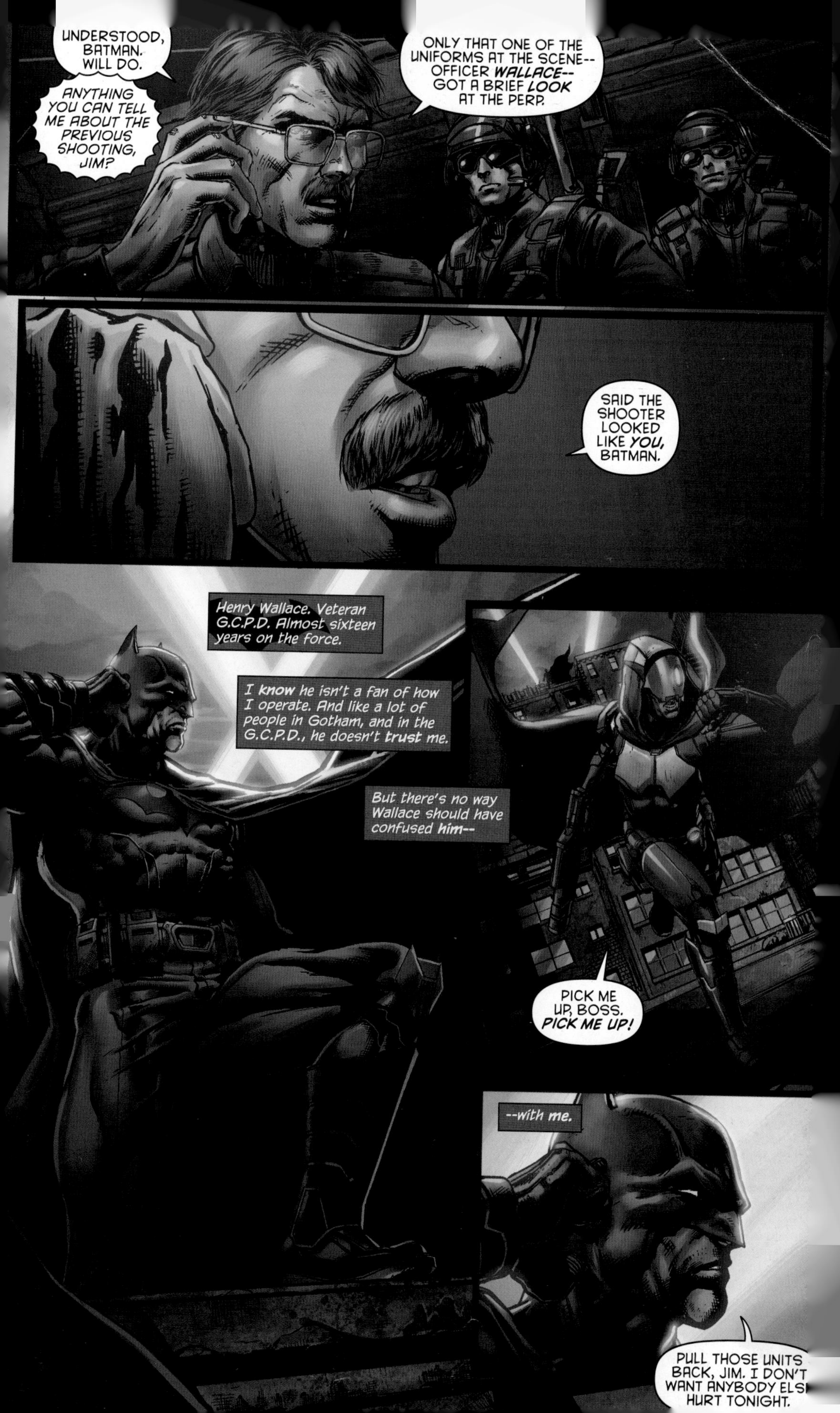
UNDERSTOOD, BATMAN. WILL DO.
ANYTHING YOU CAN TELL ME ABOUT THE PREVIOUS SHOOTING, JIM?
ONLY THAT ONE OF THE UNIFORMS AT THE SCENE-- OFFICER WALLACE-- GOT A BRIEF LOOK AT THE PERP.
SAID THE SHOOTER LOOKED LIKE YOU, BATMAN.
Henry Wallace. Veteran G.C.P.D. Almost sixteen years on the force.
I know he isn't a fan of how I operate. And like a lot of people in Gotham, and in the G.C.P.D., he doesn't trust me.
But there's no way Wallace should have confused him--
PICK ME UP, BOSS. PICK ME UP!
--with me.
PULL THOSE UNITS BACK, JIM. I DON'T WANT ANYBODY ELS HURT TONIGHT.

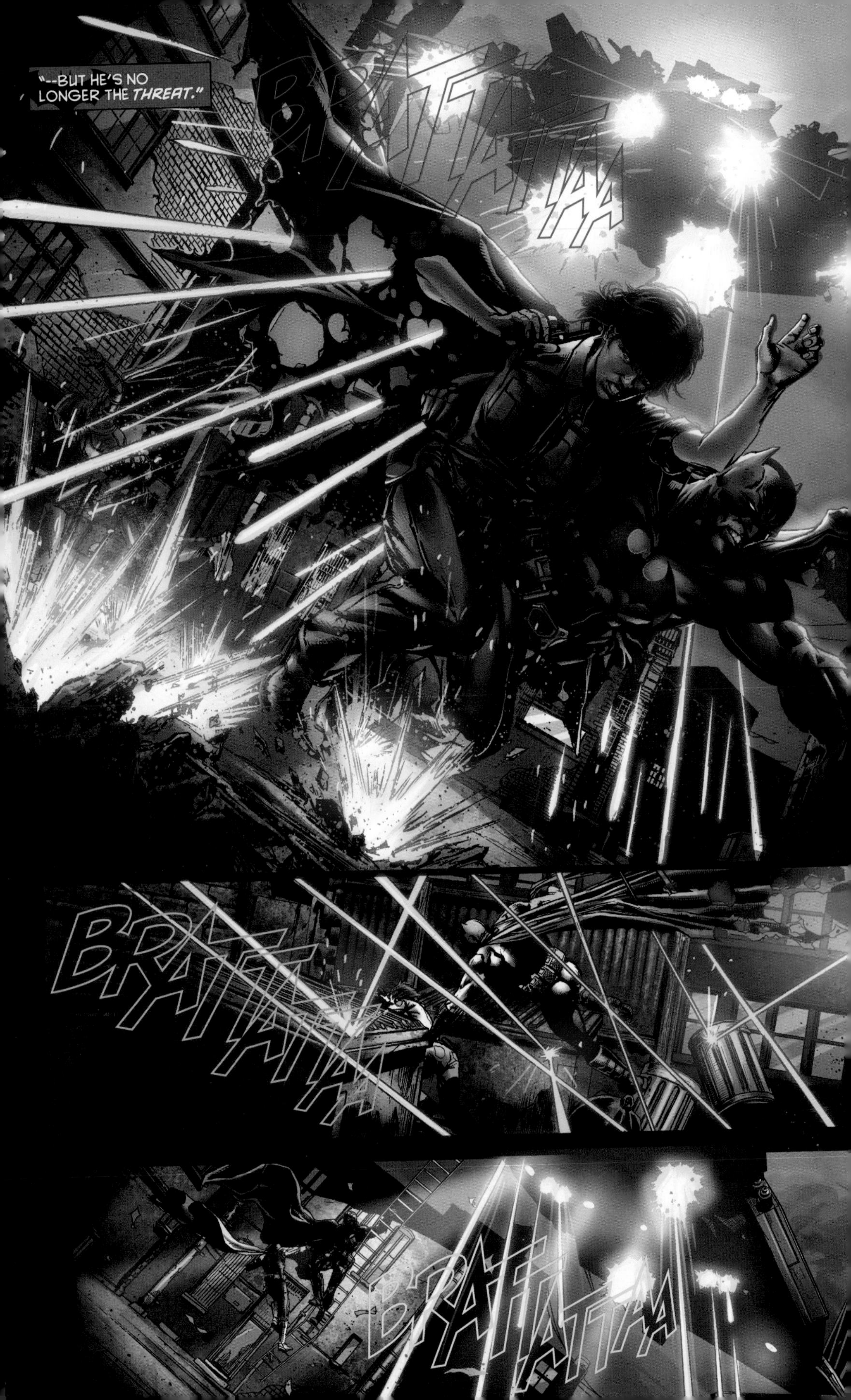
"--BUT HE'S NO LONGER THE *THREAT.*"

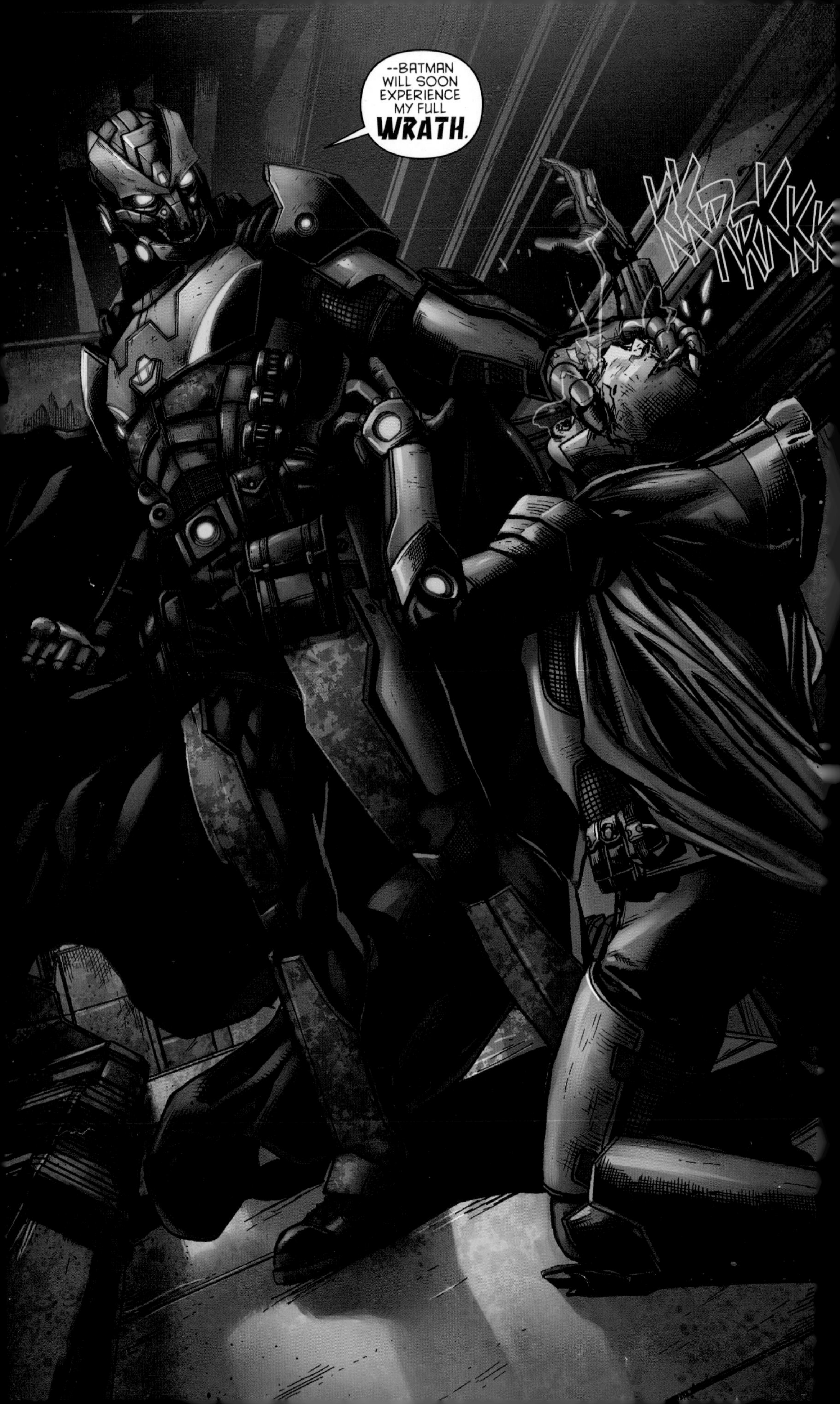
--BATMAN WILL SOON EXPERIENCE MY FULL **WRATH**.

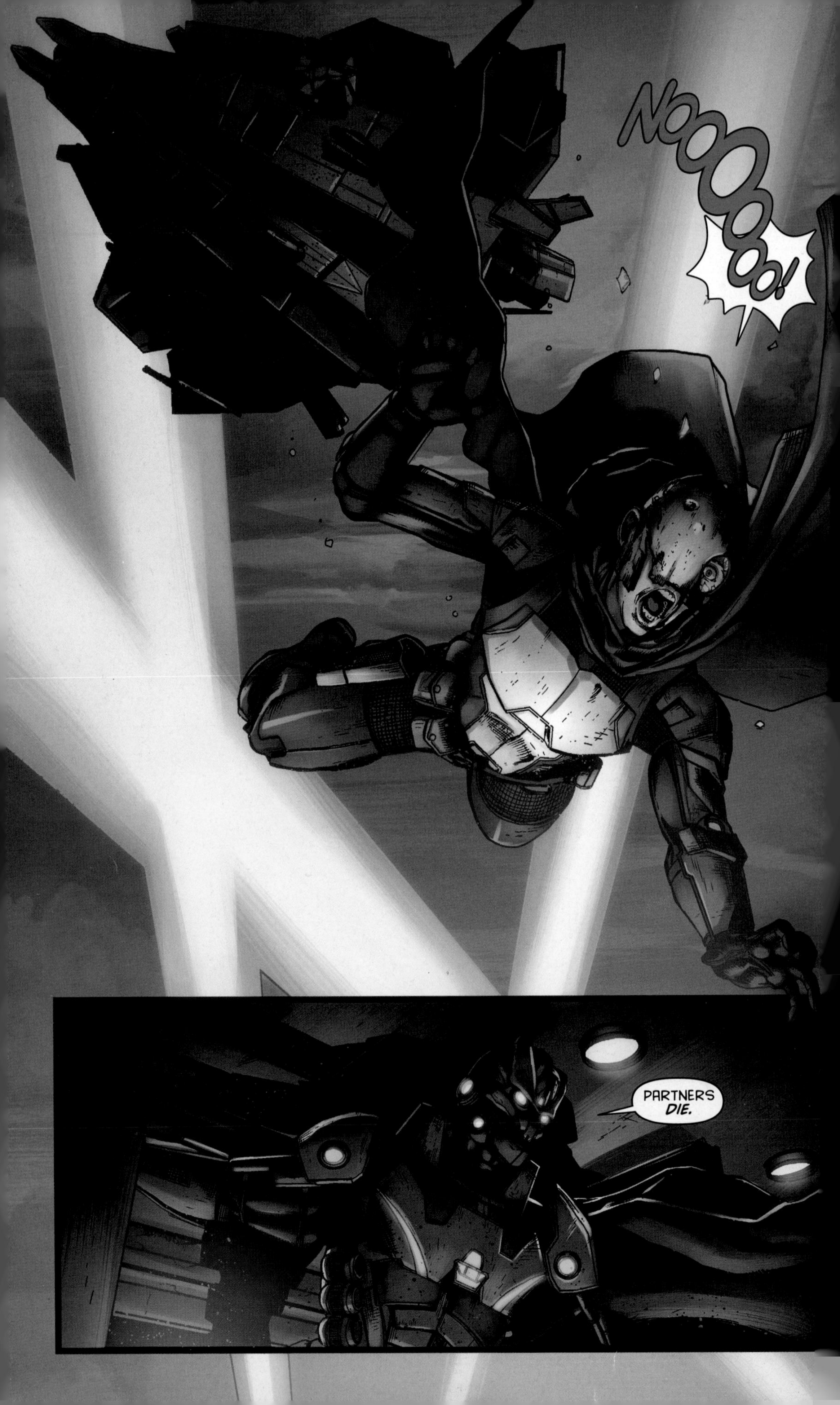
NOOOOOOOO!
PARTNERS DIE.

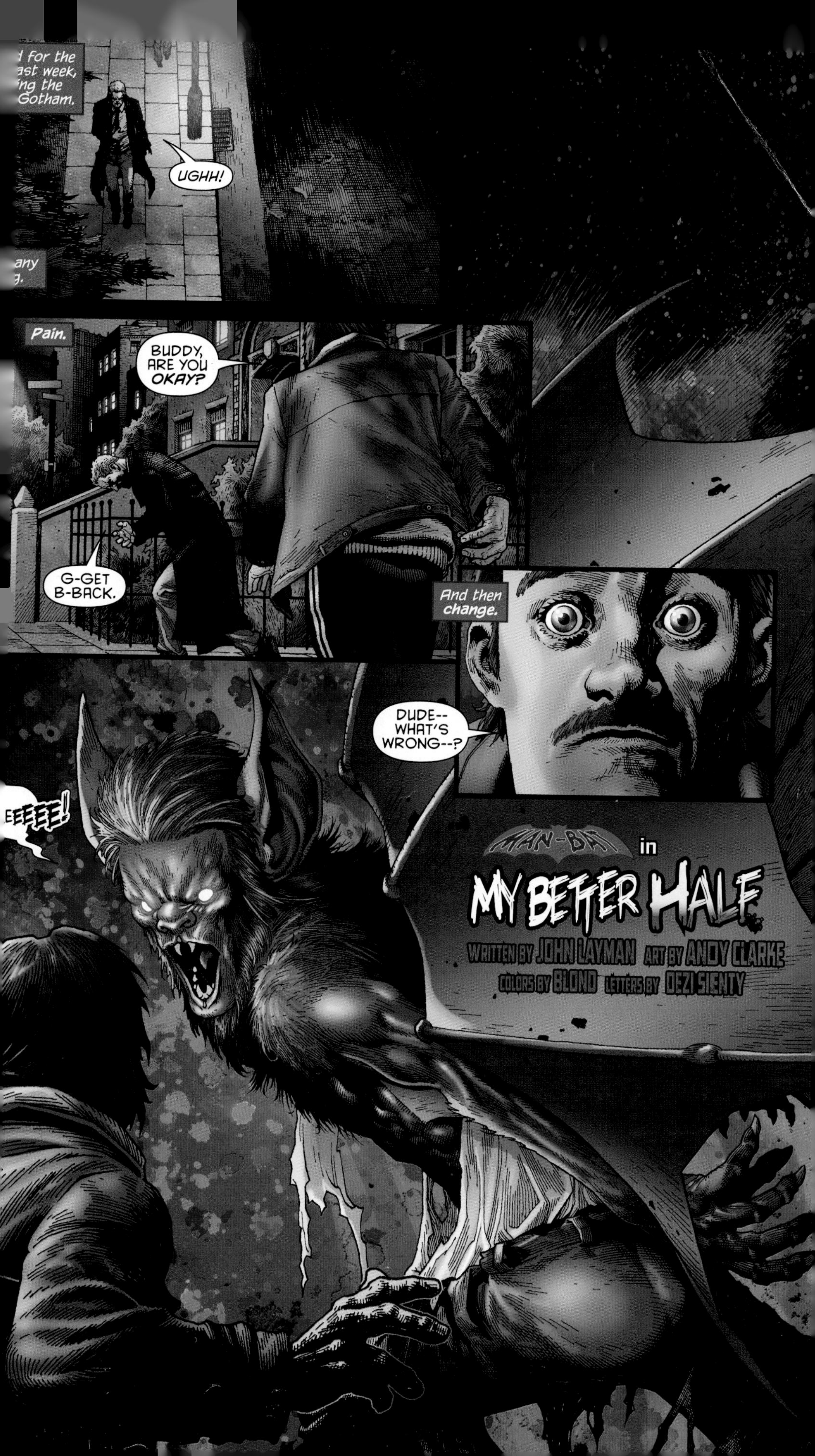
d for the
ast week,
ing the
Gotham.
UGHH!
any
g.
Pain.
BUDDY, ARE YOU OKAY?
G-GET B-BACK.
And then change.
DUDE-- WHAT'S WRONG--?
EEEEE!
MAN-BAT in
MY BETTER HALF
WRITTEN BY JOHN LAYMAN ART BY ANDY CLARKE
COLORS BY BLOND LETTERS BY DEZI SIENTY

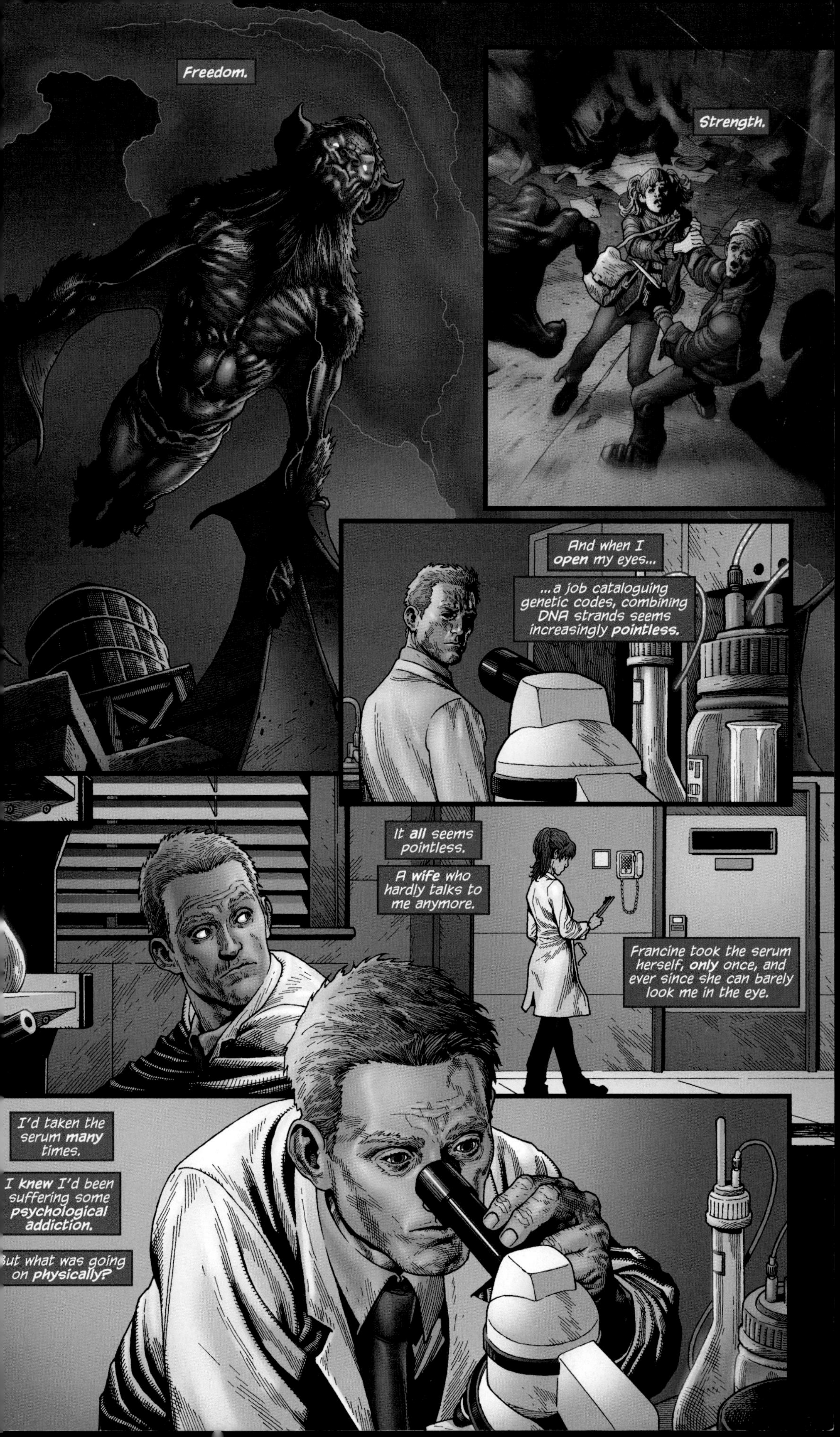
Freedom.
Strength.
And when I open my eyes...
...a job cataloguing genetic codes, combining DNA strands seems increasingly pointless.
It all seems pointless.
A wife who hardly talks to me anymore.
Francine took the serum herself, only once, and ever since she can barely look me in the eye.
I'd taken the serum many times.
I knew I'd been suffering some psychological addiction.
But what was going on physically?

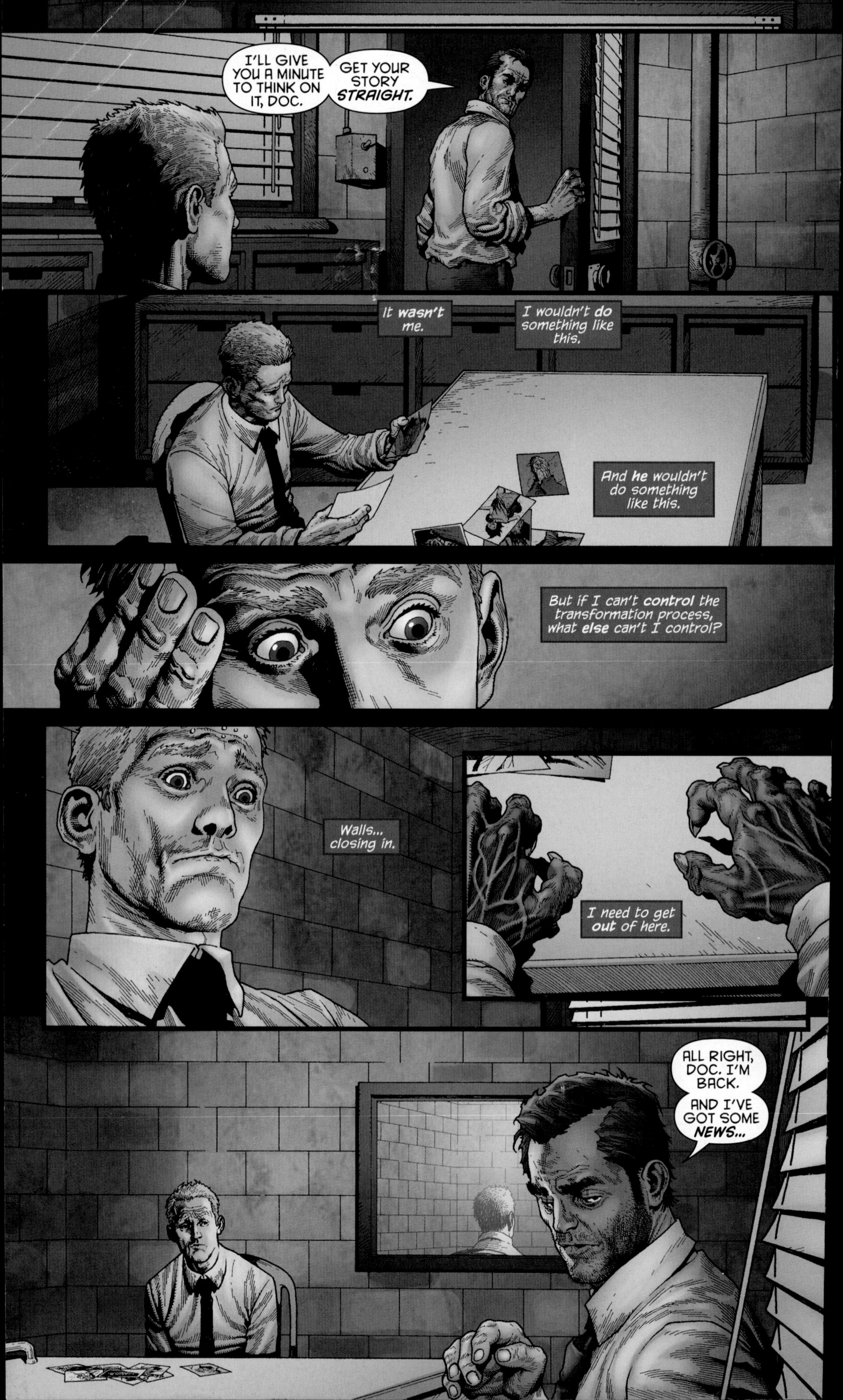

I'LL GIVE YOU A MINUTE TO THINK ON IT, DOC.
GET YOUR STORY *STRAIGHT.*
It **wasn't** me.
I wouldn't **do** something like this.
And **he** wouldn't do something like this.
But if I can't **control** the transformation process, what **else** can't I control?
Walls... closing in.
I need to get **out** of here.
ALL RIGHT, DOC. I'M BACK.
AND I'VE GOT SOME *NEWS...*

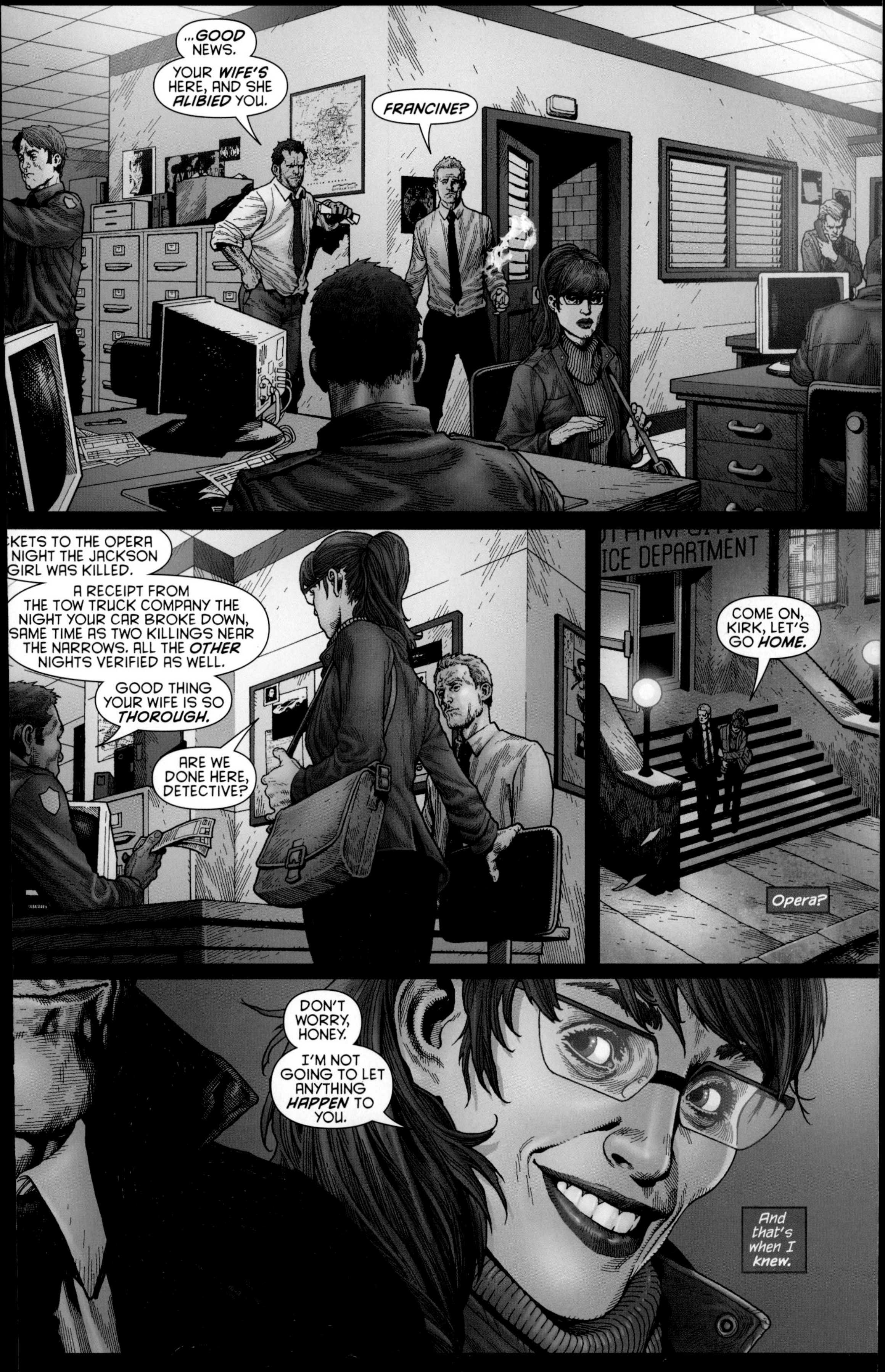
...GOOD NEWS.
YOUR WIFE'S HERE, AND SHE ALIBIED YOU.
FRANCINE?
CKETS TO THE OPERA NIGHT THE JACKSON GIRL WAS KILLED.
A RECEIPT FROM THE TOW TRUCK COMPANY THE NIGHT YOUR CAR BROKE DOWN, SAME TIME AS TWO KILLINGS NEAR THE NARROWS. ALL THE OTHER NIGHTS VERIFIED AS WELL.
GOOD THING YOUR WIFE IS SO THOROUGH.
ARE WE DONE HERE, DETECTIVE?
ICE DEPARTMENT
COME ON, KIRK, LET'S GO HOME.
Opera?
DON'T WORRY, HONEY.
I'M NOT GOING TO LET ANYTHING HAPPEN TO YOU.
And that's when I knew.

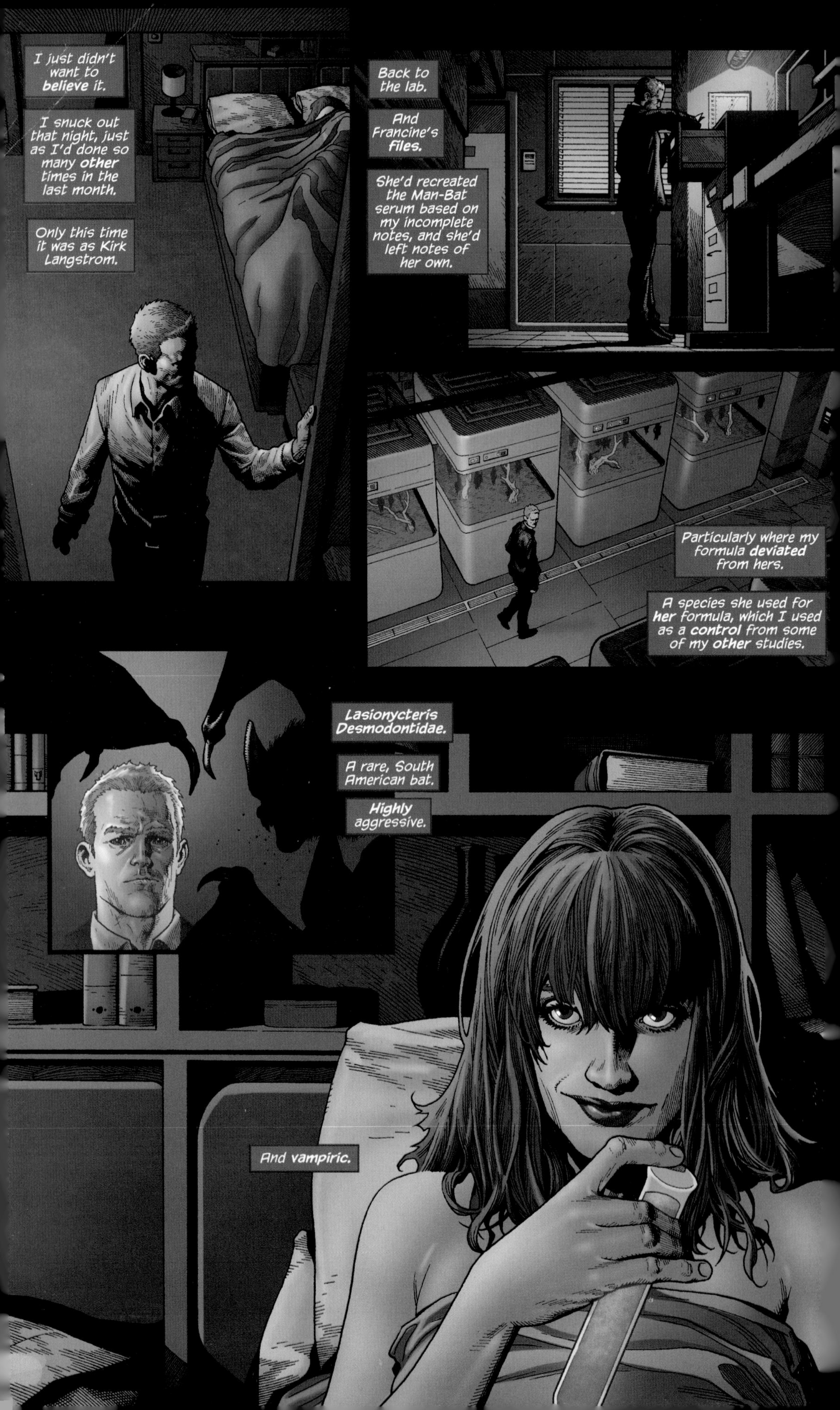
I just didn't want to **believe** it.
I snuck out that night, just as I'd done so many **other** times in the last month.
Only this time it was as Kirk Langstrom.
Back to the lab.
And Francine's **files.**
She'd recreated the Man-Bat serum based on my incomplete notes, and she'd left notes of her own.
Particularly where my formula **deviated** from hers.
A species she used for **her** formula, which I used as a **control** from some of my **other** studies.
Lasionycteris Desmodontidae.
A rare, South American bat.
Highly aggressive.
And **vampiric.**

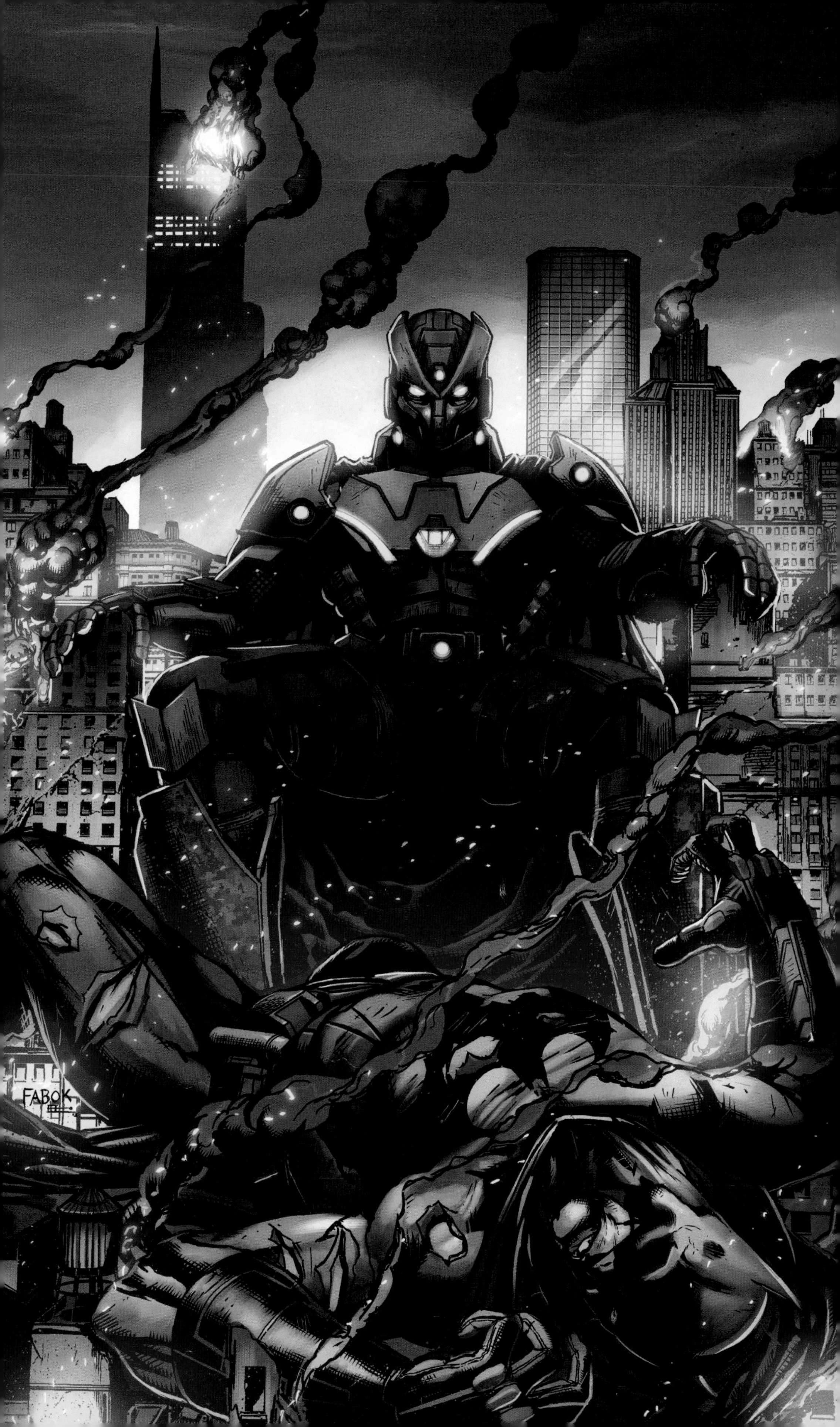
FABOK

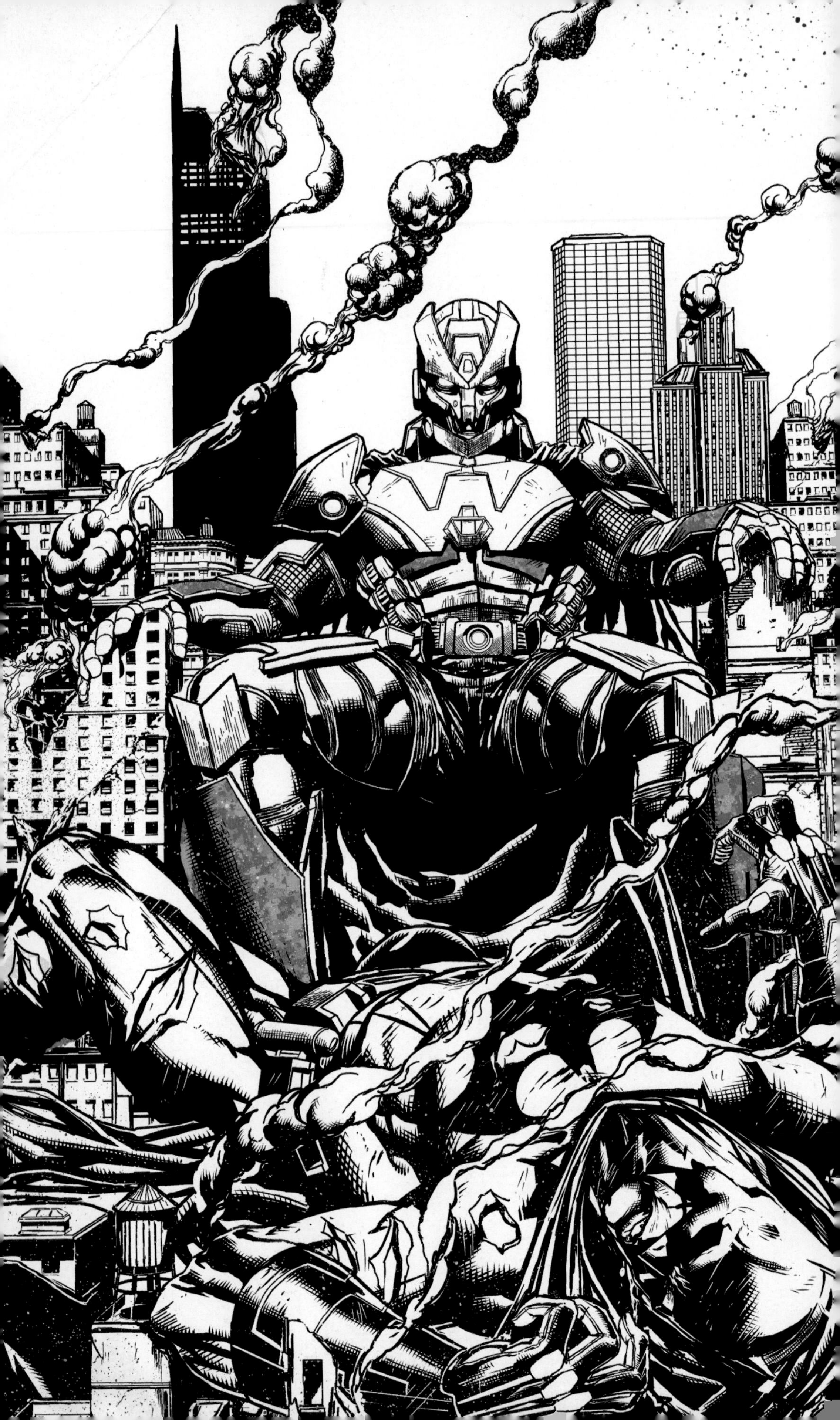

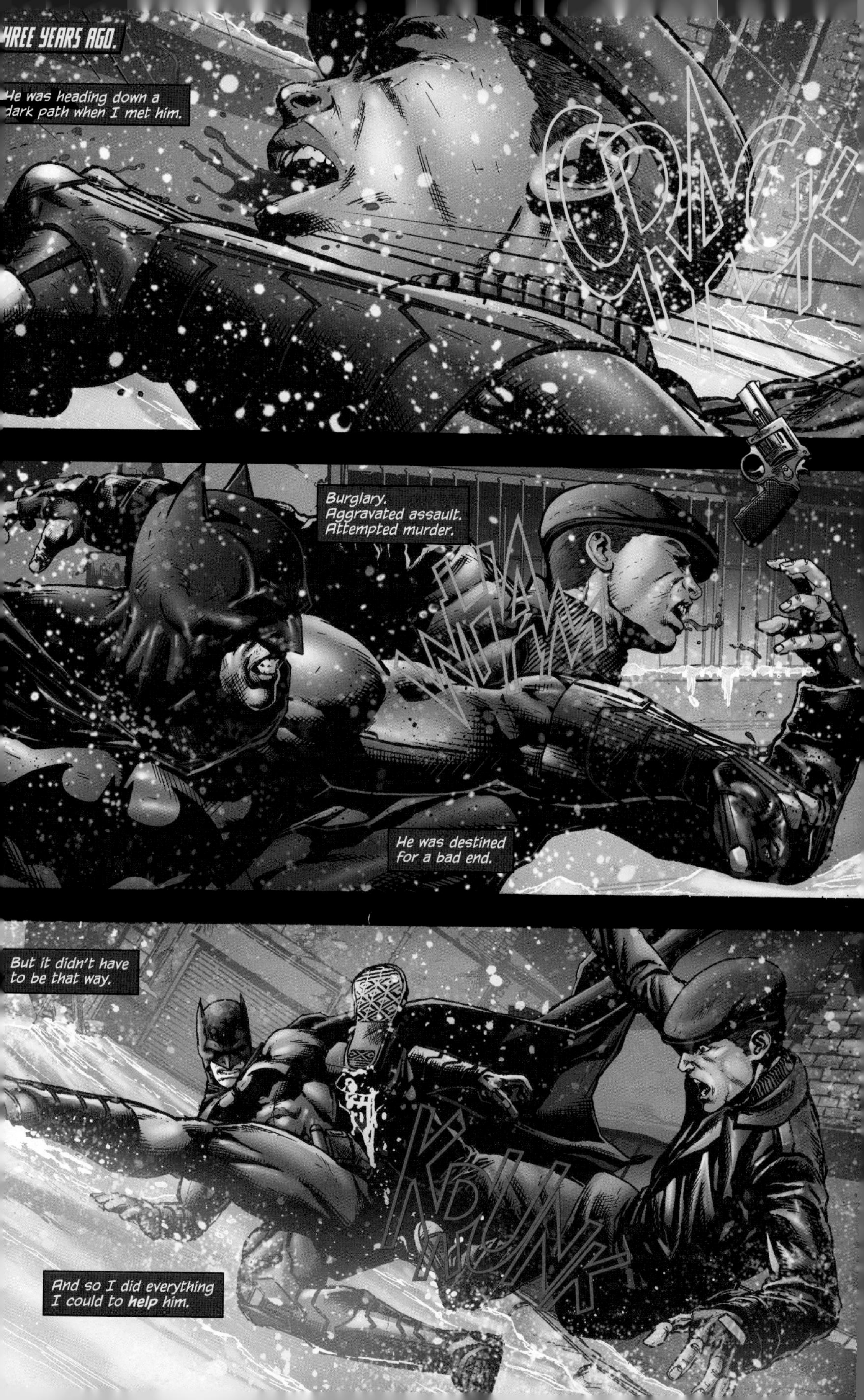
HREE YEARS AGO.
He was heading down a dark path when I met him.
CRACK
Burglary. Aggravated assault. Attempted murder.
He was destined for a bad end.
But it didn't have to be that way.
And so I did everything I could to **help** him.

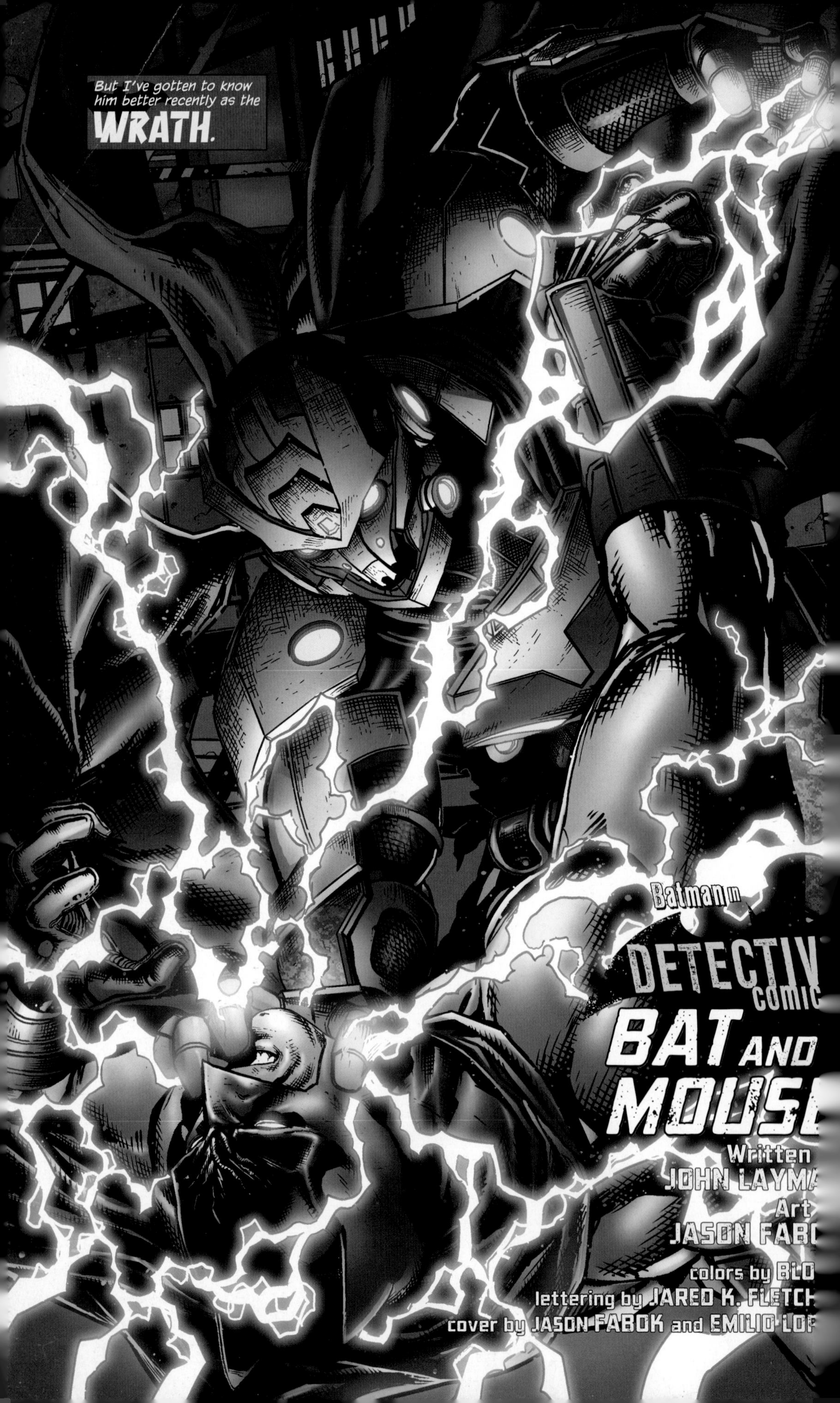
But I've gotten to know him better recently as the WRATH.
Batman in
DETECTIV
comic
BAT AND
MOUS
Written
JOHN LAYMA
Art
JASON FABO
colors by BLO
lettering by JARED K. FLETCH
cover by JASON FABOK and EMILIO LOF

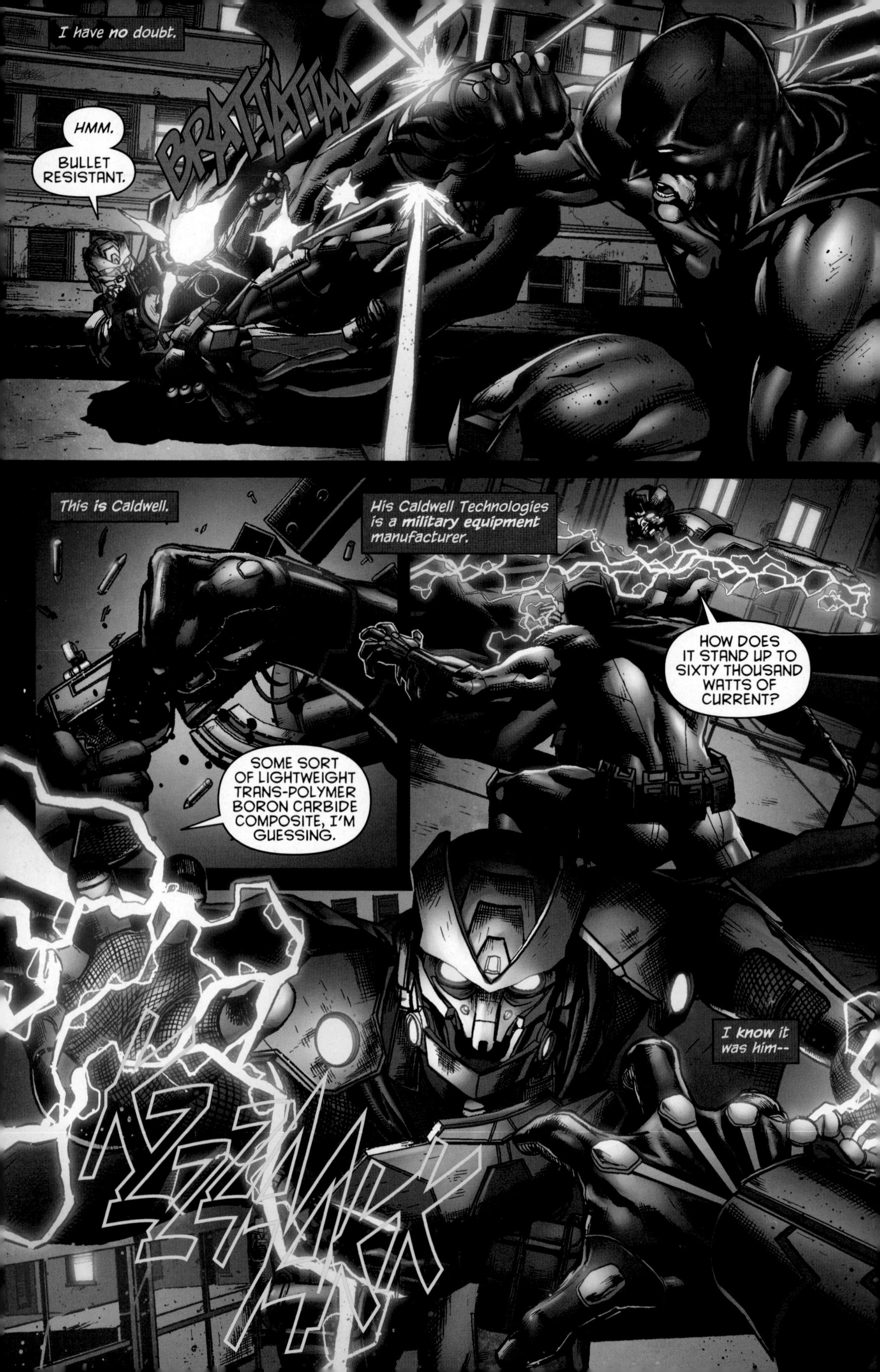
I have no doubt.
HMM.
BULLET RESISTANT.
BRATTATTAA
This is Caldwell.
His Caldwell Technologies is a military equipment manufacturer.
HOW DOES IT STAND UP TO SIXTY THOUSAND WATTS OF CURRENT?
SOME SORT OF LIGHTWEIGHT TRANS-POLYMER BORON CARBIDE COMPOSITE, I'M GUESSING.
I know it was him--

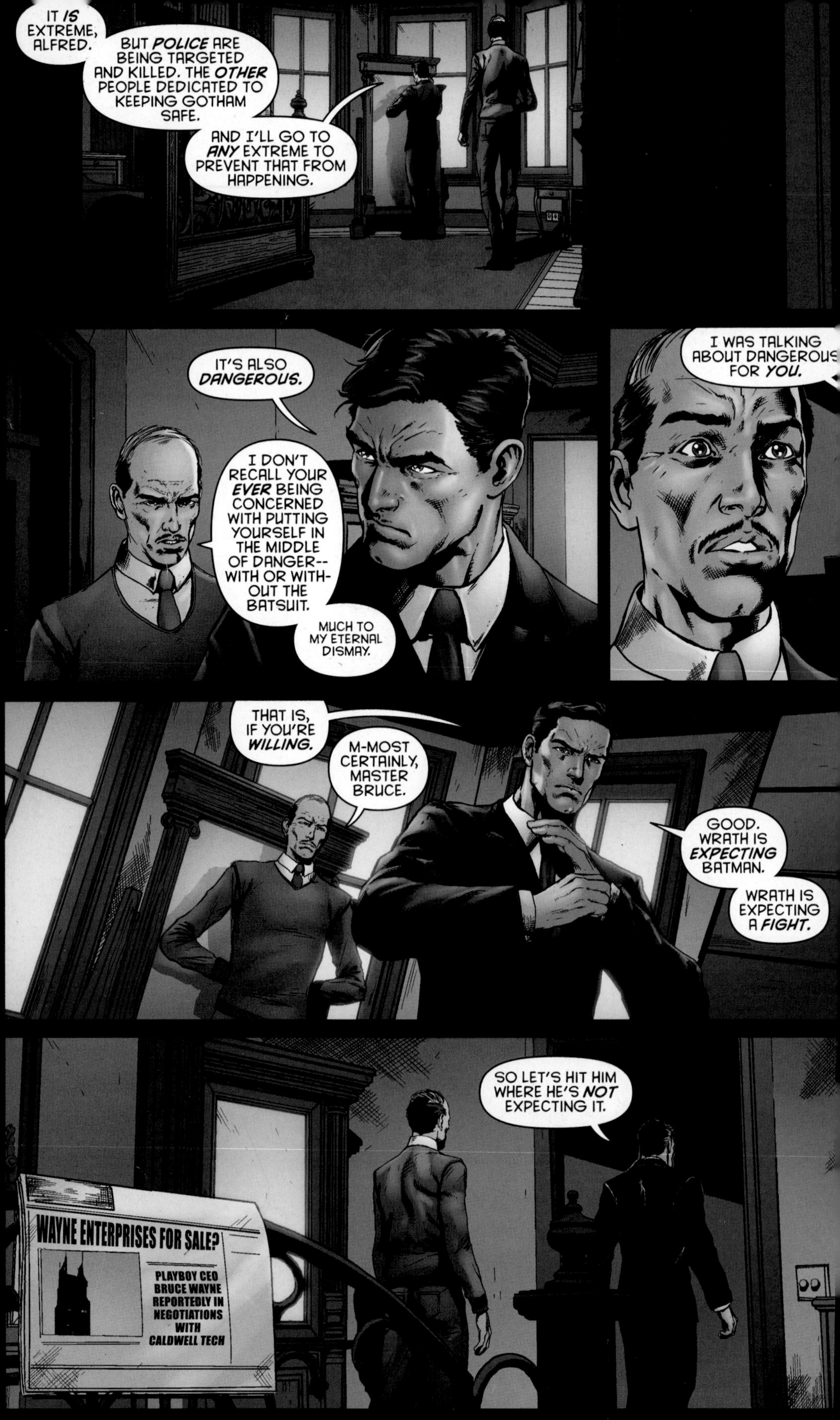
IT IS EXTREME, ALFRED.
BUT POLICE ARE BEING TARGETED AND KILLED. THE OTHER PEOPLE DEDICATED TO KEEPING GOTHAM SAFE.
AND I'LL GO TO ANY EXTREME TO PREVENT THAT FROM HAPPENING.
IT'S ALSO DANGEROUS.
I DON'T RECALL YOUR EVER BEING CONCERNED WITH PUTTING YOURSELF IN THE MIDDLE OF DANGER-- WITH OR WITHOUT THE BATSUIT.
MUCH TO MY ETERNAL DISMAY.
I WAS TALKING ABOUT DANGEROUS FOR YOU.
THAT IS, IF YOU'RE WILLING.
M-MOST CERTAINLY, MASTER BRUCE.
GOOD. WRATH IS EXPECTING BATMAN.
WRATH IS EXPECTING A FIGHT.
SO LET'S HIT HIM WHERE HE'S NOT EXPECTING IT.
WAYNE ENTERPRISES FOR SALE?
PLAYBOY CEO BRUCE WAYNE REPORTEDLY IN NEGOTIATIONS WITH CALDWELL TECH

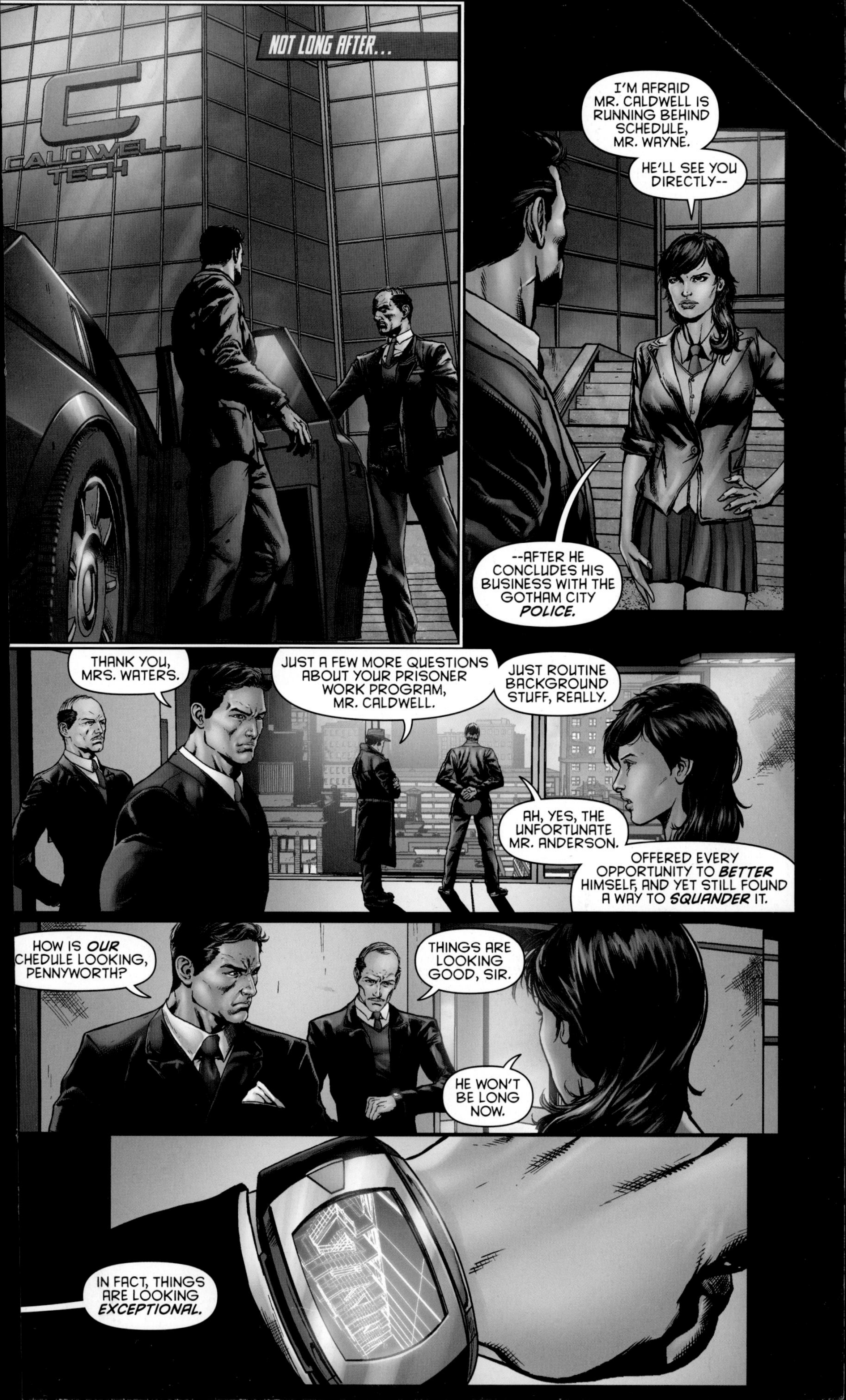
NOT LONG AFTER...
CALDWELL TECH
I'M AFRAID MR. CALDWELL IS RUNNING BEHIND SCHEDULE, MR. WAYNE.
HE'LL SEE YOU DIRECTLY--
--AFTER HE CONCLUDES HIS BUSINESS WITH THE GOTHAM CITY *POLICE.*
THANK YOU, MRS. WATERS.
JUST A FEW MORE QUESTIONS ABOUT YOUR PRISONER WORK PROGRAM, MR. CALDWELL.
JUST ROUTINE BACKGROUND STUFF, REALLY.
AH, YES, THE UNFORTUNATE MR. ANDERSON.
OFFERED EVERY OPPORTUNITY TO *BETTER* HIMSELF, AND YET STILL FOUND A WAY TO *SQUANDER* IT.
HOW IS *OUR* CHEDULE LOOKING, PENNYWORTH?
THINGS ARE LOOKING GOOD, SIR.
HE WON'T BE LONG NOW.
IN FACT, THINGS ARE LOOKING *EXCEPTIONAL.*

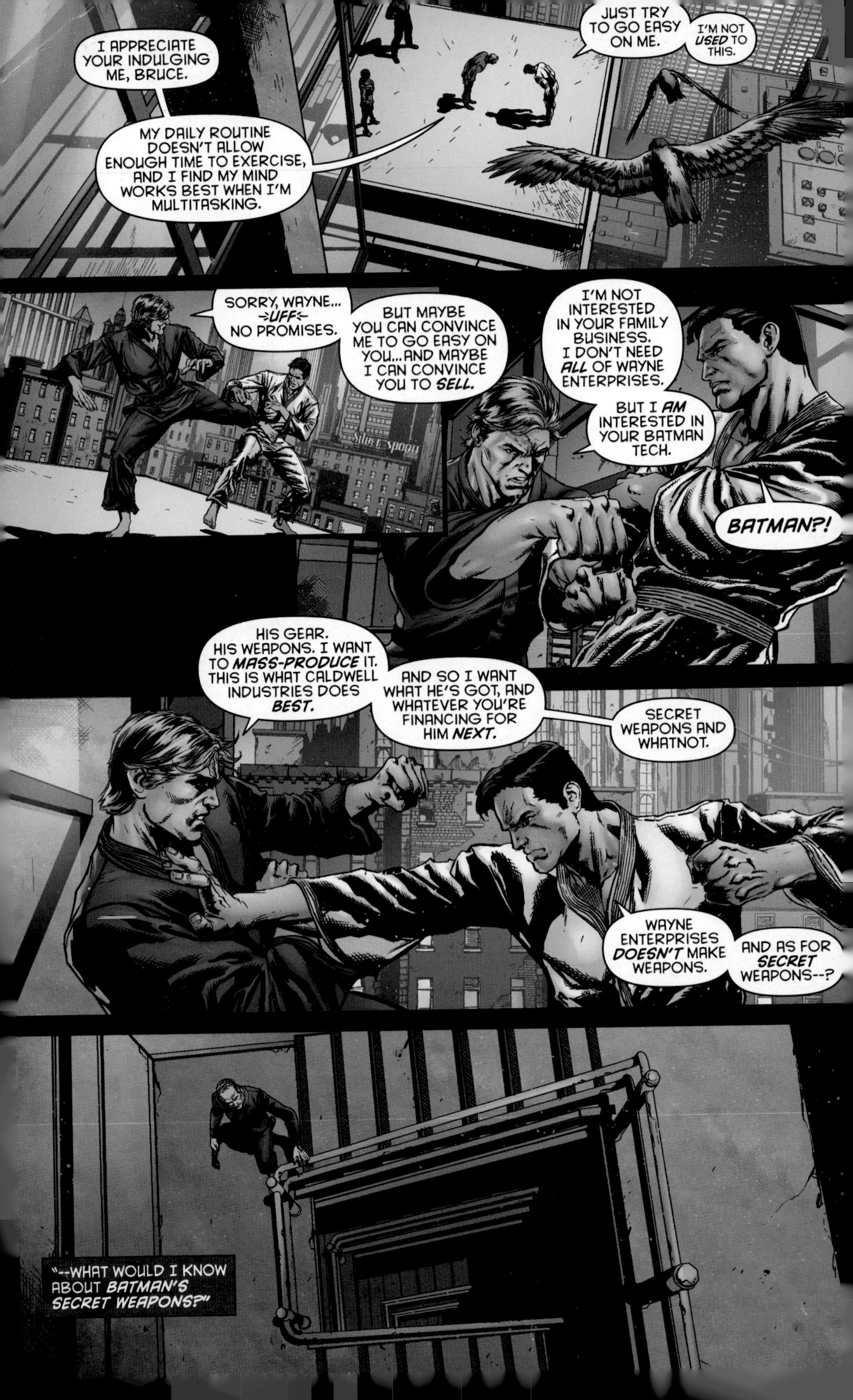
I APPRECIATE YOUR INDULGING ME, BRUCE.
MY DAILY ROUTINE DOESN'T ALLOW ENOUGH TIME TO EXERCISE, AND I FIND MY MIND WORKS BEST WHEN I'M MULTITASKING.
JUST TRY TO GO EASY ON ME.
I'M NOT *USED* TO THIS.
SORRY, WAYNE... *UFF* NO PROMISES.
BUT MAYBE YOU CAN CONVINCE ME TO GO EASY ON YOU...AND MAYBE I CAN CONVINCE YOU TO *SELL.*
I'M NOT INTERESTED IN YOUR FAMILY BUSINESS. I DON'T NEED *ALL* OF WAYNE ENTERPRISES.
BUT I *AM* INTERESTED IN YOUR BATMAN TECH.
BATMAN?!
HIS GEAR. HIS WEAPONS. I WANT TO *MASS-PRODUCE* IT. THIS IS WHAT CALDWELL INDUSTRIES DOES *BEST.*
AND SO I WANT WHAT HE'S GOT, AND WHATEVER YOU'RE FINANCING FOR HIM *NEXT.*
SECRET WEAPONS AND WHATNOT.
WAYNE ENTERPRISES *DOESN'T* MAKE WEAPONS.
AND AS FOR *SECRET* WEAPONS--?
"--WHAT WOULD I KNOW ABOUT *BATMAN'S SECRET WEAPONS?*"

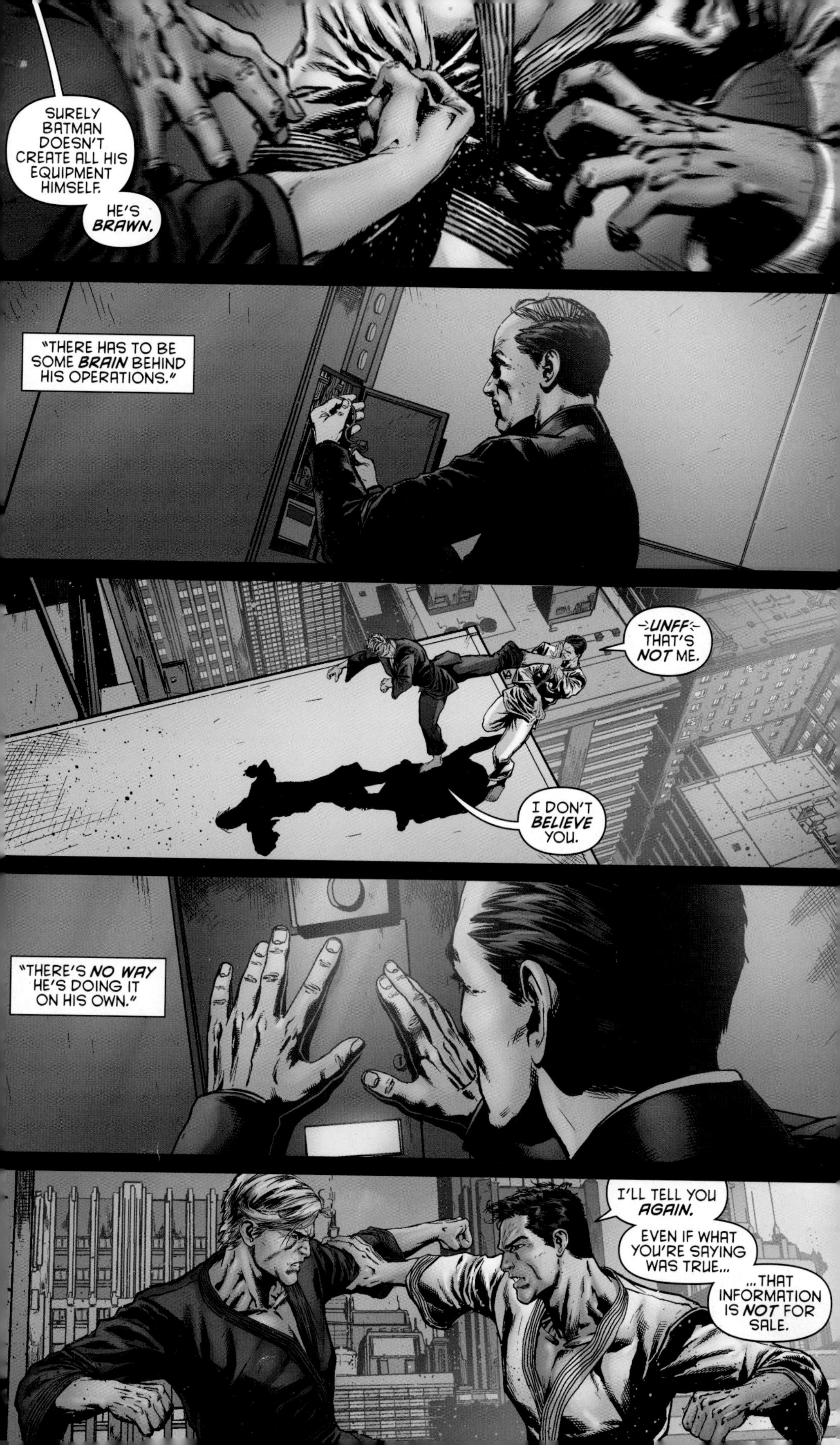
SURELY BATMAN DOESN'T CREATE ALL HIS EQUIPMENT HIMSELF.
HE'S BRAWN.
"THERE HAS TO BE SOME BRAIN BEHIND HIS OPERATIONS."
-UNFF- THAT'S NOT ME.
I DON'T BELIEVE YOU.
"THERE'S NO WAY HE'S DOING IT ON HIS OWN."
I'LL TELL YOU AGAIN.
EVEN IF WHAT YOU'RE SAYING WAS TRUE...
...THAT INFORMATION IS NOT FOR SALE.

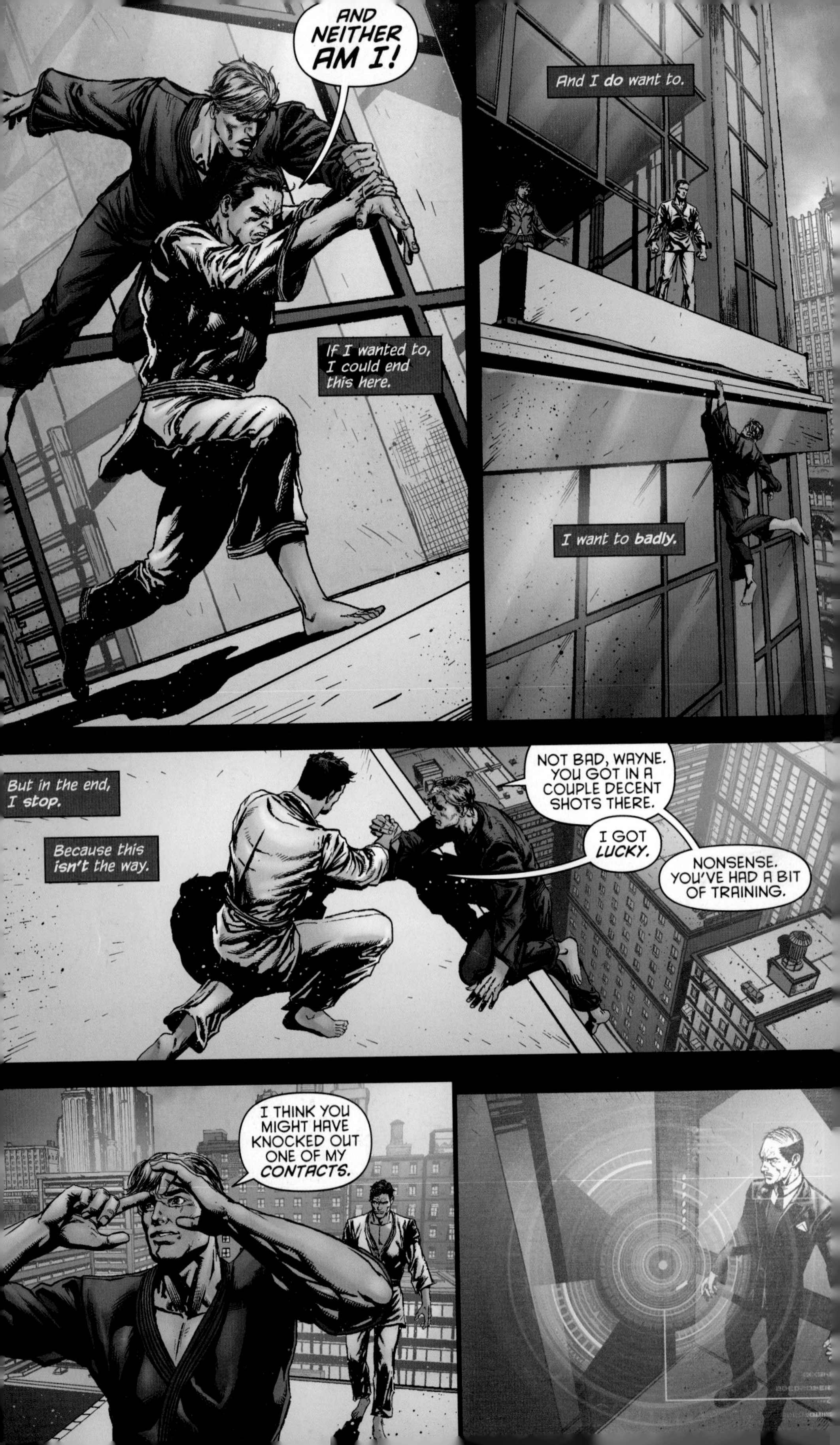
AND NEITHER AM I!
If I wanted to, I could end this here.
And I do want to.
I want to badly.
But in the end, I stop.
Because this isn't the way.
NOT BAD, WAYNE. YOU GOT IN A COUPLE DECENT SHOTS THERE.
I GOT LUCKY.
NONSENSE. YOU'VE HAD A BIT OF TRAINING.
I THINK YOU MIGHT HAVE KNOCKED OUT ONE OF MY CONTACTS.

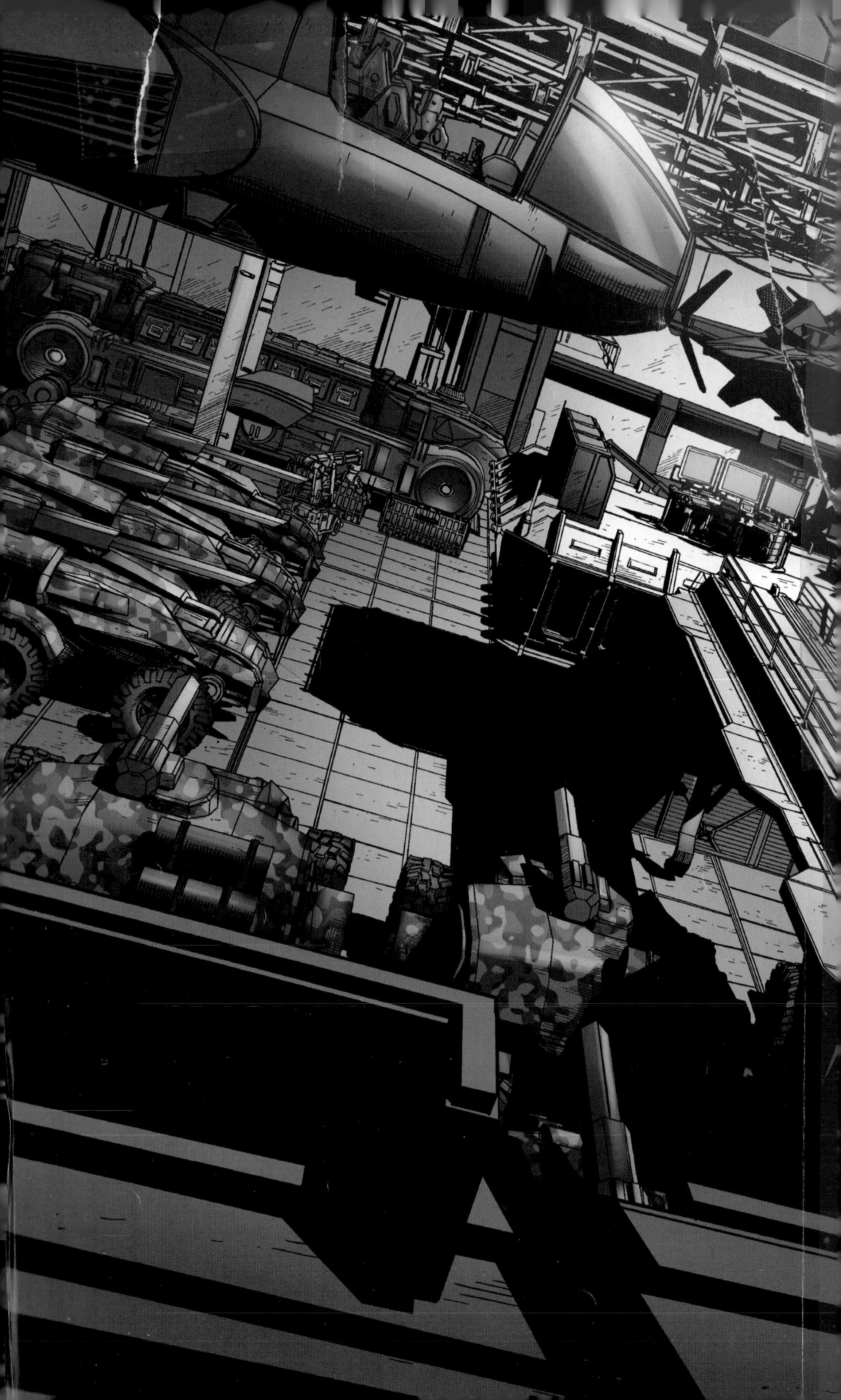

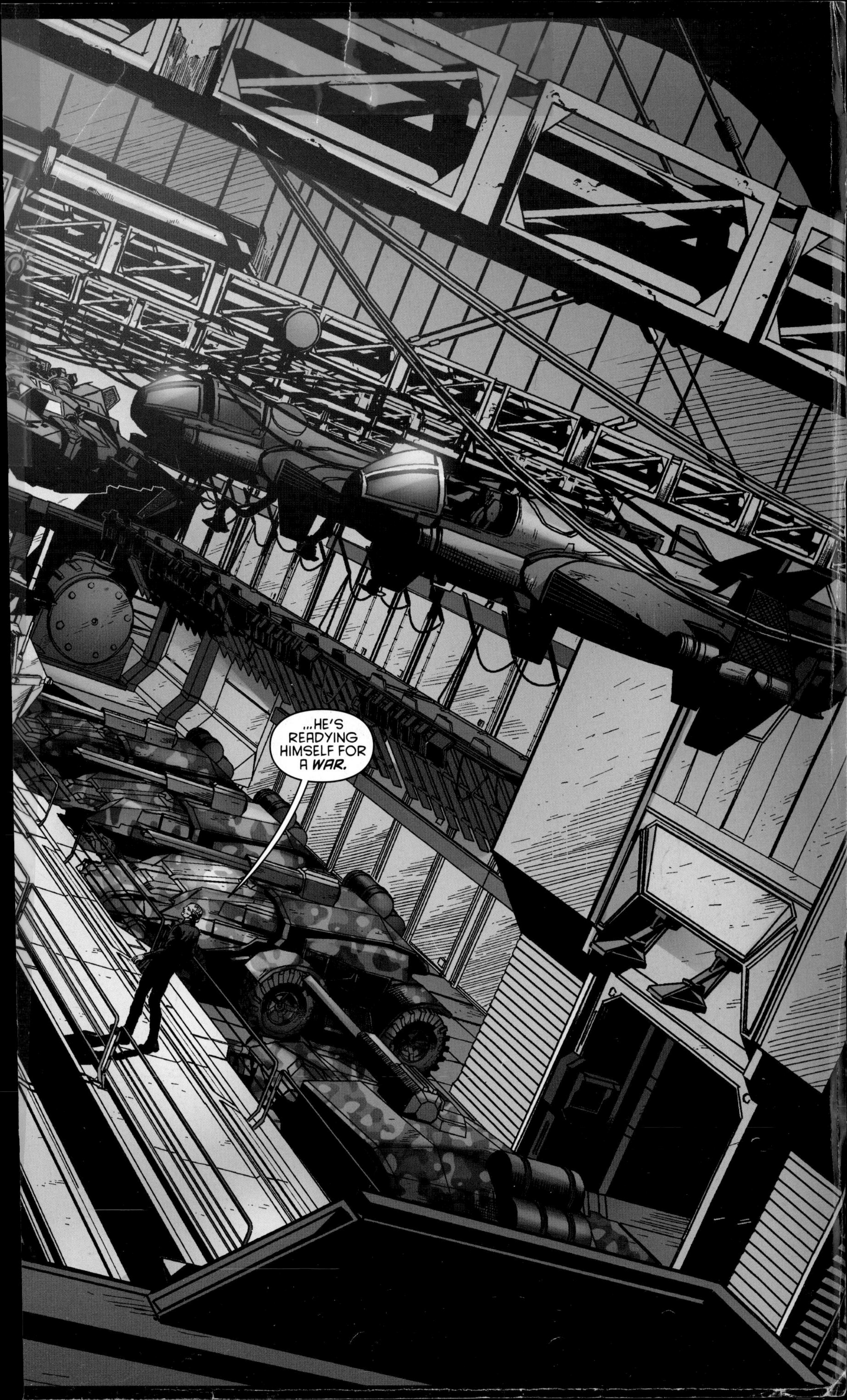
...HE'S READYING HIMSELF FOR A *WAR.*

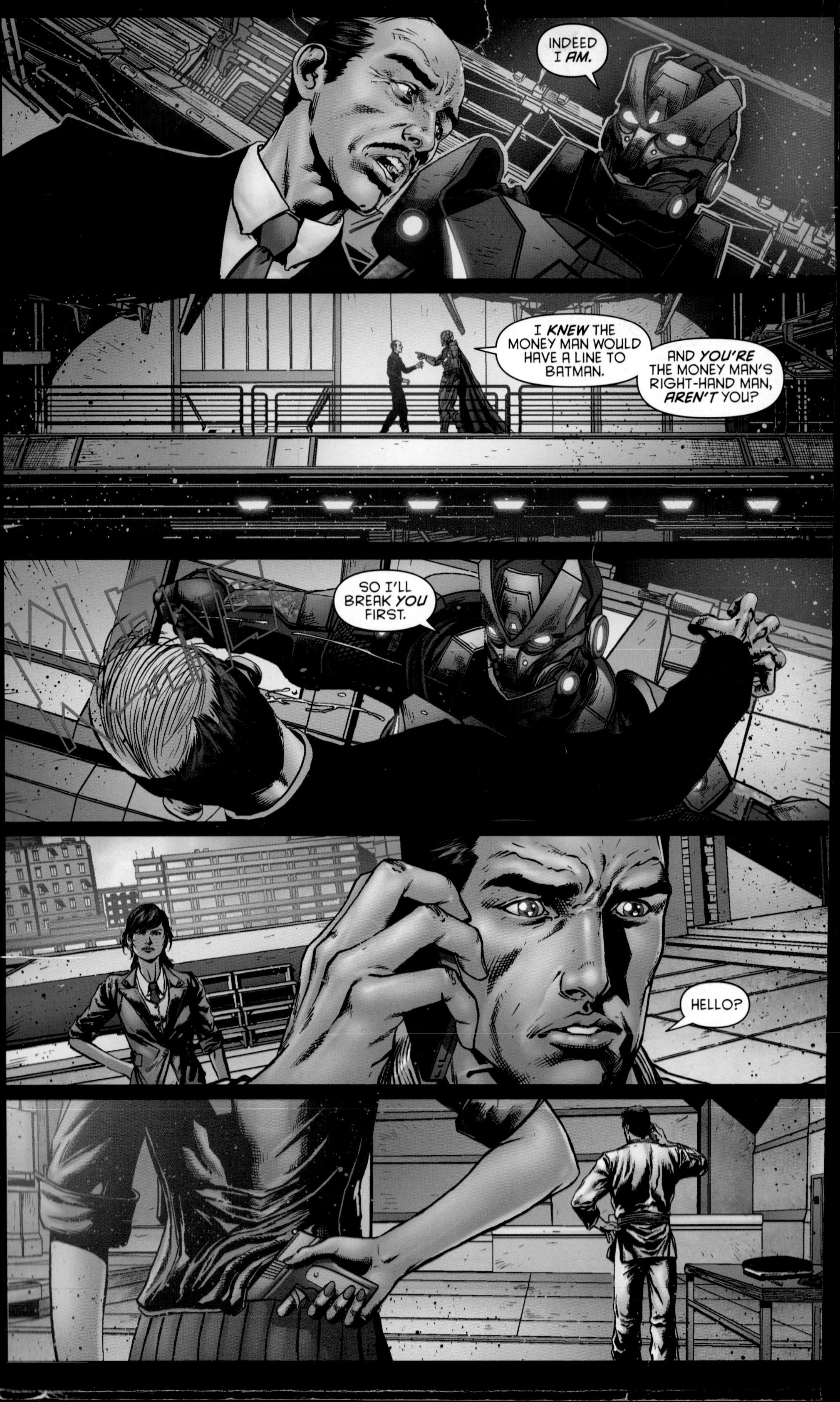
INDEED I **AM.**
I **KNEW** THE MONEY MAN WOULD HAVE A LINE TO BATMAN.
AND **YOU'RE** THE MONEY MAN'S RIGHT-HAND MAN, **AREN'T** YOU?
SO I'LL BREAK **YOU** FIRST.
HELLO?

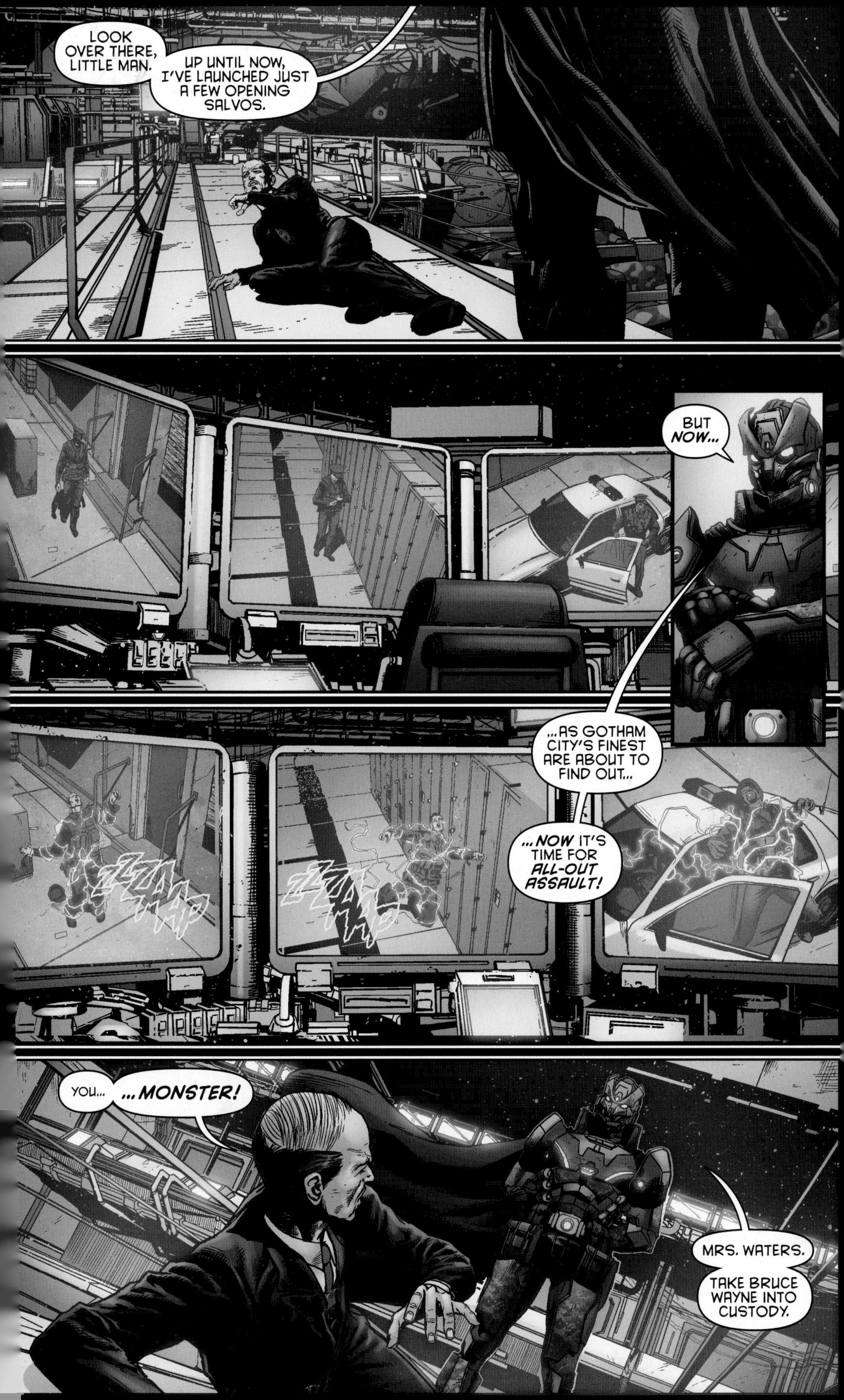
LOOK OVER THERE, LITTLE MAN.
UP UNTIL NOW, I'VE LAUNCHED JUST A FEW OPENING SALVOS.
BUT NOW...
...AS GOTHAM CITY'S FINEST ARE ABOUT TO FIND OUT...
...NOW IT'S TIME FOR ALL-OUT ASSAULT!
ZZZAP
ZZZAP
YOU...
...MONSTER!
MRS. WATERS.
TAKE BRUCE WAYNE INTO CUSTODY.

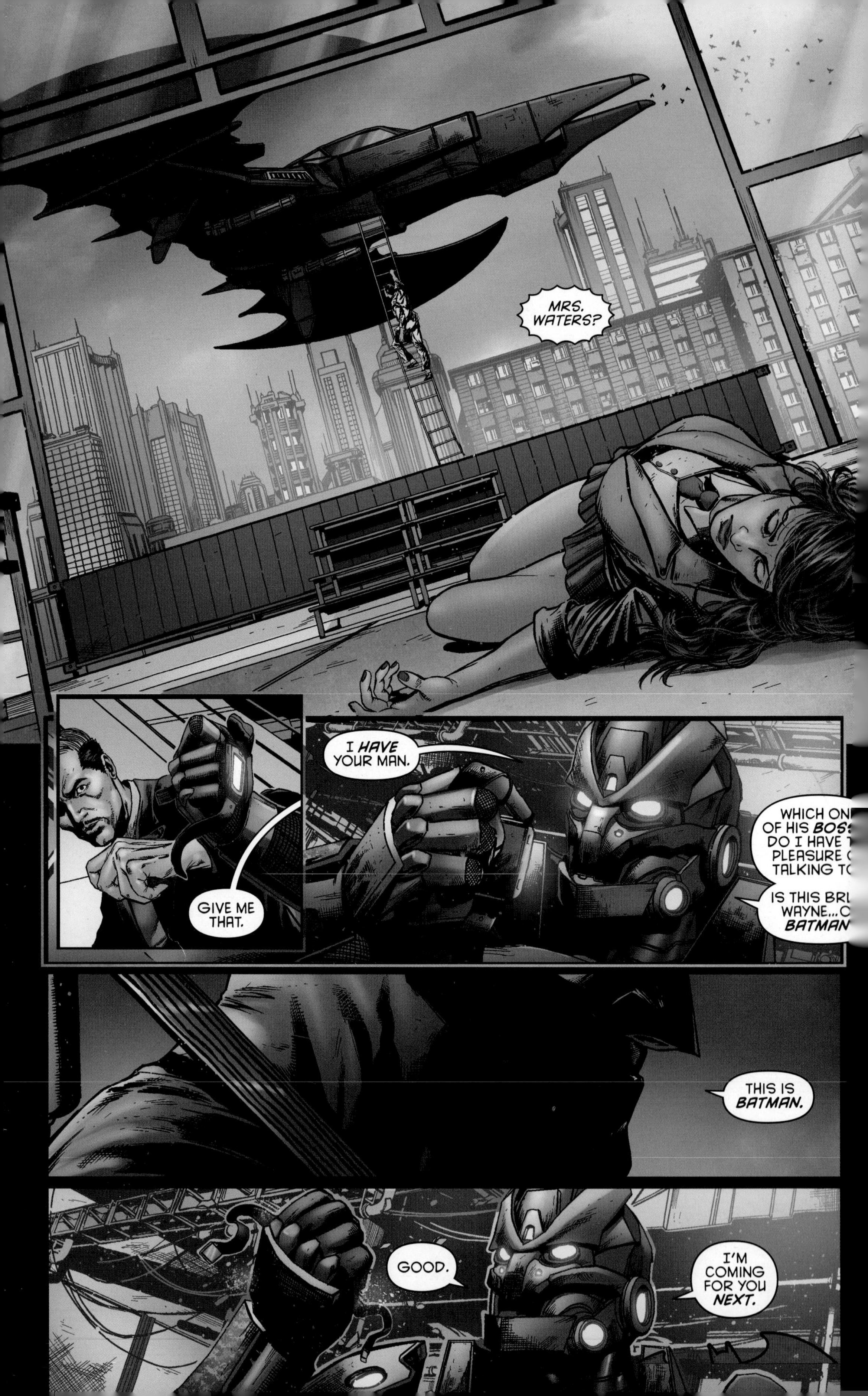

MRS. WATERS?
GIVE ME THAT.
I *HAVE* YOUR MAN.
WHICH ON
OF HIS *BOS*
DO I HAVE T
PLEASURE O
TALKING TO
IS THIS BRU
WAYNE...O
BATMAN
THIS IS *BATMAN.*
GOOD.
I'M COMING FOR YOU *NEXT.*

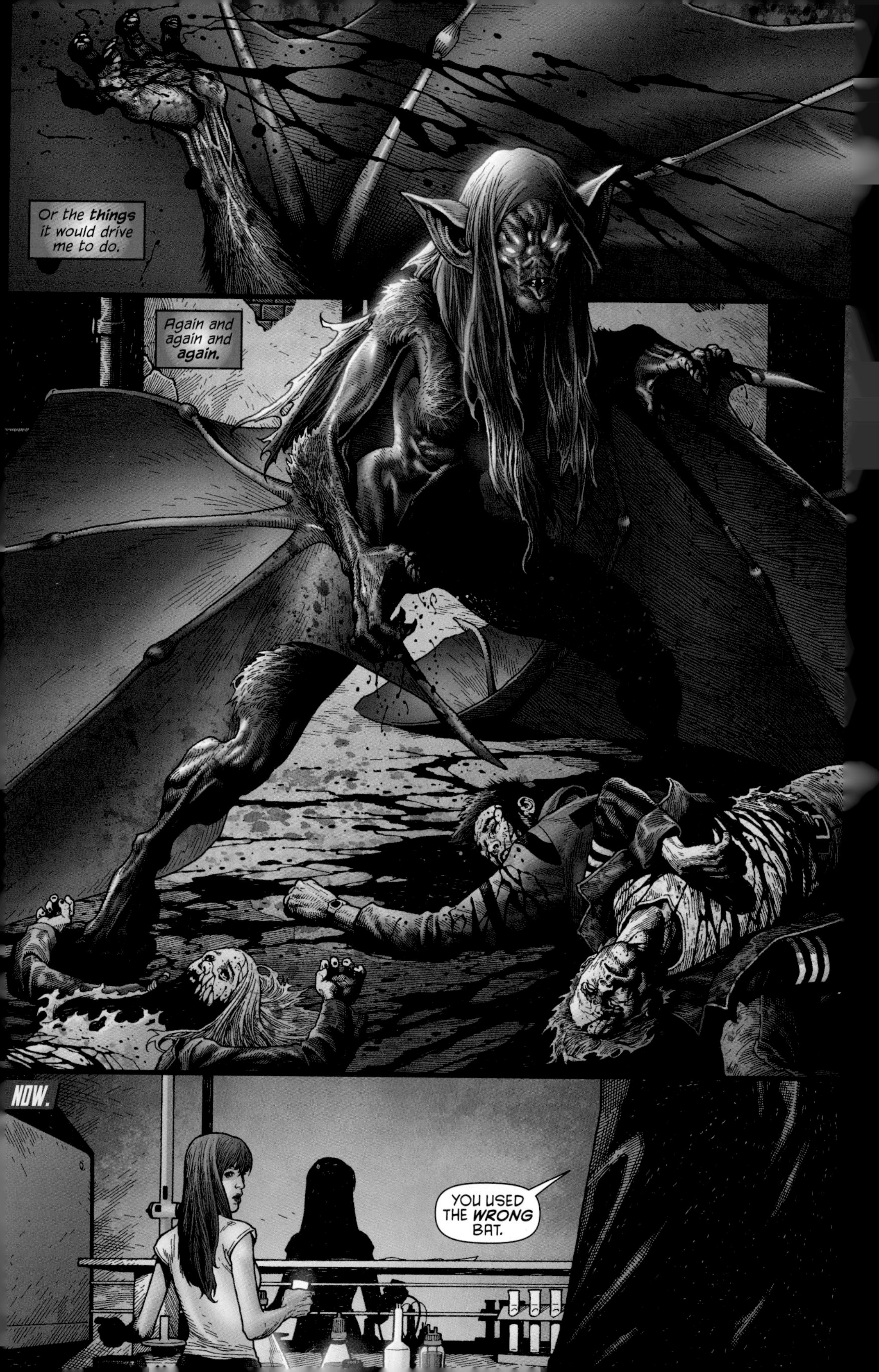
Or the things it would drive me to do.
Again and again and again.
NOW.
YOU USED THE WRONG BAT.

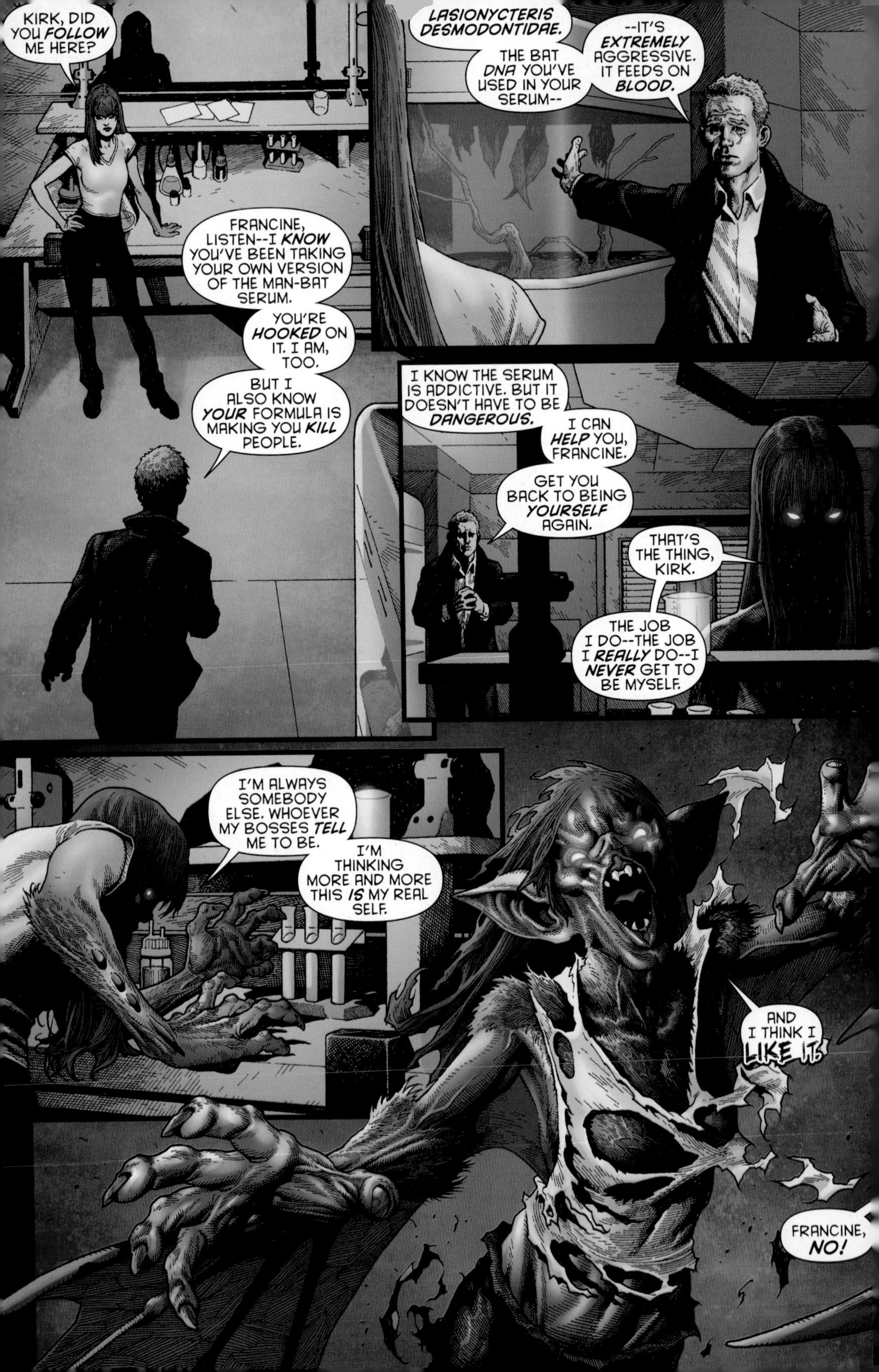
KIRK, DID YOU FOLLOW ME HERE?
LASIONYCTERIS DESMODONTIDAE.
THE BAT DNA YOU'VE USED IN YOUR SERUM--
--IT'S EXTREMELY AGGRESSIVE. IT FEEDS ON BLOOD.
FRANCINE, LISTEN--I KNOW YOU'VE BEEN TAKING YOUR OWN VERSION OF THE MAN-BAT SERUM.
YOU'RE HOOKED ON IT. I AM, TOO.
BUT I ALSO KNOW YOUR FORMULA IS MAKING YOU KILL PEOPLE.
I KNOW THE SERUM IS ADDICTIVE. BUT IT DOESN'T HAVE TO BE DANGEROUS.
I CAN HELP YOU, FRANCINE.
GET YOU BACK TO BEING YOURSELF AGAIN.
THAT'S THE THING, KIRK.
THE JOB I DO--THE JOB I REALLY DO--I NEVER GET TO BE MYSELF.
I'M ALWAYS SOMEBODY ELSE. WHOEVER MY BOSSES TELL ME TO BE.
I'M THINKING MORE AND MORE THIS IS MY REAL SELF.
AND I THINK I LIKE IT.
FRANCINE, NO!

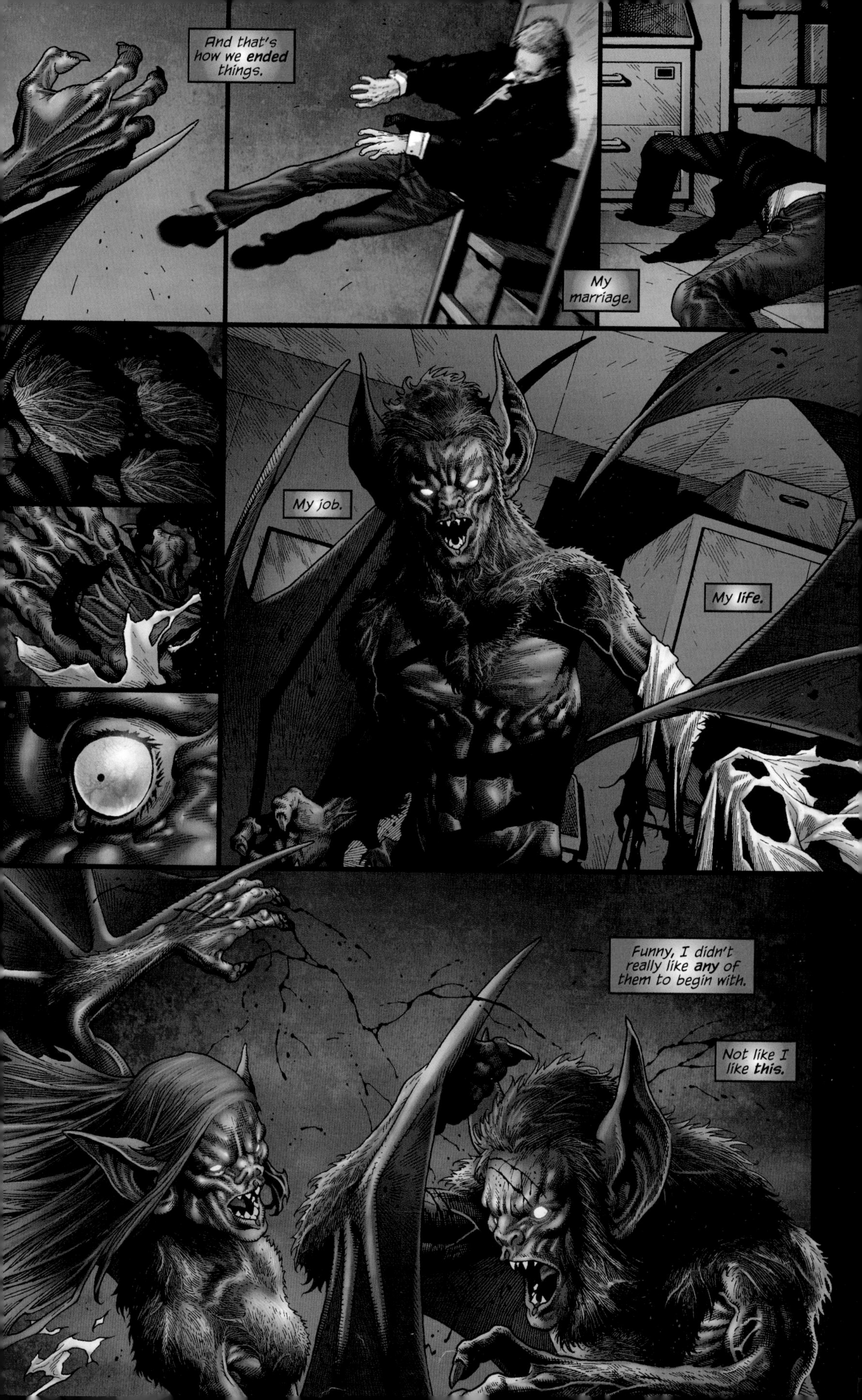
And that's how we **ended** things.
My marriage.
My job.
My *life.*
Funny, I didn't really like **any** of them to begin with.
Not like I like **this.**

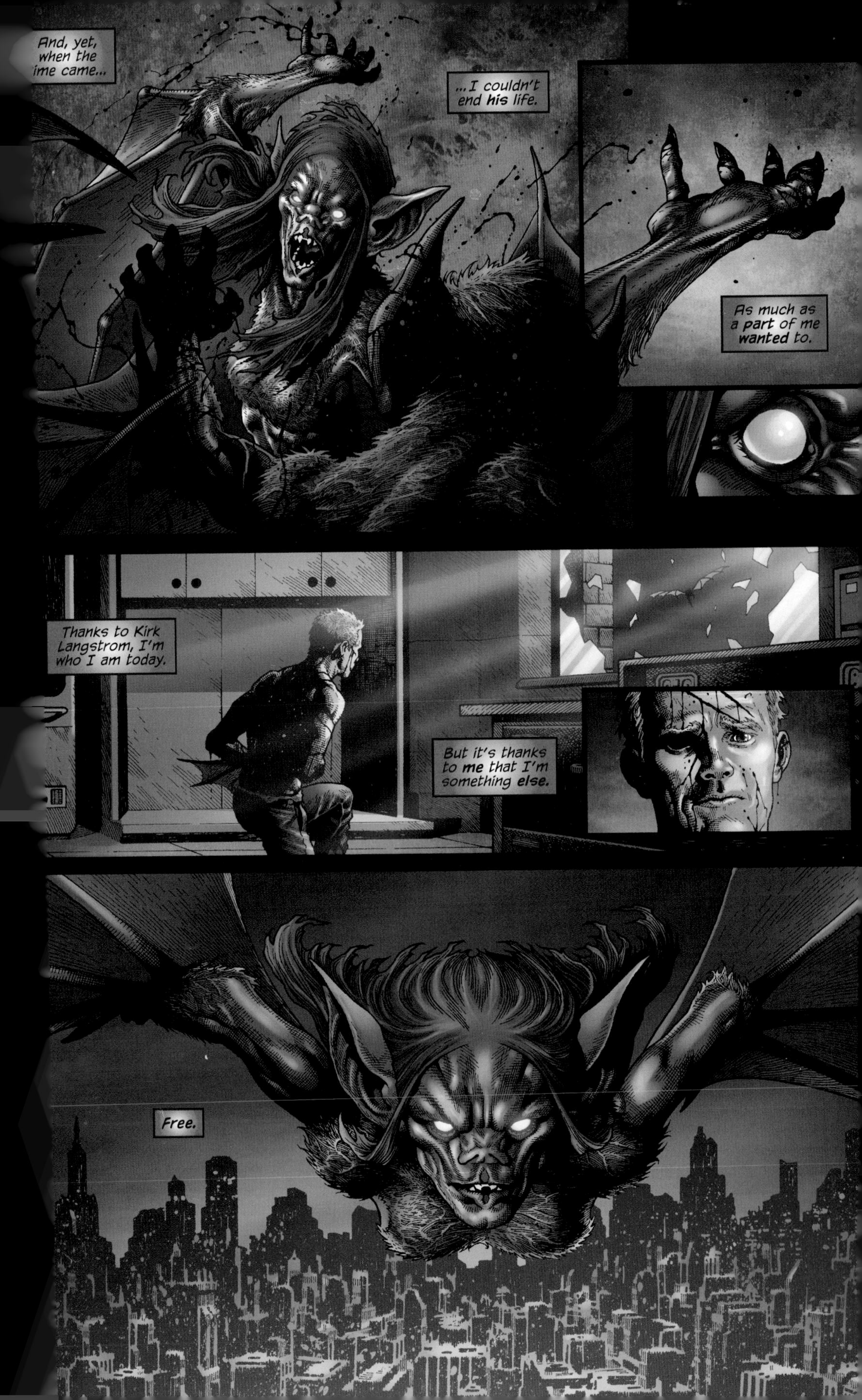

And, yet, when the ime came...
...I couldn't end his life.
As much as a part of me wanted to.
Thanks to Kirk Langstrom, I'm who I am today.
But it's thanks to me that I'm something else.
Free.

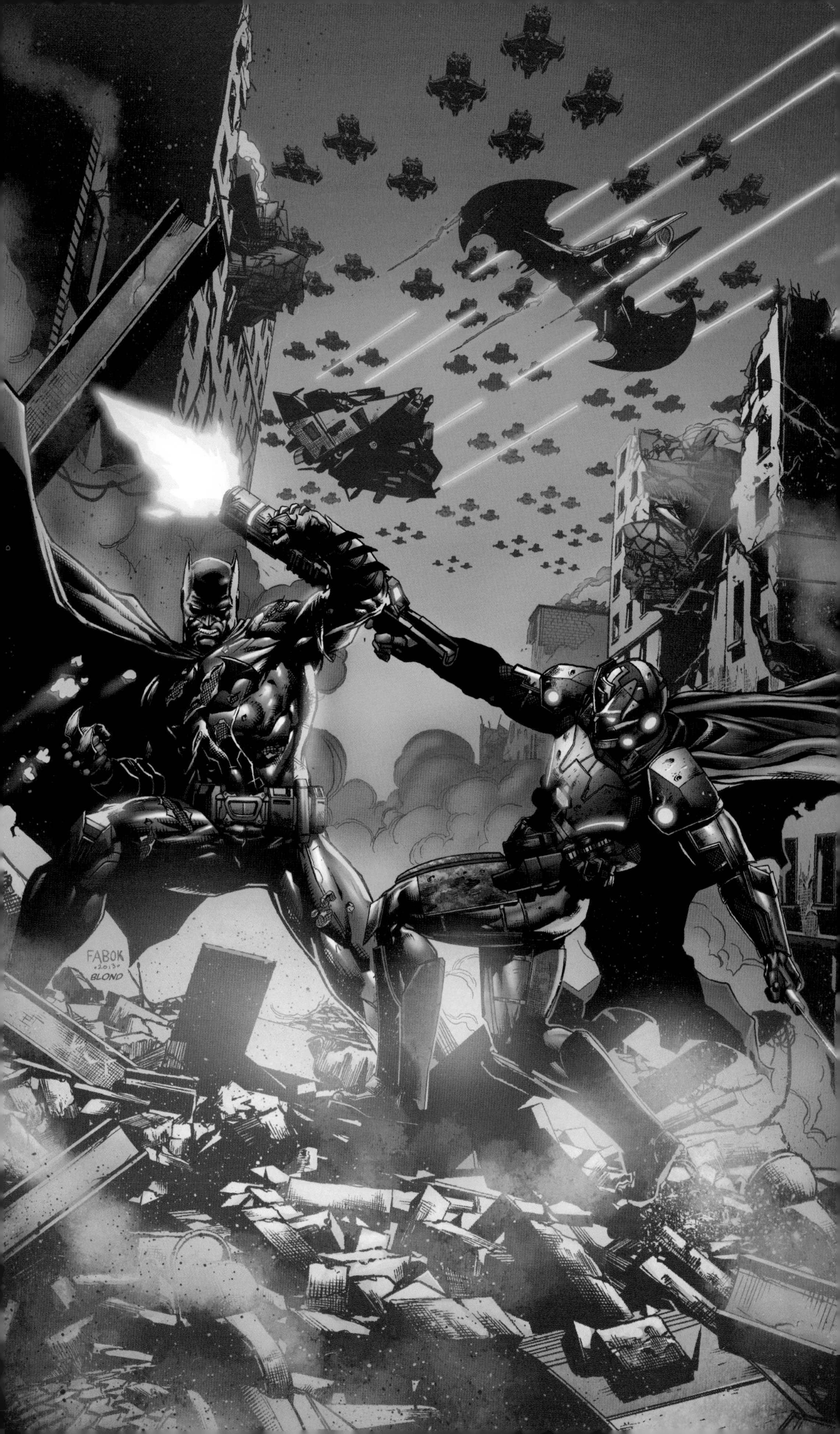
FABOK
2013
BLOND

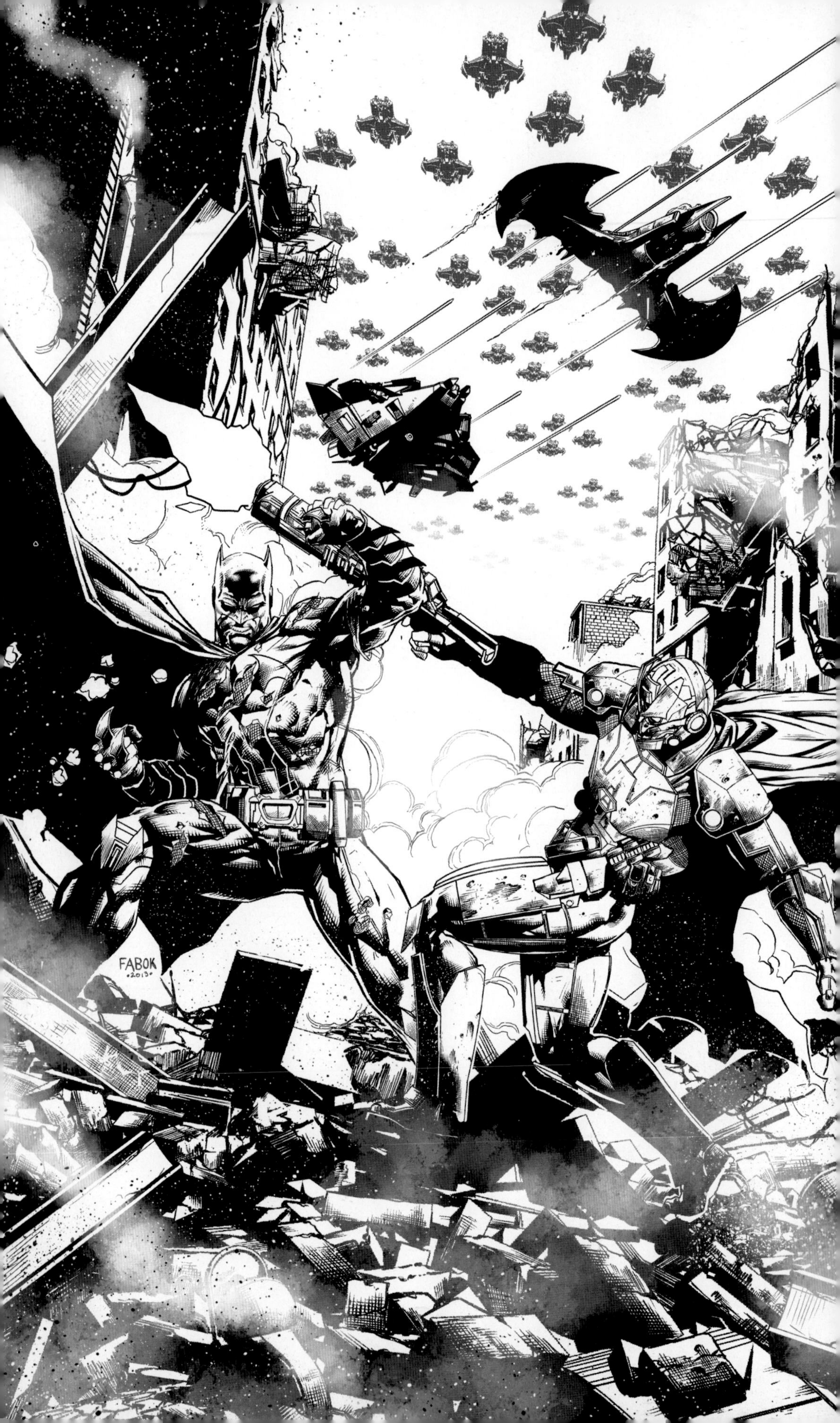
FABOK
2013

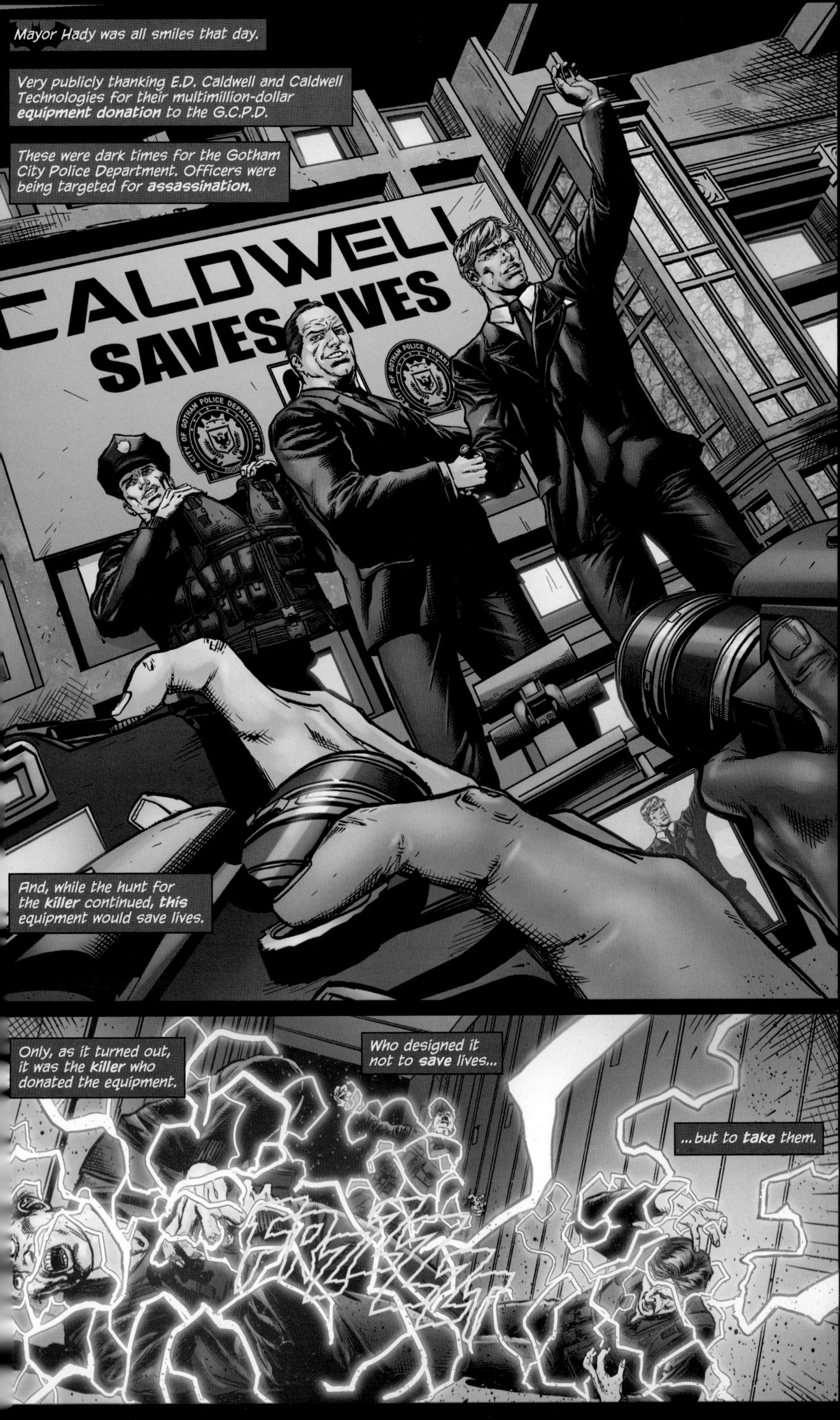
Mayor Hady was all smiles that day.
Very publicly thanking E.D. Caldwell and Caldwell Technologies for their multimillion-dollar **equipment donation** to the G.C.P.D.
These were dark times for the Gotham City Police Department. Officers were being targeted for **assassination.**
CALDWELL
SAVES LIVES
CITY OF GOTHAM POLICE DEPARTMENT
And, while the hunt for the **killer** continued, **this** equipment would save lives.
Only, as it turned out, it was the **killer** who donated the equipment.
Who designed it not to **save** lives...
...but to **take** them.

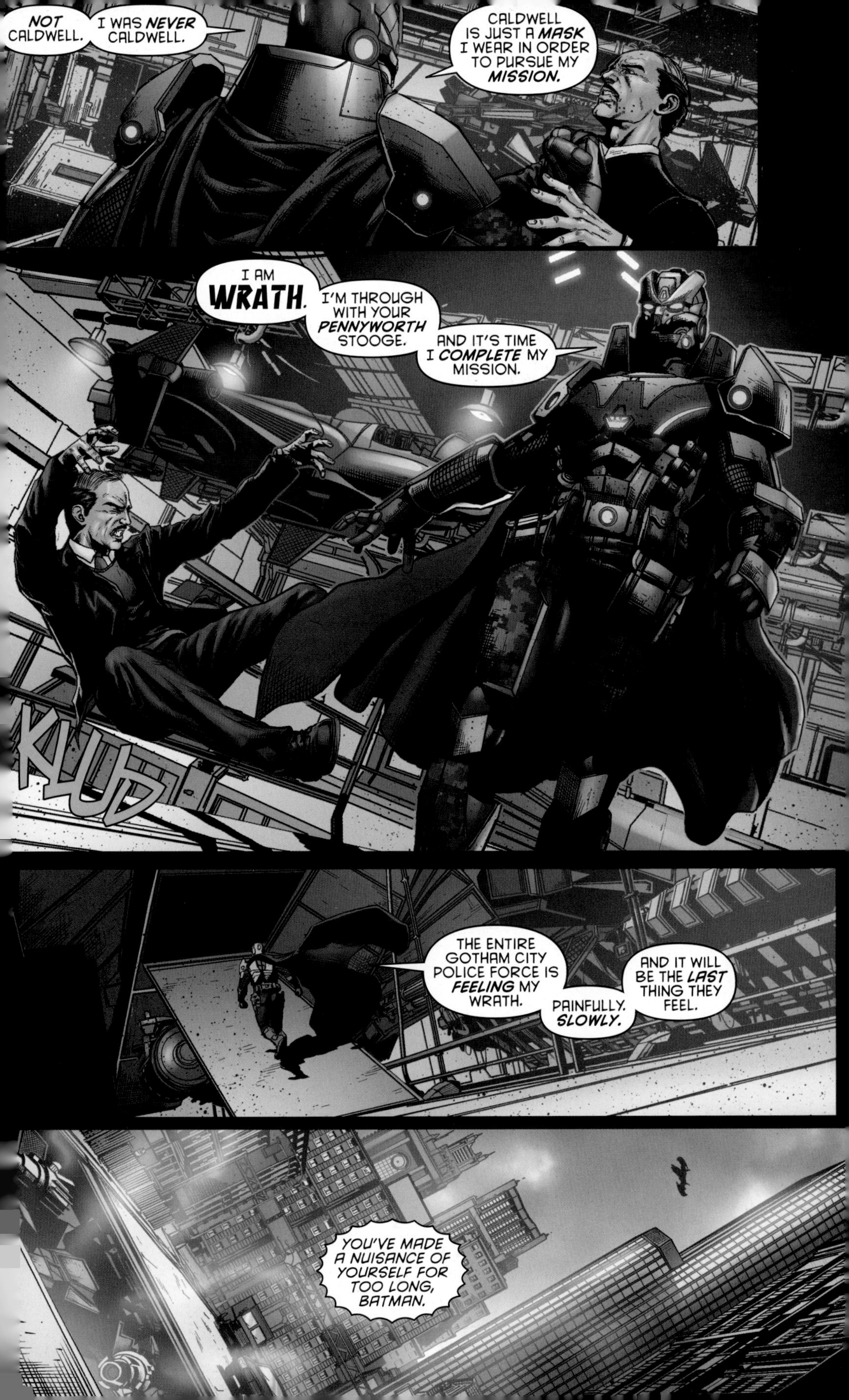
NOT CALDWELL.
I WAS NEVER CALDWELL.
CALDWELL IS JUST A MASK I WEAR IN ORDER TO PURSUE MY MISSION.
I AM WRATH.
I'M THROUGH WITH YOUR PENNYWORTH STOOGE.
AND IT'S TIME I COMPLETE MY MISSION.
KLUD
THE ENTIRE GOTHAM CITY POLICE FORCE IS FEELING MY WRATH.
PAINFULLY. SLOWLY.
AND IT WILL BE THE LAST THING THEY FEEL.
YOU'VE MADE A NUISANCE OF YOURSELF FOR TOO LONG, BATMAN.

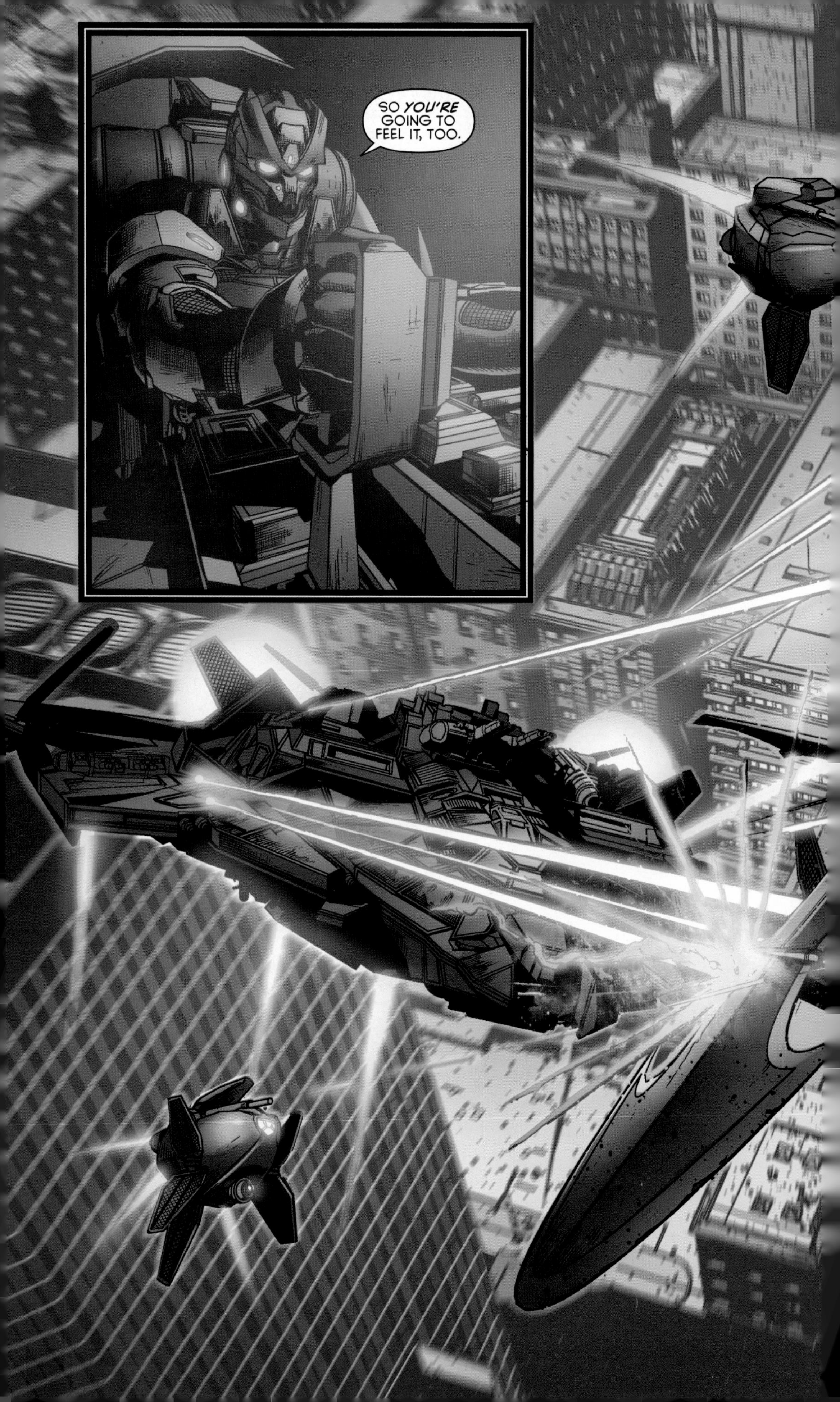
SO *YOU'RE* GOING TO FEEL IT, TOO.

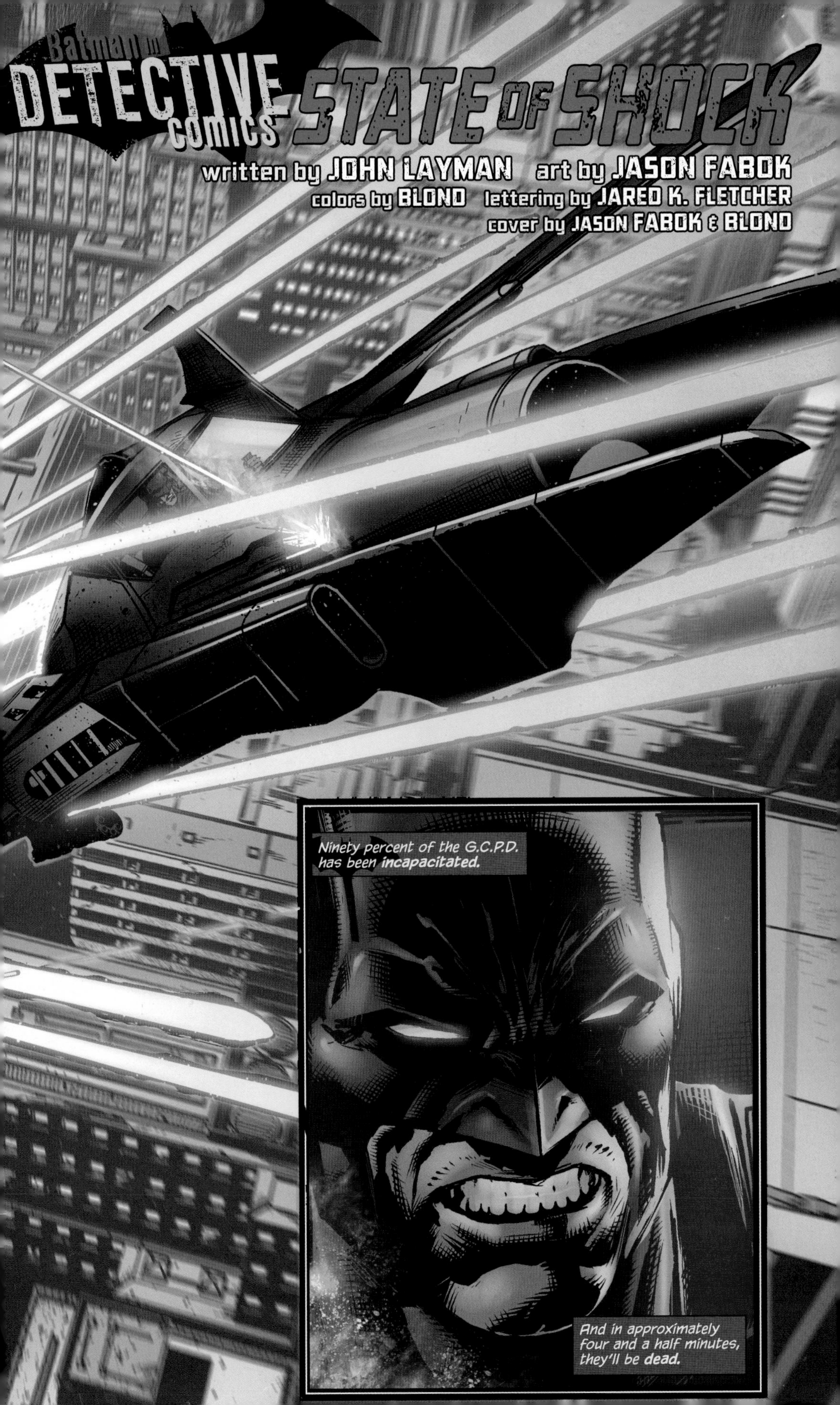
Batman in DETECTIVE COMICS
STATE OF SHOCK
written by JOHN LAYMAN art by JASON FABOK
colors by BLOND lettering by JARED K. FLETCHER
cover by JASON FABOK & BLOND
Ninety percent of the G.C.P.D. has been incapacitated.
And in approximately four and a half minutes, they'll be dead.

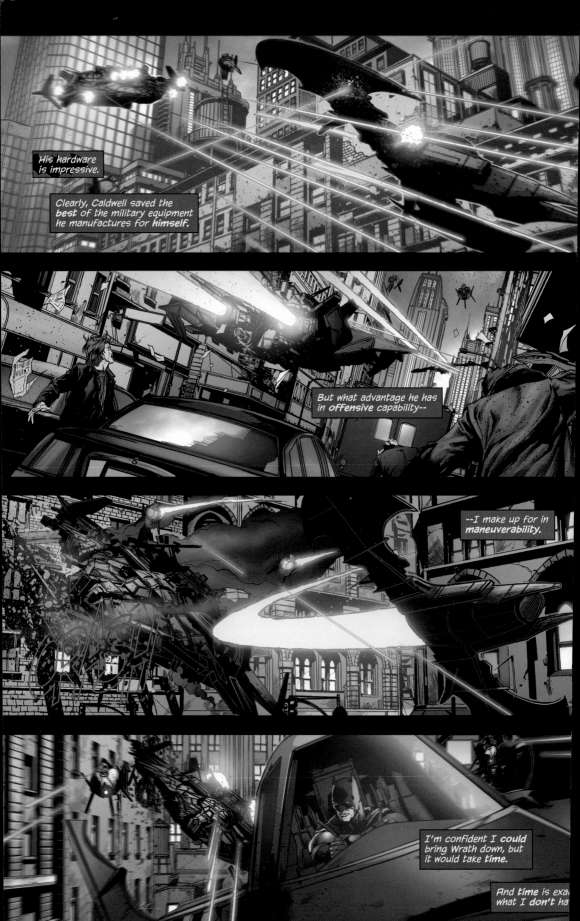

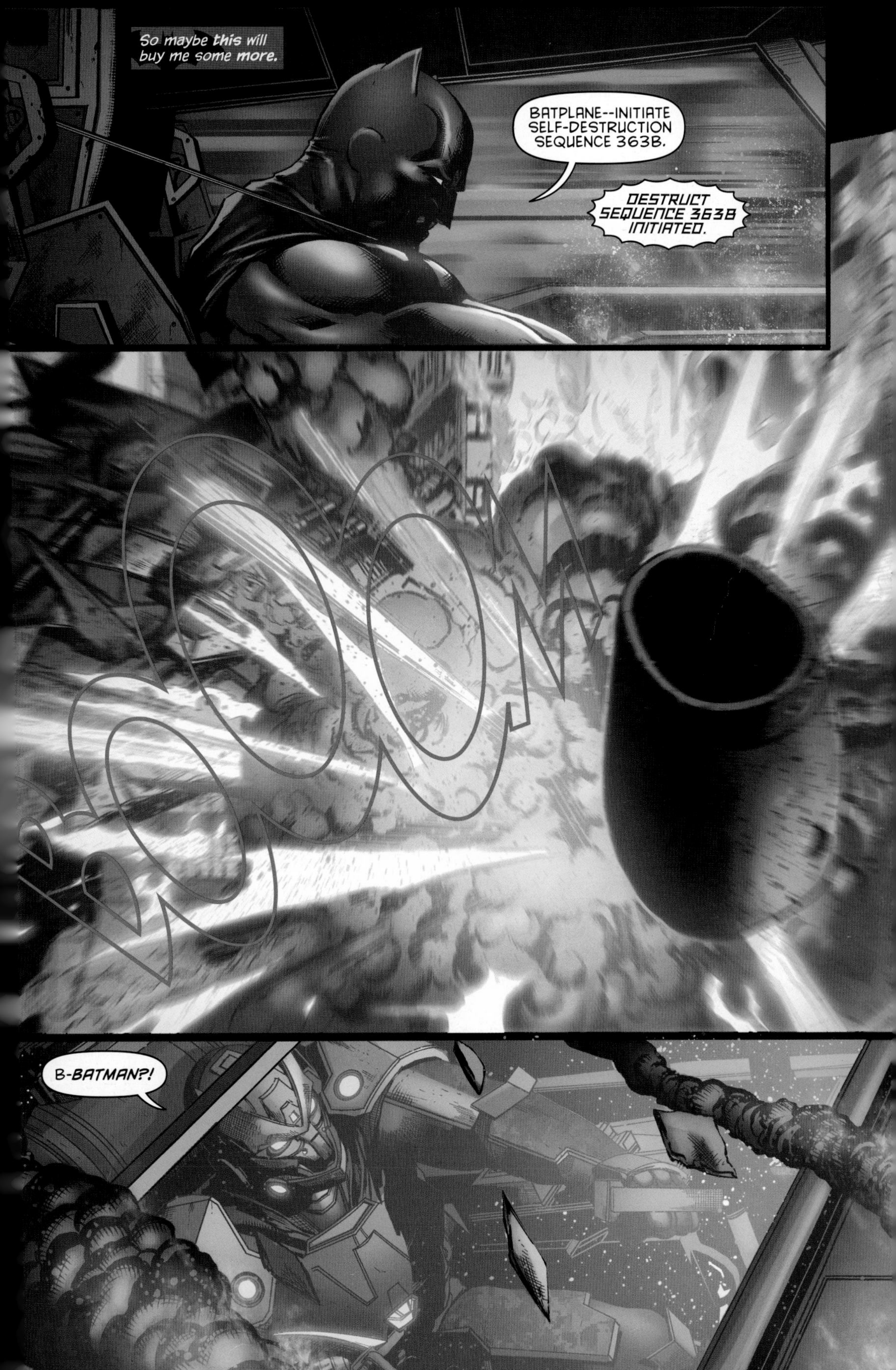
So maybe this will buy me some more.
BATPLANE--INITIATE SELF-DESTRUCTION SEQUENCE 363B.
DESTRUCT SEQUENCE 363B INITIATED.
BOOOOM
B-BATMAN?!

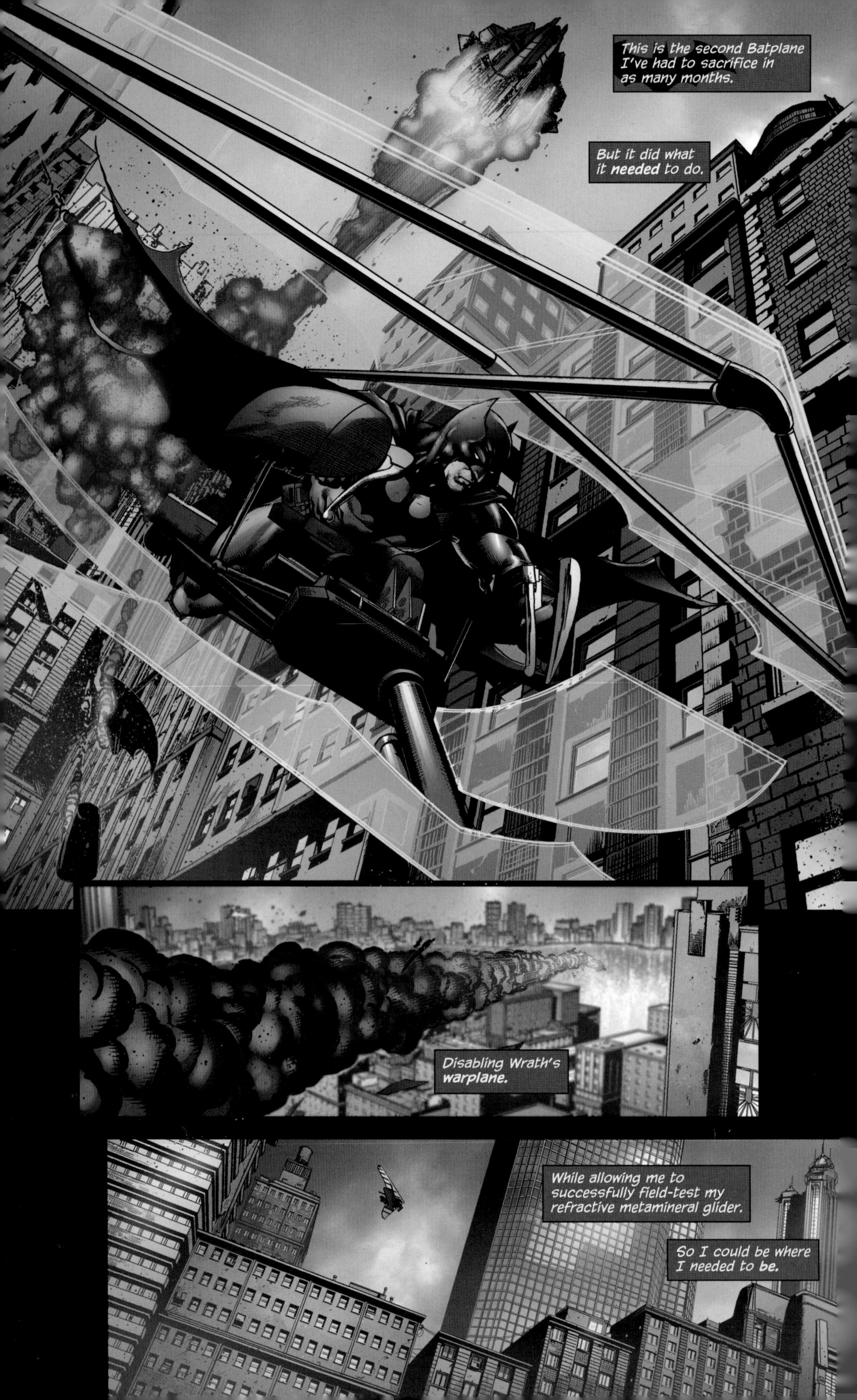
This is the second Batplane I've had to sacrifice in as many months.
But it did what it needed to do.
Disabling Wrath's warplane.
While allowing me to successfully field-test my refractive metamineral glider.
So I could be where I needed to be.

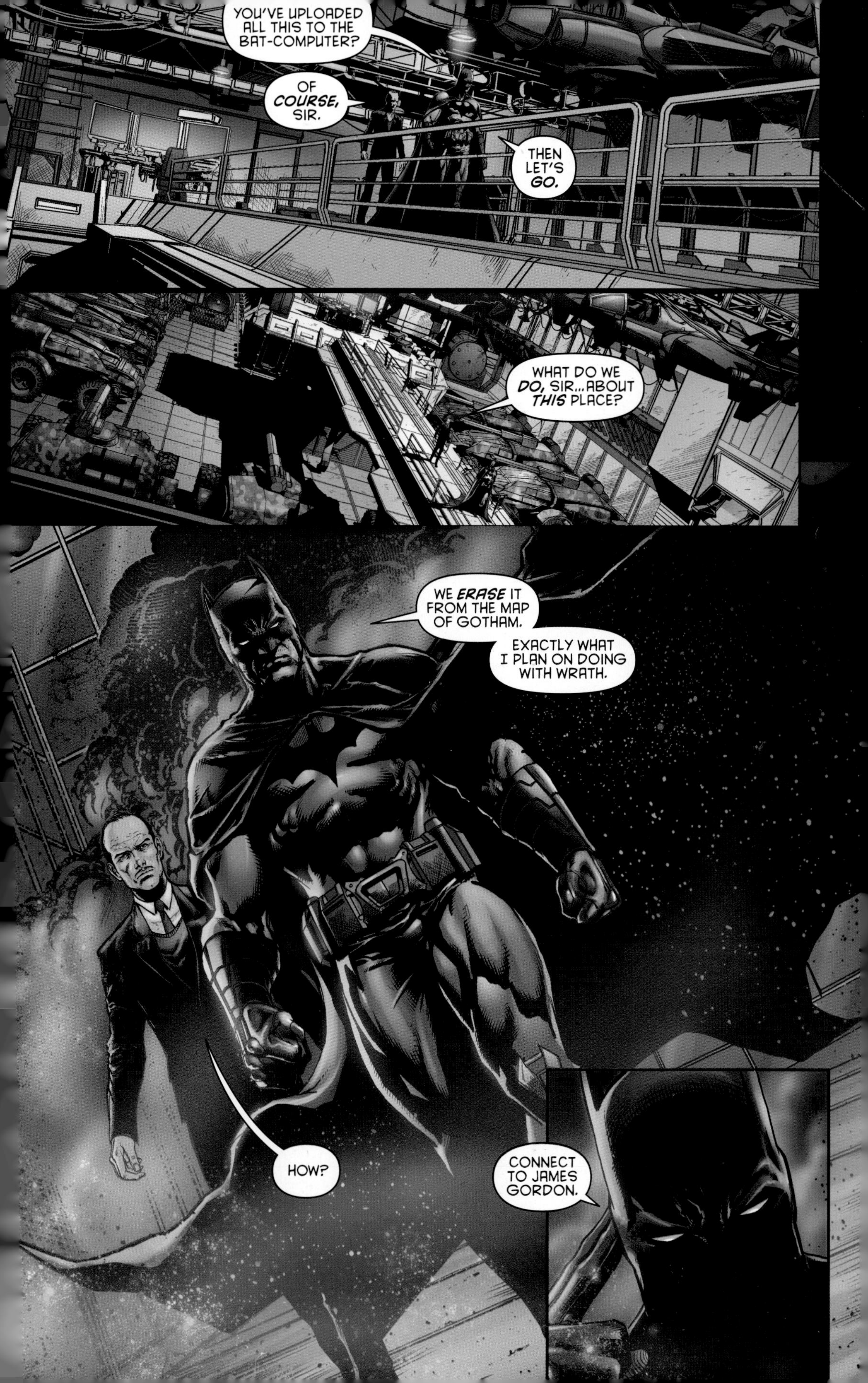
YOU'VE UPLOADED ALL THIS TO THE BAT-COMPUTER?
OF COURSE, SIR.
THEN LET'S GO.
WHAT DO WE DO, SIR...ABOUT THIS PLACE?
WE ERASE IT FROM THE MAP OF GOTHAM.
EXACTLY WHAT I PLAN ON DOING WITH WRATH.
HOW?
CONNECT TO JAMES GORDON.

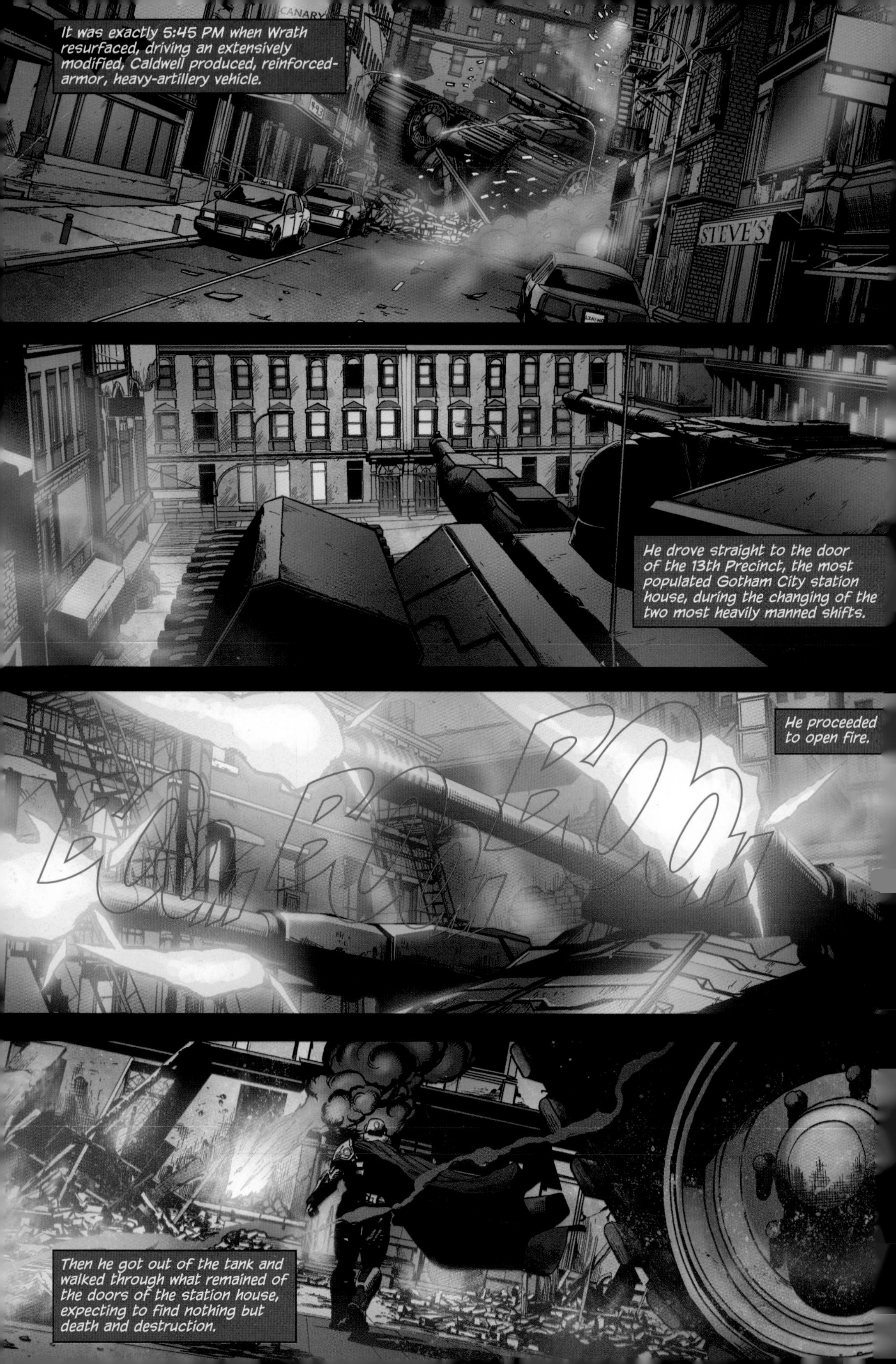
It was exactly 5:45 PM when Wrath resurfaced, driving an extensively modified, Caldwell produced, reinforced-armor, heavy-artillery vehicle.
CANARY
STEVE'S
He drove straight to the door of the 13th Precinct, the most populated Gotham City station house, during the changing of the two most heavily manned shifts.
He proceeded to open fire.
Then he got out of the tank and walked through what remained of the doors of the station house, expecting to find nothing but death and destruction.

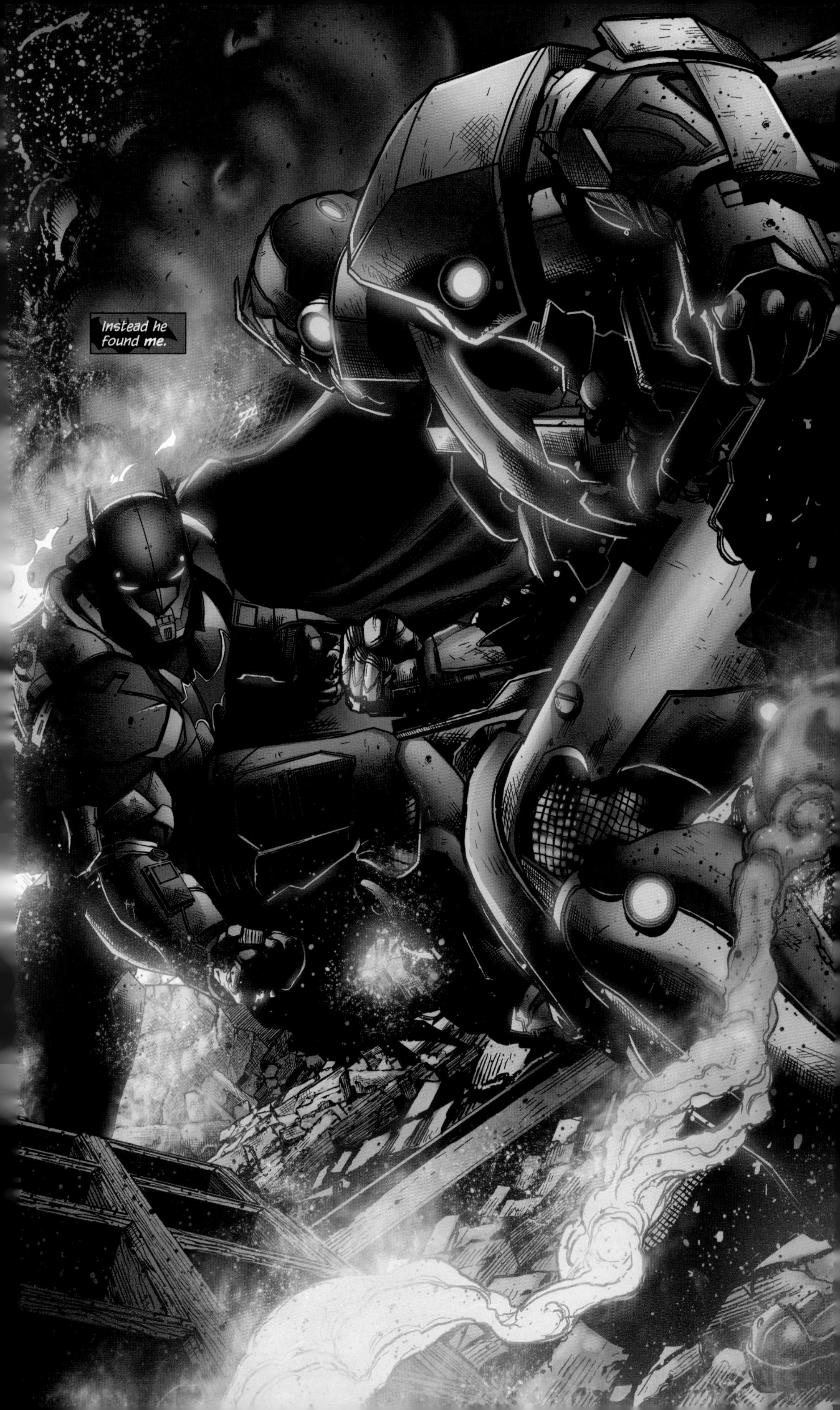
Instead he found me.

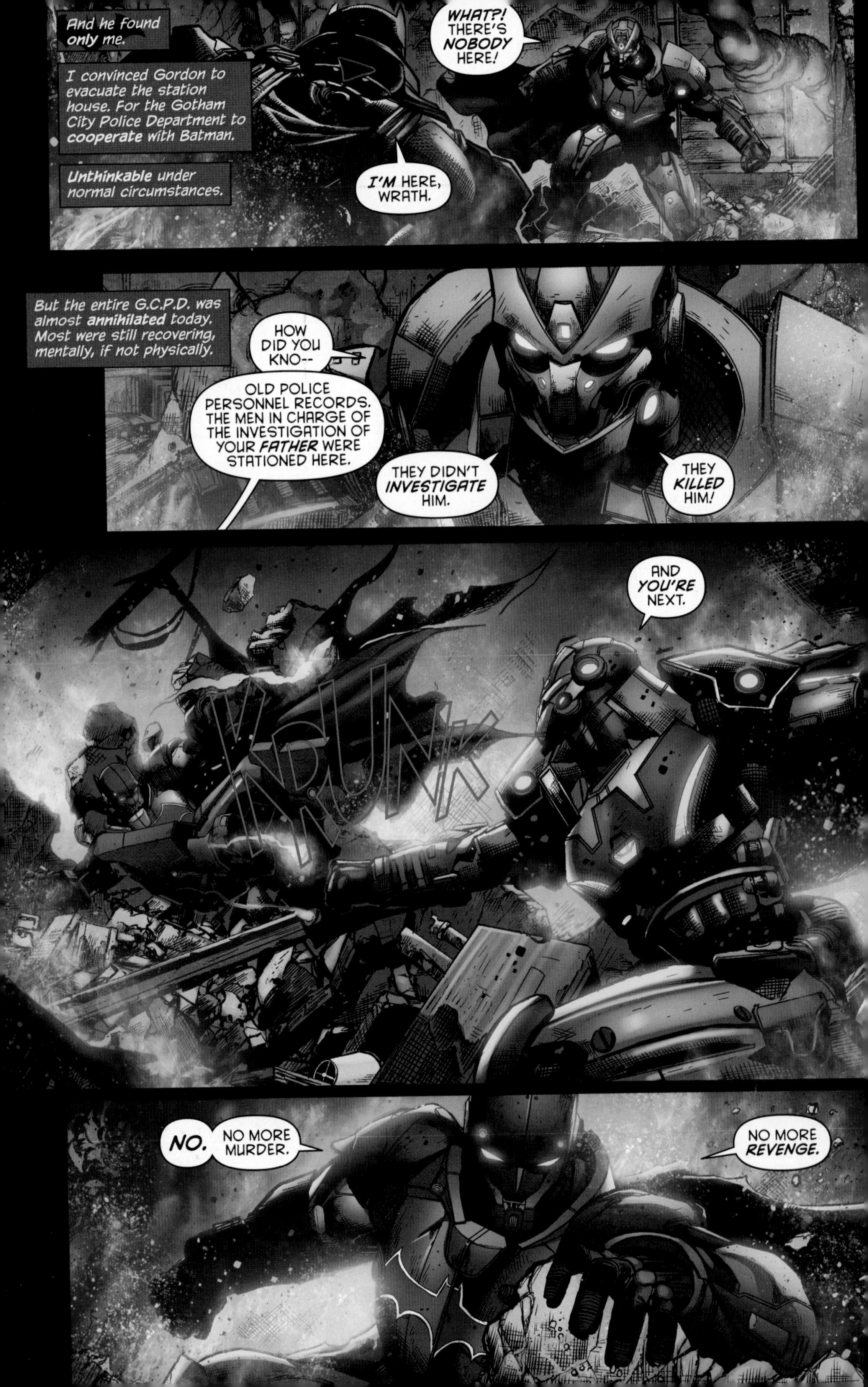
And he found **only** me.
I convinced Gordon to evacuate the station house. For the Gotham City Police Department to **cooperate** with Batman.
Unthinkable under normal circumstances.
WHAT?! THERE'S **NOBODY** HERE!
I'M HERE, WRATH.
But the entire G.C.P.D. was almost **annihilated** today. Most were still recovering, mentally, if not physically.
HOW DID YOU KNO--
OLD POLICE PERSONNEL RECORDS. THE MEN IN CHARGE OF THE INVESTIGATION OF YOUR **FATHER** WERE STATIONED HERE.
THEY DIDN'T **INVESTIGATE** HIM.
THEY **KILLED** HIM!
AND **YOU'RE** NEXT.
KRUNK
NO. NO MORE MURDER.
NO MORE **REVENGE.**

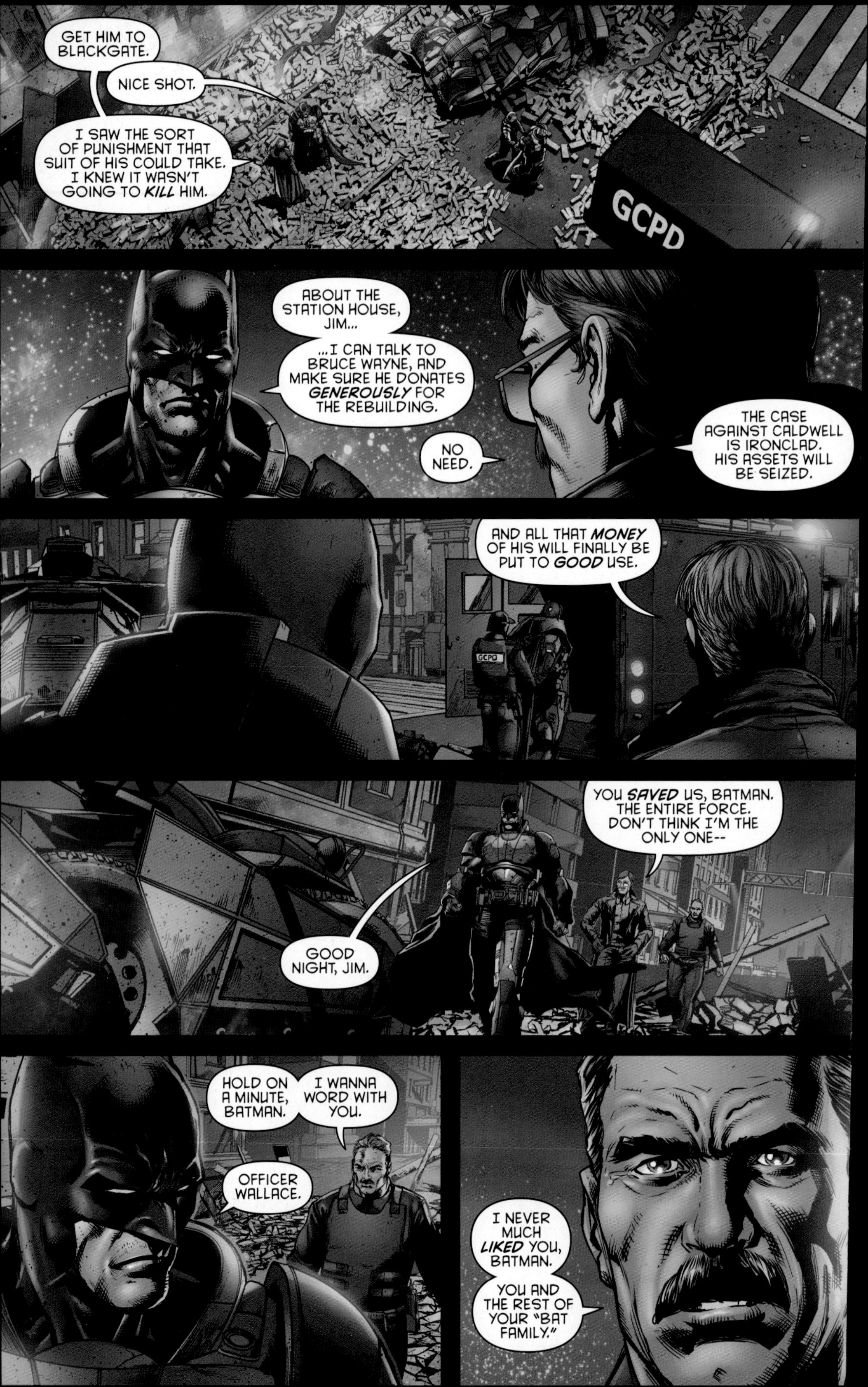
GET HIM TO BLACKGATE.
NICE SHOT.
I SAW THE SORT OF PUNISHMENT THAT SUIT OF HIS COULD TAKE. I KNEW IT WASN'T GOING TO *KILL* HIM.
ABOUT THE STATION HOUSE, JIM...
...I CAN TALK TO BRUCE WAYNE, AND MAKE SURE HE DONATES *GENEROUSLY* FOR THE REBUILDING.
NO NEED.
THE CASE AGAINST CALDWELL IS IRONCLAD. HIS ASSETS WILL BE SEIZED.
GCPD
AND ALL THAT *MONEY* OF HIS WILL FINALLY BE PUT TO *GOOD* USE.
GCPD
YOU *SAVED* US, BATMAN. THE ENTIRE FORCE. DON'T THINK I'M THE ONLY ONE--
GOOD NIGHT, JIM.
HOLD ON A MINUTE, BATMAN.
I WANNA WORD WITH YOU.
OFFICER WALLACE.
I NEVER MUCH *LIKED* YOU, BATMAN.
YOU AND THE REST OF YOUR "BAT FAMILY."

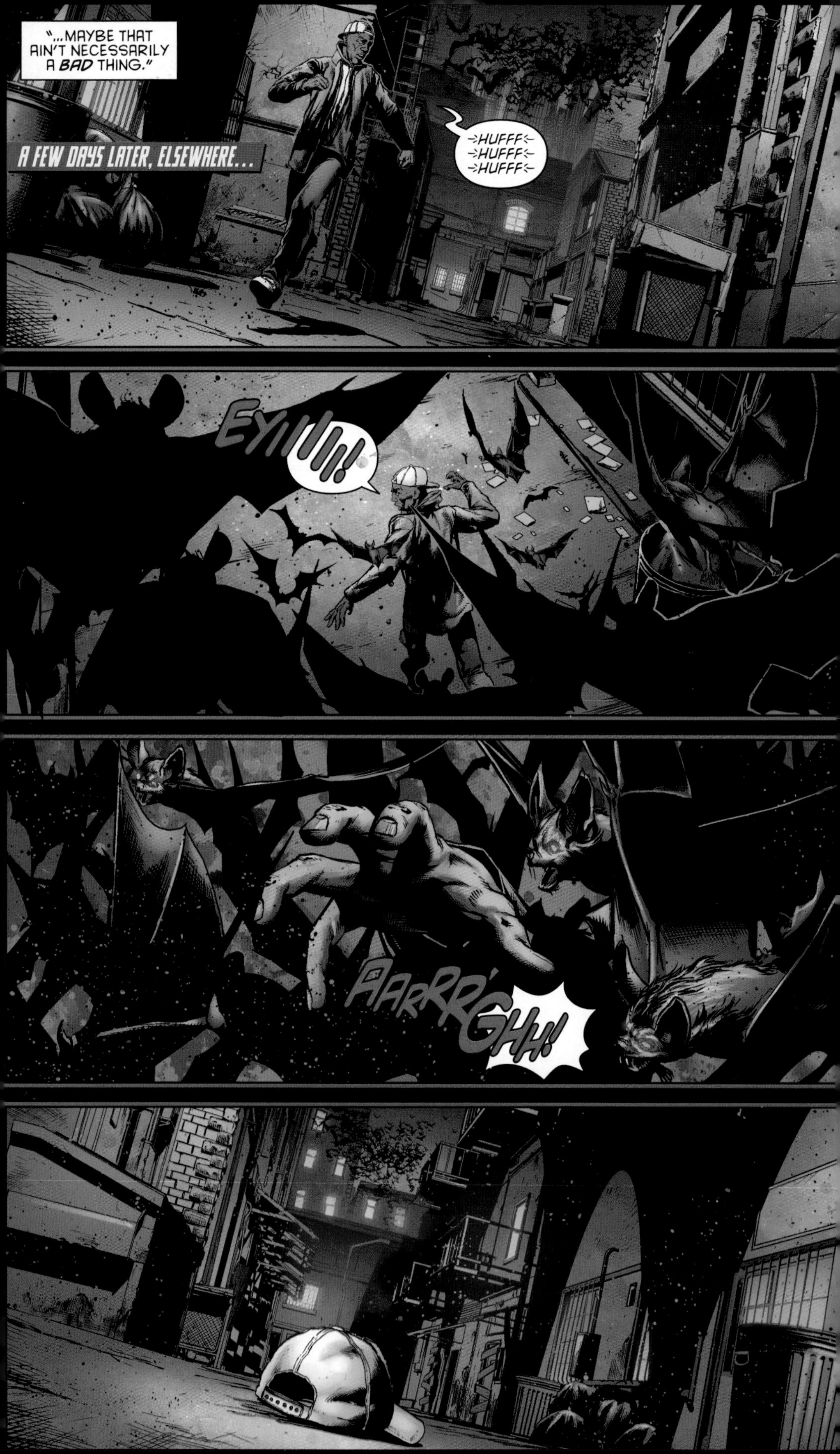
"...MAYBE THAT AIN'T NECESSARILY A BAD THING."
A FEW DAYS LATER, ELSEWHERE...
HUFFF HUFFF HUFFF
EYIIIIII!
AARRRGHH!

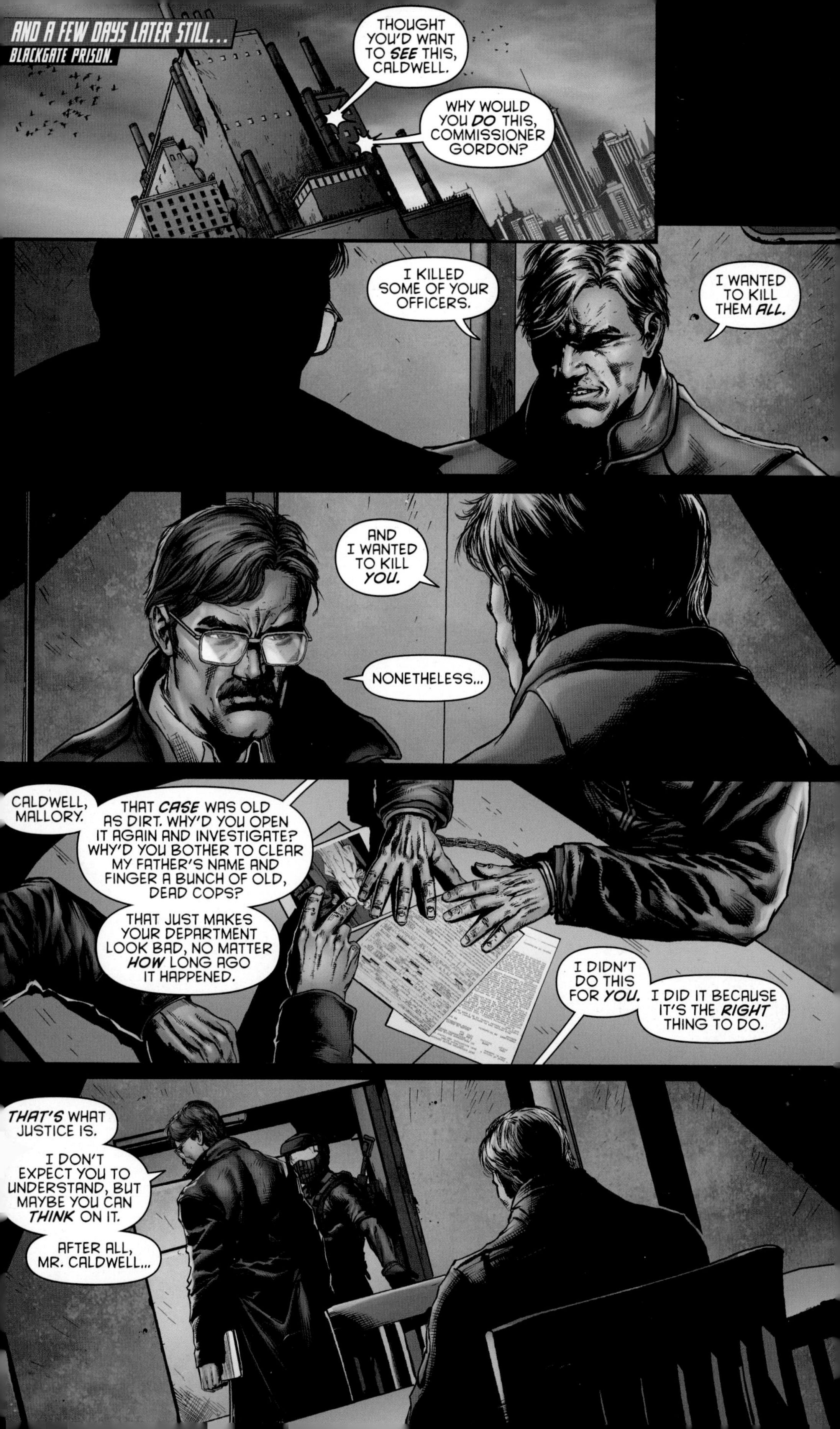
AND A FEW DAYS LATER STILL...
BLACKGATE PRISON.
THOUGHT YOU'D WANT TO SEE THIS, CALDWELL.
WHY WOULD YOU DO THIS, COMMISSIONER GORDON?
I KILLED SOME OF YOUR OFFICERS.
I WANTED TO KILL THEM ALL.
AND I WANTED TO KILL YOU.
NONETHELESS...
CALDWELL, MALLORY.
THAT CASE WAS OLD AS DIRT. WHY'D YOU OPEN IT AGAIN AND INVESTIGATE? WHY'D YOU BOTHER TO CLEAR MY FATHER'S NAME AND FINGER A BUNCH OF OLD, DEAD COPS?
THAT JUST MAKES YOUR DEPARTMENT LOOK BAD, NO MATTER HOW LONG AGO IT HAPPENED.
I DIDN'T DO THIS FOR YOU.
I DID IT BECAUSE IT'S THE RIGHT THING TO DO.
THAT'S WHAT JUSTICE IS.
I DON'T EXPECT YOU TO UNDERSTAND, BUT MAYBE YOU CAN THINK ON IT.
AFTER ALL, MR. CALDWELL...

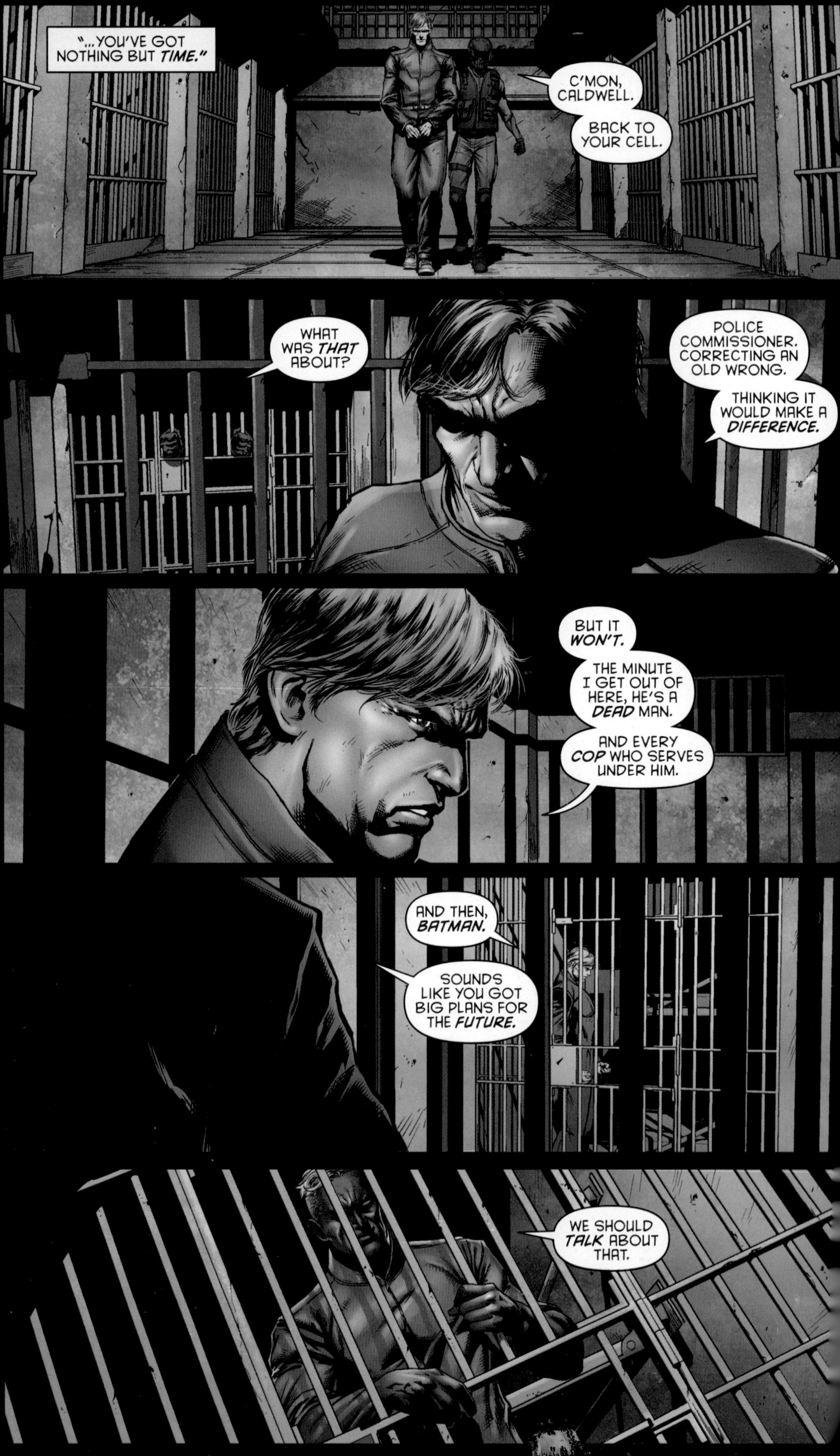
"...YOU'VE GOT NOTHING BUT *TIME.*"
C'MON, CALDWELL.
BACK TO YOUR CELL.
WHAT WAS *THAT* ABOUT?
POLICE COMMISSIONER. CORRECTING AN OLD WRONG.
THINKING IT WOULD MAKE A *DIFFERENCE.*
BUT IT *WON'T.*
THE MINUTE I GET OUT OF HERE, HE'S A *DEAD* MAN.
AND EVERY *COP* WHO SERVES UNDER HIM.
AND THEN, *BATMAN.*
SOUNDS LIKE YOU GOT BIG PLANS FOR THE *FUTURE.*
WE SHOULD *TALK* ABOUT THAT.

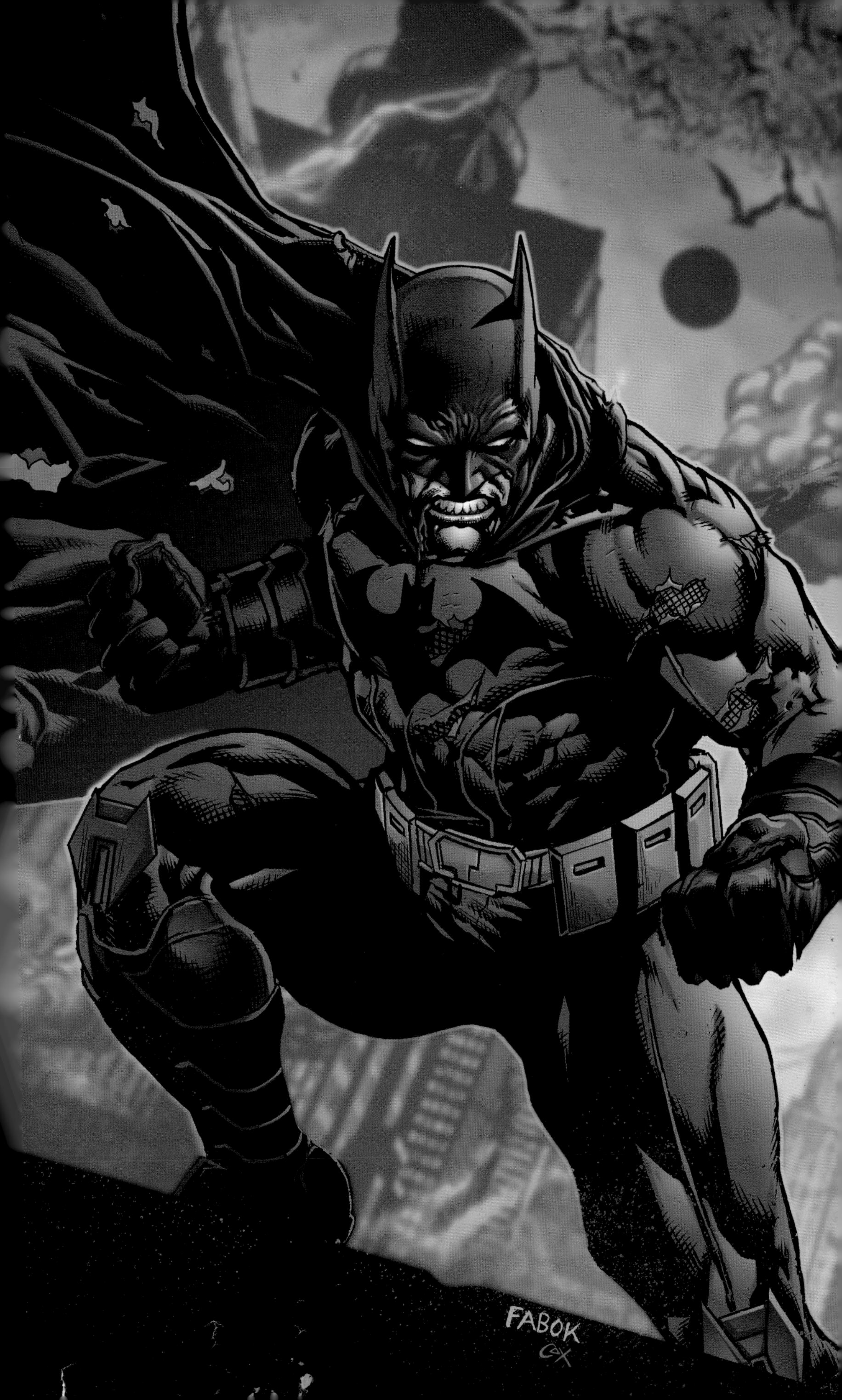
FABOK
COX

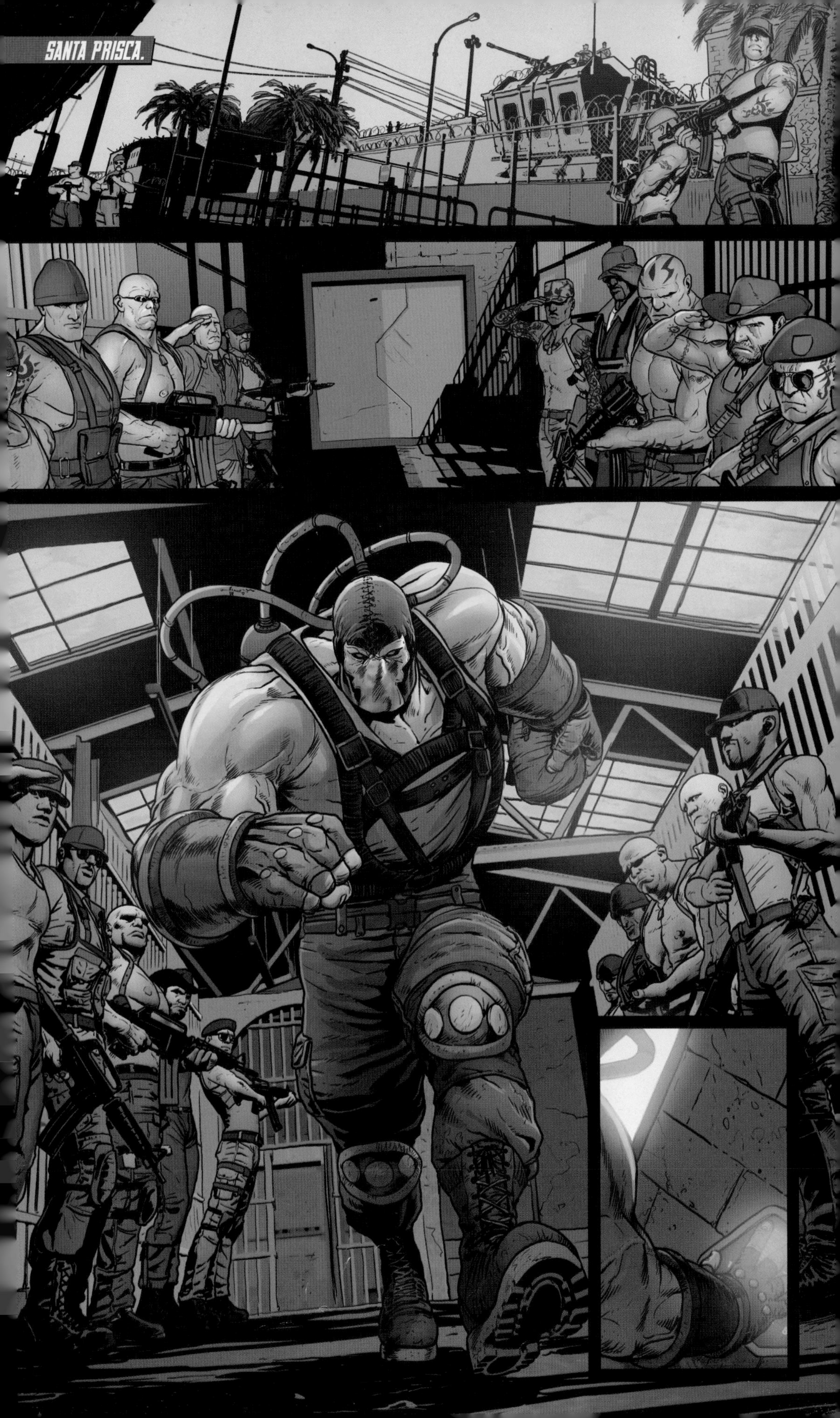
SANTA PRISCA.

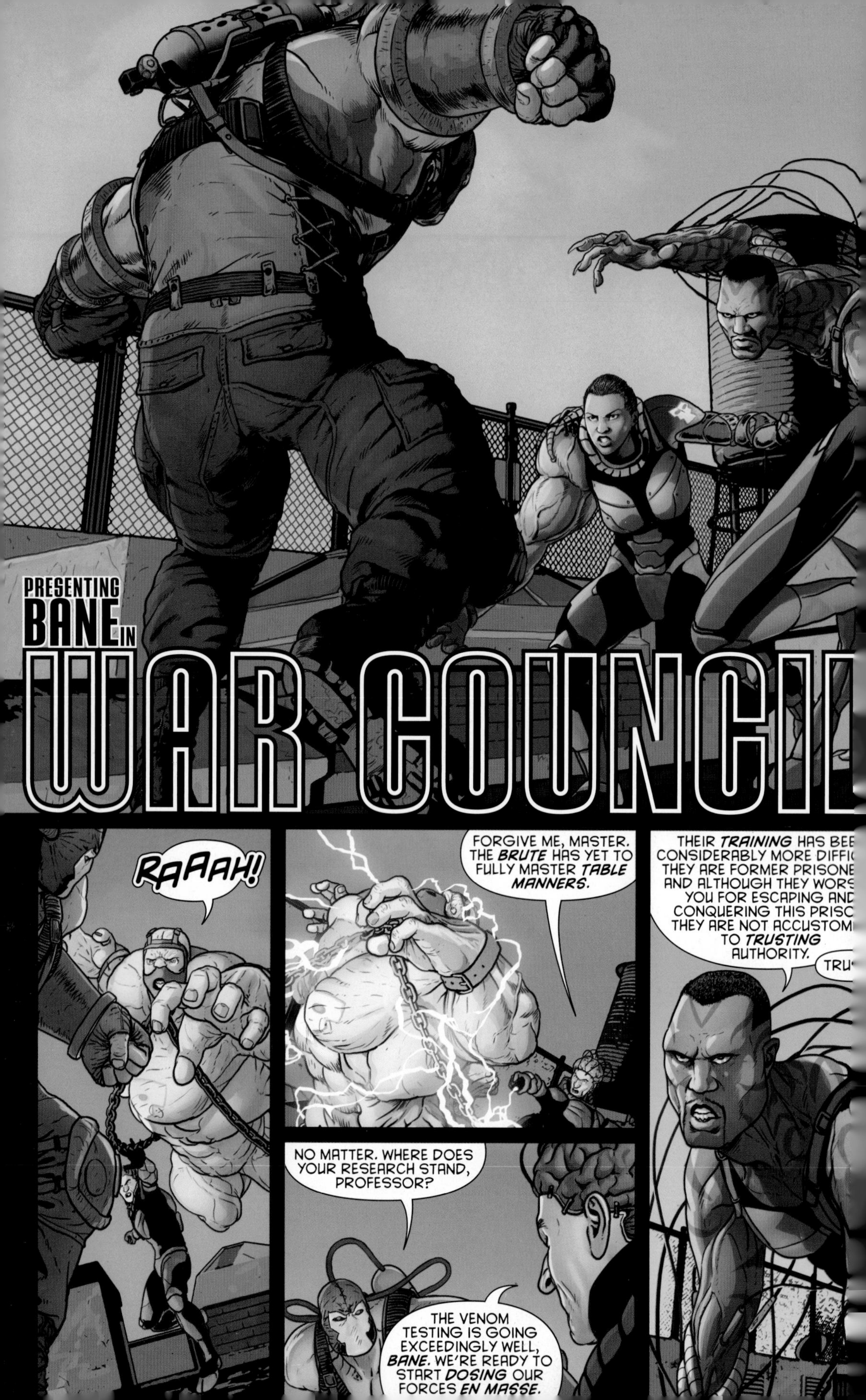
PRESENTING
BANE IN
WAR COUNCIL
RAAAH!
FORGIVE ME, MASTER. THE BRUTE HAS YET TO FULLY MASTER TABLE MANNERS.
THEIR TRAINING HAS BEE
CONSIDERABLY MORE DIFFI
THEY ARE FORMER PRISONE
AND ALTHOUGH THEY WORS
YOU FOR ESCAPING AND
CONQUERING THIS PRISO
THEY ARE NOT ACCUSTOM
TO TRUSTING AUTHORITY.
TRU
NO MATTER. WHERE DOES YOUR RESEARCH STAND, PROFESSOR?
THE VENOM TESTING IS GOING EXCEEDINGLY WELL, BANE. WE'RE READY TO START DOSING OUR FORCES EN MASSE.

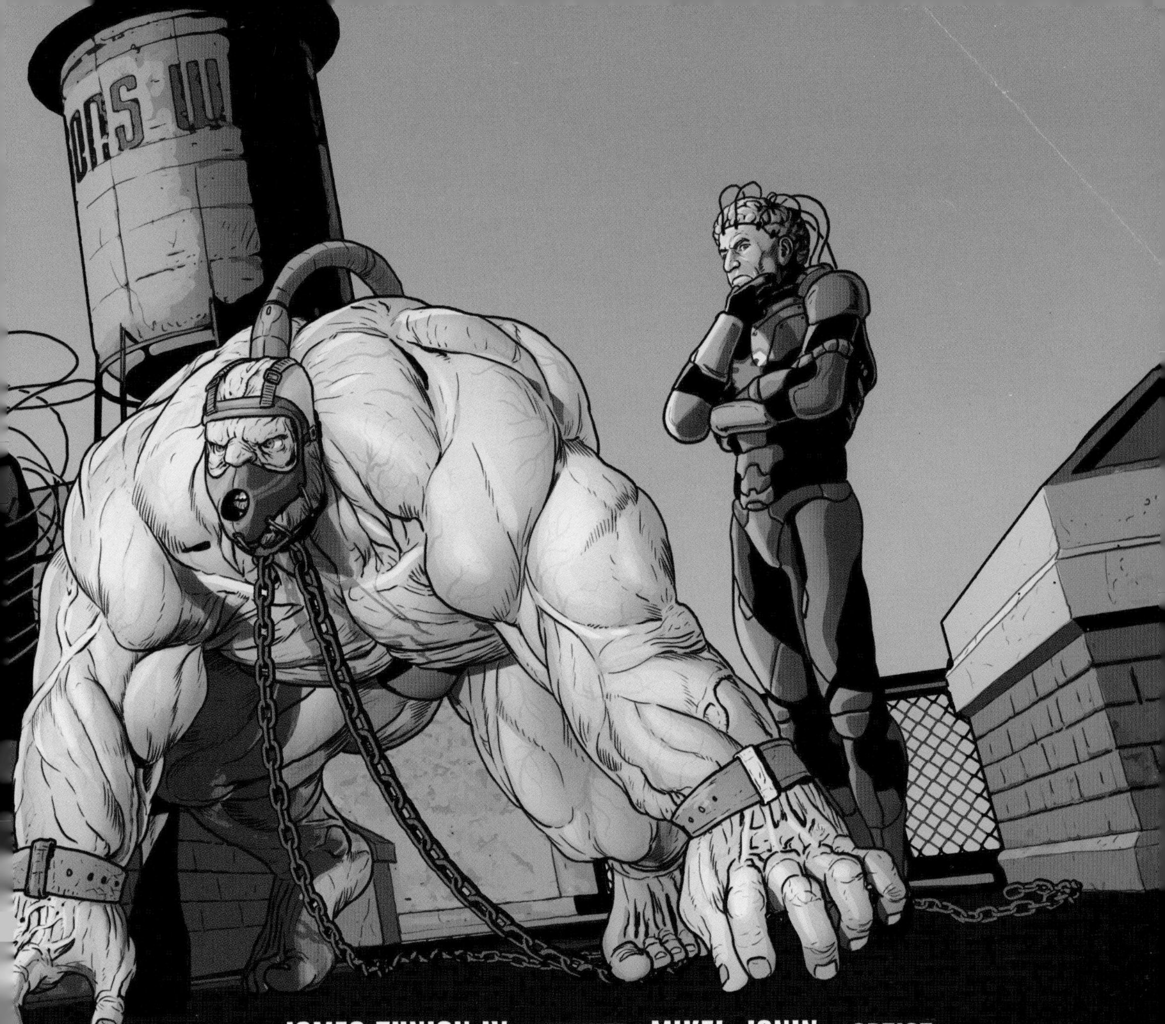

JAMES TYNION IV - WRITER MIKEL JANIN - ARTIST
DAVE McCAIG and BRAD ANDERSON - COLORISTS SAL CIPRIANO - LETTERER

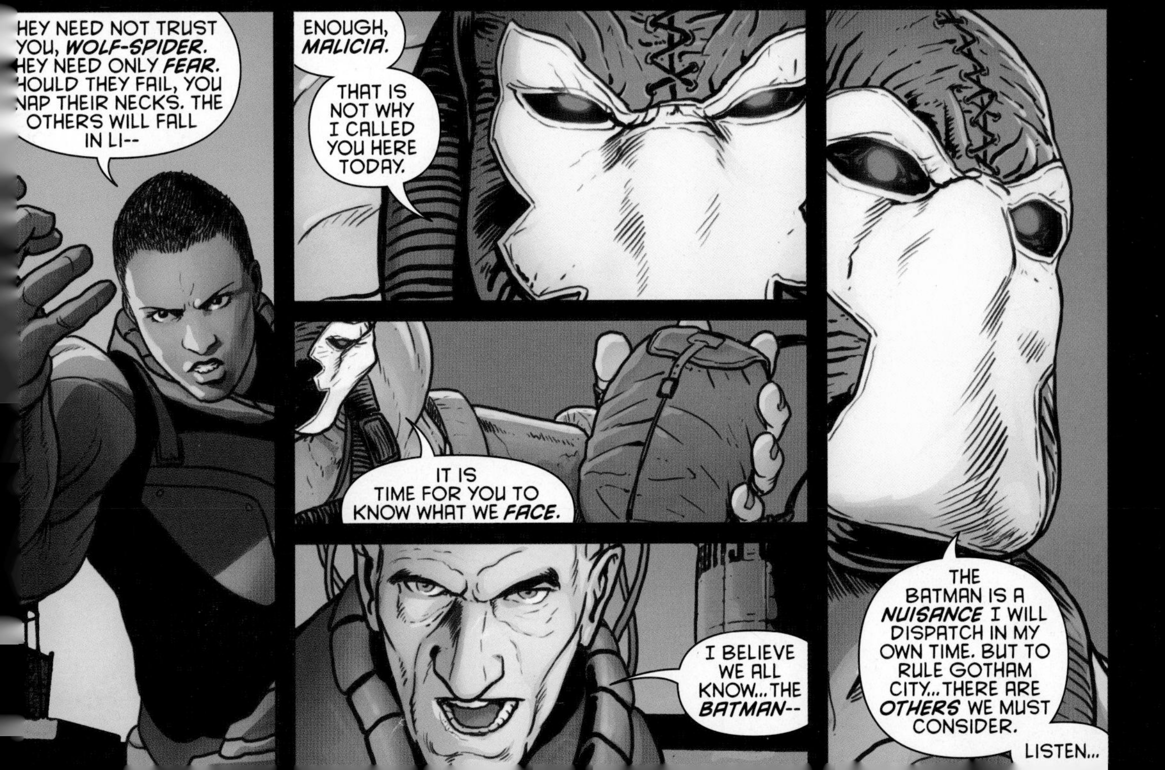
HEY NEED NOT TRUST YOU, *WOLF-SPIDER.* HEY NEED ONLY *FEAR.* HOULD THEY FAIL, YOU NAP THEIR NECKS. THE OTHERS WILL FALL IN LI--
ENOUGH, *MALICIA.*
THAT IS NOT WHY I CALLED YOU HERE TODAY.
IT IS TIME FOR YOU TO KNOW WHAT WE *FACE.*
I BELIEVE WE ALL KNOW... THE *BATMAN*--
THE BATMAN IS A *NUISANCE* I WILL DISPATCH IN MY OWN TIME. BUT TO RULE GOTHAM CITY... THERE ARE *OTHERS* WE MUST CONSIDER.
LISTEN...

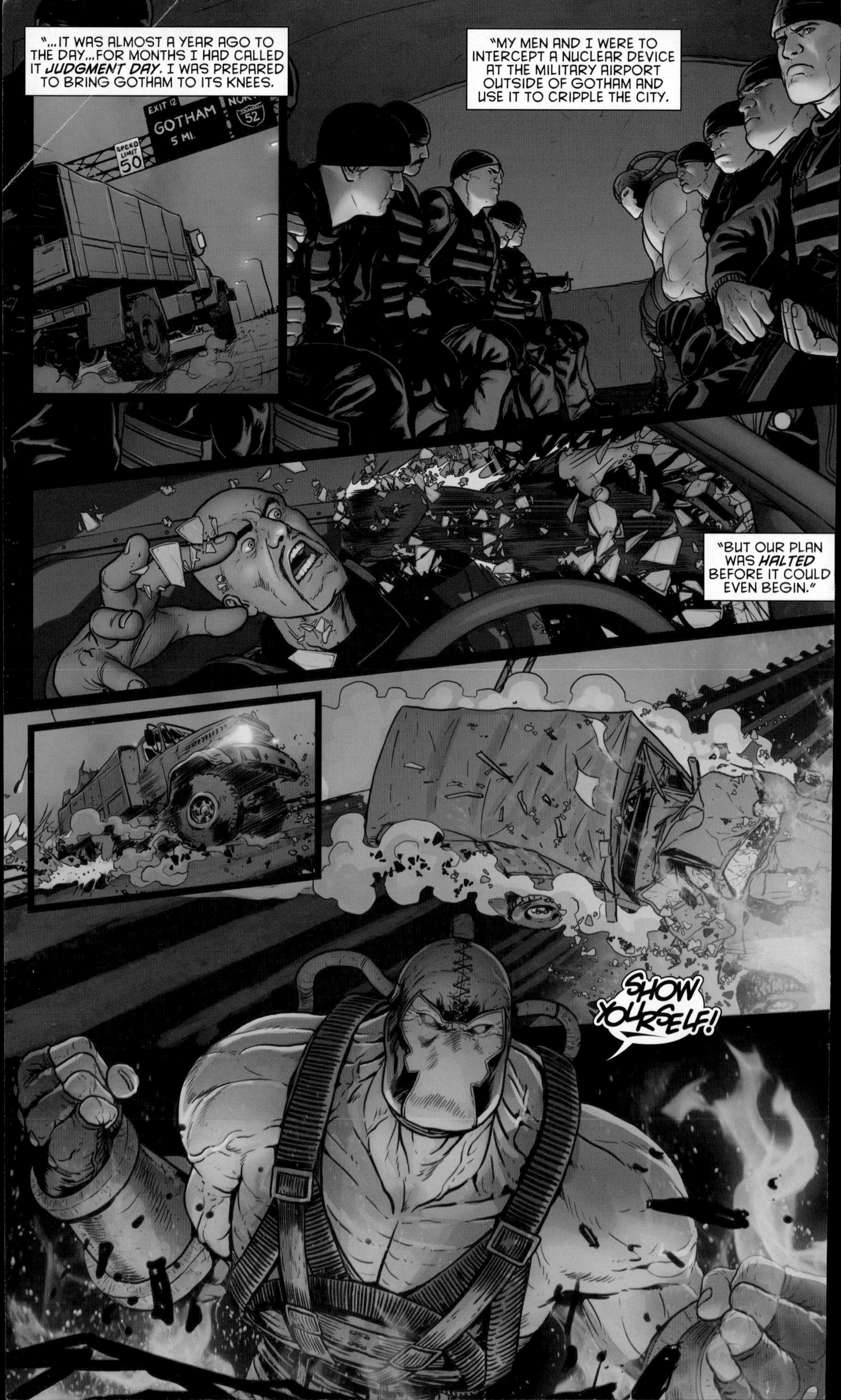
"...IT WAS ALMOST A YEAR AGO TO THE DAY...FOR MONTHS I HAD CALLED IT JUDGMENT DAY. I WAS PREPARED TO BRING GOTHAM TO ITS KNEES.
EXIT 12
GOTHAM
5 MI.
SPEED LIMIT 50
52
"MY MEN AND I WERE TO INTERCEPT A NUCLEAR DEVICE AT THE MILITARY AIRPORT OUTSIDE OF GOTHAM AND USE IT TO CRIPPLE THE CITY.
"BUT OUR PLAN WAS HALTED BEFORE IT COULD EVEN BEGIN."
SHOW YOURSELF!

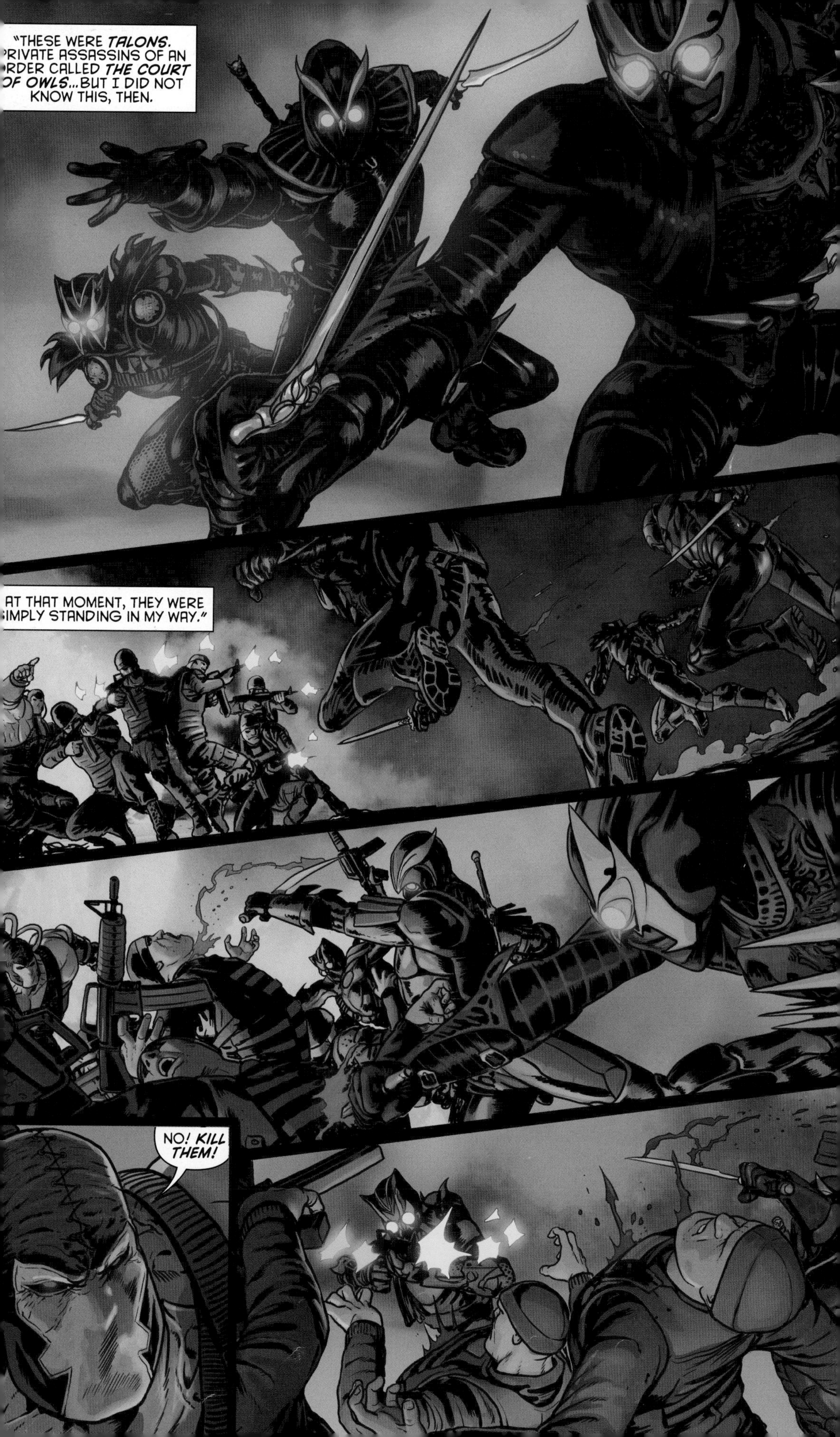
"THESE WERE TALONS. PRIVATE ASSASSINS OF AN ORDER CALLED THE COURT OF OWLS...BUT I DID NOT KNOW THIS, THEN.
AT THAT MOMENT, THEY WERE SIMPLY STANDING IN MY WAY."
NO! KILL THEM!

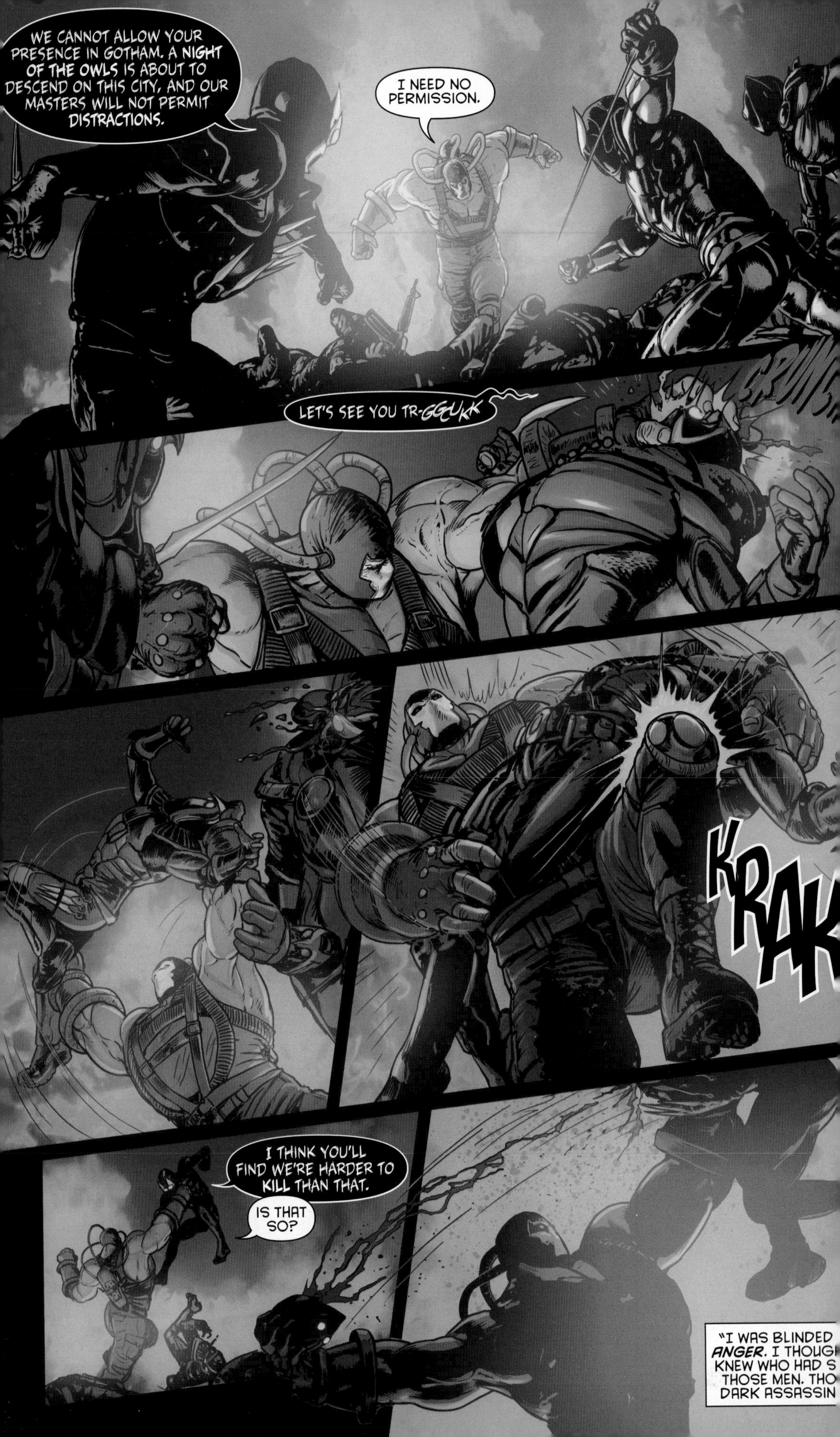
WE CANNOT ALLOW YOUR PRESENCE IN GOTHAM. A NIGHT OF THE OWLS IS ABOUT TO DESCEND ON THIS CITY, AND OUR MASTERS WILL NOT PERMIT DISTRACTIONS.
I NEED NO PERMISSION.
LET'S SEE YOU TR-GGUKK
KRAK
I THINK YOU'LL FIND WE'RE HARDER TO KILL THAN THAT.
IS THAT SO?
"I WAS BLINDED
ANGER. I THOUG
KNEW WHO HAD S
THOSE MEN. THO
DARK ASSASSIN

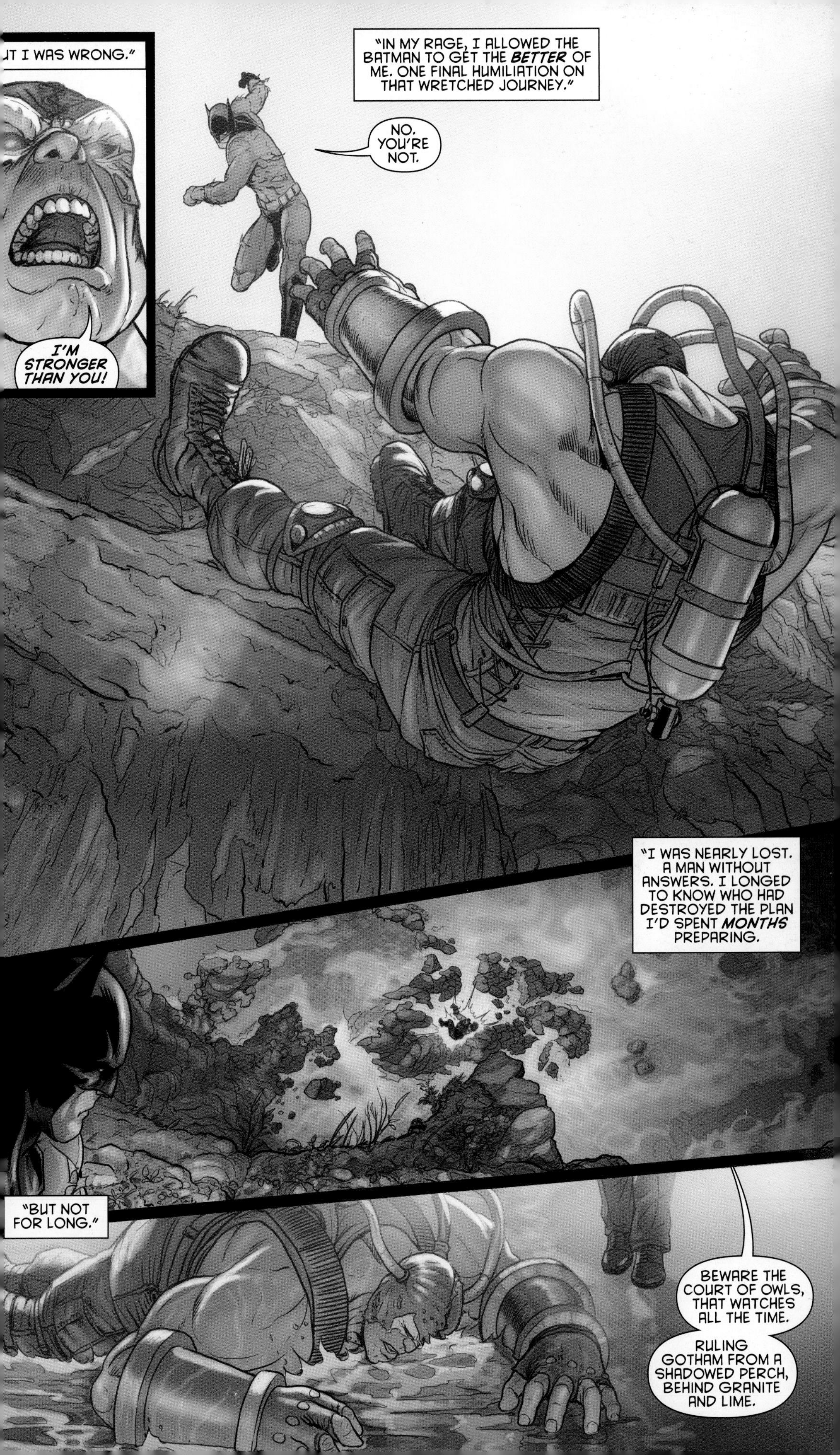
"...UT I WAS WRONG."
I'M STRONGER THAN YOU!
"IN MY RAGE, I ALLOWED THE BATMAN TO GET THE *BETTER* OF ME. ONE FINAL HUMILIATION ON THAT WRETCHED JOURNEY."
NO. YOU'RE NOT.
"I WAS NEARLY LOST. A MAN WITHOUT ANSWERS. I LONGED TO KNOW WHO HAD DESTROYED THE PLAN I'D SPENT *MONTHS* PREPARING.
"BUT NOT FOR LONG."
BEWARE THE COURT OF OWLS, THAT WATCHES ALL THE TIME.
RULING GOTHAM FROM A SHADOWED PERCH, BEHIND GRANITE AND LIME.

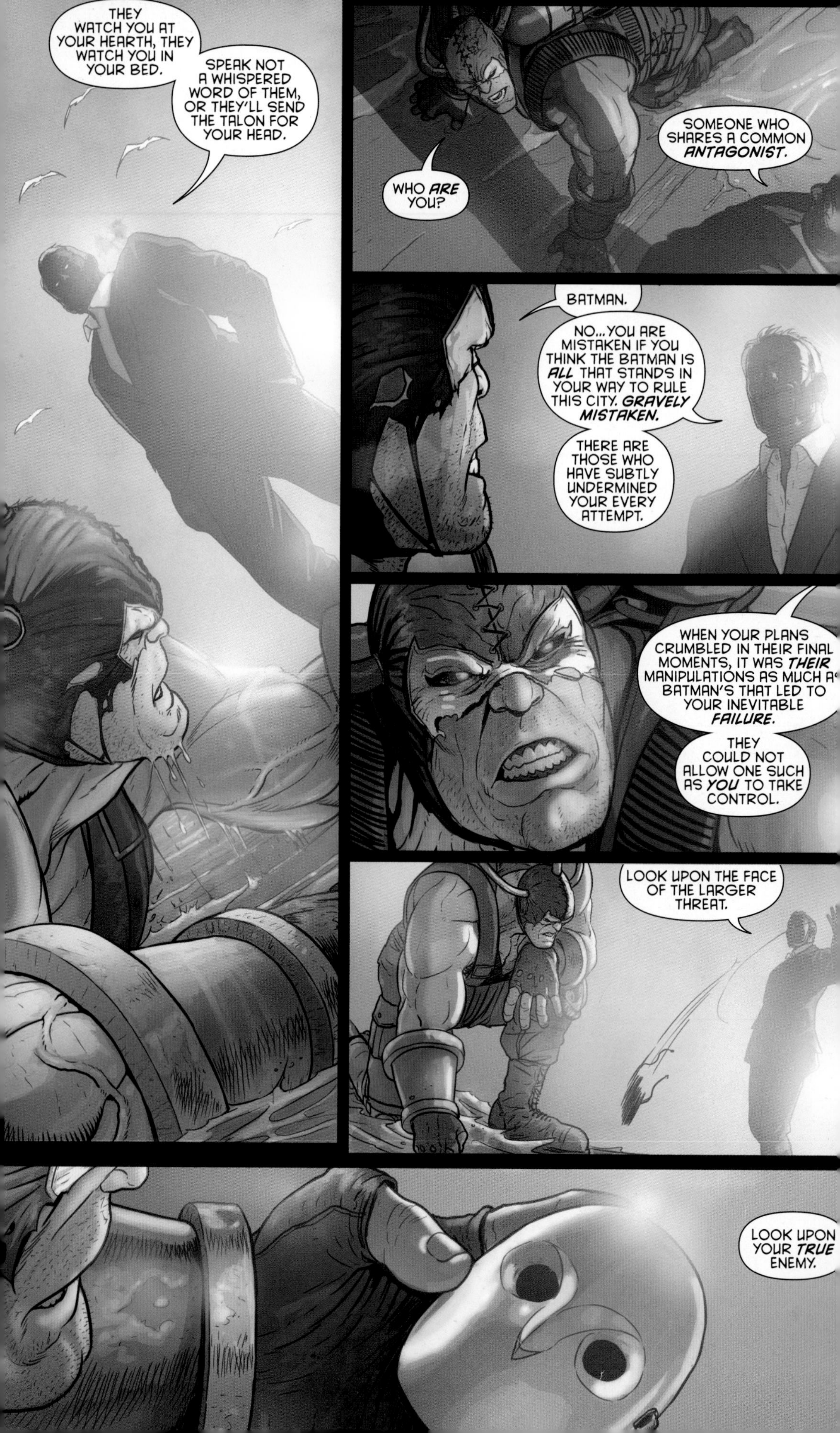
THEY WATCH YOU AT YOUR HEARTH, THEY WATCH YOU IN YOUR BED.
SPEAK NOT A WHISPERED WORD OF THEM, OR THEY'LL SEND THE TALON FOR YOUR HEAD.
WHO *ARE* YOU?
SOMEONE WHO SHARES A COMMON *ANTAGONIST*.
BATMAN.
NO...YOU ARE MISTAKEN IF YOU THINK THE BATMAN IS *ALL* THAT STANDS IN YOUR WAY TO RULE THIS CITY. *GRAVELY MISTAKEN.*
THERE ARE THOSE WHO HAVE SUBTLY UNDERMINED YOUR EVERY ATTEMPT.
WHEN YOUR PLANS CRUMBLED IN THEIR FINAL MOMENTS, IT WAS *THEIR* MANIPULATIONS AS MUCH A BATMAN'S THAT LED TO YOUR INEVITABLE *FAILURE*.
THEY COULD NOT ALLOW ONE SUCH AS *YOU* TO TAKE CONTROL.
LOOK UPON THE FACE OF THE LARGER THREAT.
LOOK UPON YOUR *TRUE* ENEMY.

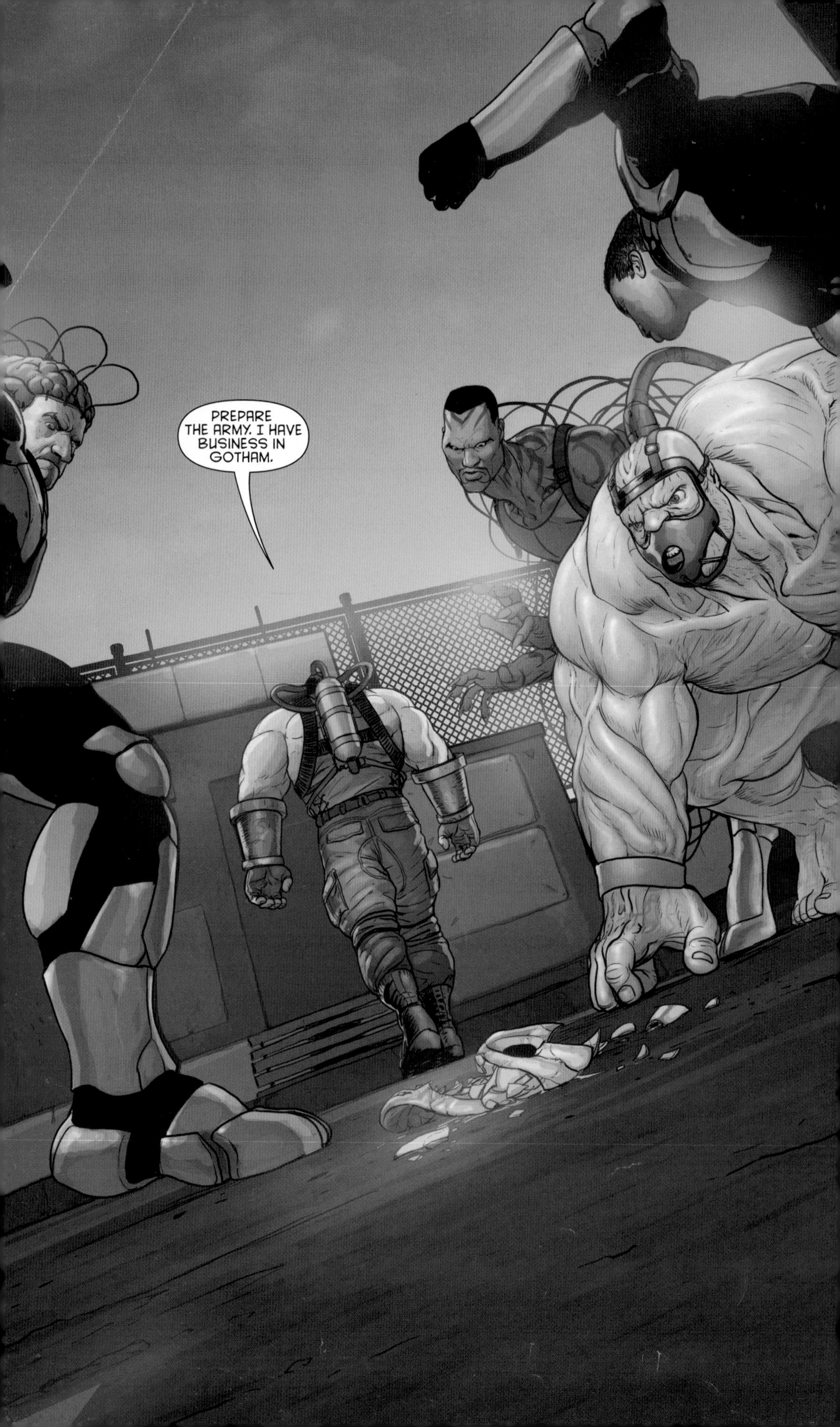
PREPARE THE ARMY. I HAVE BUSINESS IN GOTHAM.

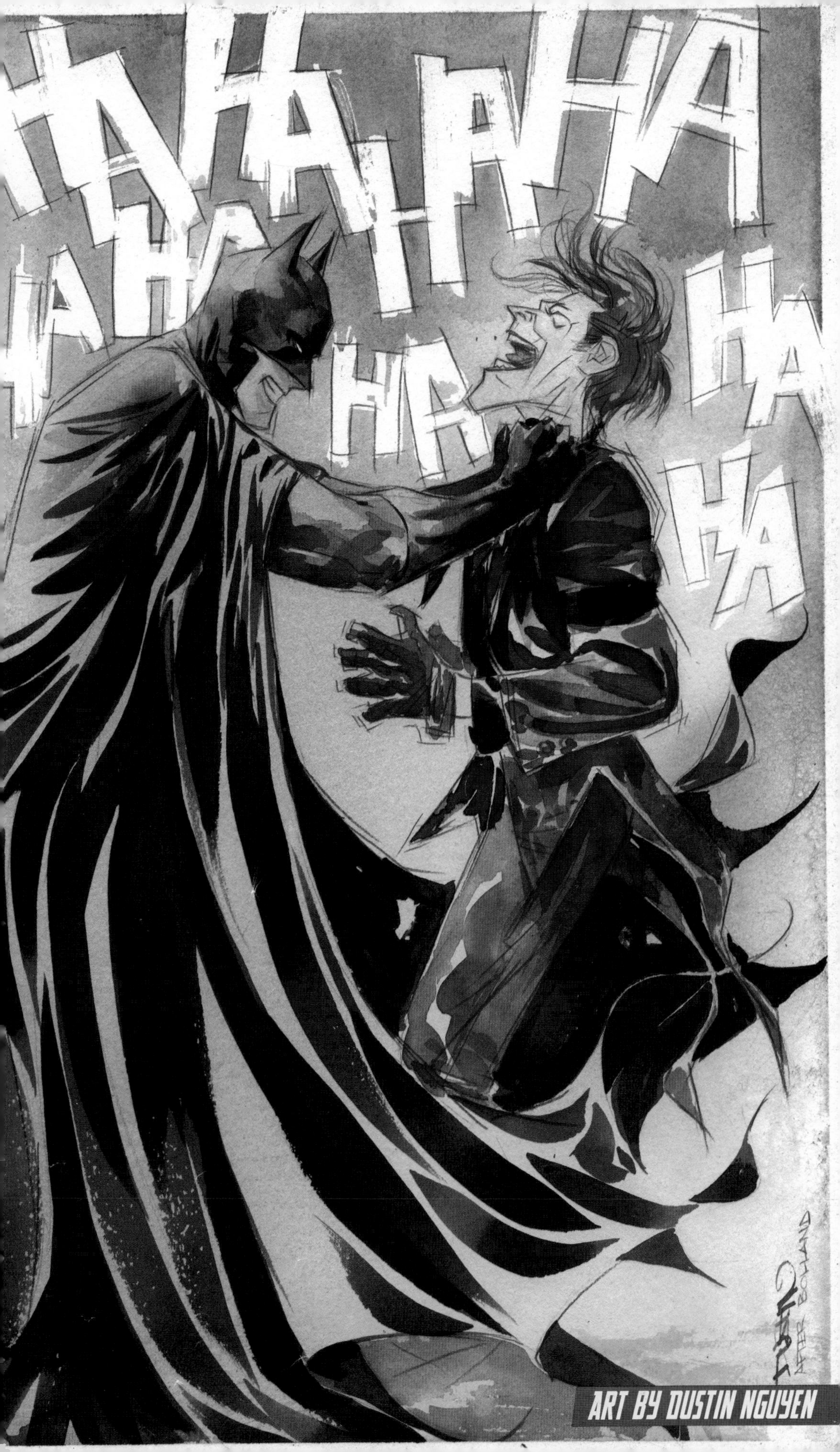
HA HA HA
HA HA HA
HA
HA
AFTER BOLLAND

ART BY DUSTIN NGUYEN

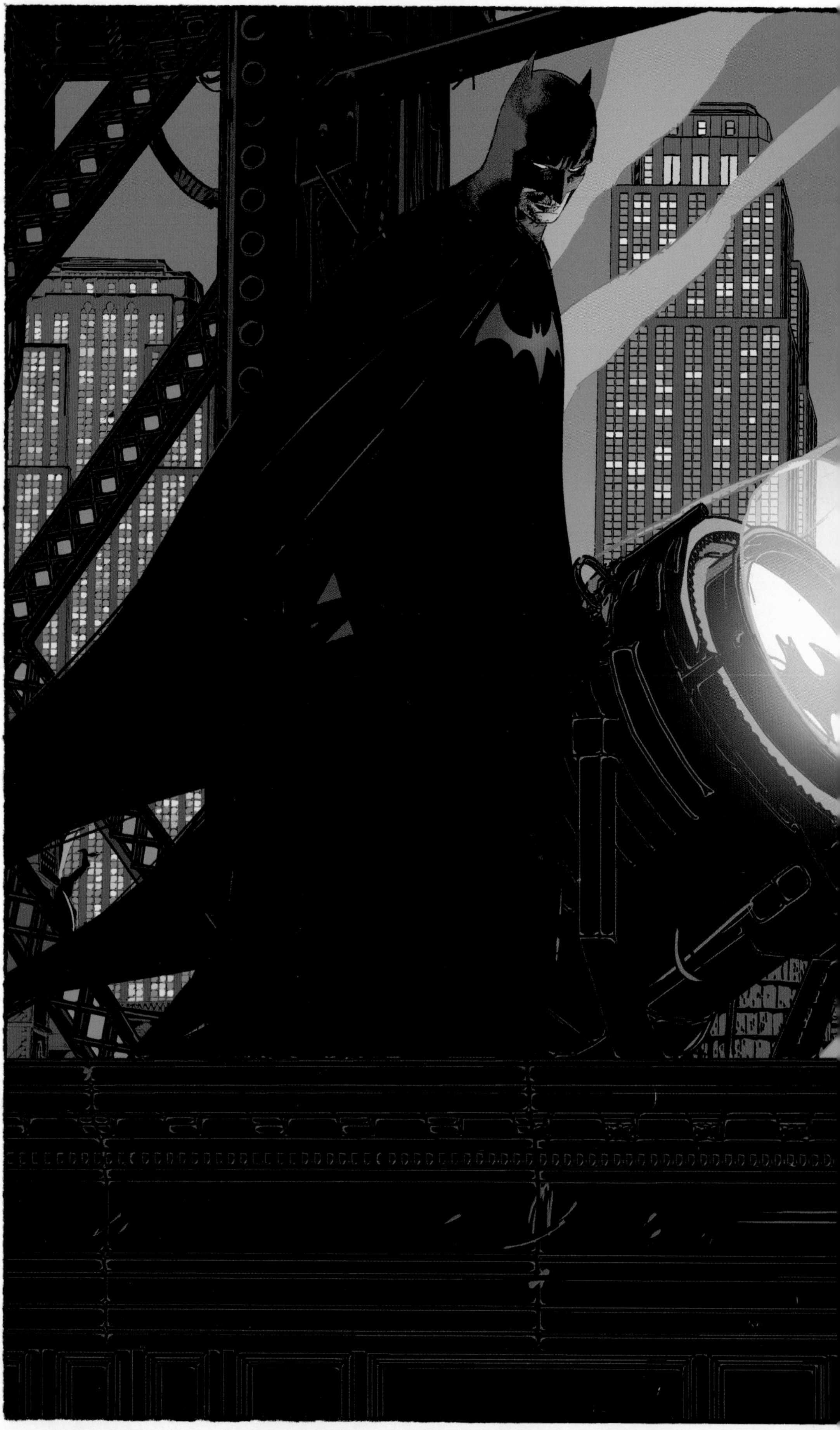

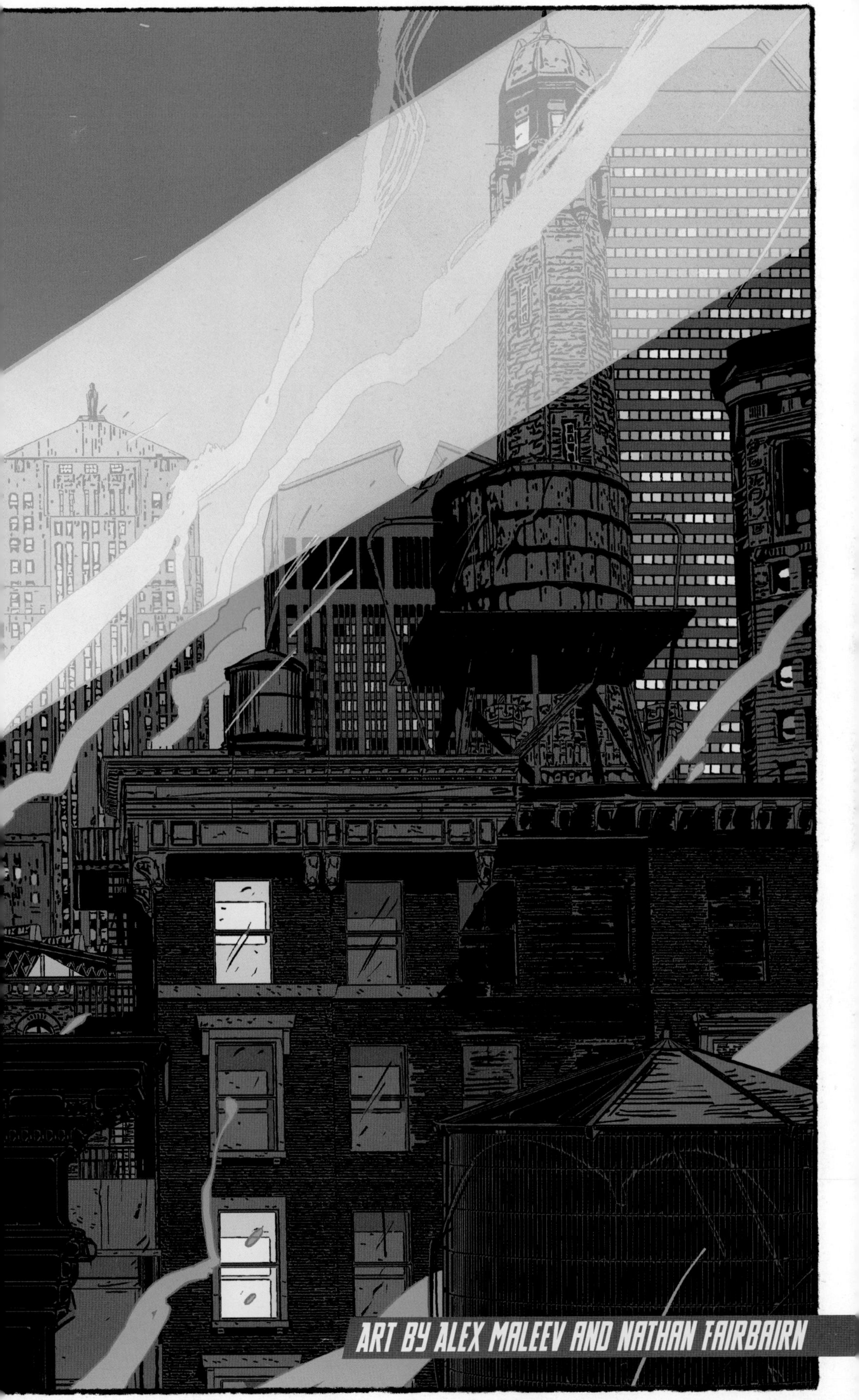
ART BY ALEX MALEEV AND NATHAN FAIRBAIRN

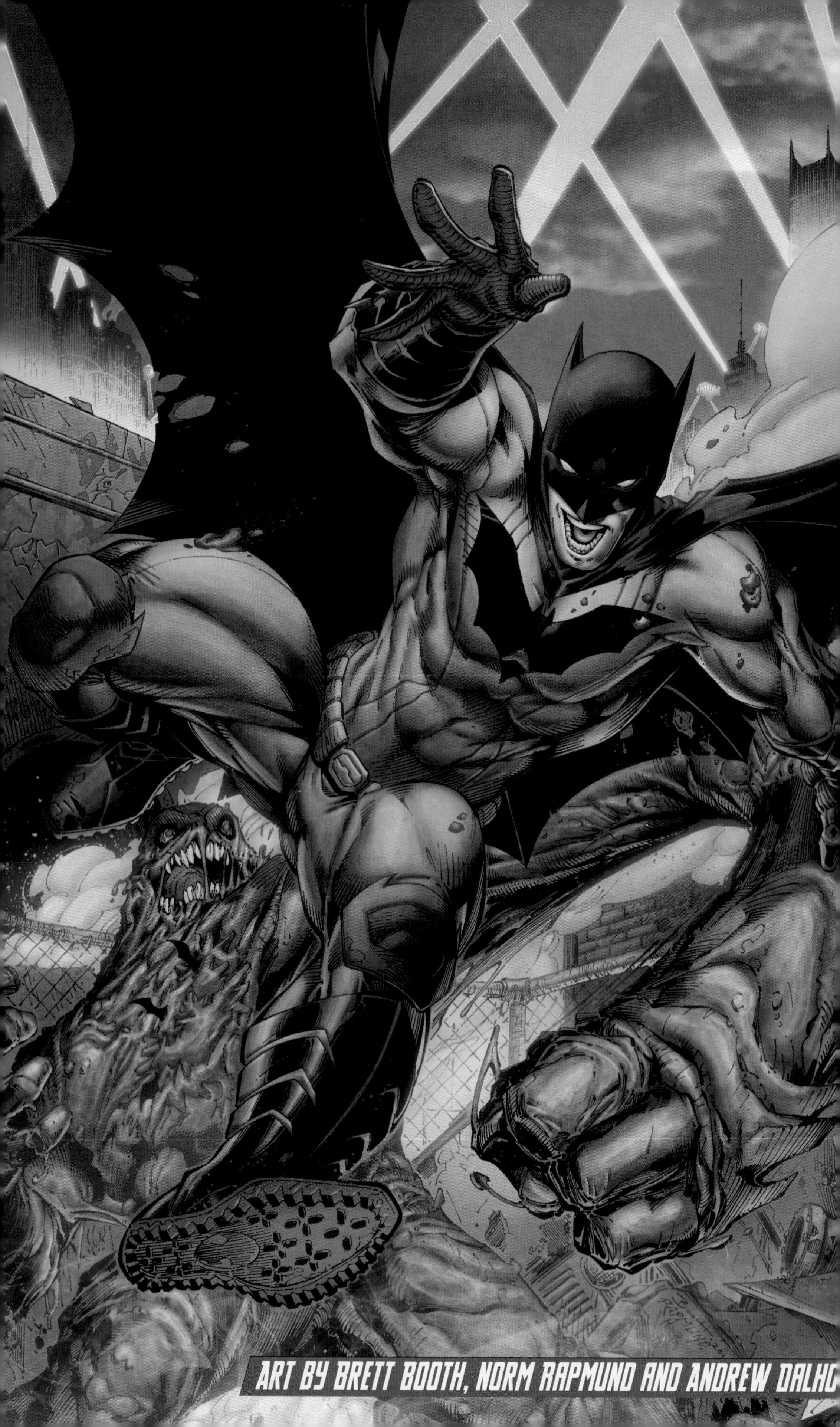

ART BY BRETT BOOTH, NORM RAPMUND AND ANDREW DALHO

ART BY CHRIS BURNHAM AND NATHAN FAIRBAIRN

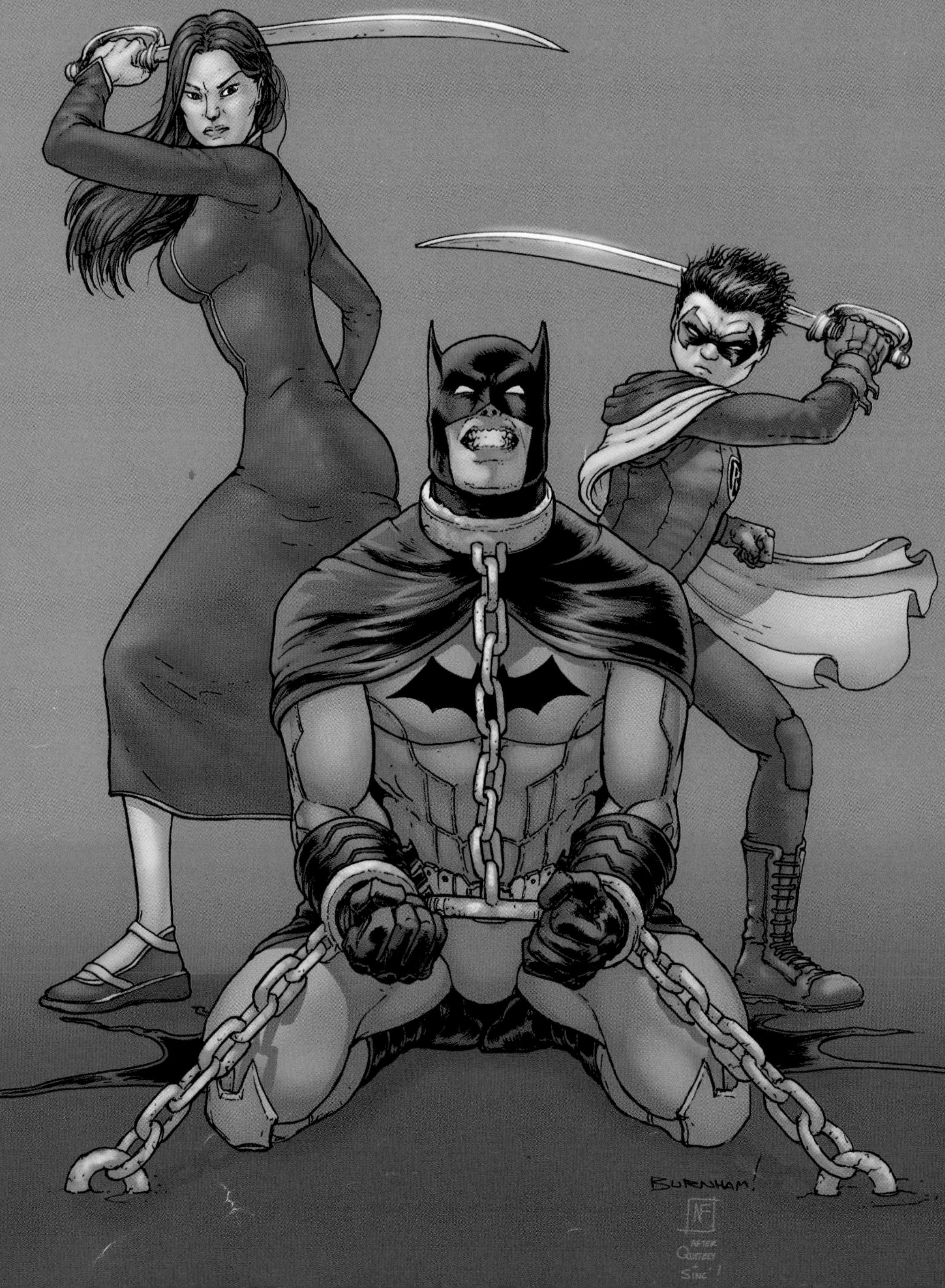
BURNHAM!

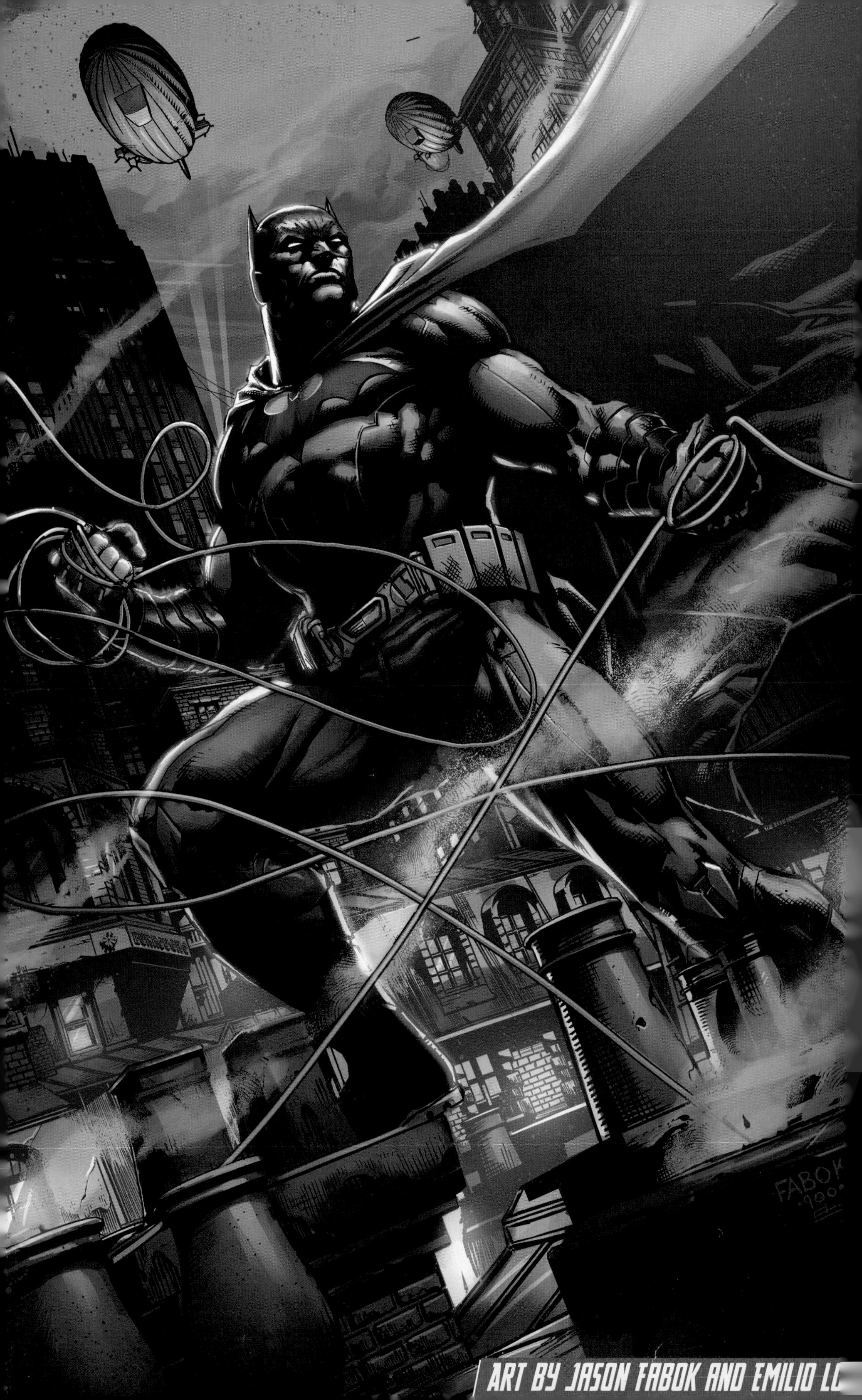

ART BY JASON FABOK AND EMILIO LC

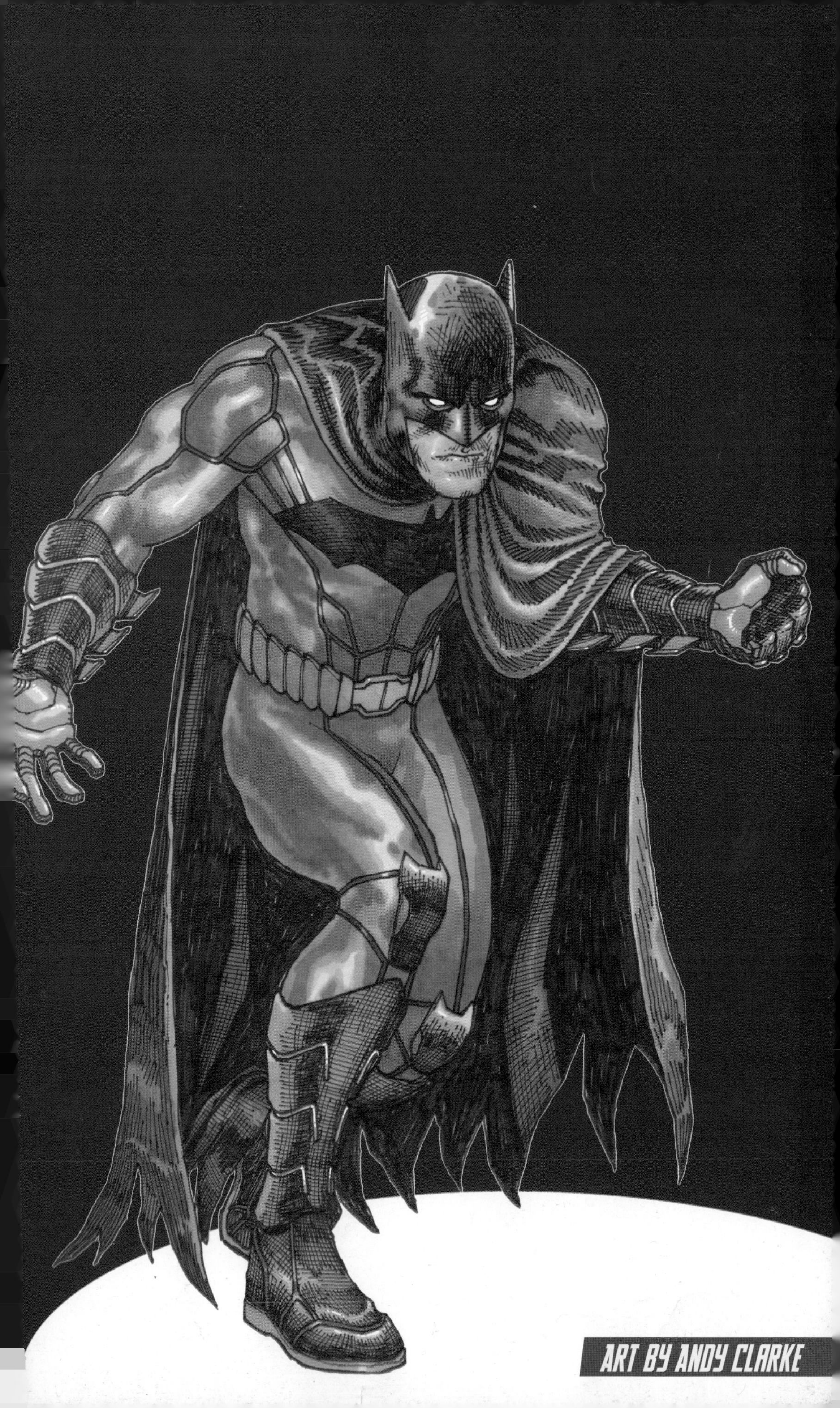
ART BY ANDY CLARKE

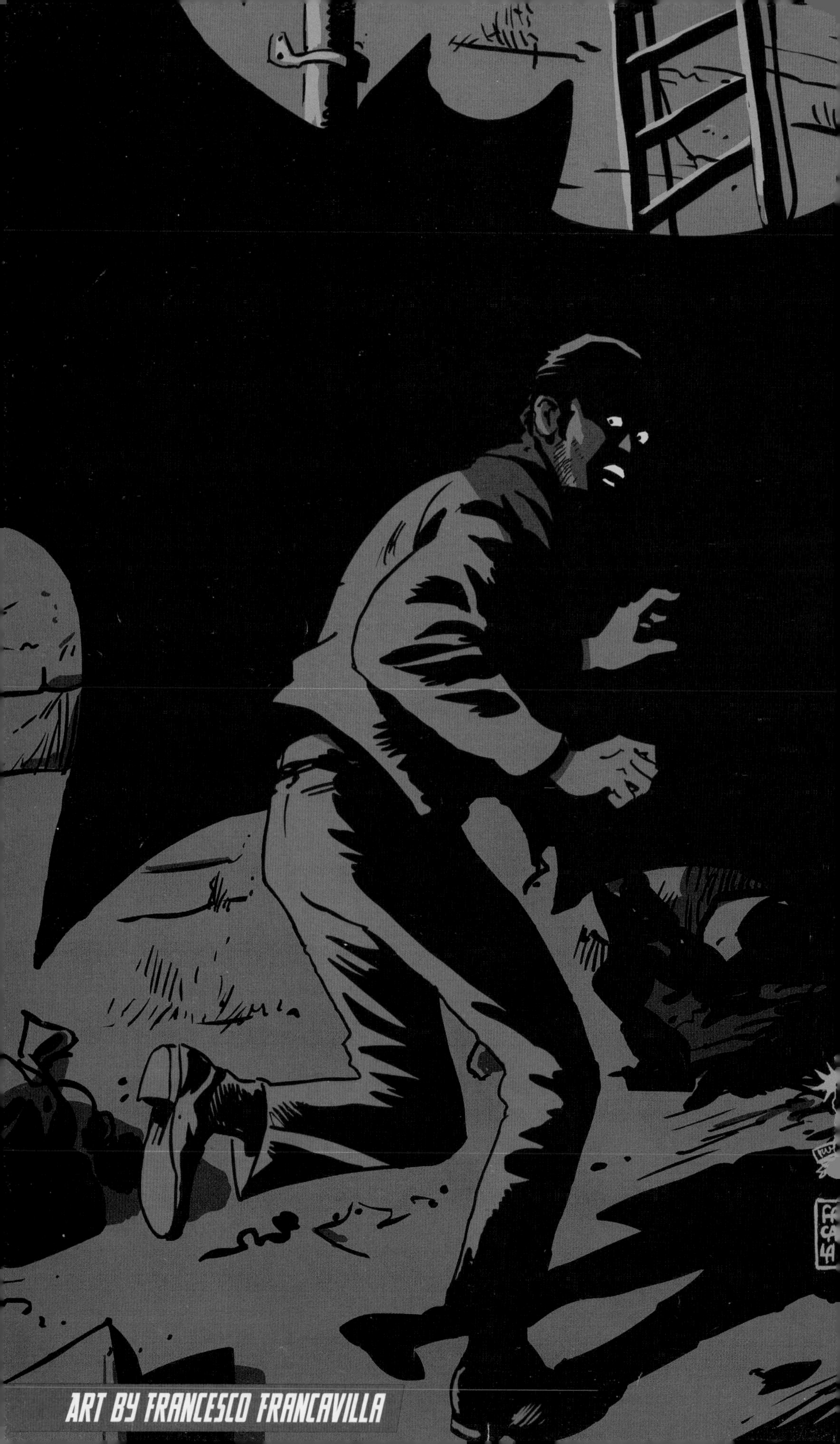

ART BY FRANCESCO FRANCAVILLA

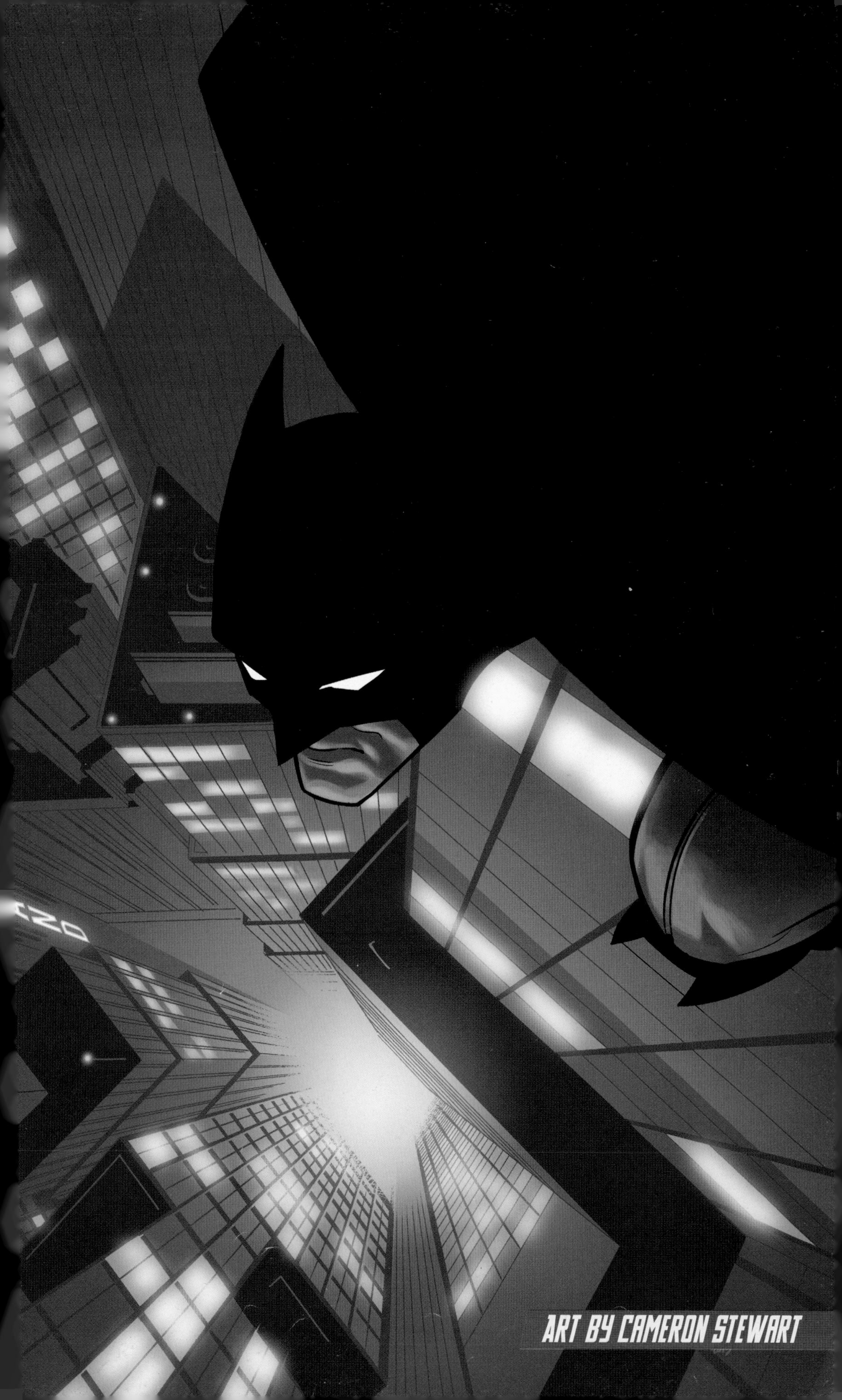

ART BY CAMERON STEWART

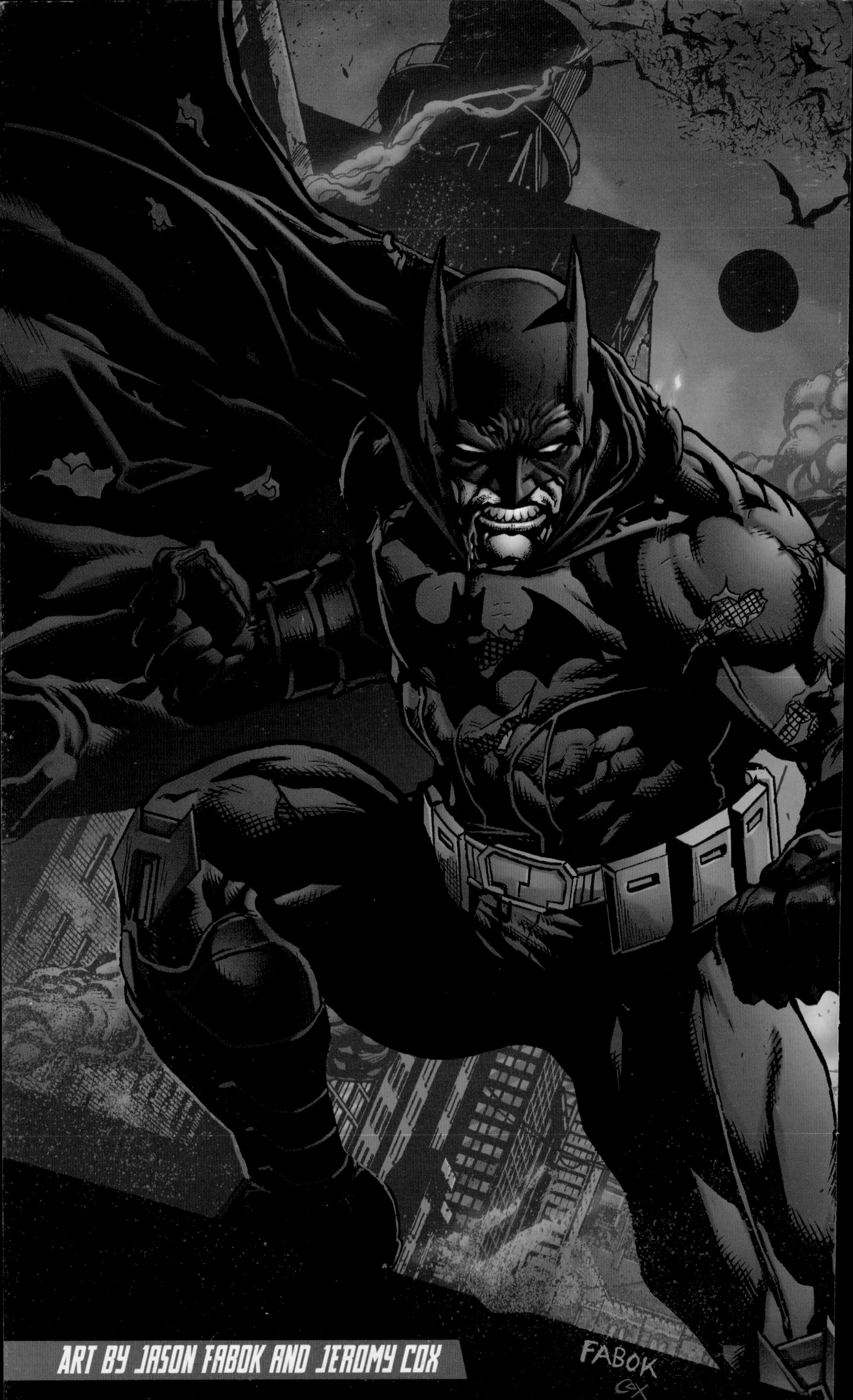
FABOK
COX

ART BY JASON FABOK AND JEROMY COX

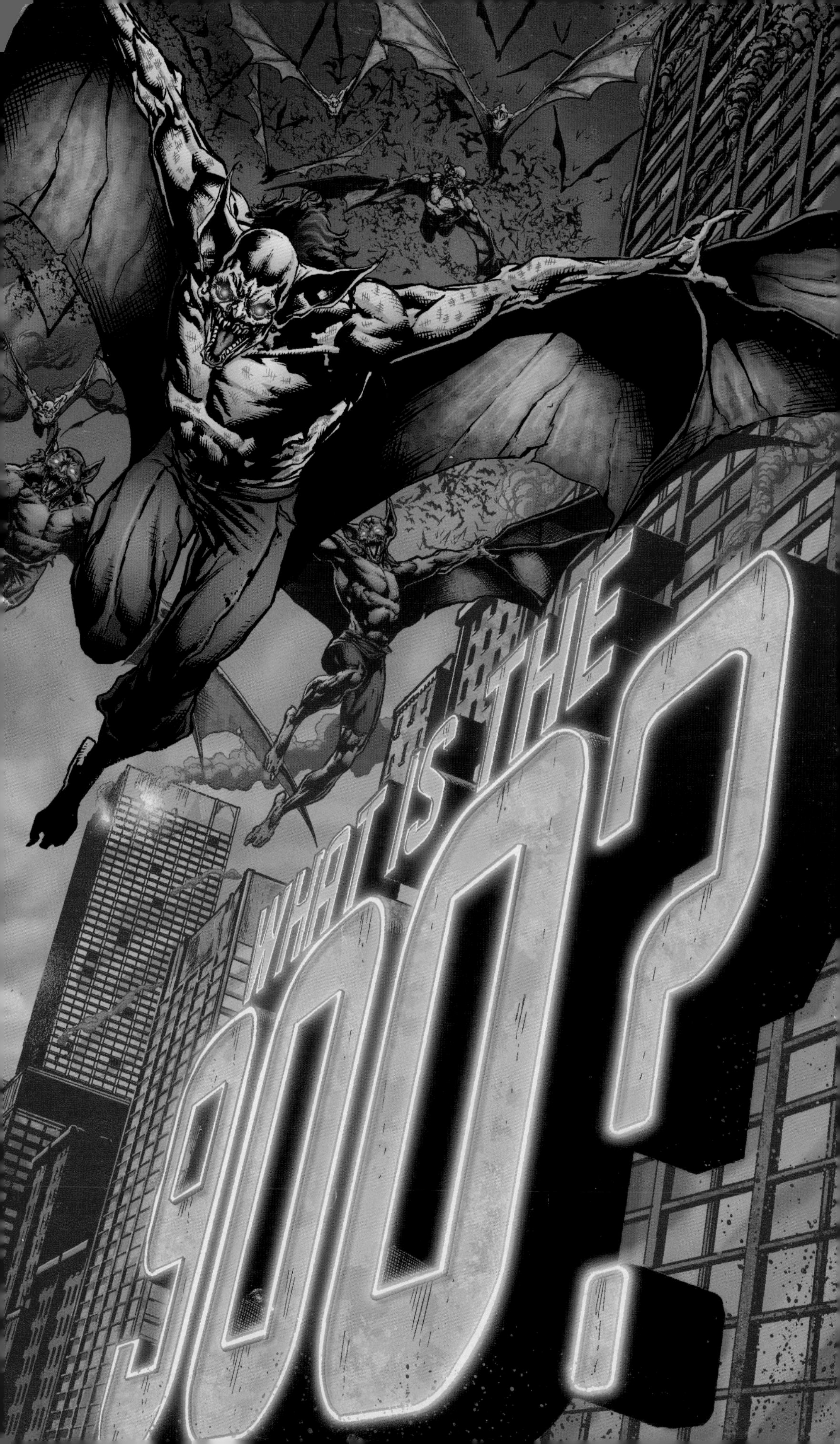
WHAT IS THE
900?

Issue #19 Variant Cover by Tom Richmond

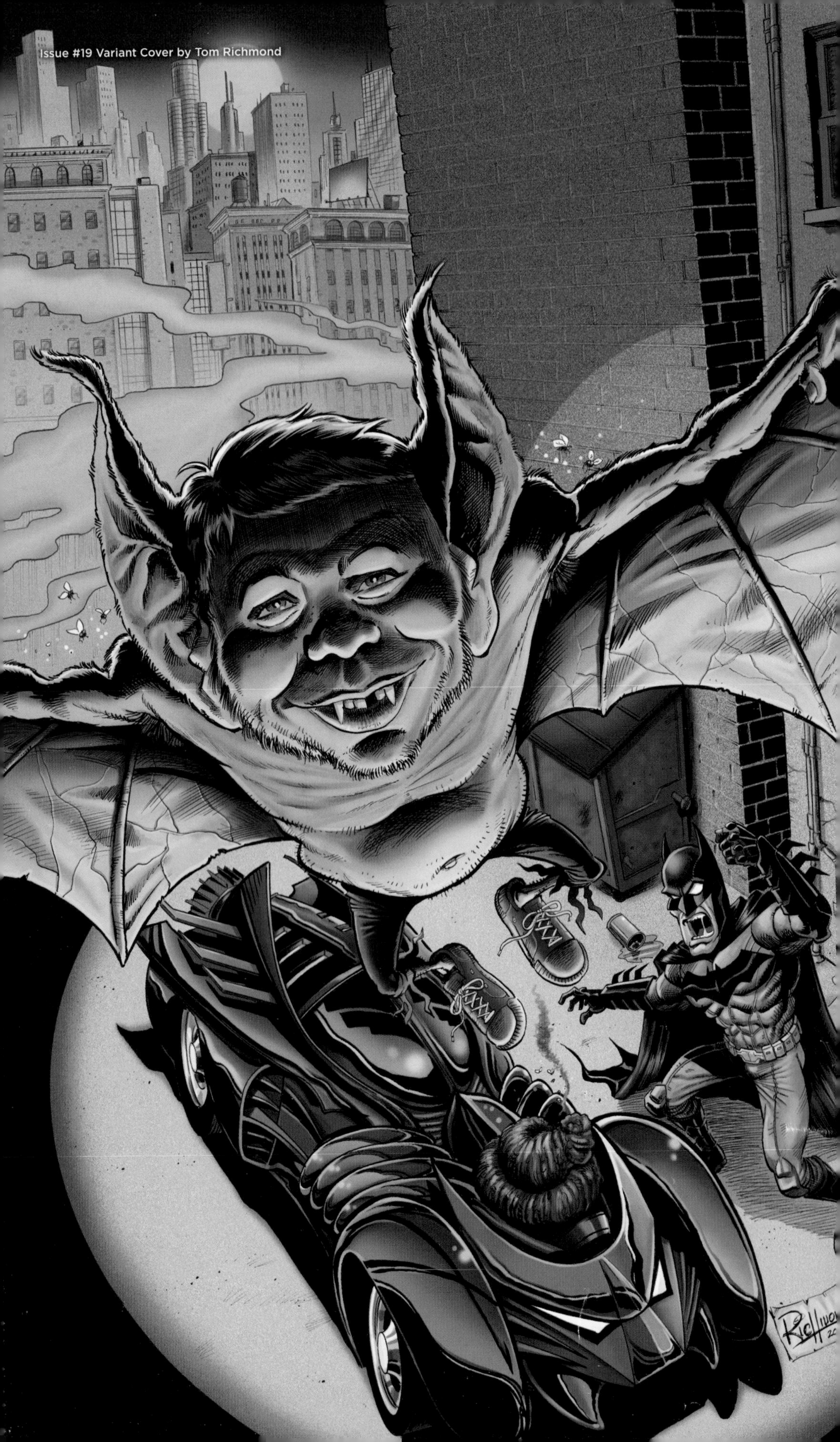